EVERYONE A TEACHER

EVERYONE A TEACHER

Edited by

MARK SCHWEHN

UNIVERSITY OF NOTRE DAME PRESS

Notre Dame, Indiana

Library of Congress Cataloging-in-Publication Data

Everyone a teacher / edited by Mark Schwehn.
    p. cm. — (The ethics of everyday life)
    Includes bibliographical references.
    ISBN 0-268-04209-8 (alk. paper) — ISBN 0-268-04210-1 (pbk. : alk. paper)
        1. Teaching.   2. Learning.   3. Teachers.   4. Education—Aims and objectives.
I. Schwehn, Mark. R., 1945–   II. Series.

LB1025.3 .E87 2000
371.102—dc21

                                                                00-023412

THE ETHICS OF EVERYDAY LIFE
Preface to the Series

This book is one of a series of volumes devoted to the ethics of everyday life. The series has been produced by a group of friends, united by a concern for the basic moral aspects of our common life and by a desire to revive public interest in and attention to these matters, now sadly neglected. We have met together over the past five years, under the auspices of the Institute of Religion and Public Life and supported by a generous grant from the Lilly Endowment. We have been reading and writing, conversing and arguing, always looking for ways to deepen our own understanding of the meaning of human life as ordinarily lived, looking also for ways to enable others to join in the search. These anthologies of selected readings on various aspects of everyday life—courting and marrying, teaching and learning, working, leading, and dying—seem to us very well suited to the task. This preface explains why we think so.

We begin by remembering that every aspect of everyday life is ethically charged. Nearly everything that we do, both as individuals and in relations with others, is colored by sentiments, attitudes, customs, and beliefs concerning "how to live." At work or at play, in word or in deed, with kin or with strangers, we enact, often unthinkingly and albeit imperfectly, our ideas of what it means to live a decent and worthy life. Notions and feelings regarding better and worse, good and bad, right and wrong, noble and base, just and unjust, decent and indecent, honorable and dishonorable, or human and inhuman always influence the way we speak to one another, the way we do our work, the way we control our passions, rear our children, manage our organizations, respond to injustice, treat our neighbors, teach the young, care for the old, court our beloved, and face our deaths.

For many centuries and up through the early part of the twentieth century, there was in the West (as in the East) a large and diverse literature on "living the good life," involving manners, patterns of civility, and the meaning of decency, honor, and virtue as these are manifested in daily life. Moralists, both philosophical and religious, wrote voluminously on the moral dimensions of the life cycle (e.g., growing up and coming of age, courting and marrying, rearing the young, aging and dying); on the virtues of everyday life (e.g., courage, endurance, self-command, generosity, loyalty, forbearance, modesty, industry, neighborliness, patience, hope, forgiveness, repentance); on the moral passions or sentiments (e.g., shame, guilt, sympathy, joy, envy, anger, awe) and their proper expression; on the activities of everyday life (e.g., loving, working, caring, giving, teaching, talking, eating); and on basic moral phenomena (e.g., responsibility, obligation, vocation, conscience, praise and blame). These topics, which once held the attention of great thinkers like Aristotle, Erasmus, and Adam Smith, are now sorely neglected, with sorry social consequences.

The ethics of everyday life have been left behind despite—or perhaps because of—the burgeoning attention given these past few decades to professional ethics and public ethics. Mention ethics today, and the discussion generally turns to medical ethics, legal ethics, journalistic ethics, or some other code of behavior that is supposed to guide the activities of professionals. Or it turns to the need to establish codes of conduct to address and curtail the mischief and malfeasance of members of Congress, generals, bureaucrats, or other public officials. In both cases, the concern for ethics is largely instrumental and protective. The codes are intended to tell people how to stay out of trouble with their professional colleagues and with the law. The latter is especially important in a world in which it is increasingly likely that a challenge or disagreement will be engaged not by civil conversation but by an uncivil lawsuit.

Today's proliferation of codes of ethics, while an expression of moral concern, is at the same time an expression of moral poverty. We write new rules and regulations because we lack shared customs and understandings. Yet the more we resort to such external and contrived codes, the less we can in fact take for granted. "Ethics" and "morality" have their source in "ethos" and "mores," words that refer to the ways and attitudes, manners and habits, sensibilities and customs that shape and define a community. Communities are built on shared understandings, usually tacitly conveyed, not only of what is right and wrong or good and bad, but also of who we are, how we stand, what things mean. These matters are not well taught by ethics codes.

Neither are they communicated, or even much noticed, by the current fashions in the academic study and teaching of ethics or by the proliferating band of professional ethicists. The dominant modes of contemporary ethical discourse and writing, whether conducted in universities or in independent ethics centers, are, by and large, highly abstract, analytically philosophic, interested only in principles or arguments, often remote from life as lived, divorced from the way most people face and make moral decisions, largely deaf to questions of character and moral feeling or how they are acquired, unduly influenced by the sensational or extreme case, hostile to insights from the religious traditions, friendly to fashionable opinion but deaf to deeper sources of wisdom, heavily tilted toward questions of law and public policy, and all too frequently marked by an unwillingness to take a moral stand. Largely absent is the older—and we think richer—practice of moral reflection, which is concrete, rooted in ordinary experience, engaged yet thoughtful, attuned to human needs and sentiments as well as to "rational principles of justification," and concerned for institutions that cultivate and promote moral understanding and moral education. Absent especially is the devoted search for moral wisdom regarding the conduct of life—philosophy's original meaning and goal, and a central focus of all religious thought and practice—a search that takes help from wherever it may be found and that gives direction to a life seriously lived.

Many academic teachers of ethics, formerly professors of moral wisdom, are today purveyors of moral relativism. In the colleges and universities ethics is often taught cafeteria style, with multiple theories and viewpoints, seemingly equal, offered up for the picking. But this apparently neutral approach often coexists with ideologically intolerant teaching. Students are taught that traditional views must give way to the "enlightened" view that all views—except, of course, the "enlightened" one—are culture-bound, parochial, and absolutely dependent on your *point*-of-viewing. The morally charged "givens" of human life—e.g., that we have bodies or parents and neighbors—tend to be regarded not as gifts but as impositions, obstacles to the one true good, unconstrained personal choice. Moral wisdom cannot be taught or even sought, because we already know that we must not constrain freedom, must not "impose" morality. Thus, we insist that our "values" are good because we value them, not that they are valued because they are good. Abstract theories of individual autonomy and self-creation abound, while insights into real life as lived fall into obscurity or disappear altogether. To be sure, not all academic teachers of ethics share these opinions and approaches. But experience and study of the literature convinces us that these generalizations are all too accurate.

The current fashions of ethical discourse are of more than merely academic interest. When teachings of "autonomy" or "self-creation" are disconnected from attention to mores and the cultural ethos and from the search for moral wisdom, we come to know less and less what we are supposed to do and how we are supposed to be. Neither can we take for granted that others know what they are supposed to do and be. Being morally unfettered and unformed may make us feel liberated albeit insecure or lost; but seeing that others are morally unfettered and unformed is downright threatening. Thus, despite our moral codes of ethics with penalties attached, despite the boom in the demand for ethicists and in ethics courses in our colleges, our everyday life declines into relationships of narrow-eyed suspicion. No one can argue that we are as a nation morally better off than we were before professional and academic ethics made such a big splash. Americans of widely differing views recognize the growing incivility and coarseness of public discourse and behavior, the sorry state of sexual mores, the erosion of family life, the disappearance of neighborliness, and the growing friction among, and lack of respect for, peoples of differing ages, races, religions, and social classes. To be sure, contemporary ethicists are not responsible for our cultural and moral difficulties. But they have failed to provide us proper guidance or understanding, largely because they neglect the ethics of everyday life and because they have given up on the pursuit of wisdom.

How to provide a remedy? How to offer assistance to the great majority of decent people who still care about living the good life? How to answer the ardent desires of parents for a better life for their children or the deep longings of undergraduates for a more meaningful life for themselves? How to supply an intellectual defense for the now beleaguered and emaciated teachings of decency and virtue? Any answer to these questions depends on acquiring—or at least seeking—a richer and more profound understanding of the structure of human life and the prospects for its flourishing and enhancement. This series of readings on the ethics of everyday life offers help to anyone seeking such understanding.

The topics considered in the several volumes are central to everyday life. Most of us marry, nearly all of us work (and play and rest), all of us lose both loved ones and our own lives to death. In daily life, many of us teach and all of us learn. In civic life, some of us lead, many of us follow, and, in democratic societies, all of us are called upon to evaluate those who would lead us. Yet rarely do we reflect on the nature and meaning of these activities. The anthologized readings—collected from poets and prophets, philosophers and preachers, novelists and anthropologists, scholars and statesmen; from authors ancient, modern, and contemporary—provide rich materials for such reflection. They are moral, not moralistic; they can yield insights, not maxims. The reader will find here no rules for catching a husband, but rather explorations of the purposes of courting and marrying; no prescriptions for organizing the workplace, but competing accounts of the meaning of work; no discussions of "when to pull the plug," but examinations of living in the face of death; no formulae for "effective leadership," but critical assessments of governance in democratic times; no advice on how to teach, but various meditations on purposes and forms of instruction. The different volumes reflect the differences in their subject matter, as well as the different tastes and outlooks of their editors. But they share a common moral seriousness and a common belief that proper ethical reflection requires a "thick description" of the phenomena of everyday life, with their inherent anthropological, moral, and religious colorations.

The readings in this series impose no morality. Indeed, they impose nothing; they only propose. They propose different ways of thinking about our common lives, sometimes in the form of stories, sometimes in the form of meditations, sometimes in the form of arguments. Some of these proposals will almost certainly "impose" themselves upon the reader's mind and heart as being more worthy than others. But they will do so not because they offer simple abstractable ethical principles or suggest procedures for solving this or that problem of living. They will do so because they will strike the thoughtful reader as wiser, deeper, and more true. We ourselves have had this experience with our readings, and we hope you will also. For the life you examine in these pages is—or could become—your own.

Timothy Fuller
Amy A. Kass
Leon R. Kass
Gilbert C. Meilaender
Richard John Neuhaus
Mark Schwehn

CONTENTS

EVERYONE A TEACHER
Introduction

1.

All of us teach. Most of our teaching is woven so routinely into the fabric of our daily lives that we scarcely notice it. We point very deliberately to a can of peas, holding it perhaps too close to the toddler's eyes, and we say—ever so carefully—"peeeeeeeze; p—e—a—s: peeeeeeeze." The child repeats, "peas," and we respond with an approving smile, seldom wondering whether the child has connected the sound she has uttered and the letters we have pronounced to the can itself, the picture on the can, or the finger pointing to it. Or again, we teach a young boy how to drive a standard shift automobile, and we are barely aware that our teaching of this seemingly simple practice may nonetheless consist of a number of complicated actions: explaining, demonstrating, exhorting, encouraging, inventing, correcting, sympathizing, judging, and discerning. So too with teaching how to play a musical instrument, how to read a map, how to tie shoes, how to cook a seven-course meal or how to eat it properly: all of these are complicated endeavors, tied together by family resemblances to one another, part and parcel of everyday life, yet strangely difficult to understand fully once we begin to think about them.

These efforts to teach someone how to do something or other are often parts of much larger, even life-long practices of imparting a tradition or "training up children in the way they should grow" or forming characters or witnessing to a way of life. These more global activities are also in some sense cases of teaching, even though many of them may be more inadvertent or habitual than deliberate and carefully planned. To the extent that this is so, to the extent that parents should come to think of the examples of good or bad, noble or ignoble conduct that they embody before their children every day as cases of "teaching," pedagogy may be the most pervasive of all human activities. And though we may be tempted to say that our understanding of teaching has by now become *too* broad, we should first ponder the similarities between the "simplest" of our examples so far, teaching a toddler the meaning of a word and how to spell it, and the most "complex," i.e., teaching someone the difference between right and wrong. We may notice, for example, that both endeavors involve horizons of meaning and value, clear standards, and the hope that our "students" will be able to learn how to use our help to meet situations and

1

cases (of spelling, language use, and moral judgment) that we could not in principle "spell out" for them in advance.

We may wonder as well about the connection between these several kinds of teaching and the correlative activity of learning. Our vocabulary is rich with words that attempt to describe those people and activities involved in learning. Words like student, disciple, apprentice, novice, beginner, neophyte, and amateur begin to express the range of different ways in which the activity of learning has been related, socially and psychologically, to the activity of teaching. All of these various expressions that we use to try to capture a precise, fixed, and simple connection between teaching and learning attest both to our uncertainty about whether such a clear statement of the matter is possible and to the presence in our minds of an unresolved question: do human beings really learn *from* teachers, or do they learn through them or with them or by virtue of their questions? Or, to put the matter a bit differently, does our learning depend more on what is already within each of us than it does upon anything that any teacher could *give* us?

Though these matters of teaching and learning once seemed terribly abstract, they have become instead for me, as a parent, a citizen, and a college teacher of thirty years, some of the most immediate and concrete of all the things I daily encounter and learn to live with and love. This book is accordingly informed by my seemingly paradoxical convictions that from one point of view all of us are most definitely teachers, and from another none of us are. These convictions are rooted in my experience of teaching, not in abstract theorizing about it. On the one hand, I can sense that I have gotten better and better at understanding the books and the subjects that I teach, at formulating questions, at leading discussion, at planning syllabi, and at figuring out how and when to teach my children something worthwhile. So I have no doubts about whether I am in fact teaching.

On the other hand, I have come increasingly to think that good teaching depends as much on the character of the teacher as it does upon his or her grasp of the subject matter. And like most human beings, I have doubts about my own possession of those virtues like humility, honesty, patience, good judgment, practical wisdom, charity, and courage that are essential to good teaching. I therefore am frequently doubtful about the quality of my teaching. My doubts are even more fundamental, however. As I daily witness learning in others, as I watch my children improve skills, reckon sums, treat one another (once in a while) more kindly, and speak more clearly; as I watch my students interpret complicated passages, unravel difficult arguments, and justify with greater confidence and wisdom their own opinions, I feel less and less sure that I can truthfully attribute the many signs of positive growth in grace and understanding within my children and my students to my own teaching. So I have over the years come to believe that most of learning depends upon the learners themselves and upon transcendent powers and agencies that I only dimly comprehend. In view of these convictions, I have come to doubt whether anyone of us ever teaches in most of the ordinary senses of the word. Contrary to our unexamined notions that we teach whenever we actively impart information or tell someone how to do something, it is probably more truthful to say, reformulating a line of John Milton's poetry, that those mainly teach who only stand (in awe) and wait.

The main point of this book is not, however, to brood over paradoxes and mysteries. The book attempts to consider the closely related activities of teaching and learning, to acknowledge and investigate some of their more mysterious aspects, and to provide instructive and inspiring examples of good teaching as a part of the everyday life of human beings. The hope is for the kind of edification that will lead to improvement of our own teaching practice. The book therefore sets out several instances of teaching that are designed to give us all more experience in watching others teach as well as more guidance than we customarily receive in reflecting critically upon these experiences. Two of the virtues that good teachers must have are, as stated earlier, the virtues of practical wisdom and good judgment. The cultivation of both of these virtues depends in part upon experience. And since we cannot have directly all of the experience that we need to be the best teachers, we must acquire some of it vicariously through acts of imagination as we enter into the teaching and the learning of others. The texts in this book provide some of these occasions, experiences, and examples. Whether or not we learn from them and through them depends as much upon us as it does upon the teachers in the readings.

2.

Though it is true that we all teach, this fact is often forgotten, since many in our society are professional teachers, people who earn a living by teaching, and we have grown accustomed to reserving the designation "teacher" for them. Education is, however, a part of the business of everyday life for all citizens when we regularly transmit some of what we know to others, and whenever we support schools, vocational training institutes, and other institutions whose business is education.

This much may seem self-evident to us now, but it has not always been so clear. Thirty-five years ago, a distinguished American historian, Bernard Bailyn, published a small essay that reminded his generation of students of these obvious truths while explaining how most academics had temporarily lost sight of them. Entitled *Education in the Forming of American Society,* the essay argued that education should not be reduced to "schooling" but that it should instead be regarded as "the entire process by which a culture transmits itself across the generations." Having defended the latter view, Bailyn proceeded to show that schools in the English colonies of the seventeenth century arose in response to the reconfiguration of other institutions—indentured servanthood, apprenticeship, the family, and the church—that had long been the primary agents of cultural transmission.

Today, the experiences of my colleagues who teach in colleges and universities demonstrate the extent to which their work is in part defined by the operation of institutions of cultural transmission other than the school. We notice that more and more students show the effects of abuse, neglect, and divorce. We all worry over the quality of secondary and elementary schools. Few of us have not complained at one time or another about the decline of cultural literacy among our students and the rise in a certain kind of visual sophistication. We find ourselves asked repeatedly to "minister to the whole student" or to "educate the whole person," when this often means increasing expenditures for support services like psychological counseling and drug abuse centers. All of these experiences remind us of the extent to which the allocation of our resources, the shape of our curriculum, our choice of study materials, our level of expectation, our vocabulary, and even our teaching styles are shaped by a multitude of social institutions outside of the academy that are themselves for better or for worse involved in education.

Although professional teachers would instantly agree, on the basis of experience if nothing else, that education should not be and cannot be reduced to schooling, many of us probably nevertheless think, at least in our unguarded moments, that teaching refers to something like "classroom activity." In other words, though we are disposed to a more broadly cultural understanding of education, we are also disposed toward a more narrowly professional understanding of teaching. Indeed, this latter disposition was precisely what led to the confused and confusing situation that Bernard Bailyn sought to clarify in his pathbreaking book.

The history of education, according to Bailyn, fell into the hands of professional teachers of education sometime around the turn of the twentieth century. And once that happened, the whole purpose of histories of education became, in Bailyn's words, "to dignify a new self-conscious profession by arguing that modern education was a cosmic force leading mankind to a full realization of itself." This self-serving agenda led these historians of education to "direct their attention almost exclusively to the part of the educational process carried on in formal institutions of instruction." By so limiting their subject, they "lost the capacity to see it in its full context and hence to assess the variety and magnitude of the burdens it had borne and to judge its historical importance."

At this point in our history we are in danger of losing our capacity to see the full context of teaching and to judge its historical, indeed its human, importance. This book therefore argues, in its conception, its arrangement, and its substance, that unless we remind ourselves that teaching is a vocation that extends far beyond departments of education and self-contained classrooms, we risk misunderstanding both its nature and its purposes. If we think of teaching simply as classroom activity or even more broadly but still restrictively as a schooling activity, we will be inclined to make one of two fundamental errors. We will either reduce it to a set of methods and techniques or we will mystify it by turning it into an occult practice that defies rational appraisal or description. This book suggests that good thinking by citizens about the everyday practice of good teaching begins with the recognition that teaching is a basic human activity whose excellence depends upon the exercise of certain intellectual, moral, and spiritual virtues. It also suggests that though teaching is closer to an art than it is to a technique, and though it certainly involves mysterious transactions, it is nevertheless a public activity that is improvable through practice, questioning, and the consideration of good examples.

3.

We might be convinced by now that we are all teachers, but on what grounds, if any, can we hope that a careful reading of a book like this one will improve our teaching? We need to ask ourselves first what good teaching is, and second, how we already try to improve our teaching in everyday life. Take a moment to think about the three people whom you would regard as your best teachers, and ask yourself what these three people had in common. When a large and diverse group of citizens recently pondered these latter questions, few of them included more than one professionally trained teacher in their list of three; they listed instead parents, spouses, friends, neighbors, pastors, siblings, and other relatives. So much for professionalism! But more important, almost no one, in answer to the second question about what the three teachers had in common, listed techniques or teaching styles. On the contrary. The three teachers selected were invariably very different from one another in terms of what they taught and how they taught it and even in terms of how well they knew or appeared to know what they taught. But they invariably had in common certain attitudes toward their craft or subject and toward their pupils as well. Moreover they had certain qualities of character in common—integrity, truthfulness, compassion, dedication, empathy, attentiveness, and love were frequently mentioned. In brief, people know good teaching when they see it, and when they try to describe it they rarely if ever do so in terms of some favored technique, even though a great deal of literature about teaching until quite recently emphasized technique over almost everything else.

These observations suggest that if we want to develop a rich account of good teaching, we must think about what the lives of professional teachers have in common with the lives of grandparents teaching their grandchildren how to sew or how to fish and with riverboat pilots teaching apprentices how to read a river. A book like Mark Twain's *Old Times on the Mississippi* might, in other words, have more to say to professionals about the excellences of teaching than the most recent publication on classroom pedagogy. And conversely, some books about teaching that have been written by professionals might improve the quality of teaching that all of us do as part of our everyday lives.

4.

This book is organized around assumptions like the ones we have been suggesting: that professional and nonprofessional teachers have a great deal to learn from one another; that before we can think well about how to teach anything in particular, we need to think about those qualities of character and mind that make good teaching of any kind possible; and that we can improve our own teaching through critical consideration of the teaching of others. This latter assumption points out a special feature of this whole book, perhaps its most important feature. The "teachings" contained here, readings gathered from a wide variety of people, times, and places, are "teachings" in two senses of the word. First, they are themselves something taught. Second, they are themselves acts of teaching. We all therefore find ourselves in a somewhat unusual position with respect to these texts. We can learn from reading them and in reading them.

An example drawn from one of the readings will make this point clearer. It comes from a dialogue of Plato, entitled *Meno*, that is included in its entirety as the first selection in Part II. Socrates attempts to show Meno something about teaching and learning by inviting Meno to examine the process by which Socrates helps a slave boy learn something about geometry, through asking the boy questions:

> S: Tell me now, boy, you know that a square figure is like this?—I do.
> S: A square then is a figure in which all these four sides are equal?—Yes indeed.
> S: And it also has these lines through the middle equal?—Yes.
> S: And such a figure could be larger or smaller?—Certainly.
> S: If then this side were two feet, and this other side two feet, how many feet would the whole be? Consider it this way: if it were two feet this way, and only one foot that way, the figure would be once two feet?—Yes.

S: But if it is two feet also that way, it would surely be twice two feet?—Yes.

S: How many feet is twice two feet? Work it out and tell me.—Four, Socrates.

S: Now let us have another figure twice the size of this one, with the four sides equal like this one.—Yes.

S: How many feet will that be?—Eight.

S: Come now, try to tell me how long each side of this will be. The side of this is two feet. What about each side of the one which is its double?—Obviously, Socrates, it will be twice the length.

S: You see, Meno, that I am not teaching the boy anything, but all I do is question him. And now he thinks he knows the length of the line on which an eight-foot figure is based. Do you agree?—I do.

S: And does he know?—Certainly not.

S: He thinks it is a line twice the length?—Yes. . . .

On further questioning the slave boy recognizes that the side of an "eight-foot square" cannot be either four (twice two) feet in length, or three feet in length, and he admits he is at a loss.

S: You realize, Meno, what point he has reached in his recollection. At first he did not know what the basic line of the eight-foot square was; even now he does not yet know, but then he thought he knew, and answered confidently as if he did know, and he did not think himself at a loss, but now he does think himself at a loss, and as he does not know, neither does he think he knows.—That is true.

S: So he is now in a better position with regard to the matter he does not know.

M: I agree with that too.

S: Have we done him any harm by making him perplexed and numb as the torpedo fish does?—I do not think so. . . .

S: Look then how he will come out of his perplexity while searching along with me. I shall do nothing more than ask questions and not teach him. Watch whether you find me teaching and explaining things to him instead of asking for his opinion.

S: You tell me, is this not a four-foot figure? You understand?—I do.

S: We add to it this figure which is equal to it?—Yes.

S: And we add this third figure equal to each of them?—Yes.

S: Could we then fill in the space in the corner?—Certainly.

S: So we have these four equal figures?—Yes.

S: Well, then, how many times is the whole figure larger than this one?—Four times.

S: But we should have had one that was twice as large, or do you not remember?—I certainly do.

S: Does not this line from one corner to the other cut each of these figures in two?—Yes.

S: So these are four equal lines which enclose this figure?—They are.

S: Consider now: how large is the figure?—I do not understand.

S: Each of these lines cuts off half of each of the four figures inside it, does it not?—Yes.

S: How many of this size are there in this figure?—Four.

S: How many in this?—Two.

S: What is the relation of four to two?—Double.

S: How many feet in this?—Eight.

S: Based on what line?—This one.

S: That is, on the line that stretches from corner to corner of the four-foot figure?—Yes.—Clever men call this the diameter, so that if diameter is its name, you say that the double figure would be that based on the diameter?—Most certainly, Socrates.

S: So what do you think, Meno? Has he, in his answers, expressed any opinion that was not his own?

M: No, they were all his own.

S: And yet, as we said, he did not know a short time ago?—That is true.

S: So these opinions were in him, were they not?—Yes.

S: So the man who does not know has within himself true opinions about the things that he does not know?—So it appears.

S: These opinions have now just been stirred up like a dream, but if he were repeatedly asked these same questions in various ways, you know that in the end his knowledge about these things would be as accurate as anyone's.—It is likely.

S: And he will know it without having been taught but only questioned, and find the knowledge within himself?—Yes.

S: And is not finding knowledge within oneself recollection?—Certainly.

S: Must he not either have at some time acquired the knowledge he now possesses, or else have always possessed it?—Yes.

S: If he always had it, he would always have known. If he acquired it, he cannot have done so in his present life. Or has someone taught him geometry? For he will perform in the same way about all geometry, and all other knowledge. Has someone taught him everything? You should know, especially as he has been born and brought up in your house.

M: But I know that no one has taught him.

S: Yet he has these opinions, or doesn't he?

M: That seems indisputable, Socrates.

S: If he has not acquired them in his present life, is it not clear that he had them and had learned them at some other time?—It seems so.

S: Then that was the time when he was not a human being?—Yes.

S: If then, during the time he exists and is not a human being he will have true opinions which, when stirred by questioning, become knowledge, will not his soul have learned during all time? For it is clear that during all time he exists, either as a man or not.—So it seems.

S: Then if the truth about reality is always in our soul, the soul would be immortal so that you should always confidently try to seek out and recollect what you do not know at present—that is, what you do not recollect?

M: Somehow, Socrates, I think that what you say is right.

S: I think so too, Meno. I do not insist that my argument is right in all other respects, but I would contend at all costs both in word and deed as far as I could that we will be better men, braver and less idle, if we believe that one must search for the things one does not know, rather than if we believe that it is not possible to find out what we do not know and that we must not look for it.

M: In this too I think you are right, Socrates.

S: Since we are of one mind that one should seek to find out what one does not know, shall we try to find out together what virtue is?

Notice that at several points during the course of Socrates' helping the slave boy to learn some geometrical truths, Socrates interrogates Meno about the process of teaching and learning. And as we study Meno watching Socrates and the slave boy, we too are drawn into the process of learning with Plato, the author of the dialogue, as our teacher. Many of the texts in this book will position us relative to certain characters who are teaching or learning in a place very like the one Meno occupies relative to Socrates and the slave boy in *Meno*. In those instances, we will have to learn to ask ourselves questions about the teaching and the learning very much like the questions that Socrates asks Meno. Those questions should include the following: are we learning something through these readings and the teaching and learning the readings represent to us? What exactly are we learning? From whom?

5.

This anthology is designed to do two things at once: first, to set before all of us a number of images of teaching and learning; second, to involve us in a process of learning about teaching through thinking about the ideas that these images bring to mind. Its organization is itself based on the pedagogical assumption that we learn how to do many things, in this case teach, by (a) imitating others and (b) asking the right questions in the right order about the studied subject or practice. With respect to teaching in particular, there must be another dimension to our learning as well. We must strive to be self-critical and self-aware. We must, in other words, learn to study and question ourselves as we study others teaching. In the case of our example above, we must ask ourselves whether the slave boy learns anything, whether Meno learns anything, and whether and how we ourselves learn anything by reading the entire account. Are we more like the slave boy or like Meno? Which of the several teachers whose teaching is represented in the readings sets the best example? How do we arrive at that judgment? What would it mean to follow that example in our own teaching?

The book divides the readings into four parts. The first part is a study of "the aims of education" through the dramatic exploration of the seven most common answers to the question, why do we teach? In some of the readings, we study the endeavors of a teacher seeking to realize one or another of these purposes of teaching—to civilize, to provide training for a job, or to inform. In others, like the excerpts from the *Joy of Cooking*, we immediately experience the purposive endeavors of a teacher to help us learn something. Though many of us have grown to believe that there are sharp and significant distinctions among these several aims or goods, the readings have been selected and arranged in order to invite us to reexamine critically that assumption. Is providing job training really and truly and completely different from evoking self-knowledge or civilizing or informing or cultivating arts and skills? And how, if at all, do these several aims inform the manner and the art of the teaching that goes on in an effort to realize them?

Having considered the aims of teaching, we turn in Part II, the most demanding of the four parts, to a consideration of the nature of teaching and learning. The four readings will compare and contrast two ancient accounts of teaching and learning to two contemporary ones. These contrasts will enable us to see and perhaps to begin to understand how and why the ancients placed a sense of transcendent mystery close to the heart of their explorations of teaching and learning. In the contemporary presentations such a sense is wholly absent. Readers will need to decide for themselves which of the accounts gets closest to the heart of teaching and learning as these activities are represented throughout the other sections of the book.

Having examined the nature of teaching, we turn in Part III to the many forms teaching has assumed and continues to assume in everyday life. This broad sampling of teaching is designed to remind us of how pervasive teaching has been and still is, and to expand our conception of what teaching includes. At the same time, the readings invite us to consider what common features hold them together. *All* of these examples address readers directly as those who might learn through engagement with them. We move from the experience of learning about teaching indirectly by studying others who are teaching and learning (Part I), through more abstract discussions about the nature of teach-

ing (Part II), to the experience of learning about teaching directly by studying how we ourselves learn in response to several forms of teaching (Part III).

Part IV leads us literally through those places where most of us have done the majority of our learning. We move from the home to the elementary school to the secondary school and finally to the college. These five readings dramatize teachers at work in the home and in the classroom in ways that both deepen the insights offered by preceding readings and call them sharply into question. The domestic scenes point to elements of teaching that are fundamental, seldom discussed, and rarely understood—awe, trust, fear, hope, and love. These scenes end with children literally being sent off to school. At the schools, we will meet three teachers teaching. They leave us, in this age of a renewed interest in "home schooling," with a sense of how difficult and profound the work of teaching really is and how permeable are the boundaries between home and school.

Even though there is a logical progression from Part I through Part IV, the book is organized to encourage readers to allow their own interests to guide the order of their reading and learning. The readings taken as a whole constitute a complex field of human endeavor—the activities of teaching and learning—that is best understood as a web of interconnected practices. Thus, a given reading from one section will illuminate a reading in another section in surprising ways. The introductions to each section point out some of these interconnections and invite readers to work out their own paths of learning through the material.

Both in its organization and in its contents, the book suggests that we cannot learn about teaching unless we also learn about learning. However, it seeks to promote this reflection about learning not for its own sake, but for the sake of improving our teaching. This explains in part why it does not include essays about cognitive psychology and other related sciences of learning. The other part of the explanation for this omission of cognitive theory is contained in the concluding reading in the volume, a lecture delivered by Eva Brann entitled "Depth and Desire." We have sought, as she has, not to provide a method or state a theory or solve a problem, but to provoke questioning and so to demonstrate both teaching and learning.

Part I

WHY TEACH?
THE GAINS AND LOSSES
OF LEARNING

The selections in Part I develop extended "answers" to the basic question, "why teach?" The answers, however, assume dramatically different forms and are often implied by the readings more than they are stated directly. All of the readings also address the question of what is lost as well as what is gained by learning something. Again, some of the readings address this question more directly than others. These particular readings have been selected because they dramatize or otherwise represent seven of the most common motives or reasons for teaching, and because they make us aware of the stakes involved in teaching and learning. We change when we learn; teachers are, among other things, agents of change in the souls and the minds, the skills and the habits, of students. Teachers therefore need to be deeply thoughtful about what can be and sometimes must be lost in the process of learning something. Is knowledge always a good thing? Or, as teachers more typically encounter such a question, is this kind of learning good for this particular student at this particular time for this particular purpose?

The first reading raises all of these questions in a profound and fundamental way. At the very end of the eighteenth century in the French Département of Aveyron a "wild boy" was found wandering at the edge of a forest where he had lived alone for many years. The boy soon became a popular sensation and a medical mystery; indeed, even today scholars disagree about what really afflicted him. Did he survive for many years utterly alone in the wild, or was he a recently abandoned "idiot," as many professionals thought at the time?

Or was there some combination of physical debility and cultural deprivation that accounted for his strange behavior?

The most skilled and humane of his diagnosticians was a young medical man named Jean-Marc-Gaspard Itard, who had been appointed as a physician at a new institution for deaf mutes shortly before he learned of the wild boy. The first selection, entitled *The Wild Boy of Aveyron,* is Itard's record of his diagnoses and of his effort to "civilize" the boy by teaching him a number of humanizing arts and skills. Itard develops several methods during the course of this complex endeavor, like multiplying the boy's needs, occasionally frightening him, and using techniques that we would today call "behavior modification." Do these techniques work? Are there some things that Itard underestimates or ignores, like the maternal love of Madame Guérin, as sources of the boy's education? In pondering the role of the affections in education, it might be profitable to compare the roles and the methods of Itard and Guérin to the roles and the methods of the two parents in the selections in Part IV from James Agee's *A Death in the Family.* How much of education depends upon the basic affections that children feel for parental figures, affections like awe, love, and trust?

Perhaps the most basic question raised by this reading is whether the boy was really better for his being civilized. It was a question that occurred again and again to Itard, who wrote in another of his reports, "Oh! How ready I was on this occasion, as on so many others, to give up my self-imposed task and regard as wasted the time that I had already given it! How many times did I regret ever having known this child, and freely condemn the sterile and inhuman curiosity of the men who *first tore him from his innocent and happy life!*" Such outbursts should remind us all that teaching is as often deeply frustrating as it is rewarding, but they should also make us wonder, in less dramatic ways perhaps, whether we do not rush too quickly to deprive children today of the play and innocence of childhood with routinized assignments that soon overwhelm them. The famous film by François Truffaut based on this reading, entitled *The Wild Child,* raises all of these issues even more powerfully and vividly. It should be required viewing for those who consider deeply this most fundamental of the answers to the question of why we should teach: "to civilize."

If civilizing is the most basic answer to the question of why we should teach, the next selection from Mark Twain's *Old Times on the Mississippi* presents the most common answer: "to provide vocational training." The selection that dramatizes this answer also presents one of the oldest educational practices, the practice of apprenticeship or, as we might say today, "on-the-job training." As with the first selection, the question of what is lost in the process of teaching and learning is a poignant one. Once the boy learns to read the

river as a pilot must read it, he loses the capacity to see it with an innocent eye. He loses to some extent the wonder, the mystery, and the beauty that seem just as much properties of the river as the more functional qualities it possesses as a medium of transportation. Is there some sense in which the boy really does retain his original sense of the river even after he comes to possess a more educated sensibility? And what of Mr. Bixby here? Is he a good teacher? What techniques does he use? Which ones of them are most effective and why?

During the course of his education, the boy learns a great deal of information about the river. But he almost always learns the information in an urgently practical context. Many people think that the main reason we teach is just "to provide information." The contrast between the Twain selection and the next reading, from Dickens's *Hard Times*, should make us wonder whether this is ever really so and whether providing information just for the sake of providing information is ever salutary. What effects does Dr. Gradgrind's view of the purpose of teaching have upon the children both inside and outside of the classroom? Must the good teacher always either awaken within the student a desire to learn the information (as Itard does) or supply a context in which the information is immediately useful (as Mr. Bixby does)? Does Dr. Gradgrind's failure to do either of these things well make him a bad teacher? Dickens's presentation of Gradgrind seems like negative caricature. Is there anything to be said on Gradgrind's behalf? What can we learn from his example to improve our own teaching?

We find a more positive example of good teaching in the next reading from *The Joy of Cooking*. In this selection, we find a fourth answer to our question of why we should teach, namely, "to cultivate arts and skills." The mother and daughter team who prepared the first edition of this book teach us quickly that there is much more to practicing any art than the right ingredients and the right recipes for success. One must also have the right attitudes, the proper understanding of the larger point and spirit of the endeavor, even an appreciation for the history of the various component practices involved in the art. In sum, the good cook exhibits many virtues, like the virtue of hospitality, that extend well beyond the skills necessary to find and blend the right ingredients at the right temperature in the right amounts at the right time. And these teachers seem to find just the right voice to convey all of this to those novices among us who mistakenly think that in order to become a good cook, we just need the right recipes. We learn here that following a recipe and practicing an art, though related, are two very different things, rather like the difference between taking information from a teacher and following her example.

By now we should have noticed the substantial overlap between the cultivation of arts and skills and the vocational training dramatized in the Twain reading. The next reading offers a fifth answer to our question about the reasons for teaching: "to initiate into a way of life." The role of the teacher in this selection from *Lame Deer: Seeker of Visions* seems to be restricted to knowing when the student is ready to undergo a particular rite of passage from one stage of life to another one, and knowing how best to prepare the student for the experience. But the point of this "teaching" is very similar to the point of teaching riverboat piloting. The latter teaching involves not simply instruction in how to read a river and maneuver a boat but also initiation into the way of life of riverboat pilots. And the art of cooking, extending as it does to cultivating at least the virtue of hospitality, shades into the formation of identity and selfhood. The transformation of Lame Deer from a boy to a man is more momentous and all-encompassing than the transformation of the novice into a cub pilot and then into a veteran riverboat pilot. Yet there is a sense in which the boy in Twain's book becomes more than just a pilot during the course of his education. And if we really attend fully to the teachings in the *Joy of Cooking,* we might find that we have become a different sort of person, not simply better cooks.

Sometimes these transformations wrought by teaching can be sudden and complete, almost like a conversion experience, rather than gradual and circumscribed. The sixth reading represents just such a moment in the life of David, the great king of Israel. Many teachers of the liberal arts would favor the answer to the question of why we should teach that is dramatized by this reading: "to evoke self-knowledge." They may resist, however, the idea that they, like the Nathan of the Bible story, should function as prophets. The pedagogical genius of Nathan here consists not so much of prophecy as of judgment. But here he accomplishes the best kind of judgment; he maneuvers the king to pass judgment upon himself.

Like the excerpts from Plato's *Meno* included in the introduction, the story of Nathan involves us in several levels of interpretation and engagement. We watch Nathan telling a story, and we watch the great king interpreting it and passing judgment upon it. We then watch the story become "living word," as clergymen might call it, a word of judgment that applies, not to remote and anonymous human beings, but to the king himself. This is an example of transformation through self-knowledge—a sudden change in character very much like the one accomplished at the center of classical tragedies where a reversal of role coincides with an insight into the truth of matters. Here the judge becomes the judged who at the same time sees himself for what he has become. But where are we in this story? What kind of teaching will it take to enable us to find ourselves in this text? And is this not one of the goals of all liberal learning, to enable students to find themselves in the works before them and to open themselves to the possibility of self-knowledge through the study of such works?

We come finally to a reason for teaching that is at once the most ambitious and the most self-effacing: "to change the world." Henry Adams once remarked that "a teacher touches eternity for he never knows where his influence stops." The poem that concludes this section also suggests that the business of teaching is a spiritual one, a religious calling that depends upon God for its successes. Echoing Henry Adams, *oma* (the grandmother) reminds the weary teacher, "you cannot know what your words / will weigh with students remembering them / in a place you will never see." Teachers may well change the world, but only through love of the work we have read about in this section: "read, talk, listen, cook, lay brick, sweep the mat when it is drenched with snow, wash the beaker, run the errand, pray for the healing of what you cannot heal." Though many of us may neither recognize nor share this Calvinist understanding of teaching as a religious vocation, we might ask ourselves which alternative accounts of teaching better capture the stark contrast between our natural sense of how much is potentially at stake in our teaching and how little we seem to be able to control the outcome of it.

Readings in Part I

1. Jean-Marc-Gaspard Itard, *The Wild Boy of Aveyron*, translated by George and Muriel Humphrey (Englewood Cliffs, N.J.: Prentice-Hall, 1962), pp. xxi–xxiv, 3–51. The diagnosis and treatment of this "wild boy" were controversial at the very beginning of the nineteenth century, and they remain so today. Itard's record of his clinical work with what some contemporaries believed to be an embodiment of Rousseau's "noble savage" raises some of the most fundamental and thought-provoking questions about the nature and purposes of education.

2. Mark Twain, *Old Times on the Mississippi*, in *The Portable Mark Twain*, edited by Bernard de Voto (New York: Viking Press, 1969), pp. 58–88. This book and its enlargement, *Life on the Mississippi*, feature some of the best passages in American literature on what was once the dominant form of "professional" or "vocational" education, namely, apprenticeship. The extended metaphor of the river represented as a book to be read invites comparisons between so-called vocational training and liberal learning, between teaching someone to read aspects of the world for practical purposes and teaching someone to read texts for the purposes of furnishing and strengthening the mind.

3. Charles Dickens, *Hard Times*, Norton Critical Edition (New York: W. W. Norton, 1987), pp. 1–11. Dickens's literal-minded Thomas Gradgrind has become

perhaps the most memorable caricature in all of English literature of the educator who believes that all good teaching is simply the inculcation of factual
information.

4. Irma S. Rombauer and Marion Rombauer Becker, *The Joy of Cooking*
(Indianapolis: Bobbs-Merrill, 1964), pp. 9–12, 14, 16–17, 163–165. This classic of
the culinary arts demonstrates as well as any text available how the very best
teaching of arts and skills must include the loving transmission of traditions
of thought and practice.

5. John (Fire) Lame Deer and Richard Erdoes, *Lame Deer: Seeker of Visions*
(New York: Washington Square Press, 1978), pp. 1–6. This selection raises the
question of whether teaching can be sometimes understood as a collective endeavor that is carried out primarily through rituals and communal story-telling.

6. 2 Samuel 11–12:15. This well-known story from the Bible presents the
prophet Nathan as being concerned in his teaching of the king with a number
of issues, including truth, justice, and the state of David's soul. It demonstrates
an especially effective way of teaching when, from one vantage point at least,
the pupil is much more powerful than the teacher.

7. Lionel Basney, "Dream of the School," in *Keeping Faith: Embracing the
Tensions in Christian Higher Education,* edited by Ronald Wells (Grand Rapids,
Mich.: William B. Eerdmans, 1996). The poem was presented on the occasion
of the inauguration of Gaylen J. Byker as president of Calvin College. It expresses very well some of the myriad connections between communities of
faith and communities of teaching and learning.

Jean-Marc-Gaspard Itard, *The Wild Boy of Aveyron*

Foreword by the Author

Cast upon this globe without physical strength or innate ideas, incapable in himself of obeying the fundamental laws of his nature which call him to the supreme place in the universe, it is only in the heart of society that man can attain the preeminent position which is his natural destiny. Without the aid of civilization he would be one of the feeblest and least intelligent of animals—a statement which has been many times repeated, it is true, but which has never yet been strictly proved. The philosophers who first made this statement, those who later upheld and taught it, have pointed to the physical and mental state of certain wandering tribes, which they regard as uncivilized because they are not civilized in our particular manner, and from which they have deduced the primitive characteristics of man as he exists in the pure state of nature. No, in spite of all assertions to the contrary, this is not the place to seek and study Man. In the most vagrant and barbarous horde as well as in the most civilized nation of Europe, man is only what he is made. Necessarily brought up by his own kind, he has acquired from them his habits and his needs; nor are his ideas any longer his own. He has enjoyed the fairest prerogative of his kind, the capacity of developing his understanding by the power of imitation and the influence of society.

The really wild type of man, one who owes nothing to his peers, ought then to be sought elsewhere. He ought to be reconstructed from the specific histories of a small number of individuals who, in the course of the seventeenth and beginning of the eighteenth centuries, have been found at different intervals living isolated in the woods, where they had been abandoned at a very early age.

But in those unenlightened times so retarded was the progress of science—given up as it was to the mania for explanation, the uncertainty of hypothesis, and to investigation undertaken exclusively in the armchair—that actual observation counted for nothing and these valuable facts concerning the natural history of man were lost. The accounts left of them by contemporary authors are reduced to a few insignificant details, from which the most striking and most general conclusion to be drawn is that these individuals were susceptible to no very marked improvement. This was doubtless because the ordinary method of social instruction was applied to their education, without consideration for the difference of their organs. If the application of this method was entirely successful with the wild girl found in France towards the beginning of the last century, it is because, having lived in the woods with a companion, she already owed to that simple association a certain development of her intellectual faculties. This gave her a real education, such as Condillac grants when he supposes two children abandoned in a profound solitude to whom the mere influence of cohabitation would naturally give scope for memory, imagination and even the invention of a few signs. This is an ingenious supposition fully justified by the story of the girl in question, in whom memory was found to be developed to the point where she could retrace in great detail some of the circumstances of her sojourn in the woods and above all, the violent death of her companion.

Deprived of these advantages the other children found in a state of individual isolation have brought to society only extremely sluggish powers. Their faculties were such that even if an attempt had been made to educate them, they would inevitably have defeated all the efforts of a metaphysics which was only just coming to life, and which was still hindered by the established doctrine of innate ideas. This metaphysics, united to a system of medicine fettered by entirely mechanical doctrines, could not rise to a philosophic treatment of the mind. Lighted by the torch of analysis and lending each other a mutual support, these two sciences have in our day laid aside their old errors and made immense progress. So it was reasonable to hope that if ever there appeared a creature similar to those of whom we have spoken, the sciences in question would bring to bear *all the resources of their present knowledge in order to develop him physically and morally,* or, at least, if this proved impossible or fruitless, there would be found in this age of observation someone who, *carefully collecting the history of so surprising a creature, would determine what he is and would deduce from what he lacks the hitherto uncalculated sum of knowledge and ideas which man owes to his education.*

Dare I confess that I have proposed to myself both of these two great undertakings? But let no one ask me if I have reached my goal. This would be a very premature question which I could only answer at a time yet far distant. Nevertheless I might have waited in silence without wishing to trouble the public with an account of my labors, if it had not been a necessity as much as an obligation for me to prove, by my first successes, that the child with whom I have been concerned is not, as is generally believed, a hopeless imbecile but an interesting being, and one who merits from every point of view both the attention of observers and the particular care which is being devoted to him by the solicitude of an enlightened and philanthropic administration.

First Developments of the Young Savage of Aveyron

A child of eleven or twelve who some years before had been seen completely naked in the Caune Woods seeking acorns and roots to eat, was met in the same place toward the end of September 1799 by three sportsmen who seized him as he was climbing into a tree to escape from their pursuit. Conducted to a neighboring hamlet and confided to the care of a widow, he broke loose at the end of a week and gained the mountains, where he wandered during the most rigorous winter weather, draped rather than covered with a tattered shirt. At night he retired to solitary places but during the day he approached the neighboring villages, where of his own accord he entered an inhabited house situated in the Canton of St. Sernin.

There he was retaken, watched and cared for during two or three days and transferred to the hospital of Saint-Afrique, then to Rodez where he was kept for several months. During his sojourn in these different places he remained equally wild and shy, impatient and restless, continually seeking to escape. He furnished material for most interesting observations, which were collected by credible witnesses whose accounts I shall not fail to report in this essay where they can be displayed to the best advantage. A minister of state with scientific interests believed that this event would throw some light upon the science of the mind. Orders were given that the child should be brought to Paris. He arrived there towards the end of September 1800 under the charge of a poor respectable old man who, obliged to part from the child shortly after, promised to come and take him again and act as a father to him should the Society ever abandon him.

The most brilliant and irrational expectations preceded the arrival of the Savage of Aveyron at Paris. A number of inquisitive people looked forward with delight to witnessing the boy's astonishment at the sights of the capital. On the other hand many people otherwise commendable for their insight, forgetting that human organs are by so much less flexible, and imitation made by so much more difficult, in proportion as man is removed from society and from his infancy, believed that the education of this child would only be a question of some months, and that he would soon be able to give the most interesting information about his past life. In place of all this what do we see? A disgustingly dirty child affected with spasmodic movements and often convulsions who swayed back and forth ceaselessly like certain animals in the menagerie, who bit and scratched those who opposed him, who showed no sort of affection for those who attended him; and who was in short, indifferent to everything and attentive to nothing.

It can easily be understood that a creature of this kind could excite only a momentary curiosity. People ran in crowds, they saw him without observing him, they passed judgment on him without knowing him, and spoke no more about him. In the midst of this general indifference the administrators of the National Institute of the Deaf and Dumb and its celebrated director never forgot that society, in taking over this unfortunate youth, had contracted towards him binding obligations that must be fulfilled. Sharing then the hopes which

I founded upon a course of medical treatment, they decided that this child should be confided to my care.

But before the details and results of this decision are presented I must begin with an account of our starting point and recall and describe this first period, in order that the progress we have made may be better appreciated. By thus contrasting the past with the present, we can determine what ought to be expected from the future. Obliged then to return to facts already known, I will state these briefly; and that I may not be suspected of having exaggerated for the purpose of contrast, I will venture here to give a careful analysis of the description given of the boy, in a meeting to which I had the honor of being admitted, by a doctor whose genius for observation is as famous as his profound knowledge of mental diseases.

Proceeding first with an account of the sensory functions of the young savage, citizen Pinel showed that his senses were reduced to such a state of inertia that the unfortunate creature was, according to his report, quite inferior to some of our domestic animals. His eyes were unsteady, expressionless, wandering vaguely from one object to another without resting on anybody; they were so little experienced in other ways and so little trained by the sense of touch, that they never distinguished an object in relief from one in a picture. His organ of hearing was equally insensible to the loudest noises and to the most touching music. His voice was reduced to a state of complete muteness and only a uniform guttural sound escaped him. His sense of smell was so uncultivated that he was equally indifferent to the odor of perfumes and to the fetid exhalation of the dirt with which his bed was filled. Finally, the organ of touch was restricted to the mechanical function of the grasping of objects. Proceeding then to the state of the intellectual functions of this child, the author of the report presented him to us as being quite incapable of attention (except for the objects of his needs) and consequently of all those operations of the mind which attention involves. He was destitute of memory, of judgment, of aptitude for imitation, and was so limited in his ideas, even those relative to his immediate needs, that he had never yet succeeded in opening a door or climbing upon a chair to get the food that had been raised out of reach of his hand. In short, he was destitute of all means of communication and attached neither expression nor intention to his gestures or to the movements of his body. He passed rapidly and without any apparent motive from apathetic melancholy to the most immoderate peals of laughter. He was insensible to every kind of moral influence. His perception was nothing but a computation prompted by gluttony, his pleasure an agreeable sensation of the organ of taste and his intelligence the ability to produce a few incoherent ideas relative to his wants. In a word, his whole life was a completely animal existence.

Later, reporting several cases collected at Bicêtre of children incurably affected with idiocy, citizen Pinel established very strict parallels between the condition of these unfortunate creatures and that of the child now under con- sideration, and convincingly established a complete and perfect identity be- tween these young idiots and the Savage of Aveyron. This identity led to the inevitable conclusion that, attacked by a malady hitherto regarded as incurable, he was not capable of any kind of sociability or instruction. This was the con- clusion which citizen Pinel drew but which, nevertheless, he accompanied by that philosophic doubt which pervades all his writings, and which accompa- nies the predictions of the man who estimates the science of prognosis at its true worth, seeing in it nothing but a more or less uncertain calculation of probabilities and conjectures.

I never shared this unfavorable opinion and in spite of the truth of the picture and the justice of the parallels I dared to conceive certain hopes. I founded them for my part upon the double consideration of the cause and the curability of this apparent idiocy. I cannot go further without dwelling a mo- ment upon these two considerations. Moreover, they bear upon the present and depend upon a series of facts which I must relate, and to which I shall see myself obliged more than once to add my own reflections.

If it were proposed to solve the following problem of metaphysics: *to de- termine what would be the degree of intelligence and the nature of the ideas of an adolescent, who, deprived from his childhood of all education, had lived entirely separated from individuals of his own species,* unless I am greatly mistaken the solution of the problem would be found as follows. There should first be as- signed to that individual nothing but an intelligence relative to the small num- ber of his needs and one which was deprived, by abstraction, of all the simple and complex ideas we receive by education, which combine in our mind in so many ways solely by means of our knowledge of signs, or reading. Well, the mental picture of this adolescent would be that of the Wild Boy of Aveyron and the solution of the problem would consist in exhibiting the extent and the cause of his intellectual state.

But in order to justify still further my opinion of the existence of this cause, it is necessary to prove that it has operated for a number of years, and to reply to the objection that can be made and that has already been made to me, that the so-called savage was merely a poor imbecile whom his parents in disgust had recently abandoned at the entrance to some woods. Those who lend themselves to such a supposition had not observed the child shortly after his arrival in Paris. They would have seen that all his habits bore the mark of a wandering and solitary life. He had an insurmountable aversion to society and to its customs, to our clothing, our furniture, to living in houses and to the preparation of our food. There was a profound indifference to the objects of our pleasures and of our fictitious needs; there was still in his present state, in spite of his new needs and dawning affections, so intense a passion for the freedom of the fields that during a short sojourn at Montmorency he would certainly have escaped into the forest had not the most rigid precautions been taken, and twice he did escape from the house of the Deaf and Dumb in spite of the supervision of his governess. His locomotion was extraordinary, literally heavy after he wore shoes, but always remarkable because of his difficulty in adjusting himself to our sober and measured gait, and because of his constant tendency to trot and to gallop. He had an obstinate habit of smelling at anything that was given to him, even the things which we consider void of smell; his mastication was equally astonishing, executed as it was solely by the sudden action of the incisors, which because of its similarity to that of certain rodents was a sufficient indication that our savage, like these animals, most commonly lived on vegetable products. I said most commonly, for it appeared by the following incident that in certain circumstances he had devoured small dead animals. A dead canary was given him and in an instant the bird was stripped of its feathers big and little, opened with his nail, sniffed at and thrown away.

Other indications of an entirely isolated, precarious and wandering life are the nature and the number of scars with which the child's body is covered. To say nothing of the scar which is visible on his throat and which I shall mention elsewhere as having another origin and meriting particular attention, there could be counted four upon his face, six along his left arm, three at some distance from the right shoulder, four at the margin of the pubis, one upon the left buttock, three on one leg and two on the other which makes twenty-three altogether. Of these some appeared to be due to bites of animals and the others to scratches which were more or less large and deep, forming numerous and ineffaceable evidences of the long and total abandonment of this unfortunate creature. When considered from a more general and philosophic point of view, these scars bear witness equally against the feebleness and insufficiency of man when left entirely to himself, and in favor of the resources of nature which, following apparently contradictory laws, work openly to repair and conserve that which she tends secretly to impair and to destroy.

Let us add to all these facts derived from observation those not less authentic to which the inhabitants of the country near the woods in which he was found have testified. We shall find that in the first days following his entrance into society, his only nourishment was acorns, potatoes and raw chestnuts, that he made no sort of sound, that in spite of the most active supervision he succeeded several times in escaping, that he showed a great repugnance to sleeping in a bed, etc. We shall find above all that he had been seen more than five years before entirely naked and fleeing at the approach of men, which presupposes that he was already, at the time of his first appearance, habituated to this manner of life, which could only be the result of at least two years' sojourn in uninhabited places. Thus this child had lived in an absolute solitude from his seventh almost to his twelfth year, which is the age he may have been when he was taken in the Caune woods. It is then probable, and almost proved, that he had been abandoned at the age of four or five years, and that if, at this time, he already owed some ideas and some words to the beginning of an education, this would all have been effaced from his memory in consequence of his isolation.

This is what appeared to me to be the cause of his present state. It can be seen why I augured favorably from it for the success of my treatment. Indeed, considering the short time he was among people, the Wild Boy of Aveyron was much less an adolescent imbecile than a child of ten or twelve months, and a child who would have the disadvantage of anti-social habits, a stubborn inattention, organs lacking in flexibility and a sensibility accidentally dulled. From this last point of view his situation became a purely medical case, and one the treatment of which belonged to mental science, that sublime art created in England by Willis and Crichton, and newly spread in France by the success and writings of Professor Pinel.

Guided much less by the spirit of their doctrine than by their precepts, which could not be adapted to this unforeseen case, I classified under five principal aims the mental and moral education of the Wild Boy of Aveyron.

1st Aim. To interest him in social life by rendering it more pleasant to him than the one he was then leading, and above all more like the life which he had just left.

2nd Aim. To awaken his nervous sensibility by the most energetic stimulation, and occasionally by intense emotion.

3rd Aim. To extend the range of his ideas by giving him new needs and by increasing his social contacts.

4th Aim. To lead him to the use of speech by inducing the exercise of imitation through the imperious law of necessity.

5th Aim. To make him exercise the simplest mental operations upon the objects of his physical needs over a period of time afterwards inducing the application of these mental processes to the objects of instruction.

I

First Aim. *To interest him in social life by rendering it more pleasant to him than the one he was then leading and above all more like the life which he had just left.*

This sudden change in his manner of life, the continued pestering of inquisitive people, a certain amount of ill-natured treatment which was the inevitable effect of living with children of his own age, seemed to have extinguished all hope of civilizing him. His petulant activity had insensibly degenerated into a dull apathy which had produced yet more solitary habits. Thus, except for the occasions when hunger took him to the kitchen, he was always to be found squatting in a corner of the garden or hidden in the attic behind some builders' rubbish. It was in this unfortunate condition that certain inquisitive persons from Paris saw him, and after an examination of some minutes judged him fit to be sent to an asylum; as if society had the right to tear a child away from a free and innocent life, and send him to die of boredom in an institution, there to expiate the misfortune of having disappointed public curiosity. I believed that there was a simpler and above all, a more humane method, namely, to treat him kindly and to exercise great consideration for his tastes and inclinations. Madame Guérin, to whom the authorities had confided the special care of this child, has performed and is still performing this exacting task with all the patience of a mother and the intelligence of an enlightened teacher. Far from opposing his habits, she has been able somehow to compromise with them and in that way to realize this first aim.

As far as one could judge of the past life of this child by his present inclinations, it was clear that, like certain savages from hot countries, his knowledge was limited to four things, viz. sleeping, eating, doing nothing and running about the fields. It was necessary then to make him happy in his own way, by putting him to bed at the close of day, supplying him abundantly with foods to his taste, respecting his indolence, and by accompanying him whenever possible for walks, or rather scampers, no matter what the weather was. These rural excursions seemed even more pleasing to him when a sudden or violent change in the weather occurred, so true it is that whatever condition he may be in, man is greedy for new sensations. Thus, for example, when watched inside his own room he was seen swaying with a tiresome monotony, turning his eyes constantly towards the window, looking sadly over the airy plains outside. If at such a time a stormy wind chanced to blow, if the sun behind the clouds showed itself suddenly illuminating the atmosphere more brightly, there were loud bursts of laughter, an almost convulsive joy, during which all his movements backwards and forwards very much resembled a kind of leap he would like to take, in order to break through the window and dash into the garden. Sometimes instead of these joyous movements there was a kind of frantic rage, he writhed his arms, pressed his closed fists upon his eyes, gnashed his teeth audibly and became dangerous to those who were near him.

One morning when there had been a heavy fall of snow while he was in bed, on awakening he uttered a cry of joy, left the bed, ran to the window, then to the door, going and coming with impatience from one to the other and finally escaped half dressed and gained the garden. There, giving vent to his delight by the most piercing cries, he ran, rolled himself in the snow and gathered it by handfuls, feasting on it with eagerness.

But it was not always that his sensations would be expressed in such a lively and noisy manner at the sight of these grand effects of nature. It is worthy of notice that in certain cases they appeared to assume the stillness of regret and of melancholy—a very hazardous conjecture and one doubtless much opposed to the opinions of metaphysicians, but one which could not be gainsaid when this unfortunate youth was observed carefully and in certain circumstances. Thus, when the inclemency of the weather drove everybody from the garden, that was the moment when he chose to go there. He went round it several times and finished by sitting upon the edge of the pond.

I have often stopped for hours with inexpressible delight to consider him in this situation. I noticed how all these spasmodic movements and this continual swaying of his whole body diminished, subsiding by degrees and giving place to a more tranquil attitude. By what imperceptible stages his face, vacant or grimacing, took on a very decided expression of sadness or of melancholy reverie, as his eyes clung fixedly to the surface of the water, while from time to time he threw in some debris or dried leaves! During the night by the beautiful light of the moon, when the rays of this heavenly body penetrated into his room, he rarely failed to waken and place himself before the window. He stayed there, according to the report of his governess, for part of the night, standing motionless, his neck bent, his eyes fixed upon the moon-lit fields giving himself up to a sort of contemplative ecstasy, the silence and immobility of which were only interrupted at long intervals by deep inspirations nearly always accompanied by a plaintive little sound. It would have been as useless as inhuman to try to oppose these new habits and it even entered into my mind to associate them with his new existence in order to render it more agreeable. It was different with such habits as had the disadvantage of exercising his stomach and muscles continuously, thus leaving the sensibilities of the nerves and the faculties of the brain without action. Thus I made it my aim, and gradually succeeded in my attempt, to render his excursions less frequent, his meals fewer and less plentiful, his time in bed much shorter, and his days more profitable from the instructional point of view.

II

Second Aim. *To awaken his nervous sensibility by the most energetic stimulation, and sometimes by intense emotion.*

Certain modern physiologists have suspected that sensitiveness is directly proportional to civilization. I do not believe that a stronger proof of this could be given than the dullness of the Wild Boy of Aveyron's sense organs. The reader may convince himself by a glance at the description that I have already given which rests on facts drawn from the most authentic source. Relative to the same subject I will add here some of my most striking observations.

Several times during the course of the winter I have seen him crossing the garden of the Deaf and Dumb, squatting half naked upon the wet ground, remaining thus exposed for hours on end to a cold and wet wind. It was not only to cold but also to intense heat that the organ of the skin and touch showed no sensitivity. When he was near the fire and the glowing embers came rolling out of the hearth it was a daily occurrence for him to seize them with his fingers and replace them without any particular haste upon the flaming fire. He has been discovered more than once in the kitchen picking out in the same way potatoes which were cooking in boiling water, and I can guarantee that he had, even at that time, a fine and velvety skin.

I have often succeeded in filling the exterior cavities of his nose with snuff without making him sneeze. The inference is that between the organ of smell, which was very highly developed in other respects, and those of respiration and sight, there did not exist any of those sympathetic relations which form an integral part of our sensibility, and which in this case would have caused sneezing or the secretion of tears. Still less was the secretion of tears connected with feelings of sadness, and in spite of innumerable annoyances, in spite of the bad treatment to which his new manner of life had exposed him during the first months, I have never discovered him weeping. Of all his senses, the ear appeared the least sensitive. It was found, nevertheless, that the sound of a cracking walnut or other favorite eatable never failed to make him turn round. This observation is quite accurate: yet, nevertheless, this same organ showed itself insensible to the loudest noises and the explosion of firearms. One day I fired two pistol shots near him, the first appeared to rouse him a little, the second did not make him even turn his head.

I have collated a number of similar cases where the lack of mental attention was taken for a lack of sensibility in the organ, but found, however, that this nervous sensibility was singularly weak in most of the other sense organs as well. Consequently it became part of my plan to develop it by all possible means, and to prepare the mind for attention by preparing the senses to receive keener impressions. Of the various means I employed, the effect of heat appeared to me best to fulfill this purpose. It is admitted by physiologists and political theorists that the inhabitants of the South owe their exquisite sensibility, so superior to that of the northerners, entirely to the action of heat upon the skin. I employed this stimulus in all possible ways. Not only was he clothed, put to bed, and housed warmly, but every day I gave him, and at a very high temperature, a bath lasting two or three hours during which frequent douches with the same water were administered to him on the head. I did not observe that the warmth and the frequency of the baths were followed by the debilitating effect attributed to them.

I should even have been glad if such had happened, convinced that in such a case the nervous sensibility would gain by the loss of muscular strength. But if the one effect did not follow, at least the other did not disappoint my expectations. After some time our young savage showed himself sensitive to the action of cold, made use of his hand to find out the temperature of the bath, and refused to enter when it was only lukewarm. For the same reason he soon began to appreciate the utility of clothes which until then he had only endured with much impatience. This utility once recognized, it was only a step to make him dress himself. This end was attained after some days by leaving him each morning exposed to the cold within reach of his clothes until he himself knew how to make use of them. A very similar expedient sufficed to give him at the same time habits of cleanliness and the certainty of passing the night in a cold wet bed accustomed him to get up in order to satisfy his needs. To the administration of the baths I added the use of dry frictions along the spine and even ticklings of the lumbar region. This last means was more exciting than most. I even found myself obliged to reject it, when its effects were no longer limited to producing movements of pleasure but appeared to extend further to the generative organs and to add the threat of perversion to the first stirrings of an already precocious puberty.

To these various stimulants I had to add emotional stimulants which were no less exciting. Those to which he was susceptible at this time were confined to two, joy and anger. The latter I only provoked at long intervals, for its attack was most violent and always apparently justified. I remarked sometimes that in the force of his passion his intelligence seemed to acquire a sort of extension which furnished him with some ingenious expedient in order to get himself out of trouble. Once when we wanted to make him take a bath which was as yet only lukewarm and our reiterated entreaties had made him violently angry, seeing that his governess was not convinced of the coolness of the water by the frequent tests that he made with the tips of his own fingers, he turned towards her quickly, seized her hand and plunged it into the bath.

Let me relate another act of the same nature. One day when he was in my study sitting upon a sofa I came to sit at his side and placed between us a Leyden jar lightly charged. A slight shock which he had received from it the day before had made him familiar with its effect. Seeing the uneasiness which the approach of the instrument caused him I thought he would move it further away by taking hold of the handle. He took a more prudent course which was to put his hands in the opening of his waistcoat, and to draw back some inches so that his leg would no longer touch the covering of the bottle. I drew near him a second time and again replaced it between us. Another movement on his part, another adjustment on mine. This little maneuvre continued until, driven into a corner at the end of the sofa, he found himself bounded by the wall behind, by a table in front, and at my side by the troublesome machine.

It was no longer possible for him to make any movement. It was then that, seizing the moment when I advanced my arm in order to guide his, he very adroitly lowered my wrist upon the knob of the bottle. I received the discharge.

But if sometimes in spite of the intense interest this young orphan inspired in me I took upon myself to excite his anger, I let no occasion pass of procuring happiness for him: and certainly this was neither difficult nor costly. A ray of sun reflected upon a mirror in his room and turning about on the ceiling, a glass of water let fall drop by drop from a certain height upon his finger tips while he was in the bath, and, a wooden porringer containing a little milk placed at the end of his bath, which the oscillations of the water drifted, little by little, amid cries of delight, into his grasp, such simple means were nearly all that was necessary to divert and delight this child of nature almost to the point of ecstasy.

Such were, among a host of others, the stimulations, both physical and mental, with which I endeavored to develop the sensibilities of his organs. These methods produced after three months a general excitement of all the senses. His touch showed itself sensitive to the impression of hot or cold substances, smooth or rough, yielding or resistant. At that time I wore velvet breeches over which he seemed to take pleasure in passing his hand. It was with this exploratory organ that he nearly always assured himself of the degree to which his potatoes were cooked. Taking them from the pot with a spoon he would apply his fingers to them several times and decide according to their state of softness or resistance whether to eat them or throw them back again into the boiling water. When he was given a candle to light with some paper, he did not always wait until the fire had caught the wick before throwing the paper away hurriedly, although the flame was not yet near his fingers. If he was forced to push or to carry anything he would sometimes abandon it suddenly although it was neither hard nor heavy, in order to look at the ends of his fingers which were certainly neither bruised nor hurt, after which he would put his hand gently in the opening of his waistcoat. The sense of smell had also gained by this improvement. The least irritation of this organ provoked sneezing, and I judged by the fright that seized him the first time this happened, that this was a new experience to him. He immediately ran away and threw himself on his bed.

The refinement of the sense of taste was even more marked. The eating habits of this child shortly after he arrived at Paris were disgusting in the extreme. He dragged his food into the corners and kneaded it with his filthy hands.

But at the time of which I am now speaking it frequently happened that he would throw away in a temper all the contents of his plate if any foreign substance fell on it; and when he had broken his walnuts under his feet, he fastidiously wiped the nuts clean.

Finally disease itself, that irrefutable and troublesome witness of the characteristic sensitiveness of civilized man, came at this point to attest the development of this principle of life. Towards the first days of spring, our young savage had a violent cold in the head and some weeks later two catarrhal affections, one almost immediately succeeding the other.

Nevertheless, all his organs did not respond so quickly. Those of sight and hearing did not participate in the improvement, doubtless because these two senses, much less simple than the others, had need of a particular and longer education as may be seen by what follows.

The simultaneous improvement of the three senses, touch, taste and smell, resulting from the stimulants applied to the skin whilst these last two remained unaffected is a valuable fact, worthy of being drawn to the attention of physiologists. It seems to prove, what from other sources appears probable, that the senses of touch, smell and taste are only a modification of the organ of the skin; whereas those of hearing and sight, more subjective, enclosed in a most complicated physical apparatus, are subject to other laws and ought in some measure to form a separate class.

III

Third Aim. *To extend the range of his ideas by giving him new needs and by social contacts.*

If the progress of this child towards civilization and my success in developing his intelligence have hitherto been so slow and so difficult, I must attribute this more particularly to the innumerable obstacles I have met in accomplishing this third aim. I have successively shown him toys of all kinds; more than once I have tried for whole hours to teach him how to use them and I have seen with sorrow that, far from attracting his attention, these various objects always ended by making him so impatient that he came to the point of hiding them or destroying them when the occasion offered itself. Thus, one day when he was alone in his room he took upon himself to throw into the fire a game of ninepins with which we had pestered him and which had been shut up for a long time in a night commode, and he was found gaily warming himself before his bonfire.

However, I succeeded sometimes in interesting him in amusements which had connection with his appetite for food. Here is one, for example, which I often arranged for him at the end of the meal when I took him to dine with me in town. I placed before him without any symmetrical order, and upside down, several little silver cups, under one of which was placed a chestnut. Quite sure of having attracted his attention, I raised them one after the other excepting that which covered the nut. After having thus shown him that they contained nothing, and having replaced them in the same order, I invited him by signs to seek in his turn. The first cup under which he searched was precisely the one under which I had hidden the little reward due to him. Thus far, there was only a feeble effort of memory. But I made the game insensibly more complicated. Thus after having by the same procedure hidden another chestnut, I changed the order of all the cups, slowly, however, so that in this general inversion he was able, although with difficulty, to follow with his eyes and with his attention the one which hid the precious object. I did more; I placed nuts under two or three of the cups and his attention, although divided between these three objects, still followed them none the less in their respective changes, and directed his first searches towards them. Moreover, I had a further aim in mind. This judgment was after all only a calculation of greediness. To render his attention in some measure less like an animal's, I took away from this amusement everything which had connection with his appetite, and put under the cups only such objects as could not be eaten. The result was almost as satisfactory and this exercise became no more than a simple game of cups, not without advantage in provoking attention, judgment, and steadiness in gaze.

With the exception of amusements which like this lent themselves to his physical wants, it has not been possible for me to inspire in him a taste for those of his age. I am almost certain that if I could have done so I should have had great success. To appreciate this, one should remember the powerful influence exerted on the first development of thought by the games of childhood as well as by the little pleasures of the palate.

I have also done everything to awaken these last tendencies by means of the dainties most coveted by children and which I hoped to use as a new means of recompense, punishment, encouragement and instruction. But the aversion which he showed for all sweet substances and for our most delicate dishes was insurmountable. I then thought it advisable to try the use of seasoned dishes as being most suitable to arouse a sense necessarily dulled by rough foods. This was not any more successful and I offered him in vain, at such times when he was hungry and thirsty, strong liquors and spiced foods. Despairing at last of being able to inspire in him any new tastes, I cultivated the few to which he was limited by accompanying them with all accessories that could increase his pleasure in them.

It was with this intention that I often took him to dine with me in town. On such occasions there was on the table a complete collection of his favorite dishes. The first time that he found himself at such a feast there were transports of joy amounting almost to frenzy. Doubtless he thought that he would not do so well at supper time as he had just done at dinner, for on leaving the house that evening it was not his fault that he did not carry away with him a plate of lentils that he had pilfered from the kitchen. I congratulated myself on this first outcome. I had just procured him a pleasure; I had only to repeat it several times to make it a necessity. Which is what I actually did. I did more. I was careful to precede our expeditions by certain preparations which he would notice; these were to enter his home about four o'clock, my hat upon my head, his shirt folded in my hand. These preparations soon came to be for him the signal of departure. I scarcely appeared before I was understood; he dressed himself hurriedly and followed me with much evidence of satisfaction. I do not give this fact as proof of a superior intelligence and there is no one who will not object that the most ordinary dog will do at least as much. But in admitting this intellectual equality one is obliged to acknowledge a great change, and those who saw the Wild Boy of Aveyron at the time of his arrival in Paris, know that he was very inferior on the score of discernment to this most intelligent of our domestic animals.

It was impossible when I took him with me to go on foot. It would have been necessary for me to run with him or else to use most tiring violence in order to make him walk in step with me. We were obliged, then, to go out only in a carriage, another new pleasure that he connected more and more with his frequent excursions. In a short time these days ceased to be merely holidays to which he gave himself up with the liveliest pleasure, but were real necessities the privation of which, when there was too long an interval between them, made him sad, restless and capricious.

How the pleasure was increased when these parties took place in the country! I took him not long ago to the country house of citizen Lachabeaussiére in the valley of Montmorency. It was a most curious sight, and I venture to say one of the most touching, to see the joy that was pictured in his eyes at the sight of the little hills and woods of that laughing valley. It seemed as if the eagerness of his gaze could not be satisfied through the windows of the carriage. He leaned now towards the one, now towards the other, and showed the liveliest anxiety when the horses went more slowly or were about to stop. He spent two days in this country house and such was the effect of these outside influences, of these woods, these hills, with which he could never satisfy his eyes, that he appeared more impatient and wild than ever, and, in the midst of the most assiduous and kind attention and most affectionate care, seemed to be occupied only with the desire to take flight. Entirely captivated by this dominant idea which absorbed all his faculties and even the consciousness of his needs, he scarcely found time to eat. He would get up from the table every minute and run to the window in order to escape into the park if it was open; or if it was shut, to contemplate, at least through the panes, all those objects towards which he was irresistibly attracted by still recent habits and perhaps even by the memory of an independent life, happy and regretted. I therefore resolved never again to submit him to similar tests. But in order not to sever him entirely from his country tastes, he was taken continually to walk in some neighboring gardens, of which the straight and regular arrangement had nothing in common with the great landscapes of which wild nature is composed, and which so strongly attach primitive man to the place of his childhood. Thus Madame Guérin took him sometimes to the Luxembourg and almost daily to the Observatory gardens where the kindness of citizen Lemeri has accustomed him to go every day for a lunch of milk. By means of these new habits, of certain recreations of his own choosing and finally, of all the kind treatment with which his new existence was surrounded, he finished by liking it all. This was the beginning of the intense affection which he has acquired for his governess and which he sometimes expresses in a most touching manner. He never leaves her without reluctance nor does he rejoin her without signs of satisfaction.

Once when he had escaped from her in the streets, he shed many tears on seeing her again. Some hours after, he still had a high and broken respiration and a kind of feverish pulse. When Madame Guérin reproached him, he interpreted her tone so well that he began to weep. The friendship which he had for me was much less strong, and justifiably so. The care which Madame Guérin takes of him is of a kind which is immediately appreciated, and what I give him is of no obvious use to him. That this difference is unquestionably due to the cause indicated is shown by the fact that there are times when he welcomes me and they are the times which I have never used for his instruction. For example, when I go to the house in the evening just after he has gone to bed, his first movement is to sit up for me to embrace him, then to draw me to him by seizing my arm and making me sit upon his bed, after which he usually takes my hand, carries it to his eyes, his forehead, the back of his head, and holds it with his upon these parts for a very long time. At other times he gets up with bursts of laughter and comes beside me to caress my knees in his own way which consists of feeling them, rubbing them firmly in all directions for some minutes, and then sometimes in laying his lips to them two or three times. People may say what they like, but I will confess that I lend myself without ceremony to all this childish play.

I shall perhaps be understood if my readers will remember the paramount influence exerted upon a child's mind by the inexhaustible delights and the maternal triflings that nature has put into the heart of a mother and which make the first smiles flower and bring to birth life's earliest joys.

IV

Fourth Aim. *To lead him to the use of speech by inducing the exercise of imitation through the imperious law of necessity.*

If I had wished to relate only happy results I should have suppressed from this account this fourth aim, the means I have employed in order to reach it and the slight success I have obtained in it. But my object is to give an account not so much of my own labors as of the first mental developments of the *Savage of Aveyron*, and I ought not to omit anything that can have the least bearing on this. I shall even be obliged to introduce certain theoretical ideas here and I hope that they will be pardoned when it is seen how careful I have been to found them on nothing but facts and when it is recognized that I was obliged to reply to the everlasting objections. *"Does the Savage speak? If he is not deaf why does he not speak?"*

It is easily conceived that in the midst of the forest and far from the society of all thinking beings, the sense of hearing of our savage did not experience any other impressions than those which a small number of noises made upon him, and particularly those which were connected with his physical needs. Under these circumstances his ear was not an organ for the appreciation of sounds, their articulations and their combinations; it was nothing but a simple means of self-preservation which warned of the approach of a dangerous animal or the fall of wild fruit. These are without doubt the functions to which his hearing was limited, judging by the slight response obtained from the organ given a year ago to all sounds and noises except those bearing upon his individual needs; and judging on the other hand, by the exquisite sensibility which this sense showed for such sounds as had some such connection with his interests. When a chestnut or a walnut was cracked without his knowledge and as gently as possible; if the key of the door which held him captive was merely touched, he never failed to turn quickly and run towards the place whence the sound came. If the organ of hearing did not show the same susceptibility for the sounds of the voice, even for the explosion of firearms, it was because he was necessarily little sensitive and little attentive to all other impressions than those to which he had been long and exclusively accustomed.

It is understandable then why the ear, well qualified to perceive certain noises however slight, would not be apt to appreciate the articulation of sounds. Moreover in order to speak it is not sufficient to perceive the sound of the voice, it is necessary also to appreciate the articulation of that sound, two very distinct operations which require different conditions on the part of the organ. For the first a certain degree of sensibility of the auditory nerve is sufficient, for the second there must be a special modification of this same sensibility. It is possible then that certain well-organized and very quick ears may be unable to seize the articulation of words. Many mutes have been found among the Cretins who are nevertheless not deaf. Among the pupils of citizen Sicard there are two or three children who hear perfectly the sound of the clock, clapping of hands, the lowest tones of the flute and violin, but who have however never been able to imitate the pronunciation of a word even though it may be articulated very loudly and slowly. Thus one might say that speech is a species of music to which certain ears, although perfectly constituted otherwise, may be insensible. Will it be the same with the child here in question? I do not think so, although my hopes have not much foundation. It is true that my efforts here have not been very numerous and that for a long time, uncertain as to the line I ought to take, I restricted myself to the rôle of observer. This then is what I have noticed. During the first four or five months of his sojourn in Paris, the *Savage of Aveyron* only showed himself sensitive to different noises which had for him the association I have indicated. During the current November he has appeared to hear the human voice and when two people conversed loudly in the corridor adjacent to his room it occurred to him to go up to the door in order to reassure himself that it was quite closed; he also closed an inside swinging door, taking the precaution to put his finger on the latch to secure its fastening still better. I noticed sometime after that he distinguished the voice of the deaf and dumb, or rather the gutteral cry which continually escapes them in their games. He even seemed to recognize the place where the sound came from, for if he heard it on coming down the stairs he never failed to go up again or come down more quickly according as whether the cry came from above or below. At the beginning of December I made a most interesting observation. One day when he was in the kitchen occupied with cooking potatoes two people had a sharp dispute behind him, without his appearing to pay the least attention. A third arrived unexpectedly, who, joining in the discussion, commenced all his replies with these words,—"Oh, that is different." I noticed that every time that this person let his favorite "Oh!" escape, the *Savage of Aveyron* quickly turned his head. That evening when he went to bed I made some experiments upon this sound and obtained almost the same results. I went over all the other simple sounds known as vowels but without any success. This preference for "O" obliged me to give him a name which terminated with this vowel. I chose Victor. This name remains his and when it is called he rarely fails to turn his head or to run up.

It is perhaps for the same reason that in the sequel he has understood the significance of the negative *Non* which I often used to correct him when he made mistakes in his little exercises.

In the middle of these slow but obvious developments of the organ of hearing his voice remained mute and refused to render those articulate sounds which his ear appeared to appreciate. However, the vocal organs in their exterior conformation presented no trace of imperfection and there was no reason for suspecting it in their interior organization. It is true that there is visible on his throat a very extended scar which might throw some doubt upon the soundness of the underlying parts if one were not reassured by the appearance of the scar. In fact it looks like a wound made by a sharp instrument but from its linear appearance one is inclined to believe that the wound was only a superficial one and that it would have reunited at the first attempt, or to use the technical term, by first intention. It is to be presumed that a hand with the will rather than the habit of crime had wished to make an attempt on the life of this child, and that, left for dead in the woods, he will have owed the prompt recovery of his wound to the help of nature alone. This recovery could not have been effected so happily if the muscular and cartilaginous parts of the organ of speech had been severed. Because of these considerations, when he did not repeat the sounds which his ear began to perceive, I did not conclude that this was due to an organic lesion, but merely to unfavorable circumstances. Complete absence of exercise renders our organs unfit for their functions; and if those already trained are so powerfully affected by this inaction, what will become of those which grow and develop without any incentive to put them into play? At least eighteen months of careful education are necessary before a child stammers a few words; and a rough inhabitant of the woods who has been in society for only fourteen or fifteen months, of which he has spent five or six among deaf mutes, is expected to be in a condition to talk! Not only is that impossible, but much more time and much more trouble will be necessary before coming to this important point in his education than would be needed for the least precocious of children. Such a child knows nothing, but he possesses in a marked degree the capacity of learning everything, an innate propensity to imitation, and extreme flexibility and sensibility of all organs, perpetual mobility of the tongue, an almost gelatinous consistency of the larynx. In short, everything cooperates to produce in him that continuous babbling which is the involuntary apprenticeship of the voice and which is assisted also by coughing, sneezing, the cries of that age, and even the tears, tears that must be considered not only as the indications of a ready excitability, but in addition as a powerful motive perpetually applied at the time most expedient for the simultaneous development of the organs of respiration, voice, and speech. Grant me these great advantages and I will guarantee the same result. Even admitting as I do that such a result can no longer be expected of the young adolescent Victor, it must also be realized that Nature is prolific enough to create new means of education when accidental causes intervene to deprive her of those that she had primitively arranged. Here are some facts at least which may justify this hope.

I said at the beginning of the fourth section that I proposed to lead him to the use of speech *by inducing the exercise of imitation through the imperious law of necessity.* By the considerations put forth in the last two paragraphs, and by another equally conclusive one which I will shortly set forth, I was convinced that a tardy functioning of the larynx must be expected and that I ought to accelerate its activity by coaxing it with something he wanted, I had reason to believe that the vowel "O," having been the first heard would be the first pronounced, and I found it very favorable to my plan that this simple pronunciation was, at least with respect to the sound, the sign of one of the most ordinary needs of the child. Nevertheless, I was unable to derive any advantage from this favorable coincidence. When his thirst was most intense, it was in vain that I held before him a glass of water, crying frequently *"eau" "eau."* Then I gave the glass to someone else who pronounced the same word beside him, asking for it back in the same way. But the unfortunate creature, tormented on all sides, waved his arms about the glass almost convulsively, producing a kind of hiss but not articulating any sound. It would have been inhuman to insist further. I changed the subject without, however, changing the method. It was upon the word *lait* that I carried out my next experiments.

On the fourth day of this next experiment I succeeded to my heart's content, and I heard Victor pronounce distinctly, though rather uncouthly it is true, the word *lait,* and he repeated it almost immediately. It was the first time that an articulate sound left his mouth and I did not hear it without the most intense satisfaction.

Nevertheless I made a reflection which in my eyes much diminished the advantage of this first success. It was not until the moment when, despairing of success, I came to pour the milk into the cup which he gave me, that the word *lait* escaped him with great demonstrations of pleasure; and it was only after I had poured it again as a reward that he pronounced it a second time. It can be seen why this result was far from fulfilling my intentions. The word pronounced instead of being the sign of his need was, relative to the time when it had been articulated, merely an exclamation of pleasure. If this word had been uttered before the thing which he desired had been granted, success was ours, the real use of speech was grasped by Victor, a point of communication established between him and me, and the most rapid progress would spring from this first triumph. Instead of all this, I had just obtained a mere expression, insignificant to him and useless to us, of the pleasure which he felt. Strictly speaking, it was certainly a vocal sign, the sign of possession. But this sign, I repeat, did not establish any relation between us. It had soon to be neglected because it was useless to the needs of the individual and was swamped by a multitude of irrelevancies, like the ephemeral and variable sentiment for which it had become the sign. The subsequent results of this misuse of the word have been such as I feared.

It was generally only during the enjoyment of the beverage that the word *lait* was heard. Sometimes he happened to pronounce it before and at other times a little after but always without purpose. I attach no more importance to this spontaneous repetition than to his repetition of it even now during the night when he happens to wake. Following this result I have entirely given up the method by which I obtained it. Awaiting the moment when circumstances will allow me to substitute another which I believe to be more efficacious, I have given over his vocal organs to the influence of imitation which, although feeble, is nevertheless not extinct, if judged by some slight subsequent and spontaneous progress.

The word *lait* has been for Victor the root of two other monysyllables *la* and *li*, to which he certainly attaches even less meaning. He has since modified the latter a little by adding a second *l* and pronouncing both like the *gli* in Italian. He is often heard to repeat *lli lli* with an inflection of voice not without sweetness. It is surprising that the liquid *l* which for children is one of the most difficult sounds to pronounce, should be one of the first that he has articulated. I am somewhat inclined to believe that in this painful linguistic labor there is a sort of feeling after the name of Julie, a young girl of eleven or twelve who comes to spend Sundays with Madame Guérin, her mother. Certain it is that on this particular day the exclamations *lli, lli,* become more frequent and, according to the account of his governess, are even heard during the night, at times when there is reason to believe that he is sleeping soundly. The cause and value of this last fact cannot be exactly determined. It is necessary to postpone its classification and description until a more advanced puberty has allowed us to make more observations. The latest accomplishment of his vocal organs is somewhat more considerable and is composed of two syllables which equal three because of the way he pronounces the last.

It is the exclamation *"Oh Dieu!"* which he has taken from Madame Guérin, and which he lets escape frequently in moments of great happiness. He pronounces it by leaving out the *u* in *Dieu,* and laying stress on the *i* as if it were double and in such a way as to be heard to cry distinctly, *Oh Dii! Oh Dii!* The *o* found in this last combination of sounds was not new to him; I had succeeded some time previously in making him pronounce it.

This is our present position with reference to the vocal organs. It is seen that all the vowels with the exception of the *u,* already enter into the small number of sounds which he articulates and that only three consonants are found *l, d,* and the liquid *l.* This progress is certainly very feeble if it is compared to that required for the complete development of the human voice; but it seems sufficient to guarantee the possibility of this development. I have already related the causes which would necessarily make this development long and difficult. There is still another which will have an equal effect in the same direction and which I ought not to pass over in silence. I allude to the facility with which our young savage expresses his few wants otherwise than by speech. Each wish manifests itself by the most expressive signs which have in some measure, as have ours, their gradations and their equivalent values. If the time for his walk has come, he appears several times before the window and before the door of his room. If he then sees that his governess is not ready, he places before her all the objects necessary for her toilet and in his impatience even goes to help her dress. That done, he goes down first and himself pulls the check string of the door. Arriving at the Observatory, his first business is to demand some milk which he does by presenting a wooden porringer which, on going out, he never forgets to put in his pocket, and with which he first provided himself the day after he had broken in the same house a china cup which had been used for the same purpose.

Then again, in order to complete the pleasure of his evenings, he has for some time past kindly been given rides in a wheelbarrow. Since then, as soon as the inclination arises, if nobody comes to satisfy it, he returns to the house, takes someone by the arm, leads him to the garden and puts in his hands the handles of the wheelbarrow, into which he then climbs. If this first invitation is resisted he leaves his seat, turns to the handles of the wheelbarrow, rolls it for some turns, and places himself in it again; imagining doubtless, that if his desires are not fulfilled after all this, it is not because they are not clearly expressed. Where meals are concerned his intentions are even less doubtful. He himself lays the cloth and gives Madame Guérin the dishes, so that she may go down to the kitchen and get the food. If he is in town dining with me, all his requests are addressed to the person who does the honors of the table; it is always to her that he turns to be served. If she pretends not to hear him, he puts his plate at the side of the particular dish which he wants and, as it were, devours with his eyes. If that produces no result, he takes a fork and strikes two or three blows with it on the brim of his plate. If she persists in further delay, then he knows no bounds; he plunges a spoon or even his hand into the dish and in the twinkling of an eye he empties it entirely in his plate. He is scarcely less expressive in his way of showing his emotions, above all impatience and boredom. A number of people visiting him out of curiosity know how, with more natural frankness than politeness, he dismisses them when, fatigued by the length of their visits, he offers to each of them, without mistake, cane, gloves and hat, pushes them gently towards the door, which he closes impetuously upon them.

In order to complete the account of this pantomime language, I must also say that Victor understands it as easily as he uses it. If Madame Guérin wishes to send him to fetch some water it is enough for her to show him the pitcher and let him see it is empty by turning it upside down.

A similar procedure was enough to make him give me a drink when we dined together. But what is more astonishing in the way he lends himself to these means of communication is that he has no need of any preliminary lesson, nor of any mutual agreement in order to make himself understood. I convinced myself of this one day by a most conclusive experiment. I chose among a number of others, an object for which there existed between him and his governess no indicating sign, as I assured myself beforehand.

Such, for example, was the comb which was used upon him and which I wished to make him bring to me. When I appeared before him with my hair rough and bristling in all directions I should have been very much surprised if he had not understood me. He did indeed do so, and immediately I had in my hands what I wanted. Many people see in these proceedings only the behavior of an animal. For my part I will confess I believe that I recognize in them the language of the human species, originally employed in the infancy of society before the work of ages had coordinated the system of speech and furnished civilized man with a prolific and sublime means of improvement which causes his thought to blossom even in the cradle, and which he uses all his life without appreciating what it is to him and what he would be without it if he found himself accidentally deprived of it, as in the case which now occupies us. Without doubt a day will come when the increased requirements of young Victor will make him feel the necessity of using new signs. The defective use which he made of his first sounds may delay this but not prevent it. It will perhaps be neither more nor less than what happens to the child who first lisps *papa*, without attaching to it any meaning and who from then on says it everywhere and on all occasions, gives it to every man he sees, and then, only after many reasonings and even abstractions, succeeds in giving it a simple and correct application.

V

Fifth Aim. *To induce him to employ the simplest mental operations over a period of time upon the objects of his physical needs, afterwards inducing the application of these mental processes to the objects of instruction.*

If we consider human intelligence at the period of earliest childhood man does not yet appear to rise above the level of the other animals. All his intellectual faculties are strictly confined to the narrow circle of his physical needs. It is upon himself alone that the operations of his mind are exercised. Education must then seize them and apply them to his instruction, that is to say to a new order of things which has no connection with his first needs. Such is the source of all knowledge, all mental progress, and the creations of the most sublime genius. Whatever degree of probability there may be in this idea, I only repeat it here as the point of departure on the path towards realization of this last aim.

I shall not enter here into details concerning the means employed to exercise the intellectual faculties of the *Savage of Aveyron* upon the objects of his appetites. These means were simply obstacles always increasing, always new, put between him and his wants, and which he could not overcome without continually exercising his attention, his memory, his judgment and all the functions of his senses.

Thus all the faculties useful in his education were developed and it was only necessary to find the easiest way to turn them to account. I could no longer count upon much assistance from the sense of hearing, for in this respect the *Savage of Aveyron* was nothing but a deaf mute. This consideration forced me to try citizen Sicard's method of instruction. I began then with the procedure ordinarily used first in that celebrated school and drew on a blackboard the outline of some objects that could best be represented by a simple drawing, such as a key, scissors, and a hammer. Repeatedly, and at such times as I saw that I was being noticed, I placed each of these objects upon its respective drawing and when I was sure that in this way he had been made to feel the connection, I endeavored to make him bring them successively to me by pointing to the drawing of the one I wanted. Nothing came of this. I repeated the experiment several times and always with as little success; he either refused stubbornly to bring the one of the three things which I indicated, or else brought the two others with it and gave them all to me at the same time. I am convinced that this was merely calculated laziness which did not let him do in detail what he found quite simple to do all at once. I bethought myself then of a means which would force him to give particular attention to each of these objects. I had noticed for some months past that he had a most decided taste for order; so much so that sometimes he would get up from his bed to put a piece of furniture or a utensil which had accidentally got moved, back again into its usual place. He was even more particular about the things hanging upon the wall: each had a nail and a particular hook, and when any of these had been changed he was not quiet until he had himself corrected them. All I had to do then was to arrange in the same way the things upon which I wished him to exercise his attention. By means of a nail I suspended each of the objects below its drawing and left them there for some time. When afterwards I came to give them to Victor they were immediately replaced in their proper order. I repeated this several times and always with the same result. Nevertheless, I was far from attributing this to his discrimination, and this classification could well be only an act of memory. To reassure myself I changed the respective positions of the drawings and this time I saw him follow the original order in the arrangement of the objects without any allowance for the transposition. As a matter of fact, nothing was easier than for him to learn the new classification necessitated by this change, but nothing more difficult than to make him reason it out. His memory alone bore the burden of each arrangement. I devoted myself then to the task of neutralizing in some way the assistance which he drew from it. I succeeded in fatiguing his memory by increasing the number of drawings and the frequency of their transpositions.

His memory now became an insufficient guide for the methodical arrangement of the numerous articles, so that one would expect his mind to find assistance by comparing the drawing with the things. What a difficult step I had overcome! I was convinced of this when I saw our young Victor fasten his gaze and successively, upon each object, choose one, and next look for the drawing to which he wished to bring it, and I soon had material proof by experimenting with the transposition of the drawings, which was followed on his part by the methodical transposition of the objects.

This result inspired in me the most brilliant hopes. I had believed there were no more difficulties to conquer, when there arose a most insuperable one which obstinately held me back and forced me to renounce my method. It is well known that in the education of the deaf and dumb this first procedure is followed by a second and much more difficult one. After having been made to feel by repeated comparisons the connection of the thing with its drawing, the letters which form the name of the object are placed on the drawing. That done, the drawing is effaced and only the alphabetical signs remain. The deaf mute sees in this second procedure only a change of drawing which continues to be for him the sign of the object. It was not so with Victor who, in spite of the most frequent repetitions, in spite of a prolonged presentation of the thing below its word, could never solve the problem. I was easily able to account for this difficulty and it was easy for me to understand why it was insurmountable. From the picture of an object to its alphabetical representation, the distance is immense and it is so much the greater for the pupil because he is faced with it during the first stages of his instruction. If deaf mutes are not held back at this point the reason is that, of all children, they are the most attentive and the most observing. Accustomed from their earliest childhood to hear and speak with their eyes, they have more practice than anyone else in the recognition of relations between visible objects. It was necessary then to look for a method more in keeping with the still torpid faculties of our young savage, a method by which the surmounting of each difficulty prepared him for a still more difficult task. It was in this spirit that I outlined my new plan. I will not stop to analyze it; it can be judged by its execution.

Upon a board, two feet square, I pasted three pieces of paper of very distinct shapes and decided colors. One was circular and red, another was triangular and blue, the third was square and black. By means of holes pierced in their centers and nails driven into the board, three pieces of cardboard of the same shapes and colors were placed there and left for some days upon their respective models pasted on the board. Then I lifted them and gave them to Victor and they were replaced without any difficulty. I assured myself by reversing the board and then changing the order of the figures, that this first result was not a matter of routine but was due to comparison. After some days I substituted another board for the first. I had pasted the same figures on it, but this time they were all of a uniform color. In the first case the pupil had the double indication of shapes and colors to aid him in recognition, in the second case he had only one guide, comparison of the shapes. At almost the same time I showed him a third where all the figures were the same but the colors different. The same tests always gave the same results, excepting that I do not count mistakes due to lack of attention. The facility with which he executed these easy comparisons obliged me to present some new ones to him. I made additions and modifications in the last two presentations. I added to the one with the different shaped figures some new shapes much less distinct and to the one with the colors some new colors which differed only in shade. There was, for example, in the first a rather long parallelogram besides a square, and in the second a pattern in sky blue beside one of grayish blue. He made some mistakes and showed some uncertainty about these, which disappeared after some days' practice.

These results emboldened me to new changes always more difficult. Each day I added, curtailed, and modified, provoking new comparisons and new judgments. At length the multiplicity and the complications of these little exercises finished by fatiguing his attention and his docility. Then those motions of impatience and rage which broke out so violently at the beginning of his sojourn in Paris, and especially when he found himself shut in his room, reappeared in all their intensity. Notwithstanding this fact, it seemed to me that the time had come when it was necessary energetically to overcome these outbreaks and no longer to mitigate them by compliance. I believed, therefore, that I ought to resist them.

So, when disgusted with some task (of which, in truth, he could not understand the end, and of which it was very natural that he should weary), he would take the pieces of cardboard, throw them on the ground with vexation and make for his bed in a fury. I let one or two minutes pass. I came again to my charge with as much *sang froid* as possible. I made him gather up all the cards scattered in his room and gave him no rest until they were properly replaced.

My persistence lasted only for a few days and was finally overcome by his independence of character. His fits of anger became more frequent, more violent, and were like the fits of madness of which I have already spoken but with this striking difference, that their effect was less directed towards persons than towards things. On such occasions he ran away and in a destructive mood bit the sheets, the blankets, and the mantelpiece, scattered the andirons, ashes and blazing embers, and ended by falling into convulsions which like those of epilepsy, involved a complete suspension of the sensorial functions. I was obliged to give up when things reached this frightful pitch; but my acquiescence only increased the evil. The paroxysms became more frequent, and apt to be renewed at the slightest opposition, often, even, without any determining cause.

My embarrassment became extreme. I foresaw the time when all my care would result only in making an unhappy epileptic of this poor child. A few more fits and force of habit would fasten upon him one of the most terrible and least curable of diseases. It was necessary then to find a remedy immediately, not in medicines which are so often fruitless, nor in gentleness from which there was nothing more to hope, but in a method of shock almost parallel to the one which Boerhaave had employed at the Hospital at Haarlem. I was convinced that if the first means I adopted should fail in its effect, the trouble would only be aggravated, and any other treatment of the same nature would become useless. In this firm conviction I chose the form which I believed would be most alarming to a creature who in his new existence had not yet experienced any kind of danger.

Some time previously when Madame Guérin was with him at the Observatory, she had taken him on the platform, which is, as is well known, very high. Scarcely had he come to within a short distance of the parapet when, seized with fright, trembling in every limb and his face covered with sweat, he returned to his governess, whom he dragged by the arm towards the door, becoming somewhat calmer only when he got to the foot of the stairs. What could be the cause of such fright? That is not what I wanted to know. It was enough for me to know the effect to make it serve my purpose. The occasion soon offered itself in the instance of violent fit, which was, I believe, caused by our resuming the exercises. Seizing the moment when the functions of the senses were not yet suspended, I violently threw back the window of his room which was situated on the fourth story and which opened perpendicularly on to a big stone court. I drew near him with every appearance of anger and seizing him forcibly by the haunches held him out of the window, his head directly turned towards the bottom of the chasm. After some seconds I drew him in again. He was pale; covered with a cold sweat, his eyes were rather tearful, and he still trembled a little which I believed to be the effect of fear. I led him to his cards. I made him gather them up and replace them all. This was done, very slowly to be sure, and badly rather than well, but at least without impatience. Afterwards he went and threw himself on his bed and wept copiously.

This was the first time, at least to my knowledge, that he shed tears. It preceded the occasions of which I have already given an account, when the grief at leaving his nurse or the pleasure of finding her again made him weep.

The account of these came first in my narrative because I have followed the plan of a methodical exposition of facts rather than one in chronological order.

This strange method succeeded, if not completely, at least sufficiently. If his distaste for work was not entirely overcome, at least it was much diminished, and ceased to be followed by such effects as those which I have just related.

On such occasions as when he was a little overtired or when he was forced to work at times set apart for his walks or his meals, he contented himself with giving signs of weariness and impatience, and uttering a plaintive murmur which ordinarily ended in tears.

This favorable change allowed us to take up again our course of exercises where we had broken it off. These I submitted to new modifications which were designed to stabilize his judgment still further. For the figures pasted on the board, which I have said were completely colored shapes representing geometrical figures, I substituted linear outlines of these same shapes. I also contented myself with indicating the colors by little irregular samples quite unlike the colored cards. I may say that these new difficulties were only a game to the child; a result which was sufficient for the end I had in mind when adopting this system of direct comparisons. The moment had come to replace this by another which was much more instructive and which would have presented insurmountable difficulties if the way had not been smoothed in advance by the success of the methods just used.

I ordered to be printed as a big character upon a piece of cardboard two inches square each of the twenty-four letters of the alphabet. I had an equal number of spaces cut in a plank a foot and a half square. Into these the pieces of cardboard could be inserted, without the use of paste, so that their places could be changed as required. I had an equal number of characters of the same dimensions made in metal. These were meant to be compared by the pupil with the printed letters, and were to be arranged in their corresponding places.

The first trial of this method was made, in my absence, by Madame Guérin. I was very much surprised on my return to learn from her that Victor distinguished all the characters and arranged them properly. He was immediately put to the test and performed his task without any mistake. Though delighted with such an immediate success I was still far from able to explain its cause, and it was only some days after that I discovered this by noting the way in which our pupil proceeded to make this arrangement. In order to make the work easier he devised of his own accord a little expedient which in this task allowed him to dispense with memory, comparison and judgment. As soon as the board was put between his hands, he did not wait until the metal letters were taken out of their places but he himself took them and piled them upon his hand, following the order of their arrangement so that the last letter, after all were taken from the board, was the first on the pile. He began with this and finished with the last of the pile, thus beginning the board at the end and proceeding always from right to left. Moreover, he was able to improve upon this procedure; for very often the pile collapsed, the characters fell out and he had to straighten everything up and put it in order by the unaided efforts of attention. So the twenty-four letters were arranged in four rows of six each, making it easier to lift them up by rows only, and even to replace them in the same way by taking letters from the second row only when the first was replaced.

I do not know whether he reasoned as I suppose, but at least it is certain that he executed the performance in the manner described. It was then a true routine, but a routine of his own invention, and one which was perhaps as much to the credit of his intelligence as was a method of arrangement hit upon shortly afterwards to the credit of his discernment. It was not difficult to set him off by giving him the characters pellmell whenever he was given the board. At last, in spite of the frequent transpositions to which I submitted the printed characters by changing their places, in spite of insidious arrangements, such as the O beside the C, the E beside the F, etc., his discrimination became infallible. In exercising it upon all these letters, the end I had in view was to prepare Victor for a primitive but correct use of the letters, namely the expression of needs which can only be made known by means of speech. Far from believing that I was already so near this great step in his education, I was led by the spirit of curiosity rather than the hope of success to try the experiment which follows.

One morning when he was waiting impatiently for the milk which he always had for breakfast, I carried to him his board which I had specially arranged the evening before with the four letters *L.A.I.T.* Madame Guérin, whom I had warned, approached, looked at the letters and immediately gave me a cup of milk which I pretended to drink myself. A moment after I approached Victor, gave him the four letters that I had lifted from the board, and pointed to it with one hand while in the other I held the jug full of milk. The letters were immediately replaced but in inverted order, so that they showed *T.I.A.L.* instead of *L.A.I.T.* I indicated the corrections to be made by designating with my finger the letters to transpose and the proper place of each. When these changes had reproduced the sign, he was allowed to have his milk.

It is difficult to believe that five or six similar attempts were sufficient, not only to make him arrange methodically the four letters of the word *Lait* but to give him the idea of the connection between the word and the thing. At least this is the justifiable inference from what happened a week later. One evening when he was ready to set out for the Observatory, he was seen to provide himself on his own initiative with the four letters in question, and to put them in his pocket; he had scarcely arrived at Citizen Lemeri's house, where as I previously said he goes every day for some milk, when he produced them and placed them on a table in such a way as to form the word *LAIT.*

It was originally my intention here to recapitulate the facts scattered throughout this work, but I thought that such a summary would never have the weight of this last achievement. I state it, naked and stripped of all reflections, so to speak, so that it may mark in a more striking way the stage which we have reached and serve as a guarantee of future achievement. In the meantime the conclusion may be drawn from the greater part of my observations, and above all from those indicated in the last two sections, that the child known under the name the *Savage of Aveyron* is endowed with the free use of all his senses; that he can compare, discern and judge, and finally apply all the faculties of his understanding to the objects related to his instruction. It is essential to note that these happy changes have occurred during the short space of nine months in a subject believed to be incapable of attention; and the conclusion will follow that his education is possible, if it is not even already guaranteed, by this early success, quite apart from any results which time may bring—time which in its unalterable course seems to give the child, in powers and development, all that it takes away from man in the decline of his life.

And meanwhile what important consequences for the philosophic and natural history of the human race already follow from this first series of observations! If they are collected, methodically classified and correctly evaluated we shall have material proof of most important truths, truths which Locke and Condillac were able to discover by the power of their genius and the depth of their meditations alone. It has appeared to me at least that the following conclusions may be drawn:

(1) That man is inferior to a large number of animals in the pure state of nature, a state of nullity and barbarism that has been falsely painted in the most seductive colors; a state in which the individual, deprived of the characteristic faculties of his kind, drags on without intelligence or without feelings, a precarious life reduced to bare animal functions.

(2) That the moral superiority said to be *natural* to man is only the result of civilization, which raises him above other animals by a great and powerful force. This force is the preëminent sensibility of his kind, an essential peculiarity from which proceed the imitative faculties and that continual urge which drives him to seek new sensations in new needs.

(3) That this imitative force, the purpose of which is the education of his organs and especially the apprenticeship of speech, and which is very energetic and very active during the first years of his life, rapidly wanes with age, with isolation, and with all the causes which tend to blunt the nervous sensibility;

from which it results that the articulation of sounds, of all the effects of imitation unquestionably the most incomprehensible and the most useful, must encounter innumerable obstacles at any age later than that of early childhood.

(4) That in the most isolated savage as in the most highly civilized man, there exists a constant relation between ideas and needs; that the increasing multiplicity of the latter in the most civilized peoples should be considered as a great means of developing the human mind; so that a general proposition may be established, namely, that all causes accidental, local, or political, which tend to augment or diminish the number of our desires, necessarily contribute to extend or to narrow the sphere of our knowledge and the domain of science, fine arts and social industry.

(5) That in the present state of our knowledge of physiology the progress of education can and ought to be illumined by the light of modern medicine which, of all the natural sciences, can help most powerfully towards the perfection of the human species by detecting the organic and intellectual peculiarities of each individual and determining therefrom what education ought to do for him and what society can expect from him.

There are still certain equally important considerations that I proposed to add to those already given; but the development which they would have required would overstep the boundaries and the plan of this short treatise. I have noticed besides in comparing my observations with the doctrines of some of our metaphysicians that I found myself in disagreement with them upon certain interesting points.

Consequently it devolves upon me to wait for more numerous and therefore more conclusive facts. A very similar reason has prevented me, when speaking of young Victor's varied development, from dwelling on the time of his puberty, which has shown itself almost explosively for some weeks, and the first phenomena of which cast much doubt upon the origin of certain tender emotions which we now regard as very "natural." Though here I have found it advisable to reserve judgment and conclusions; I am persuaded that it is impossible to allow too long a period for the ripening and subsequent confirmation of all considerations which tend to destroy those prejudices which are possibly venerable and those illusions of social life which are the sweeter because they are the most consoling.

Mark Twain, *Old Times on the Mississippi*

II. A "Cub" Pilot's Experience; or; Learning the River.

What with lying on the rocks four days at Louisville and some other delays, the poor old *Paul Jones* fooled away about two weeks in making the voyage from Cincinnati to New Orleans. This gave me a chance to get acquainted with one of the pilots, and he taught me how to steer the boat, and thus made the fascination of river life more potent than ever for me.

It also gave me a chance to get acquainted with a youth who had taken deck passage—more's the pity, for he easily borrowed six dollars of me on a promise to return to the boat and pay it back to me the day after we should arrive. But be probably died or forgot, for he never came. It was doubtless the former, since he had said his parents were wealthy and he only traveled deck passage because it was cooler.

I soon discovered two things. One was that a vessel would not be likely to sail for the mouth of the Amazon under ten or twelve years, and the other was that the nine or ten dollars still left in my pocket would not suffice for so impossible an exploration as I had planned, even if I could afford to wait for a ship. Therefore it followed that I must contrive a new career. The *Paul Jones* was now bound for St. Louis. I planned a siege against my pilot, and at the end of three hard days he surrendered. He agreed to teach me the Mississippi River from New Orleans to St. Louis for five hundred dollars, payable out of the first wages I should receive after graduating. I entered upon the small enterprise of "learning" twelve or thirteen hundred miles of the great Mississippi River with the easy confidence of my time of life. If I had really known what I was about to require of my faculties, I should not have had the courage to begin. I supposed that all a pilot had to do was to keep his boat in the river, and I did not consider that that could be much of a trick, since it was so wide.

The boat backed out from New Orleans at four in the afternoon, and it was "our watch" until eight. Mr. Bixby, my chief, "straightened her up," plowed her along past the sterns of the other boats that lay at the Levee, and then said, "Here, take her; shave those steamships as close as you'd peel an apple." I took the wheel and my heart went down into my boots; for it seemed to me that we were about to scrape the side off every ship in the line, we were so close. I held my breath and began to claw the boat away from the danger, and I had my own opinion of the pilot who had known no better than to get us into such peril, but I was too wise to express it. In half a minute I had a wide margin of safety intervening between the *Paul Jones* and the ships, and within ten seconds more I was set aside in disgrace and Mr. Bixby was going into danger again and flaying me alive with abuse of my cowardice. I was stung but I was obliged to admire the easy confidence with which my chief loafed from side to side of his wheel and trimmed the ships so closely that disaster seemed ceaselessly imminent. When he had cooled a little he told me that the easy water was close ashore and the current outside, and therefore we must hug the bank up-stream, to get the benefit of the former, and stay well out down-stream, to take advantage of the latter. In my own mind I resolved to be a down-stream pilot and leave the up-streaming to people dead to prudence.

Now and then Mr. Bixby called my attention to certain things. Said he, "This is Six-Mile Point." I assented. It was pleasant enough information but I could not see the bearing of it. I was not conscious that it was a matter of any interest to me. Another time he said, "This is Nine-Mile Point." Later he said, "This is Twelve-Mile Point." They were all about level with the water's edge; they all looked about alike to me; they were monotonously unpicturesque. I hoped Mr. Bixby would change the subject. But no, he would crowd up around a point, hugging the shore with affection, and then say: "The slack water ends here, abreast this bunch of China trees; now we cross over." So he crossed over. He gave me the wheel once or twice but I had no luck. I either came near chipping off the edge of a sugar-plantation, or I yawed too far from shore and so dropped back into disgrace again and got abused.

The watch was ended at last, and we took supper and went to bed. At midnight the glare of a lantern shone in my eyes, and the night watchman said:

"Come, turn out!"

And then he left. I could not understand this extraordinary procedure; so I presently gave up trying to and dozed off to sleep. Pretty soon the watchman was back again, and this time he was gruff. I was annoyed. I said:

"What do you want to come bothering around here in the middle of the night for? Now, as like as not, I'll not get to sleep again to-night."

The watchman said:

"Well, if this ain't good, I'm blessed."

The "off-watch" was just turning in and I heard some brutal laughter from them, and such remarks as "Hello, watchman! ain't the new cub turned out yet? He's delicate, likely. Give him some sugar in a rag and send for the chambermaid to sing 'Rock-a-by Baby,' to him."

About this time Mr. Bixby appeared on the scene. Something like a minute later I was climbing the pilothouse steps with some of my clothes on and the rest in my arms. Mr. Bixby was close behind, commenting. Here was something fresh—this thing of getting up in the middle of the night to go to work. It was a detail in piloting that had never occurred to me at all. I knew that boats ran all night but somehow I had never happened to reflect that somebody had to get up out of a warm bed to run them. I began to fear that piloting was not quite so romantic as I had imagined it was; there was something very real and worklike about this new phase of it.

It was a rather dingy night, although a fair number of stars were out. The big mate was at the wheel and he had the old tub pointed at a star and was holding her straight up the middle of the river. The shores on either hand were not much more than half a mile apart, but they seemed wonderfully far away and ever so vague and indistinct. The mate said:

"We've got to land at Jones's plantation, sir."

The vengeful spirit in me exulted. I said to myself, "I wish you joy of your job, Mr. Bixby; you'll have a good time finding Mr. Jones's plantation such a night as this, and I hope you never *will* find it as long as you live."

Mr. Bixby said to the mate:

"Upper end of the plantation, or the lower?"

"Upper."

"I can't do it. The stumps there are out of water at this stage. It's no great distance to the lower and you'll have to get along with that."

"All right, sir. If Jones don't like it, he'll have to lump it, I reckon."

And then the mate left. My exultation began to cool and my wonder to come up. Here was a man who not only proposed to find this plantation on such a night but to find either end of it you preferred. I dreadfully wanted to ask a question, but I was carrying about as many short answers as my cargo-room would admit of, so I held my peace. All I desired to ask Mr. Bixby was the simple question whether he was ass enough to really imagine he was going to find that plantation on a night when all plantations were exactly alike and all of the same color. But I held in. I used to have fine inspirations of prudence in those days.

Mr. Bixby made for the shore and soon was scraping it, just the same as if it had been daylight. And not only that but singing:

"Father in heaven, the day is declining," etc.

It seemed to me that I had put my life in the keeping of a peculiarly reckless outcast. Presently he turned on me and said:

"What's the name of the first point above New Orleans?"

I was gratified to be able to answer promptly, and I did. I said I didn't know.

"Don't *know?*"

This manner jolted me. I was down at the foot again, in a moment. But I had to say just what I had said before.

"Well, you're a smart one!" said Mr. Bixby. "What's the name of the *next* point?"

Once more I didn't know.

"Well, this beats anything. Tell me the name of any point or place I told you."

I studied awhile and decided that I couldn't.

"Look here! What do you start out from, above Twelve-Mile Point, to cross over?"

"I—I—don't know."

"You—you—don't know?" mimicking my drawling manner of speech. "What do you know?"

"I—I—nothing, for certain."

"By the great Caesar's ghost, I believe you! You're the stupidest dunderhead I ever saw or ever heard of, so help me Moses! The idea of *you* being a pilot— *you!* Why you don't know enough to pilot a cow down a lane."

Oh, but his wrath was up! He was a nervous man, and he shuffled from one side of his wheel to the other as if the floor was hot. He would boil awhile to himself and then overflow and scald me again.

"Look here! What do you suppose I told you the names of those points for?"

I tremblingly considered a moment and then the devil of temptation provoked me to say:

"Well to—to—be entertaining, I thought."

This was a red rag to the bull. He raged and stormed so (he was crossing the river at the time) that I judged it made him blind, because he ran over the steering-oar of a trading-scow. Of course the traders sent up a volley of red-hot profanity. Never was a man so grateful as Mr. Bixby was, because he was brimful and here were subjects who could *talk back*. He threw open a window, thrust his head out, and such an irruption followed as I never had heard before. The fainter and farther away the scowmen's curses drifted, the higher Mr. Bixby lifted his voice and the weightier his adjectives grew. When he closed the window he was empty. You could have drawn a seine through his system and not caught curses enough to disturb your mother with. Presently he said to me in the gentlest way:

"My boy, you must get a little memorandum-book, and every time I tell you a thing, put it down right away. There's only one way to be a pilot and that is to get this entire river by heart. You have to know it just like ABC."

That was a dismal revelation to me, for my memory was never loaded with anything but blank cartridges. However, I did not feel discouraged long. I judged that it was best to make some allowances, for doubtless Mr. Bixby was "stretching". Presently he pulled a rope and struck a few strokes on the big bell. The stars were all gone now and the night was as black as ink. I could hear the wheels churn along the bank but I was not entirely certain that I could see the shore. The voice of the invisible watchman called up from the hurricane deck:

"What's this, sir?"

"Jones's plantation."

I said to myself, "I wish I might venture to offer a small bet that it isn't." But I did not chirp. I only waited to see. Mr. Bixby handled the engine-bells and in due time the boat's nose came to the land, a torch glowed from the forecastle, a man skipped ashore, a darky's voice on the bank said: "Gimme de k'yarpet-bag, Mass' Jones," and the next moment we were standing up the river again, all serene. I reflected deeply awhile, and then said—but not aloud— "Well, the finding of that plantation was the luckiest accident that ever happened but it couldn't happen again in a hundred years." And I fully believed it *was* an accident, too.

By the time we had gone seven or eight hundred miles up the river, I had learned to be a tolerably plucky up-stream steersman, in daylight, and before we reached St. Louis I had made a trifle of progress in night work, but only a trifle. I had a note-book that fairly bristled with the names of towns, "points," bars, islands, bends, reaches, etc., but the information was to be found only in the note-book—none of it was in my head. It made my heart ache to think I had only got half of the river set down, for as our watch was four hours off and four hours on, day and night, there was a long four-hour gap in my book for every time I had slept since the voyage began.

My chief was presently hired to go on a big New Orleans boat and I packed my satchel and went with him. She was a grand affair. When I stood in her pilot-house I was so far above the water that I seemed perched on a mountain, and her decks stretched so far away, fore and aft, below me, that I wondered how I could ever have considered the little *Paul Jones* a large craft. There were other differences too. The *Paul Jones's* pilot-house was a cheap, dingy, battered rattletrap, cramped for room, but here was a sumptuous glass temple: room enough to have a dance in, showy red and gold window-curtains, an imposing sofa, leather cushions and a back to the high bench where visiting pilots sit to spin yarns and "look at the river," bright, fanciful "cuspidores" instead of a broad wooden box filled with sawdust, nice new oilcloth on the floor, a hospitable big stove for winter, a wheel as high as my head costly with inlaid work, a wire tiller-rope, bright brass knobs for the bells, and a tidy, white-aproned, black "texas-tender," to bring up tarts and ices and coffee during mid-watch, day and night. Now this was "something like," and so I began to take heart once more to believe that piloting was a romantic sort of occupation after all. The moment we were under way I began to prowl about the great steamer and fill myself with joy. She was as clean and as dainty as a drawing-room; when I looked down her long, gilded saloon, it was like gazing through a splendid tunnel; she had an oil-picture, by some gifted sign-painter, on every stateroom door; she glittered with no end of prism-fringed chandeliers; the clerk's office was elegant, the bar was marvelous, and the barkeeper had been barbered and upholstered at incredible cost. The boiler-deck (i.e., the second story of the boat, so to speak) was as spacious as a church, it seemed to me, so with the forecastle, and there was no pitiful handful of deck-hands, firemen, and roustabouts down there but a whole battalion of men. The fires were fiercely glaring from a long row of furnaces and over them were eight huge boilers! This was unutterable pomp. The mighty engines—but enough of this. I had never felt so fine before. And when I found that the regiment of natty servants respectfully "sir'd" me, my satisfaction was complete.

When I returned to the pilot-house St. Louis was gone and I was lost. Here was a piece of river which was all down in my book but I could make neither head nor tail of it: you understand, it was turned around. I had seen it when coming up-stream but I had never faced about to see how it looked when it was behind me. My heart broke again, for it was plain that I had got to learn this troublesome river *both ways*.

The pilot-house was full of pilots, going down to "look at the river." What is called the "upper river" (the two hundred miles between St. Louis and Cairo, where the Ohio comes in) was low, and the Mississippi changes its channel so constantly that the pilots used to always find it necessary to run down to Cairo to take a fresh look when their boats were to lie in port a week, that is, when the water was at a low stage. A deal of this "looking at the river" was done by poor fellows who seldom had a berth and whose only hope of getting one lay in their being always freshly posted and therefore ready to drop into the shoes of some reputable pilot for a single trip, on account of such pilot's sudden illness or some other necessity. And a good many of them constantly ran up and down inspecting the river, not because they ever really hoped to get a berth but because (they being guests of the boat) it was cheaper to "look at the river" than stay ashore and pay board. In time these fellows grew dainty in their tastes and only infested boats that had an established reputation for setting good tables. All visiting pilots were useful, for they were always ready and willing, winter or summer, night or day, to go out in the yawl and help buoy the channel or assist the boat's pilots in any way they could. They were likewise welcomed because all pilots are tireless talkers when gathered together, and as they talk only about the river they are always understood and are always interesting. Your true pilot cares nothing about anything on earth but the river, and his pride in his occupation surpasses the pride of kings.

We had a fine company of these river inspectors along this trip. There were eight or ten, and there was abundance of room for them in our great pilot-house. Two or three of them wore polished silk hats, elaborate shirt-fronts, diamond breastpins, kid gloves, and patent-leather boots. They were choice in their English, and bore themselves with a dignity proper to men of solid means and prodigious reputation as pilots. The others were more or less loosely clad, and wore upon their heads tall felt cones that were suggestive of the days of the Commonwealth.

I was a cipher in this august company and felt subdued, not to say torpid. I was not even of sufficient consequence to assist at the wheel when it was necessary to put the tiller hard down in a hurry; the guest that stood nearest did that when occasion required—and this was pretty much all the time, because of the crookedness of the channel and the scant water. I stood in a corner, and the talk I listened to took the hope all out of me. One visitor said to another:

"Jim, how did you run Plum Point, coming up?"

"It was in the night there, and I ran it the way one of the boys on the *Diana* told me; started out about fifty yards above the wood-pile on the false point and held on the cabin under Plum Point till I raised the reef—quarter less twain—then straightened up for the middle bar till I got well abreast the old one-limbed cottonwood in the bend, then got my stern on the cottonwood and head on the low place above the point, and came, through a-booming—nine and a half."

"Pretty square crossing, ain't it?"

"Yes, but the upper bar's working down fast."

Another pilot spoke up and said:

"I had better water than that and ran it lower down; started out from the false point—mark twain—raised the second reef abreast the big snag in the bend and had quarter less twain."

One of the gorgeous ones remarked:

"I don't want to find fault with your leadsmen but that's a good deal of water for Plum Point, it seems to me."

There was an approving nod all around as this quiet snub dropped on the boaster and "settled" him. And so they went on talk-talk-talking. Meantime, the thing that was running in my mind was, "Now, if my ears hear aright, I have not only to get the names of all the towns and islands and bends, and so on by heart, but I must even get up a warm personal acquaintanceship with every old snag and one-limbed cottonwood and obscure wood-pile that ornaments the banks of this river for twelve hundred miles; and more than that, I must actually know where these things are in the dark, unless these guests are gifted with eyes that can pierce through two miles of solid blackness. I wish the piloting business was in Jericho and I had never thought of it."

At dusk Mr. Bixby tapped the big bell three times (the signal to land) and the captain emerged from his drawing-room in the forward end of the "texas," and looked up inquiringly. Mr. Bixby said:

"We will lay up here all night, captain."

"Very well, sir."

That was all. The boat came to shore and was tied up for the night. It seemed to me a fine thing that the pilot could do as he pleased, without asking so grand a captain's permission. I took my supper and went immediately to bed, discouraged by my day's observations and experiences. My late voyage's note-booking was but a confusion of meaningless names. It had tangled me all up in a knot every time I had looked at it in the daytime. I now hoped for respite in sleep, but no, it reveled all through my head till sunrise again, a frantic and tireless nightmare.

Next morning I felt pretty rusty and low-spirited. We went booming along, taking a good many chances, for we were anxious to "get out of the river" (as getting out to Cairo was called) before night should overtake us. But Mr. Bixby's partner, the other pilot, presently grounded the boat and we lost so much time getting her off that it was plain the darkness would overtake us a good long way above the mouth. This was a great misfortune, especially to certain of our visiting pilots, whose boats would have to wait for their return, no matter how long that might be. It sobered the pilot-house talk a good deal. Coming up-stream, pilots did not mind low water or any kind of darkness; nothing stopped them but fog. But down-stream work was different; a boat was too nearly helpless with a stiff current pushing behind her, so it was not customary to run down-stream at night in low water.

There seemed to be one small hope, however: if we could get through the intricate and dangerous Hat Island crossing before night, we could venture the rest, for we would have plainer sailing and better water. But it would be insanity to attempt Hat Island at night. So there was a deal of looking at watches all the rest of the day and a constant ciphering upon the speed we were making; Hat Island was the eternal subject; sometimes hope was high and sometimes we were delayed in a bad crossing and down it went again. For hours all hands lay under the burden of this suppressed excitement; it was even communicated to me and I got to feeling so solicitous about Hat Island, and under such an awful pressure of responsibility, that I wished I might have five minutes on shore to draw a good, full, relieving breath and start over again. We were standing no regular watches. Each of our pilots ran such portions of the river as he had run when coming up-stream, because of his greater familiarity with it, but both remained in the pilot-house constantly.

An hour before sunset Mr. Bixby took the wheel and Mr. W. stepped aside. For the next thirty minutes every man held his watch in his hand and was restless, silent, and uneasy. At last somebody said, with a doomful sigh:

"Well, yonder's Hat Island—and we can't make it."

All the watches closed with a snap, everybody sighed and muttered something about its being "too bad, too bad—ah, if we could *only* have got here half an hour sooner!" and the place was thick with the atmosphere of disappointment. Some started to go out but loitered, hearing no bell-tap to land. The sun dipped behind the horizon, the boat went on. Inquiring looks passed from one guest to another, and one who had his hand on the door-knob and had turned it, waited, then presently took away his hand and let the knob turn back again. We bore steadily down the bend. More looks were exchanged and nods of surprised admiration—but no words. Insensibly the men drew together behind Mr. Bixby, as the sky darkened and one or two dim stars came out. The dead silence and sense of waiting became oppressive. Mr. Bixby pulled the cord and two deep, mellow notes from the big bell floated off on the night. Then a pause, and one more note was struck. The watchman's voice followed, from the hurricane-deck:

"Labboard lead, there! Stabboard lead!"

The cries of the leadsmen began to rise out of the distance and were gruffly repeated by the word-passers on the hurricane-deck.

"M-a-r-k three! M-a-r-k three! Quarter-less-three! Half twain! Quarter twain! M-a-r-k twain! Quarter-less—"

Mr. Bixby pulled two bell-ropes and was answered by faint jinglings far below in the engine-room, and our speed slackened. The steam began to whistle through the gauge-cocks. The cries of the leadsmen went on—and it is a weird sound, always, in the night. Every pilot in the lot was watching now, with fixed eyes, and talking under his breath. Nobody was calm and easy but Mr. Bixby. He would put his wheel down and stand on a spoke, and as the steamer swung into her (to me) utterly invisible marks—for we seemed to be in the midst of a wide and gloomy sea—he would meet and fasten her there. Out of the murmur of half audible talk one caught a coherent sentence now and then—such as:

"There; she's over the first reef all right!"

After a pause, another subdued voice:

"Her stern's coming down just *exactly* right, by *George!* Now she's in the marks; over she goes!"

Somebody else muttered:

"Oh, it was done beautiful—*beautiful!*"

Now the engines were stopped altogether and we drifted with the current. Not that I could see the boat drift, for I could not, the stars being all gone by this time. This drifting was the dismalest work; it held one's heart still. Presently I discovered a blacker gloom than that which surrounded us. It was the head of the island. We were closing right down upon it. We entered its deeper shadow, and so imminent seemed the peril that I was likely to suffocate, and I had the strongest impulse to do *something,* anything, to save the vessel. But still Mr. Bixby stood by his wheel, silent, intent as a cat, and all the pilots stood shoulder to shoulder at his back.

"She'll not make it!" somebody whispered.

The water grew shoaler and shoaler by the leadsman's cries, till it was down to:

"Eight-and-a-half! E-i-g-h-t feet! E-i-g-h-t feet! Seven-and—"

Mr. Bixby said warningly through his speaking-tube to the engineer: "Stand by, now!"

"Ay, ay, sir!"

"Seven-and-a-half! Seven feet! *Six*-and—"

We touched bottom! Instantly Mr. Bixby set a lot of bells ringing, shouted through the tube, "*Now*, let her have it—every ounce you've got!" then to his partner, "Put her hard down! snatch her! snatch her!" The boat rasped and ground her way through the sand, hung upon the apex of disaster a single tremendous instant, and then over she went! And such a shout as went up at Mr. Bixby's back never loosened the roof of a pilothouse before!

There was no more trouble after that. Mr. Bixby was a hero that night, and it was some little time, too, before his exploit ceased to be talked about by river-men.

Fully to realize the marvelous precision required in laying the great steamer in her marks in that murky waste of water, one should know that not only must she pick her intricate way through snags and blind reefs, and then shave the head of the island so closely as to brush the overhanging foliage with her stern, but at one place she must pass almost within arm's reach of a sunken and invisible wreck that would snatch the hull timbers from under her if she should strike it—and destroy a quarter of a million dollars' worth of steamboat and cargo in five minutes, and maybe a hundred and fifty human lives into the bargain.

The last remark I heard that night was a compliment to Mr. Bixby, uttered in soliloquy and with unction by one of our guests. He said:

"By the Shadow of Death, but he's a lightning pilot!"

III. The Continued Perplexities of Cub Piloting

At the end of what seemed a tedious while, I had managed to pack my head full of islands, towns, bars, "points," and bends, and a curiously inanimate mass of lumber it was, too. However, inasmuch as I could shut my eyes and reel off a good long string of these names without leaving out more than ten miles of river in every fifty, I began to feel that I could take a boat down to New Orleans if I could make her skip those little gaps. But of course my complacency could hardly get start enough to lift my nose a trifle into the air, before Mr. Bixby would think of something to fetch it down again. One day he turned on me suddenly with this settler:

"What is the shape of Walnut Bend?"

He might as well have asked me my grandmother's opinion of protoplasm. I reflected respectfully and then said I didn't know it had any particular shape. My gunpowdery chief went off with a bang, of course, and then went on loading and firing until he was out of adjectives.

I had learned long ago that he only carried just so many rounds of ammunition and was sure to subside into a very placable and even remorseful old smoothbore as soon as they were all gone. That word "old" is merely affectionate; he was not more than thirty-four. I waited. By and by he said:

"My boy, you've got to know the *shape* of the river perfectly. It is all there is left to steer by on a very dark night. Everything else is blotted out and gone. But mind you, it hasn't the same shape in the night that it has in the daytime."

"How on earth am I ever going to learn it, then?"

"How do you follow a hall at home in the dark? Because you know the shape of it. You can't see it."

"Do you mean to say that I've got to know all the million trifling variations of shape in the banks of this interminable river as well as I know the shape of the front hall at home?"

"On my honor, you've got to know them *better* than any man ever did know the shapes of the halls in his own house."

"I wish I was dead!"

"Now I don't want to discourage you, but—"

"Well, pile it on me; I might as well have it now as another time."

"You see, this has got to be learned, there isn't any getting around it. A clear starlight night throws such heavy shadows that, if you didn't know the shape of a shore perfectly, you would claw away from every bunch of timber, because you would take the black shadow of it for a solid cape, and you see you would be getting scared to death every fifteen minutes by the watch. You would be fifty yards from shore all the time when you ought to be within fifty feet of it. You can't see a snag in one of those shadows but you know exactly where it is, and the shape of the river tells you when you are coming to it. Then there's your pitch-dark night; the river is a very different shape on a pitch-dark night from what it is on a star-light night. All shores seem to be straight lines then, and mighty dim ones too, and you'd *run* them for straight lines, only you know better. You boldly drive your boat right into what seems to be a solid straight wall (you knowing very well that in reality there is a curve there) and that wall falls back and makes way for you. Then there's your gray mist. You take a night when there's one of these grisly, drizzly, gray mists, and then there *isn't* any particular shape to a shore. A gray mist would tangle the head of the oldest man that ever lived. Well, then, different kinds of *moonlight* change the shape of the river in different ways. You see."

"Oh, don't say any more, please! Have I got to learn the shape of the river according to all these five hundred thousand different ways? If I tried to carry all that cargo in my head it would make me stoop-shouldered."

"*No!* you only learn *the* shape of the river, and you learn it with such absolute certainty that you can always steer by the shape that's *in your head* and never mind the one that's before your eyes."

"Very well, I'll try it; but, after I have learned it, can I depend on it? Will it keep the same form and not go fooling around?"

Before Mr. Bixby could answer, Mr. W. came in to take the watch, and he said:

"Bixby, you'll have to look out for President's Island and all that country clear away up above the Old Hen and Chickens. The banks are caving and the shape of the shores changing like everything. Why, you wouldn't know the point above 40. You can go up inside the old sycamore snag, now."

So that question was answered. Here were leagues of shore changing shape. My spirits were down in the mud again. Two things seemed pretty apparent to me. One was that in order to be a pilot a man had got to learn more than any one man ought to be allowed to know, and the other was that he must learn it all over again in a different way every twenty-four hours.

That night we had the watch until twelve. Now it was an ancient river custom for the two pilots to chat a bit when the watch changed. While the relieving pilot put on his gloves and lit his cigar, his partner, the retiring pilot, would say something like this:

"I judge the upper bar is making down a little at Hale's Point; had quarter twain with the lower lead and mark twain with the other."

"Yes, I thought it was making down a little, last trip. Meet any boats?"

"Met one abreast the head of 21 but she was away over hugging the bar, and I couldn't make her out entirely. I took her for the *Sunny South*—hadn't any skylights forward of the chimneys."

And so on. And as the relieving pilot took the wheel his partner would mention that we were in such-and-such a bend, and say we were abreast of such-and-such a man's wood-yard or plantation. This was courtesy; I supposed it was *necessity*. But Mr. W. came on watch full twelve minutes late on this particular night, a tremendous breach of etiquette; in fact, it is the unpardonable sin among pilots. So Mr. Bixby gave him no greeting whatever but simply surrendered the wheel and marched out of the pilot-house without a word. I was appalled; it was a villainous night for blackness, we were in a particularly wide and blind part of the river where there was no shape or substance to anything, and it seemed incredible that Mr. Bixby should have left that poor fellow to kill the boat, trying to find out where he was. But I resolved that I would stand by him anyway. He should find that he was not wholly friendless. So I stood around and waited to be asked where we were. But Mr. W. plunged on serenely through the solid firmament of black cats that stood for an atmosphere, and never opened his mouth. "Here is a proud devil!" thought I, "here is a limb of Satan that would rather send us all to destruction than put himself under obligations to me, because I am not yet one of the salt of the earth and privileged to snub captains and lord it over everything dead and alive in a steamboat." I presently climbed up on the bench; I did not think it was safe to go to sleep while this lunatic was on watch.

However, I must have gone to sleep in the course of time, because the next thing I was aware of was the fact that day was breaking, Mr. W. gone, and Mr. Bixby at the wheel again. So it was four o'clock and all well but me; I felt like a skinful of dry bones, and all of them trying to ache at once.

Mr. Bixby asked me what I had stayed up there for. I confessed that it was to do Mr. W. a benevolence—tell him where he was. It took five minutes for the entire preposterousness of the thing to filter into Mr. Bixby's system, and then I judge it filled him nearly up to the chin; because be paid me a compliment, and not much of a one either. He said:

"Well, taking you by and large, you do seem to be more different kinds of an ass than any creature I ever saw before. What did you suppose he wanted to know for?"

I said I thought it might be a convenience to him.

"Convenience! D—nation! Didn't I tell you that a man's got to know the river in the night the same as he'd know his own front hall?"

"Well, I can follow the front hall in the dark if I know it *is* the front hall, but suppose you set me down in the middle of it in the dark and not tell me which hall it is, how am *I* to know?"

"Well, you've *got* to, on the river!"

"All right. Then I'm glad I never said anything to Mr. W."

"I should say so! Why, he'd have slammed you through the window and utterly ruined a hundred dollars' worth of window-sash and stuff."

I was glad this damage had been saved, for it would have made me unpopular with the owners. They always hated anybody who had the name of being careless and injuring things.

I went to work now to learn the shape of the river, and of all the eluding and ungraspable objects that ever I tried to get mind or hands on, that was the chief. I would fasten my eyes upon a sharp, wooded point that projected far into the river some miles ahead of me and go to laboriously photographing its shape upon my brain, and just as I was beginning to succeed to my satisfaction, we would draw up toward it and the exasperating thing would begin to melt away and fold back into the bank! If there had been a conspicuous dead tree standing upon the very point of the cape, I would find that tree inconspicuously merged into the general forest and occupying the middle of a straight shore, when I got abreast of it! No prominent hill would stick to its shape long enough for me to make up my mind what its form really was, but it was as dissolving and changeful as if it had been a mountain of butter in the hottest corner of the tropics. Nothing ever had the same shape when I was coming down-stream that it had borne when I went up. I mentioned these little difficulties to Mr. Bixby. He said:

"That's the very main virtue of the thing. If the shapes didn't change every three seconds they wouldn't be of any use. Take this place where we are now, for instance. As long as that hill over yonder is only one hill, I can boom right along the way I'm going, but the moment it splits at the top and forms a V, I know I've got to scratch to starboard in a hurry or I'll bang this boat's brains out against a rock, and then the moment one of the prongs of the V swings behind the other, I've got to waltz to larboard again or I'll have a misunderstanding with a snag that would snatch the keelson out of this steamboat as neatly as if it were a sliver in your hand. If that hill didn't change its shape on bad nights there would be an awful steamboat graveyard around here inside of a year."

It was plain that I had got to learn the shape of the river in all the different ways that could be thought of—upside down, wrong end first, inside out, fore-and-aft, and "thort-ships"—and then know what to do on gray nights when it hadn't any shape at all. So I set about it. In the course of time I began to get the best of this knotty lesson and my self-complacency moved to the front once more. Mr. Bixby was all fixed and ready to start it to the rear again. He opened on me after this fashion:

"How much water did we have in the middle crossing at Hole-in-the-Wall, trip before last?"

I considered this an outrage. I said:

"Every trip, down and up, the leadsmen are singing through that tangled place for three-quarters of an hour on a stretch. How do you reckon I can remember such a mess as that?"

"My boy, you've got to remember it. You've got to remember the exact spot and the exact marks the boat lay in when we had the shoalest water, in every one of the five hundred shoal places between St. Louis and New Orleans, and you mustn't get the shoal soundings and marks of one trip mixed up with the shoal soundings and marks of another, either, for they're not often twice alike. You must keep them separate."

When I came to myself again, I said:

"When I get so that I can do that, I'll be able to raise the dead, and then I won't have to pilot a steamboat to make a living. I want to retire from this business. I want a slush-bucket and a brush, I'm only fit for a roustabout. I haven't got brains enough to be a pilot, and if I had I wouldn't have strength enough to carry them around, unless I went on crutches."

"Now drop that! When I say I'll learn a man the river, I mean it. And you can depend on it, I'll learn him or kill him."

There was no use in arguing with a person like this. I promptly put such a strain on my memory that by and by even the shoal water and the countless crossing-marks began to stay with me. But the result was just the same. I never could more than get one knotty thing learned before another presented itself. Now I had often seen pilots gazing at the water and pretending to read it as if it were a book, but it was a book that told me nothing. A time came at last, however, when Mr. Bixby seemed to think me far enough advanced to bear a lesson on water-reading. So he began:

"Do you see that long, slanting line on the face of the water? Now, that's a reef. Moreover, it's a bluff reef. There is a solid sand-bar under it that is nearly as straight up and down as the side of a house. There is plenty of water close up to it, but mighty little on top of it. If you were to hit it you would knock the boat's brains out. Do you see where the line fringes out at the upper end and begins to fade away?"

"Yes, sir."

"Well, that is a low place; that is the head of the reef. You can climb over there and not hurt anything. Cross over, now, and follow along close under the reef—easy water there—not much current."

I followed the reef along till I approached the fringed end. Then Mr. Bixby said:

"Now get ready. Wait till I give the word. She won't want to mount the reef; a boat hates shoal water. Stand by—wait—*wait*—keep her well in hand. *Now* cramp her down! Snatch her! snatch her!"

He seized the other side of the wheel and helped to spin it around until it was hard down, and then we held it so. The boat resisted and refused to answer for a while, and next she came surging to starboard, mounted the reef, and sent a long angry ridge of water foaming away from her bows.

"Now watch her, watch her like a cat, or she'll get away from you. When she fights strong and the tiller slips a little, in a jerky, greasy sort of way, let up on her a trifle; it is the way she tells you at night that the water is too shoal; but keep edging her up, little by little, toward the point. You are well up on the bar now; there is a bar under every point, because the water that comes down around it forms an eddy and allows the sediment to sink. Do you see those fine lines on the face of the water that branch out like the ribs of a fan? Well, those are little reefs; you want to just miss the ends of them but run them pretty close. Now look out—look out! Don't you crowd that slick, greasy-looking place, there ain't nine feet there, she won't stand it. She begins to smell it; look sharp, I tell you! Oh, blazes, there you go! Stop the starboard wheel! Quick! Ship up to back! Set her back!"

The engine bells jingled and the engines answered promptly, shooting white columns of steam far aloft out of the 'scape-pipes, but it was too late. The boat had "smelt" the bar in good earnest; the foamy ridges that radiated from her bows suddenly disappeared, a great dead swell came rolling forward, and swept ahead of her; she careened far over to larboard and went tearing away toward the shore as if she were about seared to death. We were a good mile from where we ought to have been when we finally got the upper hand of her again.

During the afternoon watch the next day, Mr. Bixby asked me if I knew how to run the next few miles. I said:

"Go inside the first snag above the point, outside the next one, start out from the lower end of Higgins's woodyard, make a square crossing, and—"

"That's all right. I'll be back before you close up on the next point."

But he wasn't. He was still below when I rounded it and entered upon a piece of the river which I had some misgivings about. I did not know that he was hiding behind a chimney to see how I would perform. I went gaily along, getting prouder and prouder, for he had never left the boat in my sole charge such a length of time before. I even got to "setting" her and letting the wheel go entirely, while I vaingloriously turned my back and inspected the stern marks and hummed a tune, a sort of easy indifference which I had prodigiously admired in Bixby and other great pilots. Once I inspected rather long, and when I faced to the front again my heart flew into my mouth so suddenly that if I hadn't clapped my teeth together I should have lost it. One of those frightful bluff reefs was stretching its deadly length right across our bows! My head was gone in a moment; I did not know which end I stood on; I gasped and could not get my breath; I spun the wheel down with such rapidity that it wove itself together like a spider's web; the boat answered and turned square away from the reef, but the reef followed her! I fled but still it followed, still it kept— right across my bows! I never looked to see where I was going, I only fled. The awful crash was imminent. Why didn't that villain come? If I committed the crime of ringing a bell I might get thrown overboard. But better that than kill the boat. So in blind desperation, I started such a rattling "shivaree" down below as never had astounded an engineer in this world before, I fancy. Amidst the frenzy of the bells the engines began to back and fill in a curious way and my reason forsook its throne—we were about to crash into the woods on the other side of the river. Just then Mr. Bixby stepped calmly into view on the hurricane-deck. My soul went out to him in gratitude. My distress vanished; I would have felt safe on the brink of Niagara with Mr. Bixby on the hurricane-deck. He blandly and sweetly took his toothpick out of his mouth between his fingers, as if it were a cigar—we were just in the act of climbing an overhanging big tree and the passengers were scudding astern like rats—and lifted up these commands to me ever so gently:

"Stop the starboard! Stop the larboard! Set her back on both!"

The boat hesitated, halted, pressed her nose among the boughs a critical instant, then reluctantly began to back away.

"Stop the larboard! Come ahead on it! Stop the starboard! Come ahead on it! Point her for the bar!"

I sailed away as serenely as a summer's morning. Mr. Bixby came in and said, with mock simplicity:

"When you have a hail, my boy, you ought to tap the big bell three times before you land, so that the engineers can get ready."

I blushed under the sarcasm and said I hadn't had any hail.

"Ah! Then it was for wood, I suppose. The officer of the watch will tell you when he wants to wood up."

I went on consuming and said I wasn't after wood.

"Indeed? Why, what could you want over here in the bend, then? Did you ever know of a boat following a bend up-stream at this stage of the river?"

"No, sir—and I wasn't trying to follow it. I was getting away from a bluff reef."

"No, it wasn't a bluff reef; there isn't one within three miles of where you were."

"But I saw it. It was as bluff as that one yonder."

"Just about. Run over it!"

"Do you give it as an order?"

"Yes. Run over it!"

"If I don't, I wish I may die."

"All right; I am taking the responsibility."

I was just as anxious to kill the boat, now, as I had been to save it before. I impressed my orders upon my memory, to be used at the inquest, and made a straight break for the reef. As it disappeared under our bows I held my breath, but we slid over it like oil.

"Now, don't you see the difference? It wasn't anything but a *wind* reef. The wind does that."

"So I see. But it is exactly like a bluff reef. How am I ever going to tell them apart?"

"I can't tell you. It is an instinct. By and by you will just naturally *know* one from the other, but you never will be able to explain why or how you know them apart."

It turned out to be true. The face of the water in time became a wonderful book—a book that was a dead language to the uneducated passenger but which told its mind to me without reserve, delivering its most cherished secrets as clearly as if it uttered them with a voice. And it was not a book to be read once and thrown aside, for it had a new story to tell every day. Throughout the long twelve hundred miles there was never a page that was void of interest, never one that you could leave unread without loss, never one that you would want to skip, thinking you could find higher enjoyment in some other thing. There never was so wonderful a book written by man, never one whose interest was so absorbing, so unflagging, so sparklingly renewed with every reperusal. The passenger who could not read it was charmed with a peculiar sort of faint dimple on its surface (on the rare occasions when he did not overlook it altogether) but to the pilot that was an *italicized* passage; indeed it was more than that, it was a legend of the largest capitals with a string of shouting exclamation-points at the end of it, for it meant that a wreck or a rock was buried there that could tear the life out of the strongest vessel that ever floated. It is the faintest and simplest expression the water ever makes, and the most hideous to a pilot's eye. In truth, the passenger who could not read this book saw nothing but all manner of pretty pictures in it, painted by the sun and shaded by the clouds, whereas to the trained eye these were not pictures at all, but the grimmest and most dead-earnest of reading-matter.

Now when I had mastered the language of this water and had come to know every trifling feature that bordered the great river as familiarly as I knew the letters of the alphabet, I had made a valuable acquisition. But I had lost something, too. I had lost something which could never be restored to me while I lived. All the grace, the beauty, the poetry, had gone out of the majestic river! I still kept in mind a certain wonderful sunset which I witnessed when steamboating was new to me. A broad expanse of the river was turned to blood; in the middle distance the red hue brightened into gold, through which a solitary log came floating, black and conspicuous; in one place a long, slanting mark lay sparkling upon the water; in another the surface was broken by boiling, tumbling rings, that were as many-tinted as an opal; where the ruddy flush was faintest, was a smooth spot that was covered with graceful circles and radiating lines, ever so delicately traced; the shore on our left was densely wooded and the somber shadow that fell from this forest was broken in one place by a long, ruffled trail that shone like silver; and high above the forest wall a clean-stemmed dead tree waved a single leafy bough that glowed like a flame in the unobstructed splendor that was flowing from the sun. There were graceful curves, reflected images, woody heights, soft distances, and over the whole scene, far and near, the dissolving lights drifted steadily, enriching it every passing moment with new marvels of coloring.

I stood like one bewitched. I drank it in, in a speechless rapture. The world was new to me and I had never seen anything like this at home. But as I have said, a day came when I began to cease from noting the glories and the charms which the moon and the sun and the twilight wrought upon the river's face; another day came when I ceased altogether to note them. Then, if that sunset scene had been repeated, I should have looked upon it without rapture, and should have commented upon it inwardly after this fashion: "This sun means that we are going to have wind tomorrow; that floating log means that the river is rising, small thanks to it; that slanting mark on the water refers to a bluff reef which is going to kill somebody's steamboat one of these nights, if it keeps on stretching out like that; those tumbling 'boils' show a dissolving bar and a changing channel there; the lines and circles in the slick water over yonder are a warning that that troublesome place is shoaling up dangerously; that silver streak in the shadow of the forest is the 'break' from a new snag and he has located himself in the very best place he could have found to fish for steamboats; that tall dead tree, with a single living branch, is not going to last long, and then how is a body ever going to get through this blind place at night without the friendly old landmark?"

No, the romance and beauty were all gone from the river. All the value any feature of it had for me now was the amount of usefulness it could furnish toward compassing the safe piloting of a steamboat. Since those days, I have pitied doctors from my heart. What does the lovely flush in a beauty's cheek mean to a doctor but a "break" that ripples above some deadly disease? Are not all her visible charms sown thick with what are to him the signs and symbols of hidden decay? Does he ever see her beauty at all, or doesn't he simply view her professionally and comment upon her unwholesome condition all to himself? And doesn't he sometimes wonder whether he has gained most or lost most by learning his trade?

Charles Dickens, *Hard Times*

Book the First—Sowing
Chapter One
The One Thing Needful

"Now, what I want is, Facts. Teach these boys and girls nothing but Facts. Facts alone are wanted in life. Plant nothing else, and root out everything else. You can only form the minds of reasoning animals upon Facts; nothing else will ever be of any service to them. This is the principle on which I bring up my own children, and this is the principle on which I bring up these children. Stick to Facts, sir!"

The scene was a plain, bare, monotonous vault of a schoolroom, and the speaker's square forefinger emphasized his observations by underscoring every sentence with a line on the schoolmaster's sleeve. The emphasis was helped by the speaker's square wall of a forehead, which had his eyebrows for its base, while his eyes found commodious cellarage in two dark caves, overshadowed by the wall. The emphasis was helped by the speaker's mouth, which was wide, thin, and hard set. The emphasis was helped by the speaker's voice, which was inflexible, dry, and dictatorial. The emphasis was helped by the speaker's hair, which bristled on the skirts of his bald head, a plantation of firs to keep the wind from its shining surface, all covered with knobs, like the crust of a plum pie, as if the head had scarcely warehouse-room for the hard facts stored inside. The speaker's obstinate carriage, square coat, square legs, square shoulders— nay, his very neckcloth, trained to take him by the throat with an unaccommodating grasp, like a stubborn fact, as it was—all helped the emphasis.

"In this life, we want nothing but Facts, sir; nothing but Facts!"

The speaker, and the schoolmaster, and the third grown person present, all backed a little, and swept with their eyes the inclined plane of little vessels then and there arranged in order, ready to have imperial gallons of facts poured into them until they were full to the brim.

Chapter Two
Murdering the Innocents

THOMAS GRADGRIND, sir. A man of realities. A man of facts and calculations. A man who proceeds upon the principle that two and two are four, and nothing over, and who is not to be talked into allowing for anything over. Thomas Gradgrind, sir—peremptorily Thomas—Thomas Gradgrind. With a rule and a pair of scales, and the multiplication table always in his pocket, sir, ready to weigh and measure any parcel of human nature, and tell you exactly what it comes to. It is a mere question of figures, a case of simple arithmetic. You might hope to get some other nonsensical belief into the head of George Gradgrind, or Augustus Gradgrind, or John Gradgrind, or Joseph Gradgrind (all supposititious, nonexistent persons), but into the head of Thomas Gradgrind—no, sir!

In such terms Mr. Gradgrind always mentally introduced himself, whether to his private circle of acquaintance, or to the public in general. In such terms, no doubt, substituting the words "boys and girls" for "sir", Thomas Gradgrind now presented Thomas Gradgrind to the little pitchers before him, who were to be filled so full of facts.

Indeed, as he eagerly sparkled at them from the cellarage before mentioned, he seemed a kind of cannon loaded to the muzzle with facts, and prepared to blow them clean out of the regions of childhood at one discharge. He seemed a galvanizing apparatus, too, charged with a grim mechanical substitute for the tender young imaginations that were to be stormed away.

"Girl number twenty," said Mr. Gradgrind, squarely pointing with his square forefinger, "I don't know that girl. Who is that girl?"

"Sissy Jupe, sir," explained number twenty, blushing, standing up, and curtseying.

"Sissy is not a name," said Mr. Gradgrind. "Don't call yourself Sissy. Call yourself Cecilia."

"It's father as calls me Sissy, sir," returned the young girl in a trembling voice, and with another curtsey.

"Then he has no business to do it," said Mr. Gradgrind. "Tell him he mustn't. Cecilia Jupe. Let me see. What is your father?"

"He belongs to the horse-riding, if you please, sir."

Mr. Gradgrind frowned, and waved off the objectionable calling with his hand.

"We don't want to know anything about that, here. You mustn't tell us about that, here. Your father breaks horses, don't he?"

"If you please, sir, when they can get any to break, they do break horses in the ring, sir."

"You mustn't tell us about the ring here. Very well, then. Describe your father as a horsebreaker. He doctors sick horses, I dare say?"

"Oh, yes, sir."

"Very well, then. He is a veterinary surgeon, a farrier, and horse-breaker. Give me your definition of a horse."

(Sissy Jupe thrown into the greatest alarm by this demand.)

"Girl number twenty unable to define a horse!" said Mr. Gradgrind, for the general behoof of all the little pitchers. "Girl number twenty possessed of no facts in reference to one of the commonest of animals! Some boy's definition of a horse. Bitzer, yours."

The square finger, moving here and there, lighted suddenly on Bitzer, perhaps because he chanced to sit in the same ray of sunlight which, darting in at one of the bare windows of the intensely whitewashed room, irradiated Sissy. For, the boys and girls sat on the face of the inclined plane in two compact bodies, divided up the centre by a narrow interval; and Sissy, being at the corner of a row on the sunny side, came in for the beginning of a sunbeam, of which Bitzer, being at the corner of a row on the other side, a few rows in advance, caught the end. But, whereas the girl was so dark-eyed and dark-haired that she seemed to receive a deeper and more lustrous colour from the sun, when it shone upon her, the boy was so light-eyed and light-haired that the self-same rays appeared to draw out of him what little colour he ever possessed. His cold eyes would hardly have been eyes, but for the short ends of lashes which, by bringing them into immediate contrast with something paler than themselves, expressed their form. His short-cropped hair might have been a mere continuation of the sandy freckles on his forehead and face. His skin was so unwholesomely deficient in the natural tinge, that he looked as though, if he were cut, he would bleed white.

"Bitzer," said Thomas Gradgrind. "Your definition of a horse."

"Quadruped. Graminivorous. Forty teeth, namely twenty-four grinders, four eye-teeth, and twelve incisive. Sheds coat in the spring; in marshy countries, sheds hoofs, too. Hoofs hard, but requiring to be shod with iron. Age known by marks in mouth." Thus (and much more) Bitzer.

"Now, girl number twenty," said Mr. Gradgrind, "you know what a horse is."

She curtseyed again, and would have blushed deeper, if she could have blushed deeper than she had blushed all this time. Bitzer, after rapidly blinking at Thomas Gradgrind with both eyes at once, and so catching the light upon his quivering ends of lashes that they looked like the antennae of busy insects, put his knuckles to his freckled forehead, and sat down again.

The third gentleman now stepped forth. A mighty man at cutting and drying, he was; a government officer; in his way (and in most other people's too), a professed pugilist; always in training, always with a system to force down the general throat like a bolus, always to be heard of at the bar of his little Public-office, ready to fight all England. To continue in the fistic phraseology, he had a genius for coming up to the scratch, wherever and whatever it was, and proving himself an ugly customer. He would go in and damage any subject whatever with his right, follow up with his left, stop, exchange, counter, bore his opponent (he always fought All England) to the ropes, and fall upon him neatly. He was certain to knock the wind out of common sense, and render that unlucky adversary deaf to the call of time. And he had it in charge from high authority to bring about the great Public-office Millennium, when Commissioners should reign upon earth.

"Very well," said this gentleman, briskly smiling, and folding his arms. "That's a horse. Now, let me ask you, girls and boys, Would you paper a room with representations of horses?"

After a pause, one half of the children cried in chorus, "Yes, sir!" Upon which the other half, seeing in the gentleman's face that Yes was wrong, cried out in chorus, "No, sir!"—as the custom is, in these examinations.

"Of course, No. Why wouldn't you?"

A pause. One corpulent slow boy, with a wheezy manner of breathing, ventured the answer, Because he wouldn't paper a room at all, but would paint it.

"You *must* paper it," said the gentleman, rather warmly.

"You must paper it," said Thomas Gradgrind, "whether you like it or not. Don't tell *us* you wouldn't paper it. What do you mean, boy?"

"I'll explain to you, then," said the gentleman, after another and a dismal pause, "why you wouldn't paper a room with representations of horses. Do you ever see horses walking up and down the sides of rooms in reality—in fact? Do you?"

"Yes, sir!" from one half. "No, sir!" from the other. "Of course, No," said the gentleman, with an indignant look at the wrong half. "Why, then, you are not to see anywhere what you don't see in fact; you are not to have anywhere what you don't have in fact. What is called Taste, is only another name for Fact."

Thomas Gradgrind nodded his approbation.

"This is a new principle, a discovery, a great discovery," said the gentleman. "Now I'll try you again. Suppose you were going to carpet a room. Would you use a carpet having a representation of flowers upon it?"

There being a general conviction by this time that "No, sir!" was always the right answer to this gentleman, the chorus of No was very strong. Only a few feeble stragglers said Yes; among them Sissy Jupe.

"Girl number twenty," said the gentleman, smiling in the calm strength of knowledge.

Sissy blushed, and stood up.

"So you would carpet your room—or your husband's room, if you were a grown woman, and had a husband—with representations of flowers, would you," said the gentleman. "Why would you?"

"If you please, Sir, I am very fond of flowers," returned the girl.

"And is that why you would put tables and chairs upon them, and have people walking over them with heavy boots?"

"It wouldn't hurt them, sir. They wouldn't crush and wither if you please, sir. They would be the pictures of what was very pretty and pleasant, and I would fancy—"

"Ay, ay, ay! But you mustn't fancy," cried the gentleman, quite elated by coming so happily to his point. "That's it! You are never to fancy."

"You are not, Cecilia Jupe," Thomas Gradgrind solemnly repeated, "to do anything of that kind."

"Fact, fact, fact!" said the gentleman. And "Fact, fact, fact!" repeated Thomas Gradgrind.

"You are to be in all things regulated and governed," said the gentleman, "by fact. We hope to have before long, a board of fact, composed of commissioners of fact, who will force the people to be a people of fact, and of nothing but fact. You must discard the word Fancy altogether. You have nothing to do with it. You are not to have, in any object of use or ornament, what would be a contradiction in fact. You don't walk upon flowers in fact; you cannot be allowed to walk upon flowers in carpets. You don't find that foreign birds and butterflies come and perch upon your crockery; you cannot be permitted to paint foreign birds and butterflies upon your crockery. You never meet with quadrupeds going up and down walls; you must not have quadrupeds represented upon walls. You must use," said the gentleman, "for all these purposes, combinations and modifications (in primary colours) of mathematical figures which are susceptible of proof and demonstration. This is the new discovery. This is Fact. This is taste."

The girl curtseyed and sat down. She was very young, and she looked as if she were frightened by the matter of fact prospect the world afforded.

"Now, if Mr. M'Choakumchild," said the gentleman, "will proceed to give his first lesson here, Mr. Gradgrind, I shall be happy, at your request, to observe his mode of procedure."

Mr. Gradgrind was much obliged. "Mr. M'Choakumchild, we only wait for you."

So, Mr. M'Choakumchild began in his best manner. He and some one hundred and forty other schoolmasters had been lately turned at the same time, in the same factory, on the same principles, like so many pianoforte legs. He bad been put through an immense variety of paces, and had answered volumes of headbreaking questions. Orthography, etymology, syntax, and prosody, biography, astronomy, geography, and general cosmography, the sciences of compound proportion, algebra, land-surveying and leveling, vocal music and drawing from models, were all at the ends of his ten chilled fingers. He had worked his stony way into Her Majesty's most Honourable Privy Council's Schedule B, and had taken the bloom off the higher branches of mathematics and physical science, French, German, Latin, and Greek. He knew all about all the Water Sheds of all the world (whatever they are), and all the histories of all the peoples, and all the names of all the rivers and mountains, and all the productions, manners, and customs of all the countries, and all their boundaries and bearings on the two-and-thirty points of the compass. Ah, rather overdone, M'Choakumchild. If he had only learnt a little less, how infinitely better he might have taught much more!

He went to work, in this preparatory lesson, not unlike Morgiana in the Forty Thieves; looking into all the vessels ranged before him, one after another, to see what they contained. Say, good M'Choakumchild. When from thy boiling store thou shalt fill each jar brimful by-and-by, dost thou think that thou wilt always kill outright the robber Fancy lurking within—or sometimes only maim him and distort him?

Chapter Three
A Loophole

Mr. Gradgrind walked homewards from the school, in a state of considerable satisfaction. It was his school, and he intended it to be a model. He intended every child in it to be a model—just as the young Gradgrinds were all models.

There were five young Gradgrinds, and they were models every one. They had been lectured at, from their tenderest years; coursed, like little hares. Almost as soon as they could run alone, they had been made to run to the lecture-room. The first object with which they had an association, or of which they had a remembrance, was a large blackboard with a dry Ogre chalking ghastly white figures on it.

Not that they knew, by name or nature, anything about an Ogre. Fact forbid! I only use the word to express a monster in a lecturing castle, with Heaven knows how many beads manipulated into one, taking childhood captive, and dragging it into gloomy statistical dens by the hair.

No little Gradgrind had ever seen a face in the moon; it was up in the moon before it could speak distinctly. No little Gradgrind had ever learned the silly jingle, Twinkle, twinkle, little star; how I wonder what you are! No little Gradgrind had ever known wonder on the subject, each little Gradgrind having at five years old dissected the Great Bear like a Professor Owen, and driven Charles's Wain like a locomotive engine-driver. No little Gradgrind had ever associated a cow in a field with that famous cow with the crumpled horn who tossed the dog who worried the cat who killed the rat who ate the malt, or with that yet more famous cow who swallowed Tom Thumb; it had never heard of those celebrities, and had only been introduced to a cow as a graminivorous ruminating quadruped with several stomachs.

To his matter-of fact home, which was called Stone Lodge, Mr. Gradgrind directed his steps. He had virtually retired from the wholesale hardware trade before he built Stone Lodge, and was now looking about for a suitable opportunity of making an arithmetical figure in Parliament. Stone Lodge was situated on a moor within a mile or two of a great town—called Coketown in the present faithful guidebook.

A very regular feature on the face of the country Stone Lodge was. Not the least disguise toned down or shaded off that uncompromising fact in the landscape. A great square house, with a heavy portico darkening the principal windows, as its master's heavy brows overshadowed his eyes. A calculated, cast up, balanced, and proved house. Six windows on this side of the door, six on that side; a total of twelve in this wing, a total of twelve in the other wing; four-and-twenty carried over to the back wings. A lawn and garden and an infant avenue, all ruled straight like a botanical account-book. Gas and ventilation, drainage and water-service, all of the primest quality. Iron clamps and girders, fireproof from top to bottom; mechanical lifts for the housemaids, with all their brushes and brooms; everything that heart could desire.

Everything? Well, I suppose so. The little Gradgrinds had cabinets in various departments of science too. They had a little conchological cabinet, and a little metallurgical cabinet, and a little mineralogical cabinet; and the specimens were all arranged and labelled, and the bits of stone and ore looked as though they might have been broken from the parent substances by those tremendously hard instruments their own names; and, to paraphrase the idle legend of Peter Piper, who had never found his way into *their* nursery, If the greedy little Gradgrinds grasped at more than this, what was it, for good gracious goodness' sake, that the greedy little Gradgrinds grasped at!

Their father walked on in a hopeful and satisfied frame of mind. He was an affectionate father, after his manner; but he would probably have described himself (if he had been put, like Sissy Jupe, upon a definition) as "an eminently practical" father. He had a particular pride in the phrase eminently practical, which was considered to have a special application to him. Whatsoever the public meeting held in Coketown, and whatsoever the subject of such meeting, some Coketowner was sure to seize the occasion of alluding to his eminently practical friend Gradgrind. This always pleased the eminently practical friend. He knew it to be his due, but his due was acceptable.

He had reached the neutral ground upon the outskirts of the town, which was neither town nor country, and yet was either spoiled, when his ears were invaded by the sound of music. The clashing and banging band attached to the horse-riding establishment, which had there set up its rest in a wooden pavilion, was in full bray. A flag, floating from the summit of the temple, proclaimed to mankind that it was "Sleary's horse-riding" which claimed their suffrages. Sleary himself, a stout modern statue with a moneybox at its elbow, in an ecclesiastical niche of early Gothic architecture, took the money. Miss Josephine Sleary, as some very long and very narrow strips of printed bill announced, was then inaugurating the entertainments with her graceful equestrian Tyrolean flower-act. Among the other pleasing but always strictly moral wonders which must be seen to be believed Signor Jupe was that afternoon to "elucidate the diverting accomplishments of his highly trained performing dog Merrylegs." He was also to exhibit "his astounding feat of throwing seventy-five hundredweight in rapid succession backhanded over his head, thus forming a fountain of solid iron in mid-air, a feat never before attempted in this or any other country and which having elicited such rapturous plaudits from enthusiastic throngs it cannot be withdrawn." The same Signor Jupe was to "enliven the varied performances at frequent intervals with his chaste Shaksperean quips and retorts." Lastly, he was to wind them up by appearing in his favourite character of Mr. William Button, of Tooley Street, in "the highly novel and laughable hippocomedietta of The Tailor's Journey to Brentford."

Thomas Gradgrind took no heed of these trivialities of course, but passed on as a practical man ought to pass on, after brushing the noisy insects from his thoughts, or consigning them to the House of Correction. But, the turning of the road took him by the back of the booth, and at the back of the booth a number of children were congregated in a number of stealthy attitudes, striving to peep in at the hidden glories of the place.

This brought him to a stop. "Now, to think of these vagabonds," said he, "attracting the young rabble from a model school."

A space of stunted grass and dry rubbish being between him and the young rabble, he took his eyeglass out of his waistcoat to look for any child he knew by name, and might order off. Phenomenon almost incredible though distinctly seen, what did he then behold but his own metallurgical Louisa peeping with all her might through a hole in a deal board, and his own mathematical Thomas abasing himself on the ground to catch but a hoof of the graceful equestrian Tyrolean flower-act!

Dumb with amazement, Mr. Gradgrind crossed to the spot where his family was thus disgraced, laid his hand upon each erring child, and said:

"Louisa!! Thomas!!"

Both rose, red and disconcerted. But Louisa looked at her father with more boldness than Thomas did. Indeed, Thomas did not look at him, but gave himself up to be taken home like a machine.

"In the name of wonder, idleness, and folly!" said Mr. Gradgrind, leading each away by a hand, "what do you do here?"

"Wanted to see what it was like," returned Louisa, shortly.

"What it was like?"

"Yes, father."

There was an air of jaded sullenness in them both, and particularly in the girl; yet, struggling through the dissatisfaction of her face, there was a light with nothing to rest upon, a fire with nothing to burn, a starved imagination keeping life in itself somehow, which brightened its expression. Not with the brightness natural to cheerful youth, but with uncertain, eager, doubtful flashes, which had something painful in them, analogous to the changes on a blind face groping its way.

She was a child now, of fifteen or sixteen; but at no distant day would seem to become a woman all at once. Her father thought so as he looked at her. She was pretty. Would have been self-willed (he thought in his eminently practical way), but for her bringing-up.

"Thomas, though I have the fact before me, I find it difficult to believe that you, with your education and resources, should have brought your sister to a scene like this."

"I brought *him*, father," said Louisa, quickly. "I asked him to come."

"I am sorry to hear it. I am very sorry indeed to hear it. It makes Thomas no better, and it makes you worse, Louisa."

She looked at her father again, but no tear fell down her cheek.

"You! Thomas and you, to whom the circle of the sciences is open; Thomas and you, who may be said to be replete with facts; Thomas and you, who have been trained to mathematical exactness; Thomas and you, here!" cried Mr. Gradgrind. "In this degraded position! I am amazed."

"I was tired, father. I have been tired a long time," said Louisa.

"Tired? Of what?" asked the astonished father.

"I don't know of what—of everything, I think."

"Say not another word," returned Mr. Gradgrind. "You are childish. I will hear no more." He did not speak again until they had walked some half-a-mile in silence, when he gravely broke out with, "What would your best friends say, Louisa? Do you attach no value to their good opinion? What would Mr. Bounderby say?"

At the mention of this name, his daughter stole a look at him, remarkable for its intense and searching character. He saw nothing of it, for, before he looked at her, she had again cast down her eyes!

"What," he repeated presently, "would Mr. Bounderby say?" All the way to Stone Lodge, as with grave indignation he led the two delinquents home, he repeated at intervals, "What would Mr. Bounderby say!"—as if Mr. Bounderby had been Mrs. Grundy.

Irma S. Rombauer and Marion Rombauer Becker, *The Joy of Cooking*

Dedication

In revising and reorganizing "The Joy of Cooking" we have missed the help of my mother, Irma S. Rombauer. How grateful I am for her buoyant example, for the strong feeling of roots she gave me, for her conviction that, well-grounded, you can make the most of life, no matter what it brings! In an earlier away-from-home kitchen I acted as tester and production manager for the privately printed first edition of "The Joy." Working with Mother on its development has been for my husband, John, and for me the culmination of a very happy personal relationship. John has always contributed verve to this undertaking, but during the past ten years he has, through his constant support and crisp creative editing, become an integral part of the book. We look forward to a time when our two boys—and their wives—will continue to keep "The Joy" a family affair, as well as an enterprise in which the authors owe no obligation to anyone but themselves—and you.

Marion Rombauer Becker

Foreword and Guide

"The cook," said Saki, "was a good cook, as cooks go; and as cooks go, she went." Indeed she did go, leaving us, whether in charge of established or of fledgling families, to fend for ourselves. We are confident that after you have used this book steadily for a few months, paying due attention to our symbols . . . and especially to our "pointers to success"▶—as identified on the end papers—you will master the skills the cook walked off with. What is more, we believe that you will go on to unexpected triumphs, based on the sound principles which underlie our recipes, and actually revel in a sense of new-found freedom. You will eat at the hour of your choice. The food will be cooked and seasoned to your discriminating taste. And you will regain the priceless private joy of family living, dining and sharing. . . .

Entertaining

When you are entertaining, try not to feel that something unusual is expected of you as a hostess. It isn't. Just be yourself. Even eminent and distinguished persons are only human. Like the rest of us, they shrink from ostentation; and nothing is more disconcerting to a guest than the impression that his coming is causing a household commotion. Confine all noticeable efforts for his comfort and entertainment to the period that precedes his arrival. Satisfy yourself that you have anticipated every known emergency—the howling child, the last-minute search for cuff links, your husband's exuberance, your helper's ineptness, your own ill humor. Then relax and enjoy your guests.

If, at the last minute, something does happen to upset your well-laid plans, rise to the occasion. The mishap may be the making of your party. Capitalize on it, but not too heavily.

The procedures below present simple, dignified, current practice in table service. If you plan to serve cocktails before a meal, have glasses for drinks and nonalcoholic beverages ready on a tray. With these, you may pass some form of cracker, canape or hors d'oeuvre. If you and your guests are discriminating diners, you will keep this pick-up light. Too generous quantities of food and drink beforehand will bring jaded palates to the dinner on which you have expended such effort. Should you have the kind of guests who enjoy a long cocktail period and varied hors d'oeuvre, be sure to season your dinner food more highly than usual. Cocktail preliminaries, which have a bad habit these days of going on indefinitely, may be politely shortened by serving a delicious hot or cold consommé or soup, either near the bar area or from a tureen on a cart. Your guests are apt to welcome this transition heartily.

No matter for whom your preparations are being made, careful forethought and arrangement contribute greatly to the pleasure that results. Never forget that ❱ your family is really the most important assembly you ever entertain. Whether for them or for friends ❱ always check the freshness of the air, the temperature of the dining area and the proper heat or chill for plates, food and drinks—especially hot ones. If warming oven space is limited, use the heat cycle of your dishwasher or, if you entertain often, you may wish to install an infrared heating unit which can be raised or lowered above a heatproof counter. Be sure that each diner has plenty of elbow room, about 30 inches from the center of one plate service to the center of the next.

Formal meals, given in beautifully appointed homes, served by competent, well-trained servants—who can be artists in their own right—are a great treat. We cannot expect to have ideal conditions at all times in the average home. However, no matter what the degree of informality, always be sure that the table is attractive and immaculately clean—and always maintain an even rhythm of service. . . .

About Placing Silver and Dishes

There are certain time-honored positions for silver and equipment that result from the way food is eaten and served. So keep in mind these basic placements.

▶ Forks to the left except the very small fish fork, which goes to the right. ▶ Spoons, including iced-tea spoons, and knives to the right, with the sharp blade of the knife toward the plate. There is, of course, a practical reason for placing the knife at the diner's right, since right-handed persons, who predominate, commonly wield the knife with their favored hand, and do so early in the meal. Generally, having cut his food, the diner lays down his knife and transfers his fork to the right hand. Formal dining makes an exception to this rule; and with left-handed or ambidextrous persons the transfer seems to us, on any occasion, superfluous. ▶ Place silver that is to be used first farthest from the plate. It is also better form never to have more than three pieces of silver at either side. Bring in any other needed silver on a small tray as the course is served. The server is always careful to handle silver by the handles only, including carving and serving spoons and forks, which are placed to the right of the serving dish. . . .

When it is time to serve coffee, empty cups and saucers are placed to the right. There is a spoon on the saucer, behind the cup and parallel to the cup handle, which is turned to the diner's right. After all the cups are placed, they are filled by the server and afterward sugar and cream are offered from a small tray from the left. But the entire coffee service may be served, even for luncheon, in the living room, after the dessert. . . .

If your party is not formal, place cards may be omitted. If the party is to be for six, ten or fourteen, the host is at one end of the table, the hostess at the other. If the guests number eight or twelve, the host is at one end and the hostess just to the left at the other end.

The honor guest, if a woman, is seated to the right of the host; if a man, to the left of the hostess. At a formal meal, food is presented, but ▶ not served, to the hostess first. Food is actually offered first to the woman guest of honor. The other women are then all served. Finally, the men are served, beginning with the guest of honor. If there is no special guest of honor, you may want to reverse the direction of service every other course, so that the same people are not always served last.

While it is not the best form, some people prefer to have the hostess served first. She knows the menu and by the way she serves herself sets the pace for the other guests. This is a special help if the guest of honor is from another country. In America, it is customary for guests to wait until everyone is served and the hostess begins to eat. In Europe, however, where each individual service is usually complete in itself, it is permissible to start eating as soon as one is served. . . .

About Formal Entertainment

Most of us moderns look with amazement, not to say dismay, at the menus of traditionally formal dinners. Such meals are a vanishing breed, like the bison—but, like the bison, they manage here and there to survive. They begin with both clear and thick soups. Then comes an alternation of relevés and re-moves, each with its accompanying vegetables. The relevés are lighter in quality than the hefty joints and whole fish which make up the removes. Any one of the rather ironically titled removes could count as the equivalent of what, in current parlance, is called an entrée, or main dish.

However, in the classic formal menu, the term entrée has a quite different significance. Classic entrées occur immediately after a final remove and consist of timbales, sea foods and variety meats, served in rich pastes and with delicate sauces—trifles distinguished for their elegance.

A salad takes next place in this stately procession, and is usually made of a seasoned cooked vegetable, such as asparagus, with greens doing garnish duty only. After this, the diner may choose from a variety of cheeses.

Entremets—hot or cold sweets—succeed the cheese course and these are topped off, in turn, by both hot and cold fruits. We now have completed the major framework of a classic formal menu, in which, it goes without saying, each course is accompanied by a sympathetic wine.

We marvel at the degree of gastronomic sophistication required to appre-ciate so studied and complex a service—to say nothing of the culinary skills needed to present the menu in proper style. But, more critically, we ask, "Where do the guests stow away all that food?" Granted that a truly formal dinner lasts for hours and that each portion may be a dainty one, the total intake is still bound to be formidable. Such an array is seldom encountered in this casual and girth-conscious era. But a semiformal dinner with traces of classic service still graces the privileged household. . . .

Once the guests are seated, the server's steady but unobtrusive labor be-gins. ◗ There is a plate, filled or unfilled, before each guest throughout the meal. The server usually removes a plate from the right and replaces it imme-diately with another from the left, so that the courses follow one another in unbroken rhythm. At such a dinner, second helpings are seldom offered.

When a platter is presented, it is offered from the left to the guest by the server who holds it on a folded napkin, on the palm of his left hand and may steady it with the right. The server should always make sure that the handles of the serving tools are directed toward the diner.

The passing of crackers, breads, relishes, the refilling of water glasses and the pouring of wines take place during, not between, the appropriate courses. When the party is less formal, the host may prefer to pour the wines himself from a decanter or from a bottle. If the wine is chilled, he will wrap it in a napkin and hold a napkin in the left hand to catch any drip from the bottle. The hostess on such occasions may pass relishes to the guest at her right and the guests may continue to pass them on to one another. Also, relishes may be arranged at strategic places on the table, but must be removed with the soup. However, even with these slight assists, the work of the server is one that calls for nicely calculated timing. It is easy to see why ♦ one server should not be called on to take care of more than six or eight guests—at the most—if smooth going is expected. . . .

About Informal Entertainment

Your chances for a successful party are much greater if you key your efforts to your own belongings and service rather than struggle to meet the exacting demands of the kind of dinner which has just been described. Your standards need not be lowered in the least. ♦ Plan a menu which will simplify last-minute preparation and subsequent serving. Offer fewer courses and put several kinds of food on one platter. But please do not let your guests sit, trying to make conversation, with a gradually congealing slice of meat before them, while waiting longingly for the vegetables and the reluctant gravy boat to follow.

If you must rely on indifferent service, or if your harassed cook is trying to pinch-hit as a waitress, plan to serve the main course yourself from an attractively arranged platter. For informal meals, when the hostess may be both waitress and cook, it pays to spend lots of time planning menus that can be prepared in advance and served with little fuss. Here again, in order that food will reach the table at the right temperature, it is wise to choose cooperative equipment such as covered dishes—but do remember to allow a place to put hot lids—double dishes with provision underneath for ice or hot water, and a samovar arrangement for hot drinks.

For both service and removal, a cart may facilitate matters, especially if there are no children trained to help unobtrusively. Deputizing your guests invites chaos, and should, except in extreme emergencies, be avoided.

When service is completely lacking, it is sensible to decide well in advance what concessions will achieve the most peaceful and satisfying conditions for everyone. Plates, already prepared and garnished, can be brought into the dining area on a tray or cart. If the meal is a hot one, we find this scheme impractical for more than four people. For a larger number of guests, attractive platters and casseroles of food may be placed at each end of the table, so that serving responsibilities are divided ♦ but whatever the meal, be sure to serve hot foods hot and cold foods cold. . . .

About Casual Entertaining for One or for Many

Tray meals can be a delightful stimulant if they include a surprise element in the form of a lovely pitcher, a small flower arrangement or some seasonal delicacy. Make sure, especially if the recipient is an invalid, that all needed utensils are present, that the food is hot or cold as required, sufficient in amount and fresh and dainty looking.

A cookout, whether a mere wienie roast or a luau, can be—although it seldom is anymore—one of the least complicated ways to entertain. We suggest, unless your equipment is equal to that of a well-appointed kitchen and you can ensure your guests of comparably controlled cooking, that you choose menus which are really enhanced by outdoor cooking procedures, page 18.

Have enough covered dishes on hand to protect food from flies. Give your guests a tray or a traylike plate if there are no regular place sets or normal seating arrangements. And prepare an alternate plan of accommodation, in case of bad weather.

We remember a successful informal party that was really too big for our quarters and whose pattern might provide a substitute in case of a weather-beleaguered barbecue. The guests arrived to find no evidence of entertaining, only the most gorgeous arrangements of colchicum—those vibrant, large fall blooms which resemble vast, reticulated crocus. After drinks were served and hors d'oeuvre passed, a cart with soup tureen and cups circulated. This was followed by tray baskets containing white paper bags, each completely packaged with individual chicken salad, olives, endive filled with avocado, cocktail tomatoes, cress and cheese sandwiches, bunches of luscious grapes and foil-wrapped brownies. Coffee was served, again from the circulating cart.

In order to get an informal after-supper party rolling, young hostesses are often so eager to present the fruits of their labors that solid food is served too early for the comfort of the guests, most of whom have rather recently dined. If the party gets off to an early start, it sometimes seems too soon to start drinking alcoholic or carbonated drinks or punches. Why not suggest a tisane, page 30, to engender sociability at the take-off of an evening. Tisanes can also prove a pleasant variation for older people, who frequently refuse coffee when food is to be served later.

Here are a few parting shots—as we close this chapter on entertaining. In cooking for more people than you are normally accustomed to, allow yourself enough extra time for both food preparation and heating or cooling of food. Please read the comments on the enlarging of recipes, page 546. Be sure that your mixing and cooking equipment is scaled to take care of your group, and, ▶ most important of all, that you have the refrigerator space to protect chilled dishes and the heat surface to maintain the temperature of the hot ones. Don't hesitate to improvise steam tables or iced trays. Utilize insulated picnic boxes or buckets either way, and wheelbarrows or tubs for the cracked ice, on which to keep platters chilled.

If you entertain this way frequently, it may be worthwhile to make—as one or our friends did—a large rectangular galvanized deep tray, on which the dishes of a whole cold buffet can be kept chilled. Or try confecting an epergne-like form, such as that shown on page 46, for chilling sea foods, hors d'oeuvre or fruit.

For camping trips or boating parties, consider the safety factor in choosing the menu. No matter what the outing ▶ don't transport perishable foods in hot weather in the even hotter trunk of a car.

Not all types of entertaining—formal or casual or in between—can be detailed here. But, whatever the occasion, assemble your tried skills in menu planning so as to reflect the distinctive character of your home. Flavor the occasion with your own personality. And keep handy somewhere, for emergency use, that cool dictum attributed to Col. Chiswell Langhorne of Virginia: "Etiquette is for people who have no breeding; fashion for those who have no taste."

About Bouillabaisse and Other Fisherman's Stews

Necessity is the mother of invention; and convenience gave birth to the can and the frozen package. Use frozen or canned fish, if you must, for fisherman's stews; but remember that ▶ their fragrant, distinctive and elusive charm can only be captured if the fish which go into them are themselves freshly caught. Curnonsky reminds us of the legend that bouillabaisse, the most celebrated of fisherman's stews, was first brought by angels to the Three Marys, when they were shipwrecked on the bleak shores of the Camargue.

Divinely inspired or not, it is true that bouillabaisse can only be approximated in this country, even if its ingredients are just off the hook. For its unique flavor depends on the use of fish which are native to the Mediterranean alone: a regional rock fish, high in gelatin content, for example, which gives a slightly cloudy but still thin texture to the soup, and numberless finny tidbits, too small for market. We offer a free translation of bouillabaisse into American—realizing fully that we have succeeded only in changing poetry to rich prose.

A similar accommodation has been made for matelote or freshwater fish stew, in which eel, carp, bream, tench and perch are combined with wine. A certain amount of freewheeling must be the rule, too, in concocting chowders and stews of both sea and fresh fish, which are milk-based and often have potatoes added. Whatever fish you use, see that it is as ▶ fresh as possible and experiment with combinations of those that are most quickly available.

Bouillabaisse

8 cups

Have ready:

¼ cup finely chopped onion
4 finely julienned leeks: use the white portions only

Skin and squeeze the pulp out of and then dice:

> 4 medium-sized tomatoes

Combine:

> 5 cloves minced garlic
> 1 tablespoon finely chopped fresh fennel
> ½ to 1 teaspoon saffron
> 2 pulverized bay leaves
> 1 teaspoon grated orange rind
> 2 tablespoons tomato paste
> ⅛ teaspoon celery seed
> 3 tablespoons chopped parsley
> 1 teaspoon freshly ground pepper
> 2 tablespoons salt

Heat in a large casserole:

> ¼ to ½ cup olive oil

When the oil is hot, add the prepared ingredients above and cook until the vegetables are transparent. Meanwhile, cut into 1-inch dice and then add:

> 4 lbs. very fresh fish in combination: red snapper, halibut, pompano, sea perch, scallops; also 1-inch pieces of well-scrubbed lobster, whole shrimp, clams and mussels—all in the shell

You may prefer to leave the fish in 2-inch thick slices and use some of the smaller fish whole. If so, add the thinner pieces or small scrubbed shellfish to the pot slightly later than the thicker ones ▶ but do not disturb the boiling. Cover the fish with:

> 2½ cups hot Fumet, page 491, or water

▶ Keep the heat high and force the boiling, which should continue rapid for 15 to 20 minutes.

> **Correct the seasoning**

To serve, have ready to arrange in the bottom of 8 hot bowls:

> ¾-inch slices of French bread

Dry the bread in the oven and brush with:

> **Garlic butter**

When the bouillabaisse is ready, arrange attractively some of each kind of fish on and around the bread. You may remove the lobsters from the shell and remove the upper shells from the clams and mussels. Then pour the hot broth into the bowls and serve at once. Or, you may strain the broth onto the bread and serve the sea food on a separate platter. Plan the meal with a beverage other than wine.

About Quick Soups

When we were very young, we were more appalled than edified by "Struwwelpeter," a book of rhymed fables for children, which had been written in Germany by a Korpsbruder of our great grandfather. We remember the story of Suppenkaspar, a little boy who resolutely refused to eat his soup, wasted away for his stubbornness and was buried with a tureen as his headstone. Looking back and taking note of our wonderful present-day battery of canned, frozen and dried soups, we can see that Kaspar was born a century too soon and would, in this generation, have chosen, beyond a doubt, to live.

Know the comfort and reassurance of a larder well-stocked with processed soups. With them, you may in a jiffy lay the foundation of a good, square meal. If the unexpected guest prefers a clear soup, use a canned consomme or chicken broth with any one of several quickly confected egg-drops, page 169. If he fancies a more filling dish, serve Blender Borsch, page 166, or Quick Cucumber Soup Cockaigne, page 166.

Very special effects may be achieved in your canned and frozen soup repertory by mixing with them the meat and vegetable stocks which are the by-product of daily cooking, page 488. Put these regularly by, along with meat glazes, for just this purpose. Occasionally, too, a bouillon cube will add interest. Please read About Soup Stock and Stock Substitutes, page 488. If you have a plot or some pots of fresh herbs, now is the time to commandeer a clipping all 'round.

▶ One word of caution. Normally, we dilute ready-prepared soups considerably less than their manufacturers recommend, whether we use home-cooked stocks, milk or—less desirably—just plain water. But we find that the more concentrated the soup the more likely it is to taste oversalted. Test your mix and correct this tendency.

John (Fire) Lame Deer and Richard Erdoes, *Lame Deer: Seeker of Visions*

Alone on the Hilltop

I was all alone on the hilltop. I sat there in the vision pit, a hole dug into the hill, my arms hugging my knees as I watched old man Chest, the medicine man who had brought me there, disappear far down in the valley. He was just a moving black dot among the pines, and soon he was gone altogether.

Now I was all by myself, left on the hilltop for four days and nights without food or water until he came back for me. You know, we Indians are not like some white folks—a man and a wife, two children, and one baby sitter who watches the TV set while the parents are out visiting somewhere.

Indian children are never alone. They are always surrounded by grand-parents, uncles, cousins, relatives of all kinds, who fondle the kids, sing to them, tell them stories. If the parents go someplace, the kids go along.

But here I was, crouched in my vision pit, left alone by myself for the first time in my life. I was sixteen then, still had my boy's name and, let me tell you, I was scared. I was shivering and not only from the cold. The nearest human being was many miles away, and four days and nights is a long, long time. Of course, when it was all over, I would no longer be a boy, but a man. I would have had my vision. I would be given a man's name.

Sioux men are not afraid to endure hunger, thirst and loneliness, and I was only ninety-six hours away from being a man. The thought was comforting. Comforting, too, was the warmth of the star blanket which old man Chest had wrapped around me to cover my nakedness. My grandmother had made it es-pecially for this, my first *hanblechia,* my first vision-seeking. It was a beau-tifully designed quilt, white with a large morning star made of many pieces of brightly colored cloth. That star was so big it covered most of the blanket. If Wakan Tanka, the Great Spirit, would give me the vision and the power, I would become a medicine man and perform many ceremonies wrapped in that quilt. I am an old man now and many times a grandfather, but I still have that star blanket my grandmother made for me. I treasure it; some day I shall be buried in it.

The medicine man had also left a peace pipe with me, together with a bag of *kinnickinnick*—our kind of tobacco made of red willow bark. This pipe was even more of a friend to me than my star blanket. To us the pipe is like an open Bible. White people need a church house, a preacher and a pipe organ to get into a praying mood. There are so many things to distract you: who else is in the church, whether the other people notice that you have come, the pictures on the wall, the sermon, how much money you should give and did you bring it with you. We think you can't have a vision that way.

For us Indians there is just the pipe, the earth we sit on and the open sky. The spirit is everywhere. Sometimes it shows itself through an animal, a bird or some trees and hills. Sometimes it speaks from the Badlands, a stone, or even from the water. That smoke from the peace pipe, it goes straight up to the spirit world. But this is a two-way thing. Power flows down to us through that smoke, through the pipe stem. You feel that power as you hold your pipe; it moves from the pipe right into your body. It makes your hair stand up. That pipe is not just a thing; it is alive. Smoking this pipe would make me feel good and help me to get rid of my fears.

As I ran my fingers along its bowl of smooth red pipestone, red like the blood of my people, I no longer felt scared. That pipe had belonged to my father and to his father before him. It would someday pass to my son and, through him, to my grandchildren. As long as we had the pipe there would be a Sioux nation. As I fingered the pipe, touched it, felt its smoothness that came from long use, I sensed that my forefathers who had once smoked this pipe were with me on the hill, right in the vision pit. I was no longer alone.

Besides the pipe the medicine man had also given me a gourd. In it were forty small squares of flesh which my grandmother had cut from her arm with a razor blade. I had seen her do it. Blood had been streaming down from her shoulder to her elbow as she carefully put down each piece of skin on a handkerchief, anxious not to lose a single one. It would have made those anthropologists mad. Imagine, performing such an ancient ceremony with a razor blade instead of a flint knife! To me it did not matter. Someone dear to me had undergone pain, given me something of herself, part of her body, to help me pray and make me stronghearted. How could I be afraid with so many people—living and dead—helping me?

One thing still worried me. I wanted to become a medicine man, a *yuwipi,* a healer carrying on the ancient ways of the Sioux nation. But you cannot learn to be a medicine man like a white man going to medical school. An old holy man can teach you about herbs and the right ways to perform a ceremony where everything must be in its proper place, where every move, every word has its own, special meaning. These things you can learn—like spelling, like training a horse. But by themselves these things mean nothing. Without the vision and the power this learning will do no good. It would not make me a medicine man.

What if I failed, if I had no vision? Or if I dreamed of the Thunder Beings, or lightning struck the hill? That would make me at once into a *heyoka,* a contrarywise, an upside-down man, a clown. "You'll know it, if you get the power," my Uncle Chest had told me. "If you are not given it, you won't lie about it, you won't pretend. That would kill you, or kill somebody close to you, somebody you love."

Night was coming on. I was still lightheaded and dizzy from my first sweat bath in which I had purified myself before going up the hill. I had never been in a sweat lodge before. I had sat in the little beehive-shaped hut made of bent willow branches and covered with blankets to keep the heat in. Old Chest and three other medicine men had been in the lodge with me. I had my back against the wall, edging as far away as I could from the red-hot stones glowing in the center. As Chest poured water over the rocks, hissing white steam enveloped me and filled my lungs. I thought the heat would kill me, burn the eyelids off my face! But right in the middle of all this swirling steam I heard Chest singing. So it couldn't be all that bad. I did not cry out "All my relatives!"— which would have made him open the flap of the sweat lodge to let in some cool air—and I was proud of this. I heard him praying for me: "Oh, holy rocks, we receive your white breath, the steam. It is the breath of life. Let this young boy inhale it. Make him strong."

The sweat bath had prepared me for my vision-seeking. Even now, an hour later, my skin still tingled. But it seemed to have made my brains empty. Maybe that was good, plenty of room for new insights.

Darkness had fallen upon the hill. I knew that *hanhepiwi* had risen, the night sun, which is what we call the moon. Huddled in my narrow cave, I did not see it. Blackness was wrapped around me like a velvet cloth. It seemed to cut me off from the outside world, even from my own body. It made me listen to the voices within me. I thought of my forefathers who had crouched on this hill before me, because the medicine men in my family had chosen this spot for a place of meditation and vision-seeking ever since the day they had crossed the Missouri to hunt for buffalo in the White River country some two hundred years ago. I thought that I could sense their presence right through the earth I was leaning against. I could feel them entering my body, feel them stirring in my mind and heart.

Sounds came to me through the darkness: the cries of the wind, the whisper of the trees, the voices of nature, animal sounds, the hooting of an owl. Suddenly I felt an overwhelming presence. Down there with me in my cramped hole was a big bird. The pit was only as wide as myself, and I was a skinny boy, but that huge bird was flying around me as if he had the whole sky to himself. I could hear his cries, sometimes near and sometimes far, far away. I felt feathers or a wing touching my back and head. This feeling was so overwhelming that it was just too much for me. I trembled and my bones turned to ice. I grasped the rattle with the forty pieces of my grandmother's flesh. It also had many little stones in it, tiny fossils picked up from an ant heap. Ants collect them. Nobody knows why. These little stones are supposed to have a power in them. I shook the rattle and it made a soothing sound, like rain falling on rock. It was talking to me, but it did not calm my fears. I took the sacred pipe in my other hand and began to sing and pray: "Tunkashila, grandfather spirit, help me." But this did not help. I don't know what got into me, but I was no longer myself. I started to cry. Crying, even my voice was different. I sounded like an older man, I couldn't even recognize this strange voice. I used long-ago words in my prayer, words no longer used nowadays. I tried to wipe away my tears, but they wouldn't stop. In the end I just pulled that quilt over me, rolled myself up in it. Still I felt the bird wings touching me.

Slowly I perceived that a voice was trying to tell me something. It was a bird cry, but I tell you, I began to understand some of it. That happens sometimes. I know a lady who had a butterfly sitting on her shoulder. That butterfly told her things. This made her become a great medicine woman.

I heard a human voice too, strange and high-pitched, a voice which could not come from an ordinary, living being. All at once I was way up there with the birds. The hill with the vision pit was way above everything. I could look down even on the stars, and the moon was close to my left side. It seemed as though the earth and the stars were moving below me. A voice said, "You are sacrificing yourself here to be a medicine man. In time you will be one. You will teach other medicine men. We are the fowl people, the winged ones, the eagles and the owls. We are a nation and you shall be our brother. You will never kill or harm any one of us. You are going to understand us whenever you come to seek a vision here on this hill. You will learn about herbs and roots, and you will heal people. You will ask them for nothing in return. A man's life is short. Make yours a worthy one."

I felt that these voices were good, and slowly my fear left me. I had lost all sense of time. I did not know whether it was day or night. I was asleep, yet wide awake. Then I saw a shape before me. It rose from the darkness and the swirling fog which penetrated my earth hole. I saw that this was my great-grandfather, Tahca Ushte, Lame Deer, old man chief of the Minneconjou. I could see the blood dripping from my great-grandfather's chest where a white soldier had shot him. I understood that my great-grandfather wished me to take his name. This made me glad beyond words.

We Sioux believe that there is something within us that controls us, something like a second person almost. We call it *nagi*, what other people might call soul, spirit or essence. One can't see it, feel it or taste it, but that time on the hill—and only that once—I knew it was there inside of me. Then I felt the power surge through me like a flood. I cannot describe it, but it filled all of me. Now I knew for sure that I would become a *wicasa wakan*, a medicine man. Again I wept, this time with happiness.

I didn't know how long I had been up there on that hill—one minute or a lifetime. I felt a hand on my shoulder gently shaking me. It was old man Chest, who had come for me. He told me that I had been in the vision pit four days and four nights and that it was time to come down. He would give me something to eat and water to drink and then I was to tell him everything that had happened to me during my *hanblechia*. He would interpret my visions for me. He told me that the vision pit had changed me in a way that I would not be able to understand at that time. He told me also that I was no longer a boy, that I was a man now. I was Lame Deer.

11 In the spring of the year, the time when kings go forth to battle, David sent Jo'ab, and his servants with him, and all Israel; and they ravaged the Ammonites, and besieged Rabbah. But David remained at Jerusalem. ²It happened, late one afternoon, when David arose from his couch and was walking upon the roof of the king's house, that he saw from the roof a woman bathing; and the woman was very beautiful. ³And David sent and inquired about the woman. And one said, "Is not this Bathshe'ba, the daughter of Eli'am, the wife of Uri'ah the Hittite?" ⁴So David sent messengers, and took her; and she came to him, and he lay with her. (Now she was purifying herself from her uncleanness.) Then she returned to her house. ⁵And the woman conceived; and she sent and told David, "I am with child."

⁶So David sent word to Jo'ab, "Send me Uri'ah the Hittite." And Jo'ab sent Uri'ah to David. ⁷When Uri'ah came to him, David asked how Jo'ab was doing, and how the people fared, and how the war prospered. ⁸Then David said to Uri'ah, "Go down to your house, and wash your feet." And Uri'ah went out of the king's house, and there followed him a present from the king. ⁹But Uri'ah slept at the door of the king's house with all the servants of his lord, and did not go down to his house. ¹⁰When they told David, "Uri'ah did not go down to the house," David said to Uri'ah, "Have you not come from a journey? Why did you not go down to your house?" ¹¹Uri'ah said to David, "The ark and Israel and Judah dwell in booths; and my lord Jo'ab and the servants of my lord are camping in the open field; shall I then go to my house, to eat and to drink, and to lie with my wife? As you live, and as your soul lives, I will not do this thing." ¹²Then David said to Uri'ah, "Remain here today also, and tomorrow I will let you depart." So Uri'ah remained in Jerusalem that day, and the next. ¹³And David invited him, and he ate in his presence and drank, so that he made him drunk; and in the evening he went out to lie on his couch with the servants of his lord, but he did not go down to his house.

¹⁴In the morning David wrote a letter to Jo'ab, and sent it by the hand of Uri'ah. ¹⁵In the letter he wrote, "Set Uri'ah in the forefront of the hardest fighting, and then draw back from him, that he may be struck down, and die." ¹⁶And as Jo'ab was besieging the city, he assigned Uri'ah to the place where he knew there were valiant men. ¹⁷And the men of the city came out and fought with Jo'ab; and some of the servants of David among the people fell. Uri'ah the Hittite was slain also. ¹⁸Then Jo'ab sent and told David all the news about the fighting; ¹⁹and he instructed the messenger, "When you have finished telling all the news about the fighting to the king, ²⁰then, if the king's anger rises,

and if he says to you, 'Why did you go so near the city to fight? Did you not know that they would shoot from the wall? ²¹ Who killed Abim'elech the son of Jerub'besheth? Did not a woman cast an upper millstone upon him from the wall, so that he died at Thebez? Why did you go so near the wall?' then you shall say, 'Your servant Uri'ah the Hittite is dead also.'"

²² So the messenger went, and came and told David all that Jo'ab had sent him to tell. ²³ The messenger said to David, "The men gained an advantage over us, and came out against us in the field; but we drove them back to the entrance of the gate. ²⁴ Then the archers shot at your servants from the wall; some of the king's servants are dead; and your servant Uri'ah the Hittite is dead also." ²⁵ David said to the messenger, "Thus shall you say to Jo'ab, 'Do not let this matter trouble you, for the sword devours now one and now another; strengthen your attack upon the city, and overthrow it.' And encourage him."

²⁶ When the wife of Uri'ah heard that Uri'ah her husband was dead, she made lamentation for her husband. ²⁷ And when the mourning was over, David sent and brought her to his house, and she became his wife, and bore him a son. But the thing that David had done displeased the LORD.

12 And the LORD sent Nathan to David. He came to him, and said to him, "There were two men in a certain city, the one rich and the other poor. ² The rich man had very many flocks and herds; ³ but the poor man had nothing but one little ewe lamb, which he had bought. And he brought it up, and it grew up with him and with his children; it used to eat of his morsel, and drink from his cup, and lie in his bosom, and it was like a daughter to him. ⁴ Now there came a traveler to the rich man, and he was unwilling to take one of his own flock or herd to prepare for the wayfarer who had come to him, but he took the poor man's lamb, and prepared it for the man who had come to him." ⁵ Then David's anger was greatly kindled against the man; and he said to Nathan, "As the LORD lives, the man who has done this deserves to die; ⁶ and he shall restore the lamb fourfold, because he did this thing, and because he had no pity."

⁷ Nathan said to David, "You are the man. Thus says the LORD, the God of Israel, 'I anointed you king over Israel, and I delivered you out of the hand of Saul; ⁸ and I gave you your master's house, and your master's wives into your bosom, and gave you the house of Israel and of Judah; and if this were too little, I would add to you as much more. ⁹ Why have you despised the word of the LORD, to do what is evil in his sight? You have smitten Uri'ah the Hittite with the sword, and have taken his wife to be your wife, and have slain him with the sword of the Ammonites. ¹⁰ Now therefore the sword shall never depart from your house, because you have despised me, and have taken the wife of Uri'ah the Hittite to be your wife.' ¹¹ Thus says the LORD, 'Behold, I will raise

up evil against you out of your own house; and I will take your wives before your eyes, and give them to your neighbor, and he shall lie with your wives in the sight of this sun. [12] For you did it secretly; but I will do this thing before all Israel, and before the sun.'" [13] David said to Nathan, "I have sinned against the LORD." And Nathan said to David, "The LORD also has put away your sin; you shall not die. [14] Nevertheless, because by this deed you have utterly scorned the LORD, the child that is born to you shall die." [15] Then Nathan went to his house.

Lionel Basney, "Dream of the School"

Late, in the dead space of the night
after midnight, I heard a door click
shut behind me. I stood in the groove of a room,

its walls tight against my shoulders.
On the walls, shelves; on the shelves, books.
They stretched as far as I could see.

Then, two others. From the first I caught
the sickle cut of sweat. The other seemed,
in that gloom, to stand in a glimmer of starch.

"*Wat moet jij hier?* Do you know where you are?"
His voice seemed hoarse, as from the dust of ploughing.
"*Nosce te ipsum,*" I said. "I know where I am."

"Then why these tears?" "I've sold my life for books,"
I said. "There are too many of them,
too little wisdom for the time I've spent."

Then the other, *oma,* took my elbow
and shook me. "We gave our money
to build this place," she said. "*Kom aan.*"

Then on the wall of books I seemed
to see all those our burning cities
have sent to trudge the highways, age on age,

saw Cordelia heal the ruined king.
"Do you know what you are doing," said my guide,
"when you tell our stories? You are making

the wordless dead live out their fears again
within the long permission of God's hope."
Then on the wall, the brand of an exact number,

and an image folding to a pattern
unimaginable except by number,
like a galaxy hinging on nothing.

"Do you know what you are doing?
You reach for the stop of time itself
inside the envelope of God's intentions."

"But to what end?" I said. I felt fear, as before.
But she reached and shook me, as before.
"You cannot know," she said, "what your words

will weigh with students remembering them
in a place you will never see.
You work in the bewilderment of time.

The harrow kicks the stone away
and in a hundred years the hill is changed.
Therefore have faith, hope to do good,

love the work and its woven pattern:
read, talk, listen, cook, lay brick, sweep
the mat when it is drenched with snow,

wash the beaker, run the errand, pray
for the healing of what you cannot heal."
Then the walls in the night fell away

and I was alone. My eyes met wind,
and the dawn in fog, buildings in trees,
and on the bright plain of the campus,

people walking, from dark to light to dark
to light, under the trees, in the open.

Part II

WHAT IS TEACHING?
ANCIENT SHOWING AND
MODERN TELLING

The four selections in this section address the question of the nature of teaching. Just what does teaching entail? How can we recognize good teaching when we see it? What is the relationship between teaching and learning? Two of the selections come to us from the ancient world, one of them from Classical Greece, the other from the Roman and Early Christian period. The other two are quite contemporary, one of them by a twentieth-century British philosopher, the other by an American professor of education.

There are marked contrasts between these two pairs. The ancient texts tend to show us what teaching is; the contemporary ones tend to tell us about it. The ancient texts are, therefore, "teachings" in the double sense that we discussed in the introduction. They talk about teaching in the act of dramatizing it in dialogue form. The contemporary texts are essays, literary forms that are designed to "assay" or consider a matter of importance and complexity. The ancient texts seem less conclusive about the question of what teaching is, in part because they are designed to place more of a burden on readers to draw conclusions of their own, in part because both of them retain a sense of mystery about teaching that the more precise and circumscribed contemporary texts lack.

By far the most demanding of the four texts in this section is the *Meno*, Plato's dialogue on the subject of education. The dialogue takes up one of the oldest of all philosophical questions, the question of how human beings become excellent or virtuous. Can virtue be taught? This question shifts during the course of the dialogue. The text also broadens its focus from the question of whether virtue can be taught to questions of teaching and learning in general and then to related questions about knowledge, true opinion, recollection, and inquiry. In order to learn from the text, we must be able to follow its development actively, with questions of our own.

The key to our learning is to recognize that we are to *Meno* the text what Meno the character is to the slave boy, another character who appears in the central episode of the dialogue. Plato the author is asking us the same questions that Socrates asks Meno in the slave boy episode. When Socrates asks Meno whether the slave boy is learning anything, we must realize that we should be asking throughout the dialogue whether Meno is learning anything. What kind of a person is Meno at the beginning of the dialogue? Has he changed at all during the course of the conversation? And does Meno come to *know* anything about either teaching or virtue? Or is he at best speaking true opinions that are not yet really *his* opinions? Of the three "students" in the dialogue (Meno, the slave boy, and Anytus), which one of them learns the most? How do we know? What accounts for the relative progress in understanding each student makes?

Most of the questions about *Meno* should focus upon the figure of Socrates. What kind of a teacher is he? Are his questions genuine, i.e., does he really ask them in ignorance and from ignorance? Or are most of them rhetorical questions designed to provoke Meno or Anytus to think? Is Socrates wise to "abandon his lesson plan" when Meno objects to the order of his questions? And to the extent that Meno fails to understand something, how much of that failure is Socrates' responsibility?

Part of becoming better at teaching involves learning how to observe other teachers at work. We might profitably compare, for example, Socrates as a teacher to Mr. Bixby in *Old Times on the Mississippi* in Part I and to Vivian Paley, the author of *Wally's Stories* in Part IV. Consider the differences in teaching styles. To what extent are these differences a function of the different aims of the teaching and the different characters of the students? Are some techniques more effective than others? Which of the two teachers, Socrates or Mr. Bixby, is more responsive to his principal pupil's readiness to learn? Is Socrates' distinction between knowledge and true opinion the same as the distinction between seeing the river and reading it aright?

Plato arranges to have Socrates present some of the most critical but elusive ideas in the dialogue through stories that were told to him by religious figures. Socrates presents the theory of recollection, for example, through a religious myth. The author of the second text in this section, St. Augustine of Hippo, was and remains one of the most astute readers of Plato. In *De Magister* (*On the Teacher*), Augustine, like Plato, argues that the source of truth lies within our souls, not outside of us. And like Plato, Augustine believes that a complete account of knowledge and truth, and of teaching and learning, must be to some degree religious in character. Both writers preserve a sense of mystery at the heart of learning that more contemporary writers fail to capture.

Readers who are inclined to think that this Augustinian sense of wonder about the very possibility of teaching and learning is peculiar to the ancient world or to a religious sensibility should compare the reading from Augustine with the first reading of Part I, which is taken from the very heart of the modern Enlightenment. Both Augustine, a father of the early Christian church, and Itard, an apostle of modern science, give us the same sense of astonishment about the ineffable relationships among senses, words, and objects, between language and reality, between signs and the things that signs signify. For Plato and Augustine at least, these ineffable connections suggest that the nature of teaching is finally a kind of midwifery or evocation, a giving-birth-to or a calling forth of things or potentialities already present within the human soul. Both of the ancient writers would also agree that the failure to learn in the presence of good teaching arises not from ignorance or stupidity but from moral defects, from a weak or wicked character or a defective will.

When we enter the twentieth century through the works of Gilbert Ryle and Philip Jackson, we have come upon an altogether different world. In this world, teaching and learning have little or nothing to do with religion, and they are defined through a series of very careful conceptual and empirical distinctions. Ryle begins with puzzles, develops several distinctions, and then proceeds to "solve" or dissolve the puzzle. Jackson distinguishes teaching from any and all of the activities that collectively constitute it, in the course of his own endeavor to think more clearly about what teaching really is and how we might best recognize and appraise it. Although both of these writers traverse much of the same terrain as Plato and Augustine, as well as the authors in Part I, there is something different about their "teaching" (the manner of it) if not about the "teaching" (the matter of it).

We should not overdraw this contrast. Ryle, for example, reminds us of much of what we could observe by a careful perusal of the readings in Part I. He finds the difference between "teaching that" and "teaching how" very important. And his notion that "learning that" must consist in more than mere rote memory should remind us of Socrates' distinction between true opinion and knowledge. Compare, for instance, Ryle's discussion of what it means to know the capitals of certain countries with Socrates' discussion of what it means to "know" the road to Larissa. There are even stronger similarities between the ancient texts and Jackson's "Real Teaching." Jackson, like both Socrates and Augustine, does not pretend to be conclusive about the nature of teaching: "The teachers and I," he admits, "never did succeed in answering most of the questions we so enthusiastically and, I fear, naively wrestled with back then. Nor have I yet done so." This is genuine Socratic humility born in part from Jackson's extensive reading of Plato, Augustine, and other ancient texts.

Even after we have noticed other points of convergence between the ancient texts and the modern ones, we still have a sense of unsettling difference between them. This may stem primarily from the difference between showing and telling—between representing characters in the process of teaching and learning, and presenting arguments about teaching and learning in logical sequence. "Real Teaching" says much of what the ancient texts dramatize: teaching involves arts and skills but is more than these, the various strategies of definition all fall short of the mark, and the connections between teaching and learning remain to some extent indefinitely problematic. Even so, partly because of the presence of characters in the ancient texts, we find a more complex sense of the human soul in Plato and Augustine than in Ryle and Jackson. We should ask ourselves whether talk of methods, dispositions, and psyches does as good a job of capturing our sense of teaching and learning as talk of disciplines, virtues, the divine, and immortal souls.

The contemporary texts complement the ancient ones by raising some questions more directly and clearly. For example, "Real Teaching" helps us to think through the question of whether teaching can be said to go on at all in a given situation if no learning takes place. Both Ryle and Jackson help us to be more precise about the several different things we might mean when we use terms like teaching, training, skills, arts, and methods. We are left to wonder whether all genuine teaching is already good teaching or whether some genuine teaching is bad teaching. In other words, if we do it badly, can we be said to be teaching at all? To learn about teaching is to learn how to question and how to reckon with the fact that we always seem to be left with questions.

Readings in Part II

1. Plato, *Meno*, translated by G. M. A. Grube (Indianapolis: Hackett Publishing, 1976). This is the classic Platonic dialogue on teaching and learning. It begins by raising one of the oldest questions in philosophy, the question of whether and how human excellence or virtue can be taught. The question remains today at the heart of much contemporary controversy about the role of education in society.

2. St. Augustine, *On the Teacher*, translated by Joel Lidov, in *Plato's Meno*, edited by Malcolm Brown (Indianapolis: Bobbs-Merrill, 1976), pp. 65–89. This is an early work of Augustine drawn to some extent from his experience at

Cassiciacum near Lake Como at the foot of the Italian Alps, where he retired in 386, with his son, his mother, his brother, and his cousin, for a life of study and creative leisure.

3. Gilbert Ryle, "Teaching and Training," in Gilbert Ryle, *Collected Papers II* (New York: Barnes and Noble, 1967), pp. 451–464. This essay draws different examples from everyday life in order to clarify the distinctions that it develops among many kinds of teaching and learning.

4. Philip W. Jackson, "Real Teaching," Chapter 4 of Jackson, *The Practice of Teaching* (New York: Teachers College Press, 1986), pp. 75–97. The essay elaborates some of Ryle's distinctions in the course of Jackson's effort to interpret his observations of classroom teachers.

Plato, *Meno*

MENO: Can you tell me, Socrates, can virtue[1] be taught? Or is it not
70   teachable but the result of practice, or is it neither of these, but men possess it by nature or in some other way?

SOCRATES: Before now, Meno, Thessalians had a high reputation
among the Greeks and were admired for their horsemanship and their
b   wealth, but now, it seems to me, they are also admired for their wisdom,
not least the fellow citizens of your friend Aristippus of Larissa. The responsibility for this reputation of yours lies with Gorgias,[2] for when he
came to your city he found that the leading Aleuadae, your lover Aristippus among them, loved him for his wisdom, and so did the other leading
Thessalians. In particular, he accustomed you to give a bold and grand
c   answer to any question you may be asked, as experts are likely to do. Indeed, he himself was ready to answer any Greek who wished to question
him, and every question was answered. But here in Athens, my dear
71   Meno, the opposite is the case, as if there were a dearth of wisdom, and
wisdom seems to have departed hence to go to you. If then you want to
ask one of us that sort of question, everyone will laugh and say: "Good
stranger, you must think me happy indeed if you think I know whether
virtue can be taught or how it comes to be; I am so far from knowing
whether virtue can be taught or not that I do not even have any knowledge of what virtue itself is."

b   I myself, Meno, am as poor as my fellow citizens in this matter, and
I blame myself for my complete ignorance about virtue. If I do not know
what something is, how could I know what qualities it possesses? Or do you
think that someone who does not know at all who Meno is could know
whether he is good-looking or rich or well-born, or the opposite of these?
Do you think that is possible?

---

1. The Greek word is *aretê*. It can refer to specific virtues such as moderation, courage, et cetera,
but it is also used for *the* virtue or conglomeration of virtues that makes a man virtuous or good. In
this dialogue it is mostly used in this more general sense. Socrates himself at times (e.g., 93 b ff.) uses
"good" as equivalent to virtuous.

2. Gorgias was perhaps the most famous of the earlier generation of Sophists, those traveling
teachers who arose in the late fifth century to fill the need for higher education. They all taught rhetoric,
or the art of speaking, but as Meno tells us, Gorgias concentrated on this more than the others and
made fewer general claims for his teaching (95c). He visited Athens in 427 B.C., and his rhetorical devices
gave him an immediate success. Plato named one of his dialogues after him. Fairly substantive fragments of his writings are extant.

M: I do not; but, Socrates, do you really not know what virtue is? Are we to report this to the folk back home about you? c

S: Not only that, my friend, but also that, as I believe, I have never yet met anyone else who did know.

M: How so? Did you not meet Gorgias when he was here?

S: I did.

M: Did you then not think that he knew?

S: I do not altogether remember, Meno, so that I cannot tell you now what I thought then. Perhaps he does know; you know what he used to say, so you remind me of what he said. You tell me yourself, if you are d willing, for surely you share his views. — I do.

S: Let us leave Gorgias out of it, since he is not here. But Meno, by the gods, what do you yourself say that virtue is? Speak and do not begrudge us, so that I may have spoken a most unfortunate untruth when I said that I had never met anyone who knew, if you and Gorgias are shown to know.

M: It is not hard to tell you, Socrates. First, if you want the virtue e of a man, it is easy to say that a man's virtue consists of being able to manage public affairs and in so doing to benefit his friends and harm his enemies and to be careful that no harm comes to himself; if you want the virtue of a woman, it is not difficult to describe: she must manage the home well, preserve its possessions, and be submissive to her husband; the virtue of a child, whether male or female, is different again, and so is that of an elderly man, if you want that, or if you want that of a free man or a slave. And there are very many other virtues, so that one is not at a 72 loss to say what virtue is. There is virtue for every action and every age, for every task of ours and every one of us—and Socrates, the same is true for wickedness.

S: I seem to be in great luck, Meno; while I am looking for one virtue, I have found you to have a whole swarm of them. But, Meno, to follow up the image of swarms, if I were asking you what is the nature of b bees, and you said that they are many and of all kinds, what would you answer if I asked you: "Do you mean that they are many and varied and different from one another in so far as they are bees? Or are they no different in that regard, but in some other respect, in their beauty, for example, or their size or in some other such way?" Tell me, what would you answer if thus questioned?

M: I would say that they do not differ from one another in being bees.

S: If I went on to say: "Tell me, what is this very thing, Meno, in c which they are all the same and do not differ from one another?" Would you be able to tell me?

M: I would.

S: The same is true in the case of the virtues. Even if they are many and various, all of them have one and the same form[3] which makes them virtues, and it is right to look to this when one is asked to make clear

d   what virtue is. Or do you not understand what I mean?

M: I think I understand, but I certainly do not grasp the meaning of the question as fully as I want to.

S: I am asking whether you think it is only in the case of virtue that there is one for man, another for woman and so on, or is the same true in the case of health and size and strength? Do you think that there is one health for man and another for woman? Or, if it is health, does it

e   have the same form everywhere, whether in man or in anything else whatever?

M: The health of a man seems to me the same as that of a woman.

S: And so with size and strength? If a woman is strong, that strength will be the same and have the same form, for by "the same" I mean that strength is no different as far as being strength, whether in a man or a woman. Or do you think there is a difference?

M: I do not think so.

S: And will there be any difference in the case of virtue, as far as

73   being virtue is concerned, whether it be in a child or an old man, in a woman or in a man?

M: I think, Socrates, that somehow this is no longer like those other cases.

S: How so? Did you not say that the virtue of a man consists of managing the city well,[4] and that of a woman of managing the household? — I did.

S: Is it possible to manage a city well, or a household, or anything else, while not managing it moderately and justly? — Certainly not.

---

3. The Greek term is *eidos,* which Plato was to use for his separately existing eternal Forms. Its common meaning is stature or appearance. Socrates felt that if we apply the same name or epithet to a number of different things or actions, they must surely have a common characteristic to justify the use of the same term. A definition is then a description of this "form" or appearance, which it presents to the mind's eye. In the earlier dialogues however, as here, this form is not thought of as having a separate existence, but as immanent.

4. When discussing goodness or morality, social and political virtues would be more immediately present to the Greek mind than they are to ours. In both Plato and Aristotle a good man is above all a good citizen, whereas the modern mind thinks of goodness mainly in more individual terms, such as sobriety or sexual morals. An extreme example of this occurred in a contemporary judge's summation to the jury in the case of a woman of loose sexual behaviour who was accused of murdering her husband. He actually said: "This is a case of murder, not of morals. The morals of the accused have nothing to do with it."

S: Then if they manage justly and moderately, they must do so with   b
justice and moderation? — Necessarily.

S: So both the man and the woman, if they are to be good, need the
same things, justice and moderation. — So it seems.

S: What about a child and an old man? Can they possibly be good
if they are intemperate and unjust? — Certainly not.

S: But if they are moderate and just? — Yes.

S: So all men are good in the same way, for they become good by   c
acquiring the same qualities. — It seems so.

S: And they would not be good in the same way if they did not have
the same virtue. — They certainly would not be.

S: Since then the virtue of all is the same, try to tell me and to remember what Gorgias, and you with him, said that that same thing is.

M: What else but to be able to rule over men, if you are seeking one   d
description to fit them all.

S: That is indeed what I am seeking, but Meno, is virtue the same
in the case of a child or a slave, namely, for them to be able to rule over
a master, and do you think that he who rules is still a slave? — I do not
think so at all, Socrates.

S: It is not likely, my good man. Consider this further point: you say
that virtue is to be able to rule. Shall we not add to this *justly and not
unjustly?*

M: I think so, Socrates, for justice is virtue.

S: Is it virtue, Meno, or a virtue? — What do you mean?

S: As with anything else. For example, if you wish, take roundness,
about which I would say that it is a shape, but not simply that it is shape.
I would not so speak of it because there are other shapes.

M: You are quite right. So I too say that not only justice is a virtue
but there are many other virtues.

S: What are they? Tell me, as I could mention other shapes to you   74
if you bade me do so, so do you mention other virtues.

M: I think courage is a virtue, and moderation, wisdom, and munificence, and very many others.

S: We are having the same trouble again, Meno, though in another
way; we have found many virtues while looking for one, but we cannot
find the one which covers all the others.

M: I cannot yet find, Socrates, what you are looking for, one virtue   b
for them all, as in the other cases.

S: That is likely, but I am eager, if I can, that we should make progress, for you understand that the same applies to everything. If someone asked you what I mentioned just now: "What is shape, Meno?" and

you told him that it was roundness, and if then he said to you what I did: "Is roundness shape or a shape?" you would surely tell him that it is a shape? — I certainly would.

c   S: That would be because there are other shapes? — Yes.

S: And if he asked you further what they were, you would tell him? — I would.

S: So too, if he asked you what colour is, and you said it is white, and your questioner interrupted you, "Is white colour or a colour?" you would say that it is a colour, because there are also other colours? — I would.

S: And if he bade you mention other colours, you would mention

d   others that are no less colours than white is? — Yes.

S: Then if he pursued the argument as I did and said: "We always arrive at the many; do not talk to me in that way, but since you call all these many by one name, and say that no one of them is not a shape even though they are opposites, tell me what this is which applies as much to

e   the round as to the straight and which you call shape, as you say the round is as much a shape as the straight." Do you not say that? — I do.

S: When you speak like that, do you assert that the round is no more round than it is straight, and that the straight is no more straight than it is round?

M: Certainly not, Socrates.

S: Yet you say that the round is no more a shape than the straight is, nor the one more than the other. — That is true.

S: What then is this to which the name shape applies? Try to tell

75   me. If then you answered the man who was questioning about shape or colour: "I do not understand what you want, my man, nor what you mean," he would probably wonder and say: "You do not understand that I am seeking that which is the same in all these cases?" Would you still have nothing to say, Meno, if one asked you: "What is this which applies to the round and the straight and the other things which you call shapes and which is the same in them all?" Try to say, that you may practise for your answer about virtue.

M: No, Socrates, but you tell me.

S: Do you want me to do you this favour?

M: I certainly do.

S: And you will then be willing to tell me about virtue?

M: I will.

S: We must certainly press on. The subject is worth it.

M: It surely is.

S: Come then, let us try to tell you what shape is. See whether you will accept that it is this: Let us say that shape is that which alone of existing things always follows colour. Is that satisfactory to you, or do you look for it in some other way? I should be satisfied if you defined virtue in this way.   c

M: But that is foolish, Socrates.

S: How do you mean?

M: That shape, you say, always follows colour. Well then, if someone were to say that he did not know what colour is, but that he had the same difficulty as he had about shape, what do you think your answer would be?

S: A true one, surely, and if my questioner was one of those clever and disputatious debaters, I would say to him: "I have given my answer; if it is wrong, it is your job to refute it." Then, if they are friends as you and I are, and want to discuss with each other, they must answer in a   d manner more gentle and more proper to discussion. By this I mean that the answers must not only be true, but in terms admittedly known to the questioner. I too will try to speak in these terms. Do you call something "the end?" I mean such a thing as a limit or boundary, for all those are,   e I say, the same thing. Prodicus[5] might disagree with us, but you surely say a thing is "finished" or "completed"—that is what I want to express, nothing elaborate.

M: I do, and I think I understand what you mean.

S: Further, you call something a plane, and something else a solid,   76 as in geometry?

M: I do.

S: From this you may understand what I mean by shape, for I say this of every shape, that a shape is that which limits a solid; in a word, a shape is the limit of a solid.

M: And what do you say colour is, Socrates?

S: You are outrageous, Meno. You bother an old man to answer questions, but you yourself are not willing to recall and to tell me what Gorgias says that virtue is.

---

5. Prodicus was a well-known Sophist who was especially keen on the exact meaning of words, and he was fond of making the proper distinctions between words of similar but not identical meanings. We see him in action in the Protagoras of Plato (especially 337 a–c) where he appears with two other distinguished Sophists, Protagoras and Hippias. His insistence on the proper definition of words would naturally endear him to Socrates who, in Plato, always treats him with more sympathy than he does the other Sophists. The point here is that Prodicus would object to "end," "limit," and "boundary" being treated as "all the same thing."

M: After you have answered this, Socrates, I will tell you.

S: Even someone who was blindfolded would know from your conversation that you are handsome and still have lovers.

M: Why so?

S: Because you are forever giving orders in a discussion, as spoiled people do, who behave like tyrants as long as they are young. And perhaps you have recognized that I am at a disadvantage with handsome people, so I will do you the favour of an answer.

c

M: By all means do me that favour.

S: Do you want me to answer after the manner of Gorgias, which you would most easily follow?

S: Of course I want that.

S: Do you both say there are effluvia of things, as Empedocles[6] does? — Certainly.

S: And that there are channels through which the effluvia make their way? — Definitely.

d

S: And some effluvia fit some of the channels, while others are too small or too big?—That is so.

S: And there is something which you call sight? — There is.

S: From this, "comprehend what I state," as Pindar said, for colour is an effluvium from shapes which fits the sight and is perceived.

M: That seems to me to be an excellent answer, Socrates.

S: Perhaps it was given in the manner to which you are accustomed. At the same time I think that you can deduce from this answer what sound is, and smell, and many such things. — Quite so.

e

S: It is a theatrical answer[7] so it pleases you, Meno, more than that about shape. — It does.

S: It is not better, son of Alexidemus, but I am convinced that the other is, and I think you would agree, if you did not have to go away before the mysteries as you told me yesterday, but could remain and be initiated.

M: I would stay, Socrates, if you could tell me many things like these.

77

S: I shall certainly not be lacking in eagerness to tell you such things, both for your sake and my own, but I may not be able to tell you many. Come now, you too try to fulfill your promise to me and tell me

---

6. Empedocles (c.493–433 B.C.) of Acragas in Sicily was a famous physical philosopher. For him there were four eternal elements (earth, water, air, and fire), the intermingling and separation of which produced the physical phenomena. The reference here is to his theories of sense perception.

7. Theatrical because it brings in the philosophical theories of Empedocles and a quotation from Pindar, instead of being in simple terms such as Socrates' definition of shape.

the nature of virtue as a whole and stop making many out of one, as jokers say whenever someone breaks something; but allow virtue to remain whole and sound, and tell me what it is, for I have given you examples.

b

M: I think, Socrates, that virtue is, as the poet says, "to find joy in beautiful things and have power." So I say that virtue is to desire beautiful things and have the power to acquire them.

S: Do you mean that the man who desires beautiful things desires good things? — Most certainly.

S: Do you assume that there are people who desire bad things, and others who desire good things? Do you not think, my good man, that all men desire good things?

c

M: I do not.

S: But some desire bad things? — Yes.

S: Do you mean that they believe the bad things to be good, or that they know they are bad and nevertheless desire them? — I think there are both kinds.

S: Do you think, Meno, that anyone, knowing that bad things are bad, nevertheless desires them? — I certainly do.

S: What do you mean by desiring? Is it to secure for oneself? — What else?

S: Does he think that the bad things benefit him who possesses them, or does he know they harm him?

d

M: There are some who believe that the bad things benefit them, others who know that the bad things harm them.

S: And do you think that those who believe that bad things benefit them know that they are bad?

M: No, that I cannot altogether believe.

S: It is clear then that those who do not know things to be bad do not desire what is bad, but they desire those things that they believe to be good but that are in fact bad. It follows that those who have no knowledge of these things and believe them to be good clearly desire good things. Is that not so? — It is likely.

S: Well then, those who you say desire bad things, believing that bad things harm their possessor, know that they will be harmed by them? — Necessarily.

S: And do they not think that those who are harmed are miserable to the extent that they are harmed? — That too is inevitable.

78

S: And that those who are miserable are unhappy? — I think so.

S: Does anyone wish to be miserable and unhappy? — I do not think so, Socrates.

S: No one then wants what is bad, Meno, unless he wants to be such. For what else is being miserable but to desire bad things and secure them?

b   M: You are probably right, Socrates, and no one wants what is bad.

S: Were you not saying just now that virtue is to desire good things and have the power to secure them? — Yes, I was.

S: The desiring part of this statement is common to everybody, and one man is no better than another in this? — So it appears.

S: Clearly then, if one man is better than another, he must be better at securing them. — Quite so.

S: This then is virtue according to your argument, the power of se-

c   curing good things.

M: I think, Socrates, that the case is altogether as you now under-stand it.

S: Let us see then whether what you say is true, for you may well be right. You say that the capacity to acquire good things is virtue? — I do.

S: And by good things you mean, for example, health and wealth?

e   M: Yes, and also to acquire gold and silver, also honours and offices in the city.

S: By good things you do not mean other goods than these?

M: No, but I mean all things of this kind.

d   S: Very well. According to Meno, the hereditary guest friend of the Great King, virtue is the acquisition of gold and silver. Do you add to this acquiring, Meno, the words justly and piously, or does it make no difference to you but even if one secures these things unjustly, you call it virtue none the less?

M: Certainly not, Socrates.

S: You would then call it wickedness? — Indeed I would.

S: It seems then that the acquisition must be accompanied by justice

e   or moderation or piety or some other part of virtue; if it is not, it will not be virtue, even though it provides good things.

M: How could there be virtue without these?

S: Then failing to secure gold and silver, whenever it would not be just to do so, either for oneself or another, is not this failure to secure them also virtue?

M: So it seems.

S: Then to provide these goods would not be virtue any more than

79   not to provide them, but apparently whatever is done with justice will be virtue and what is done without anything of the kind is wickedness.

M: I think it must necessarily be as you say.

S: We said a little while ago that each of these things was a part of virtue, namely, justice and moderation and all such things? — Yes.

S: Then you are playing with me, Meno. — How so, Socrates?

S: Because I begged you just now not to break up or fragment virtue, and I gave examples of how you should answer. You paid no attention, but you tell me that virtue is to be able to secure good things with justice,   b
and this, you say, is a part of virtue.

M: I do.

S: It follows then from what you agree to, that to act in whatever you do with a part of virtue is virtue, for you say that justice is a part of virtue, as are all such qualities. Why do I say this? Because when I begged you to tell me about virtue as a whole, you are far from telling me what it is. Rather, you say that every action is virtue if it is performed with a part of virtue, as if you had told me what virtue as a whole is, and I would already know that, even if you fragment it into parts.[8] I think you must face the same question from the beginning, my dear Meno, namely, what is virtue, if every action performed with a part of virtue is virtue? For that is what one is saying when he says that every action performed with justice is virtue. Do you not think you should face the same question again, or do you think one knows what a part of virtue is if one does not know virtue itself? — I do not think so.

S: If you remember, when I was answering you about shape, we re-   d
jected the kind of answer that tried to answer in terms still being the subject of inquiry and not yet agreed upon. — And we were right to reject them.

S: Then surely, my good sir, you must not think, while the nature of virtue as a whole is still under inquiry, that by answering in terms of the parts of virtue you can make its nature clear to anyone or make anything else clear by speaking in this way, but only that the same question must be put to you again—what do you take the nature of virtue to be   e
when you say what you say? Or do you think there is no point in what I am saying? — I think what you say is right.

S: Answer me again then from the beginning: What do you and your friend say that virtue is?

M: Socrates, before I even met you I used to hear that you are always in a state of perplexity and that you bring others to the same state, and   80
now I think you are bewitching and beguiling me, simply putting me under a spell, so that I am quite perplexed. Indeed, if a joke is in order, you seem, in appearance and in every other way, to be like the broad torpedo fish, for it too makes anyone who comes close and touches it feel numb, and you now seem to have had that kind of effect on me, for both   b

---

8. That is, Meno is including the term to be defined in the definition.

my mind and my tongue are numb, and I have no answer to give you. Yet I have made many speeches about virtue before large audiences on a thousand occasions, very good speeches as I thought, but now I cannot even say what it is. I think you are wise not to sail away from Athens to go and stay elsewhere, for if you were to behave like this as a stranger in another city, you would be driven away for practising sorcery.

S: You are a rascal, Meno, and you nearly deceived me.

M: Why so particularly, Socrates?

c   S: I know why you drew this image of me.

M: Why do you think I did?

S: So that I should draw an image of you in return. I know that all handsome men rejoice in images of themselves; it is to their advantage, for I think that the images of beautiful people are also beautiful, but I will draw no image of you in turn. Now if the torpedo fish is itself numb and so makes others numb, then I resemble it, but not otherwise, for I myself do not have the answer when I perplex others, but I am more perplexed than anyone when I cause perplexity in others. So now I do not

d   know what virtue is; perhaps you knew before you contacted me, but now you are certainly like one who does not know. Nevertheless, I want to examine and seek together with you what it may be.

M: How will you look for it, Socrates, when you do not know at all what it is? How will you aim to search for something you do not know at all? If you should meet with it, how will you know that this is the thing that you did not know?

e   S: I know what you want to say, Meno. Do you realize what a debater's argument you are bringing up, that a man cannot search either for what he knows or for what he does not know? He cannot search for what he knows—since he knows it, there is no need to search—nor for what he does not know, for he does not know what to look for.

M: Does that argument not seem sound to you, Socrates?

81   S: Not to me.

M: Can you tell me why?

S: I can. I have heard wise men and women talk about divine matters . . .

M: What did they say?

S: What was, I thought, both true and beautiful.

M: What was it, and who were they?

b   S: The speakers were among the priests and priestesses whose care it is to be able to give an account of their practices. Pindar too says it, and many others of the divine among our poets. What they say is this; see whether you think they speak the truth: They say that the human soul is immortal; at times it comes to an end, which they call dying, at times it is reborn, but it is never destroyed, and one must therefore live one's life as piously as possible:

> *Persephone will return to the sun above in the ninth year*
> *the souls of those from whom*
> *she will exact punishment for old miseries,*   c
> *and from these come noble kings,*
> *mighty in strength and greatest in wisdom,*
> *and for the rest of time men will call them sacred heroes.*

As the soul is immortal, has been born often and has seen all things here and in the underworld, there is nothing which it has not learned; so it is in no way surprising that it can recollect the things it knew before, both about virtue and other things. As the whole of nature is akin, and   d
the soul has learned everything, nothing prevents a man, after recalling one thing only—a process men call learning—discovering everything else for himself, if he is brave and does not tire of the search, for searching and learning are, as a whole, recollection. We must, therefore, not believe that debater's argument, for it would make us idle, and fainthearted men like to hear it, whereas my argument makes them energetic and keen on   e
the search. I trust that this is true, and I want to inquire along with you into the nature of virtue.

M: Yes, Socrates, but how do you mean that we do not learn, but that what we call learning is recollection? Can you teach me that this is so?

S: As I said just now, Meno, you are a rascal. You now ask me if I can teach you, when I say there is no teaching but recollection, in order   82
to show me up at once as contradicting myself.

M: No, by Zeus, Socrates, that was not my intention when I spoke, but just a habit. If you can somehow show me that things are as you say, please do so.

S: It is not easy, but I am nevertheless willing to do my best for your sake. Call one of these many attendants of yours, whichever you like, that   b
I may prove it to you in his case.

M: Certainly. You there, come forward.

S: Is he a Greek? Does he speak Greek?

M: Very much so. He was born in my household.

S: Pay attention then whether you think he is recollecting or learning from me.

M: I will pay attention.

S: Tell me now, boy, you know that a square figure is like this? — I do.

c   S: A square then is a figure in which all these four sides are equal?
— Yes indeed.

S: And it also has these lines through the middle equal?[9] — Yes.

S: And such a figure could be larger or smaller? — Certainly.

S: If then this side were two feet, and this other side two feet,
how many feet would the whole be? Consider it this way: if it were two
feet this way, and only one foot that way, the figure[10] would be once two
feet? — Yes.

d   S: But if it is two feet also that way, it would surely be twice two
feet? — Yes.

S: How many feet is twice two feet? Work it out and tell me. — Four,
Socrates.

S: Now let us have another figure twice the size of this one, with the
four sides equal like this one. — Yes.

S: How many feet will that be? — Eight.

S: Come now, try to tell me how long each side of this will be. The

e   side of this is two feet. What about each side of the one which is its
double? — Obviously, Socrates, it will be twice the length.

S: You see, Meno, that I am not teaching the boy anything, but all
I do is question him. And now he thinks he knows the length of the line
on which an eight-foot figure is based. Do you agree? — I do.

9. Socrates draws a square ABCD. The sides are of course equal, and the "lines through the
middle" are the lines joining the middle points of these sides, which also go through the center of the
square, namely EF and GH.

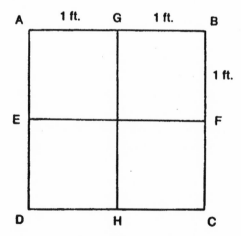

He then goes on to assume the sides to be two feet.

10. I.e., the rectangle ABFE, which is obviously two square feet.

S: And does he know? — Certainly not.

S: He thinks it is a line twice the length? — Yes.

S: Watch him now recollecting things in order, as one must recollect. Tell me, boy, do you say that a figure double the size is based on a
line double the length? Now I mean such a figure as this, not long on one   83
side and short on the other, but equal in every direction like this one, and
double the size, that is, eight feet. See whether you still believe that it will
be based on a line double the length. — I do.

S: Now the line becomes double its length if we add another of the
same length here? — Yes indeed.

S: And the eight-foot square will be based on it, if there are four
lines of that length? — Yes.

S: Well, let us draw from it four equal lines, and surely that is what   b
you say is the eight-foot square? — Certainly.

S: And within this figure are four squares, each of which is equal to
the four-foot square? — Yes.

S: How big is it then? Is it not four times as big? — Of course.

S: Is this square then, which is four times as big, its double? — No,
by Zeus.

S: How many times bigger is it? — Four times.

S: Then, my boy, the figure based on a line twice the length is not   c
double but four times as big? — You are right.

S: And four times four is sixteen, is it not? — Yes.

S: On how long a line then should the eight-foot square be based?
Is it not based on this double line? — Yes. Now this four-foot square is
based on a line half the length? — Yes.

S: Very well. Is the eight-foot square not double this one and half
that one?[11] — Yes.

S: Will it not be based on a line longer than this one and shorter
than that one? Is that not so? — I think so.   d

S: Good, you answer what you think. And tell me, was this one not
two-feet long, and that one four feet? — Yes.

S: The line on which the eight-foot square is based must then
be longer than this one of two feet, and shorter than that one of four
feet? — It must be.

S: Try to tell me then how long a line you say it is. — Three feet.   e

11. I.e., the eight-foot square is double the four-foot square and half the sixteen-foot square, double
the square based on a line two-feet long, and half the square based on a four-foot side, so it must be
based on a line between two and four feet in length. The slave naturally suggests three feet, but that
gives a nine-foot square, and is still wrong. (83e).

S: Then if it is three feet, let us add the half of this one, and it will be three feet? For these are two feet, and the other is one. And here, similarly, these are two feet and that one is one foot, and so the figure you mention comes to be? — Yes.

S: Now if it is three feet this way and three feet that way, will the whole figure be three times three feet? — So it seems.

S: How much is three times three feet? — Nine feet.

S: And the double square was to be how many feet? — Eight.

S: So the eight-foot figure cannot be based on the three-foot line? Clearly not.

84   S: But on how long a line? Try to tell us exactly, and if you do not want to work it out, show me from what line. — By Zeus, Socrates, I do not know.

S: You realize, Meno, what point he has reached in his recollection. At first he did not know what the basic line of the eight-foot square was; even now he does not yet know, but then he thought he knew, and answered confidently as if he did know, and he did not think himself at a
b   loss, but now he does think himself at a loss, and as he does not know, neither does he think he knows. — That is true.

S: So he is now in a better position with regard to the matter he does not know?

M: I agree with that too.

S: Have we done him any harm by making him perplexed and numb as the torpedo fish does? — I do not think so.

S: Indeed, we have probably achieved something relevant to finding out how matters stand, for now, as he does not know, he would be glad to find out, whereas before he thought he could easily make many fine
c   speeches to large audiences about the square of double size and said that it must have a base twice as long. — So it seems.

S: Do you think that before he would have tried to find out that which he thought he knew though he did not, before he fell into perplexity and realized he did not know and longed to know? — I do not think so, Socrates.

S: Has he then benefitted from being numbed? — I think so.

S: Look then how he will come out of his perplexity while searching along with me. I shall do nothing more than ask questions and not teach
d   him. Watch whether you find me teaching and explaining things to him instead of asking for his opinion.

S: You tell me, is this not a four-foot figure? You understand? — I do.

S: We add to it this figure which is equal to it? — Yes.

S: And we add this third figure equal to each of them? — Yes.

S: Could we then fill in the space in the corner? — Certainly.[12]

S: So we have these four equal figures? — Yes.

S: Well then, how many times is the whole figure larger than this one?[13] — Four times.   e

S: But we should have had one that was twice as large, or do you not remember? — I certainly do.

S: Does not this line from one corner to the other cut each of these figures in two?[14] — Yes.   85

S: So these are four equal lines which enclose this figure? — They are.

S: Consider now: how large is the figure? — I do not understand.

12. Socrates now builds up his sixteen-foot square by joining two four-foot squares, then a third, like this:

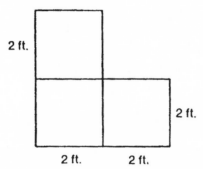

2 ft.

2 ft.

2 ft.   2 ft.

Filling "the space in the corner" will give another four-foot square, which completes the sixteen-foot square containing four four-foot squares.

13. "This one" is any one of the inside squares of four feet.

14. Socrates now draws the diagonals of the four inside squares, namely, FH, HE, EG and GF, which together form the square GFHEG. We should note that Socrates here introduces a new element, which is not the result of a question but of his own knowledge, though the answer to the problem follows from questions. The new square contains four halves of a four foot square, and is therefore eight feet.

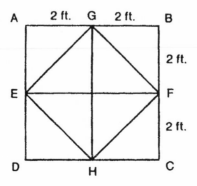

A   2 ft.   G   2 ft.   B

2 ft.

E   F

2 ft.

D   H   C

S: Each of these lines cuts off half of each of the four figures inside it, does it not? — Yes.

S: How many of this size are there in this figure? — Four.

S: How many in this? — Two.

b   S: What is the relation of four to two? — Double.

S: How many feet in this? — Eight.

S: Based on what line? — This one.

S: That is, on the line that stretches from corner to corner of the four-foot figure? — Yes. Clever men call this the diagonal, so that if diagonal is its name, you say that the double figure would be that based on the diagonal? — Most certainly, Socrates.

S: What do you think, Meno? Has he, in his answers, expressed any opinion that was not his own?

c   M: No, they were all his own.

S: And yet, as we said a short time ago, he did not know? — That is true.

S: So these opinions were in him, were they not? — Yes.

S: So the man who does not know has within himself true opinions about the things that he does not know? — So it appears.

S: These opinions have now just been stirred up like a dream, but if he were repeatedly asked these same questions in various ways, you know

d   that in the end his knowledge about these things would be as accurate as anyone's. — It is likely.

S: And he will know it without having been taught but only questioned, and find the knowledge within himself? — Yes.

S: And is not finding knowledge within oneself recollection? — Certainly.

S: Must he not either have at some time acquired the knowledge he now possesses, or else have always possessed it? — Yes.

S: If he always had it, he would always have known. If he acquired

e   it, he cannot have done so in his present life. Or has someone taught him geometry? For he will perform in the same way about all geometry, and all other knowledge. Has someone taught him everything? You should know, especially as he has been born and brought up in your house.

M: But I know that no one has taught him.

S: Yet he has these opinions, or doesn't he?

M: That seems indisputable, Socrates.

86   S: If he has not acquired them in his present life, is it not clear that he had them and had learned them at some other time? — It seems so.

S: Then that was the time when he was not a human being? — Yes.

S: If then, during the time he exists and is not a human being he will have true opinions which, when stirred by questioning, become knowledge, will not his soul have learned during all time? For it is clear that during all time he exists, either as a man or not. — So it seems.

S: Then if the truth about reality is always in our soul, the soul would be immortal so that you should always confidently try to seek out and recollect what you do not know at present—that is, what you do not recollect?[15]

M: Somehow, Socrates, I think that what you say is right.

S: I think so too, Meno. I do not insist that my argument is right in all other respects, but I would contend at all costs both in word and deed as far as I could that we will be better men, braver and less idle, if we believe that one must search for the things one does not know, rather than if we believe that it is not possible to find out what we do not know and that we must not look for it.

M: In this too I think you are right, Socrates.

S: Since we are of one mind that one should seek to find out what one does not know, shall we try to find out together what virtue is?

M: Certainly. But Socrates, I should be most pleased to investigate and hear your answer to my original question, whether we should try on the assumption that virtue is something teachable, or is a natural gift, or in whatever way it comes to men.

S: If I were directing you, Meno, and not only myself, we would not have investigated whether virtue is teachable or not before we had investigated what virtue itself is. But because you do not even attempt to rule yourself, in order that you may be free, but you try to rule me and do so, I will agree with you—for what can I do? So we must, it appears, inquire into the qualities of something the nature of which we do not yet know. However, please relax your rule a little bit for me and agree to investigate whether it is teachable or not by means of a hypothesis. I mean the way geometers often carry on their investigations. For example, if they are asked whether a specific area can be inscribed in the form of a triangle within a given circle, one of them might say: "I do not yet know whether that area has that property, but I think I have, as it were, a hypothesis that is of use for the problem, namely this: If that area is such that when one has applied it as a rectangle to the given straight line in the circle it is deficient by a figure similar to the very figure which is applied, then I

b

c

d

e

87

b

15. This is what the whole passage on recollection with the slave is intended to prove, namely, that the sophism introduced by Meno—that one cannot find out what one does not know—is false.

think one alternative results, whereas another results if it is impossible
for this to happen. So, by using this hypothesis, I am willing to tell you
what results with regard to inscribing it in the circle—that is, whether it
is impossible or not."* So let us speak about virtue also, since we do not
know either what qualities it possesses, and let us investigate whether it
is teachable or not by means of a hypothesis, and say this: Among the
things existing in the soul, of what sort is virtue, that it should be teachable or not? First, if it is another sort than knowledge, is it teachable or
c   not, or, as we were just saying, recollectable? Let it make no difference to
us which term we use: is it teachable? Or is it plain to anyone that men
cannot be taught anything but knowledge? — I think so.

S: But, if virtue is a kind of knowledge, it is clear that it could be
taught. — Of course.

S: We have dealt with that question quickly, that if it is of one kind
it can be taught, if it is of a different kind, it cannot. — We have indeed.

S: The next point to consider seems to be whether virtue is knowl-
d   edge or something else. — That does seem to be the next point to consider.

S: Well now, do we say that virtue is itself something good, and will
this hypothesis stand firm for us, that it is something good? — Of course.

S: If then there is anything else good that is different and separate
from knowledge, virtue might well not be a kind of knowledge; but if
there is nothing good that knowledge does not encompass, we would be
right to suspect that it is a kind of knowledge. — That is so.

e   S: Surely virtue makes us good? — Yes.

S: And if we are good, we are beneficent, for all that is good is beneficial. Is that not so? — Yes.

S: So virtue is something beneficial?

M: That necessarily follows from what has been agreed.

S: Let us then examine what kinds of things benefit us, taking them
up one by one: health, we say, and strength, and beauty, and also wealth.
We say that these things, and others of the same kind, benefit us, do we
not? — We do.

S: Yet we say that these same things also sometimes harm one. Do
88   you agree or not? — I do.

S: Look then, what directing factor determines in each case whether
these things benefit or harm us? Is it not the right use of them that
benefits us, and the wrong use that harms us? — Certainly.

---

*The translation here follows the interpretation of T. L. Heath, A *History of Greek Mathematics*
(Oxford: Clarendon Press, 1921), vol. I pp. 298 ff.

S: Let us now look at the qualities of the soul. There is something you call moderation, and justice, courage, intelligence, memory, munificence, and all such things? — There is.

S: Consider whichever of these you believe not to be knowledge but different from it; do they not at times harm us, at other times benefit us? Courage, for example, when it is not wisdom but like a kind of recklessness: when a man is reckless without understanding, he is harmed, when with understanding, he is benefitted. — Yes.

S: The same is true of moderation and mental quickness; when they are learned and disciplined with understanding they are beneficial, but without understanding they are harmful? — Very much so.

S: Therefore, in a word, all that the soul undertakes and endures, if directed by wisdom, ends in happiness, but if directed by ignorance, it ends in the opposite? — That is likely.

S: If then virtue is something in the soul and it must be beneficial, it must be knowledge, since all the qualities of the soul are in themselves neither beneficial nor harmful, but accompanied by wisdom or folly they become harmful or beneficial. This argument shows that virtue, being beneficial, must be a kind of wisdom. — I agree.

S: Furthermore, those other things we were mentioning just now, wealth and the like, are at times good and at times harmful. Just as for the rest of the soul the direction of wisdom makes things beneficial, but harmful if directed by folly, so in these cases, if the soul uses and directs them right it makes them beneficial, but bad use makes them harmful — Quite so.

S: The wise soul directs them right, the foolish soul wrongly? — That is so.

S: So one may say this about everything: all other human activities depend on the soul, and those of the soul itself depend on wisdom if they are to be good. According to this argument the beneficial would be wisdom, and we say that virtue is beneficial? — Certainly.

S: Virtue then, as a whole or in part, is wisdom?

M: What you say, Socrates, seems to me quite right.

S: Then, if that is so, the good are not so by nature? — I do not think they are.

S: For if they were, this would follow: if the good were so by nature, we would have people who knew which among the young were by nature good; we would take those whom they had pointed out and guard them in the Acropolis, sealing them up there much more carefully than gold so that no one could corrupt them, and when they reached maturity they would be useful to their cities. — Reasonable enough, Socrates.

b

c

d

e

89

b

S: Since the good are not good by nature, does learning make them so?

M: Necessarily, as I now think, Socrates, and clearly, on our hypothesis, if virtue is knowledge, it can be taught.

S: Perhaps, by Zeus, but may it be that we were not right to agree to this?

M: Yet it seemed to be right at the time.

S: We should not only think it right at the time, but also now and in the future if it is to be at all sound.

d   M: What is the difficulty? What do you have in mind that you do not like about it and doubt that virtue is knowledge?

S: I will tell you, Meno. I am not saying that it is wrong to say that virtue is teachable if it is knowledge, but look whether it is reasonable of me to doubt whether it is knowledge. Tell me this: if not only virtue but anything whatever can be taught, should there not be of necessity people who teach it and people who learn it? — I think so.

e   S: Then again, if on the contrary there are no teachers or learners of something, we should be right to assume that the subject cannot be taught?

M: Quite so, but do you think that there are no teachers of virtue?

S: I have often tried to find out whether there were any teachers of it, but in spite of all my efforts I cannot find any. And yet I have searched for them with the help of many people, especially those whom I believed to be most experienced in this matter. And now, Meno, Anytus here has opportunely come to sit down by us. Let us share our search with him.

90   It would be reasonable for us to do so, for Anytus, in the first place, is the son of Anthemion, a man of wealth and wisdom, who did not become rich automatically or as the result of a gift like Ismenias the Theban, who recently acquired the possessions of Polycrates, but through his own wisdom and efforts. Further, he did not seem to be an arrogant or puffed up or offensive citizen in other ways, but he was a well-mannered

b   and well-behaved man. Also he gave our friend here a good upbringing and education, as the majority of Athenians believe, for they are electing him to the highest offices. It is right then to look for the teachers of virtue with the help of men such as he, whether there are any and if so who they are. Therefore, Anytus, please join me and your guest friend Meno here, in our inquiry as to who are the teachers of virtue. Look at it in

c   this way: if we wanted Meno to become a good physician, to what teachers would we send him? Would we not send him to the physicians? — Certainly.

S: And if we wanted him to be a good shoemaker, to shoemakers? — Yes.

S: And so with other pursuits? — Certainly.

S: Tell me again on this same topic, like this: we say that we would be right to send him to the physicians if we want him to become a physician; whenever we say that, we mean that it would be reasonable to send   d
him to those who practise the craft rather than to those who do not, and to those who exact fees for this very practice and have shown themselves to be teachers of anyone who wishes to come to them and learn. Is it not with this in mind that we would be right to send him? — Yes.

S: And the same is true about flute-playing and the other crafts? It would be very foolish for those who want to make someone a flute-player   e
to refuse to send him to those who profess to teach the craft and make money at it, but to send him to make trouble for others by seeking to learn from those who do not claim to be teachers or have a single pupil in that subject which we want the one we send to learn from them? Do you not think it very unreasonable to do so? — By Zeus I do, and also very ignorant.

S: Quite right. However, you can now deliberate with me about our guest friend Meno here. He has been telling me for some time, Anytus,   91
that he longs to acquire that wisdom and virtue which enables men to manage their households and their cities well, to take care of their parents, to know how to welcome and to send away both citizens and strangers as a good man should. Consider to whom we should be right to send   b
him to learn this virtue. Or is it obvious in view of what was said just now that we should send him to those who profess to be teachers of virtue and have shown themselves to be available to any Greek who wishes to learn, and for this fix a fee and exact it?

A: And who do you say these are, Socrates?

S: You surely know yourself that they are those whom men call sophists.

A: By Heracles, hush, Socrates. May no one of my household or   c
friends, whether citizen or stranger, be mad enough to go to these people and be harmed by them, for they clearly cause the ruin and corruption of their followers.

S: How do you mean, Anytus? Are these people, alone of those who claim the knowledge to benefit one, so different from the others that they not only do not benefit what one entrusts to them but on the contrary corrupt it, even though they obviously expect to make money from the   d
process? I find I cannot believe you, for I know that one man, Protagoras,

made more money from this knowledge of his than Phidias who made such notably fine works, and ten other sculptors. Surely what you say is extraordinary, if those who mend old sandals and restore clothes would

e   be found out within the month if they returned the clothes and sandals in a worse state than they received them; if they did this they would soon die of starvation, but the whole of Greece has not noticed for forty years that Protagoras corrupts those who frequent him and sends them away in a worse moral condition than he received them. I believe that he was nearly seventy when he died and had practised his craft for forty years. During all that time to this very day his reputation has stood high; and not only Protagoras but a great many others, some born before him and

92   some still alive today. Are we to say that you maintain that they deceive and harm the young knowingly, or that they themselves are not aware of it? Are we to deem those whom some people consider the wisest of men to be so mad as that?

A: They are far from being mad, Socrates. It is much rather those among the young who pay their fees who are mad, and even more the

b   relatives who entrust their young to them and most of all the cities who allow them to come in and do not drive out any citizen or stranger who attempts to behave in this manner.

S: Has some sophist wronged you, Anytus, or why are you so hard on them?

A: No, by Zeus, I have never met one of them, nor would I allow any one of my people to do so.

S: Are you then altogether without any experience of these men?

A: And may I remain so.

c   S: How then, my good sir, can you know whether there is any good in their instruction or not, if you are altogether without experience of it?

A: Easily, for I know who they are, whether I have experience of them or not.

S: Perhaps you are a wizard, Anytus, for I wonder, from what you yourself say, how else you know about these things. However, let us not

d   try to find out who the men are whose company would make Meno wicked—let them be the sophists if you like—but tell us, and benefit your family friend here by telling him, to whom he should go in so large a city to acquire, to any worthwhile degree, the virtue I was just now describing.

e   A: Why did you not tell him yourself?

S: I did mention those whom I thought to be teachers of it, but you say I am wrong, and perhaps you are right. You tell him in your turn to whom among the Athenians he should go. Tell him the name of anyone you want.

A: Why give him the name of one individual? Any Athenian gentleman he may meet, if he is willing to be persuaded, will make him a better man than the sophists would.

S: And have these gentlemen become virtuous automatically, without learning from anyone, and are they able to teach others what they themselves never learned?

A: I believe that these men have learned from those who were gentlemen before them; or do you not think that there are many good men in this city?

S: I believe, Anytus, that there are many men here who are good at public affairs, and that there have been as many in the past, but have they been good teachers of their own virtue? That is the point we are discussing, not whether there are good men here or not, or whether there have been in the past, but we have been investigating for some time whether virtue can be taught. And in the course of that investigation we are inquiring whether the good men of today and of the past knew how to pass on to another the virtue they themselves possessed, or whether a man cannot pass it on or receive it from another. This is what Meno and I have been investigating for some time. Look at it this way, from what you yourself have said. Would you not say that Themistocles was a good man? — Yes. Even the best of men.

S: And therefore a good teacher of his own virtue if anyone was?

A: I think so, if he wanted to be.

S: But do you think he did not want some other people to be worthy men, and especially his own son? Or do you think he begrudged him this, and deliberately did not pass on to him his own virtue? Have you not heard that Themistocles taught his son Cleophantus to be a good horseman? He could remain standing upright on horseback and shoot javelins from that position and do many other remarkable things which his father had him taught and made skillful at, all of which required good teachers. Have you not heard this from your elders? — I have.

S: So one could not blame the poor natural talents of the son for his failure in virtue? — Perhaps not.

S: But have you ever heard anyone, young or old, say that Cleophantus, the son of Themistocles, was a good and wise man at the same pursuits as his father? — Never.

S: Are we to believe that he wanted to educate his son in those other things but not to do better than his neighbors in that skill which he himself possessed, if indeed virtue can be taught? — Perhaps not, by Zeus.

S: And yet he was, as you yourself agree, among the best teachers
94   of virtue in the past. Let us consider another man, Aristides, the son of
Lysimachus. Do you not agree that he was good? — I very definitely do.

S: He too gave his own son Lysimachus the best Athenian education
in matters which are the business of teachers, and do you think he made
him a better man than anyone else? For you have been in his company
b   and seen the kind of man he is. Or take Pericles, a man of such magnificent wisdom. You know that he brought up two sons, Paralus and
Xanthippus? — I know.

S: You also know that he taught them to be as good horsemen as
any Athenian, that he educated them in the arts, in gymnastics, and in
all else that was a matter of skill not to be inferior to anyone, but did he
not want to make them good men? I think he did, but this could not be
taught. And lest you think that only a few most inferior Athenians are
c   incapable in this respect, reflect that Thucydides[17] too brought up two
sons, Melesias and Stephanus, that he educated them well in all other
things. They were the best wrestlers in Athens—he entrusted the one to
Xanthias and the other to Eudorus, who were thought to be the best
wrestlers of the day, or do you not remember?

A: I remember I have heard that said.

d   S: It is surely clear that he would not have taught his boys what it
costs money to teach, but have failed to teach them what costs nothing—
making them good men—if that could be taught? Or was Thucydides
perhaps an inferior person who had not many friends among the Athenians and the allies? He belonged to a great house; he had great influence
in the city and among the other Greeks, so that if virtue could be taught
he would have found the man who could make his sons good men, be
e   it a citizen or a stranger, if he himself did not have the time because
of his public concerns. But, friend Anytus, virtue can certainly not be
taught.

A: I think, Socrates, that you easily speak ill of people. I would advise you, if you will listen to me, to be careful. Perhaps also in another
city, and certainly here, it is easier to injure people than to benefit them.
95   I think you know that yourself.

S: I think, Meno, that Anytus is angry, and I am not at all surprised.
He thinks, to begin with, that I am slandering those men, and then he
believes himself to be one of them. If he ever realizes what slander is, he

17. Not the historian but Thucydides the son of Melesias, an Athenian statesman who was an opponent of Pericles and who was ostracized in 440B.C.

will cease from anger, but he does not know it now. You tell me, are there not worthy men among your people? — Certainly.

S: Well now, are they willing to offer themselves to the young as b teachers? Do they agree they are teachers, and that virtue can be taught?

M: No, by Zeus, Socrates, but sometimes you would hear them say that it can be taught, at other times, that it cannot.

S: Should we say that they are teachers of this subject, when they do not even agree on this point? — I do not think so, Socrates.

S: Further, do you think that these sophists, who alone profess to be so, are teachers of virtue?

M: I admire this most in Gorgias, Socrates, that you would never c hear him promising this. Indeed, he ridicules the others when he hears them making this claim. He thinks one should make people clever speakers.

S: You do not think then that the sophists are teachers?

M: I cannot tell, Socrates; like most people, at times I think they are, at other times I think that they are not.

S: Do you know that not only you and the other public men at times think that it can be taught, at other times that it cannot, but that the poet d Theognis[18] says the same thing? — Where?

S: In his elegiacs: "Eat and drink with these men, and keep their company. Please those whose power is great, for you will learn goodness from the good. If you mingle with bad men you will lose even what wit e you possess." You see that here he speaks as if virtue can be taught? — So it appears.

S: Elsewhere, he changes somewhat: "if this could be done" he says, "and intelligence could be instilled," somehow those who could do this "would collect large and numerous fees," and further: "Never would a bad son be born of a good father, for he would be persuaded by wise words, but you will never make a bad man good by teaching." You realize that 96 the poet is contradicting himself on the same subject? — He seems to be.

S: Can you mention any other subject of which those who claim to be teachers not only are not recognized to be teachers of others but are not recognized to have knowledge of it themselves, and are thought to be poor in the very matter which they profess to teach? Or any other b subject of which those who are recognized as worthy teachers at one time say it can be taught and at other times that it cannot? Would you say that people who are so confused about a subject can be effective teachers of it? — No, by Zeus, I would not.

---

18. Theognis was a poet of mid-sixth century B.C. A collection of poems is extant (about twelve hundred lines), but the authenticity of a good deal of it is doubtful.

S: If then neither the sophists nor the worthy people themselves are teachers of this subject, clearly there would be no others? — I do not think there are.

S: If there are no teachers, neither are there pupils? — As you say.

c   S: And we agreed that a subject that has neither teachers nor pupils is not teachable? — We have so agreed.

S: Now there seem to be no teachers of virtue anywhere? — That is so.

S: If there are no teachers, there are no learners? — That seems so.

S: Then virtue cannot be taught?

d   M: Apparently not, if we have investigated this correctly. I certainly wonder, Socrates, whether there are no good men either, or in what way good men come to be.

S: We are probably poor specimens, you and I, Meno. Gorgias has not adequately educated you, nor Prodicus me. We must then at all costs turn our attention to ourselves and find someone who will in some way

e   make us better. I say this in view of our recent investigation, for it is ridiculous that we failed to see that it is not only under the guidance of knowledge that men succeed in their affairs, and that is perhaps why the knowledge of how good men come to be escapes us.

M: How do you mean, Socrates?

S: I mean this: we were right to agree that good men must be beneficent, and that this could not be otherwise. Is that not so? — Yes.

S: And that they will be beneficent if they give us correct guidance

97   in our affairs. To this too we were right to agree? — Yes.

S: But that one cannot guide correctly if one does not have knowledge; to this our agreement is likely to be incorrect. — How do you mean?

S: I will tell you. A man who knew the way to Larissa, or anywhere else you like, and went there and guided others would surely lead them well and correctly? — Certainly.

b   S: What if someone had had a correct opinion as to which was the way but had not gone there nor indeed had knowledge of it, would he not also lead correctly? — Certainly.

S: And as long as he has the right opinion about that of which the other has knowledge, he will not be a worse guide than the one who knows, as he has a true opinion, though not knowledge. — In no way worse.

S: So true opinion is in no way a worse guide to correct action than knowledge. It is this that we omitted in our investigation of the nature

c   of virtue, when we said that only knowledge can lead to correct action, for true opinion can do so also. — So it seems.

S: So correct opinion is no less useful than knowledge?

M: Yes, to this extent, Socrates. But the man who has knowledge will always succeed, whereas he who has true opinion will only succeed at times.

S: How do you mean? Will he who has the right opinion not always succeed, as long as his opinion is right?

M: That appears to be so of necessity, and it makes me wonder, Socrates, this being the case, why knowledge is prized far more highly than right opinion, and why they are different.   d

S: Do you know why you wonder, or shall I tell you? — By all means tell me.

S: It is because you have paid no attention to the statues of Daedalus, but perhaps there are none in Thessaly.

M: What do you have in mind when you say this?

S: That they too run away and escape if one does not tie them down but remain in place if tied down. — So what?   e

S: To acquire an untied work of Daedalus is not worth much, like acquiring a runaway slave, for it does not remain, but it is worth much if tied down, for his works are very beautiful. What am I thinking of when I say this? True opinions. For true opinions, as long as they remain, are a fine thing and all they do is good, but they are not willing to remain   98 long, and they escape from a man's mind, so that they are not worth much until one ties them down by (giving) an account of the reason why. And that, Meno my friend, is recollection, as we previously agreed. After they are tied down, in the first place they become knowledge, and then they remain in place. That is why knowledge is prized higher than correct opinion, and knowledge differs from correct opinion in being tied down.

M: Yes, by Zeus, Socrates, it seems to be something like that.

S: Indeed, I too speak as one who does not have knowledge but is   b guessing. However, I certainly do not think I am guessing that right opinion is a different thing from knowledge. If I claim to know anything else—and I would make that claim about few things—I would put this down as one of the things I know. — Rightly so, Socrates.

S: Well then, is it not correct that when true opinion guides the course of every action, it does no worse than knowledge? — I think you are right in this too.

S: Correct opinion is then neither inferior to knowledge nor less   c useful in directing actions, nor is the man who has it less so than he who has knowledge. — That is so.

S: And we agreed that the good man is beneficent. — Yes.

S: Since then it is not only through knowledge but also through right opinion that men are good, and beneficial to their cities when they d   are, and neither knowledge nor true opinion come to men by nature but are acquired—or do you think either of these comes by nature? — I do not think so.

S: Then if they do not come by nature, men are not so by nature either. — Surely not.

S: As goodness does not come by nature, we inquired next whether it could be taught. — Yes.

S: We thought it could be taught, if it was knowledge? — Yes.

S: And that it was knowledge if it could be taught? — Quite so.

e   S: And that if there were teachers of it, it could be taught, but if there were not, it was not teachable? — That is so.

S: And then we agreed that there were no teachers of it? — We did.

S: So we agreed that it was neither teachable nor knowledge? — Quite so.

S: But we certainly agree that virtue is a good thing? — Yes.

S: And that which guides correctly is both useful and good? — Certainly.

99   S: And that only these two things, true belief and knowledge, guide correctly, and that if a man possesses these he gives correct guidance. The things that turn out right by some chance are not due to human guidance, but where there is correct human guidance it is due to two things, true belief or knowledge. — I think that is so.

S: Now because it cannot be taught, virtue no longer seems to be knowledge? — It seems not.

b   S: So one of the two good and useful things has been excluded, and knowledge is not the guide in public affairs. — I do not think so.

S: So it is not by some kind of wisdom, or by being wise, that such men lead their cities, those such as Themistocles and those mentioned by Anytus just now? That is the reason why they cannot make others be like themselves, because it is not knowledge which makes them what they are.

M: It is likely to be as you say, Socrates.

S: Therefore, if it is not through knowledge, the only alternative is

c   that it is through right opinion that statesmen follow the right course for their cities. As regards knowledge, they are no different from soothsayers and prophets. They too say many true things when inspired, but they have no knowledge of what they are saying. — That is probably so.

S: And so, Meno, is it right to call divine these men who, without any understanding, are right in much that is of importance in what they say and do? — Certainly.

S: We should be right to call divine also those soothsayers and prophets whom we just mentioned, and all the poets, and we should call   d no less divine and inspired those public men who are no less under the gods' influence and possession, as their speeches lead to success in many important matters, though they have no knowledge of what they are saying. — Quite so.

S: Women too, Meno, call good men divine, and the Spartans, when they eulogize someone, say "This man is divine."

M: And they appear to be right, Socrates, though perhaps Anytus   e here will be annoyed with you for saying so.

S: I do not mind that; we shall talk to him again, but if we were right in the way in which we spoke and investigated in this whole discussion, virtue would be neither an inborn quality nor taught, but comes to those who possess it as a gift from the gods which is not accompanied   100 by understanding, unless there is someone among our statesmen who can make another into a statesman. If there were one, he could be said to be among the living as Homer said Teiresias was among the dead, namely, that "he alone retained his wits while the others flitted about like shadows." In the same manner such a man would, as far as virtue is concerned, here also be the only true reality compared, as it were, with shadows.

M: I think that is an excellent way to put it, Socrates.   b

S: It follows from this reasoning, Meno, that virtue appears to be present in those of us who may possess it as a gift from the gods. We shall have clear knowledge of this when, before we investigate how it comes to be present in men, we first try to find out what virtue in itself is. But now the time has come for me to go. You convince your guest friend Anytus here of these very things of which you have yourself been convinced, in order that he may be more amenable. If you succeed, you will also confer a benefit upon the Athenians.

St. Augustine, *On the Teacher*

VIII

AUGUSTINE. Now then, let us take up that part of the discussion in which signs designate not other signs but what we call "signifiables"—things that can be signified. First, tell me this: is a person a person?

ADEODATUS. I really don't know if you're joking.

AUG. Why do you say that?

AD. Because you think you should ask me if a person is anything other than a person.

AUG. I suppose you would likewise think you were being made fun of if I were to ask whether the first syllable of that noun is anything other than *per*, and the second other than *son*.

AD. That is surely the case.

AUG. But these two syllables joined make a *person*—or do you deny that?

AD. Who would deny it?

AUG. I am asking you, then, whether you are these two joined-up syllables.

AD. Certainly not; but I do see what you are aiming at.

AUG. Let it be said, then, so you won't think I am insulting you.

AD. You figure the conclusion to be that I am not a "person."

AUG. And don't you, too, since you have granted that everything which led up to this conclusion is true?

AD. I will not tell you what I think until you tell me whether, when you ask, "Is a person a person?" you are asking me about those two syllables or about the actual thing that they signify.

AUG. I'd rather have you answer in whichever way you take my question. For if it is ambiguous, you should have been on guard before and should not have answered me until you were sure how the question was meant.

AD. But how could this ambiguity hinder me, since my answer fits the question both ways: a "person" is in every respect a "person." For those two syllables are nothing else than those two syllables, and what they signify is nothing else than what it is.

AUG. Point well taken. But why do you only take this spoken "person" both ways and not also the other things that we said?

AD. How is it proved that I did not take the others this way too?

AUG. Other reasons aside, on the grounds that if you had taken the whole of my first question in the sense that syllables are sounds, you would not have answered me, since I would not even have seemed to you to have asked anything. As it is when I sounded three words, repeating one of them at the end, and said, "Is a person a person?" you took the first and second words as signs, but the third as that which is signified by these two. And indeed, this fact alone makes it clear that, at once, sure and confident, you assumed that the question had to be answered.

AD. That is the truth.

AUG. What, then, disposed you to take only that which was positioned last and sounded third according to both its sound and its signification?

AD. But look, now I will take the whole question only in the sense that it signifies something. For I agree with you that conversation is altogether impossible unless the mind, at the sound of words, is turned to what those words are signs of. So show me now how I was misled in that line of reasoning which concluded that I am not a person.

AUG. Instead, I will ask the same questions again, so you might find for yourself where you went astray.

AD. Very good.

AUG. Since you have now granted what I first asked, I will not repeat that question. Consider, then, more carefully whether that syllable *per* is nothing else but *per,* and whether *son* is nothing else but *son.*

AD. I can think of absolutely nothing else.

AUG. Consider also whether the joining of these two syllables makes a *person.*

AD. By no means will I concede that. For we decided—and quite rightly—that when a sign is given we turn ourselves to the thing signified, and from consideration of that we concede or deny what is said. But as for those separately pronounced syllables, since they were sound without signification, I concede that they are just this, the sound they make.

AUG. Then it seems right, and it is your firm conviction, that there are to be no answers to questions except in regard to what is signified by the words.

AD. I don't see why it shouldn't seem right, as long as there are words.

AUG. Tell me how you would rebuff that fellow who tells us, to our amusement, that he proved that a lion came out of the mouth of a man he was debating with. For he asked whether the things we say came out of our mouth, and the other could not deny it. Then, as is easily done, he managed to make him mention a lion as he spoke. When this had happened, he began to leap up ridiculously and bear down on the other, so that just because he conceded that whatever we say comes out of our mouth, and could not deny that he had mentioned a lion, the fine fellow seemed to have vomitted up a ferocious beast.

AD. There's little difficulty in answering that clown. I would not concede that whatever we say comes out of our mouth. For we signify the things we talk about; it is not the thing signified, but the sign which does the signifying that comes out of our mouth. The only exception is when the signs themselves are being signified; we spoke of that case a little while ago.

AUG. You certainly would have been well fortified against him this way. Still, what will you say if I ask whether "person" is a noun?

AD. What but a noun?

AUG. Then, since I see you, do I see a noun?

AD. No.

AUG. Shall I draw the conclusion?

AD. Please don't, for I will denounce myself: I am not a person, since I said it was a noun when you asked if "person" was a noun. Indeed, it had seemed right before to agree with or deny what is said from a consideration of the thing signified.

AUG. Yet I don't think you fell for that answer without cause; it was a law of reason, written on our minds, that overcame your vigilance. For if I were to ask, "What is a person (man)?" you would answer, perhaps, "an animal." But if I were to ask what part of speech *person* is, you could only answer rightly with "noun." Accordingly, since a person turns out to be both a noun and an animal, what is considered in the former case is the sign and, in the second, the thing signified. Therefore, if someone asks if "person" is a noun, I have no other answer than "yes." But if he asks if it is an animal, I agree much more readily, since if he were to ask only what a "person" is, with no mention of noun or animal, the mind would hasten, by that rule of speech accepted by us, to what the two syllables signify. And there would be no answer but "animal," or even the whole definition, "a mortal, rational, animal." Is this not the case?

AD. Absolutely. But since we had conceded that it was a noun, how will we avoid that quite insulting conclusion that I am not a person?

AUG. How else than by explaining that the inference does not come from the sense in which we agreed with our questioner? Or if he affirms that it does come from this sense, there is no need for fear. For why should I be afraid to confess that I am not a "person," that is to say, two syllables?

AD. Nothing is truer. Why then does it hurt our feelings to be told, "Therefore, you are not a person," since nothing truer could be said which follows from our concessions?

AUG. Why? Because it is impossible for me not to think that the conclusion refers to what is signified by these two syllables as soon as the words are sounded; impossible, in fact, by that very law, which naturally carries the greatest weight, that the thought turns, when the sign is heard, to the things signified.

AD. I fully concur.

IX

AUG. Now then, I want you to understand that the things signified are of greater worth than their signs. For whatever exists for the sake of something else is necessarily of less value than the thing it exists for—or do you figure it differently?

AD. I don't think I should agree to this rashly. When I say, "the manure (*coenum*)," I think this noun far surpasses what it signifies. For what offends us, when we hear it, has nothing to do with the sound of the word itself. Indeed, with just a slight change, "the manure" becomes "the azure (*coelum*)"; yet we see how great a distance separates what they signify! Accordingly, I would never attribute to this sign what we loathe in the thing it signifies. And so, I am right to prefer the first to the second. We prefer to hear the one than to touch on the other with any of our senses.

AUG. Extremely perceptive of you. Then it is false that all things are worth more than their signs.

AD. So it seems.

AUG. Then tell me what purpose you think they had who set a name to this foul and despicable thing. Do you approve of their action, or disapprove?

AD. I venture neither approval nor disapproval, and I do not know what they were after.

AUG. Can you know at least what you are after, when you pronounce this noun?

AD. Certainly I can. I wish to signify it, so that I can teach or warn the person I am talking to what I think he should be taught or warned about it.

AUG. What is this? To teach or warn, or to be taught and warned, things that you easily do through this word, are they not more to be cherished than the noun itself?

AD. I grant that the knowledge which results from this sign must be preferred to the sign, but I do not think the same for the thing itself.

AUG. Then in our opinion, although it is false that everything should be preferred to its sign, it is nonetheless true that everything which exists for the sake of something else is of less worth than what it exists for. For knowledge of manure, for the sake of which the name was given to it, must be considered of more value than the name itself, which, in turn, must be preferred (as we have discovered) to the actual substance. The knowledge, certainly, is not preferred to the sign in question for any other reason than that the latter exists, irrefutably, for the sake of the former, and not *vice-versa*. Thus when a certain glutton—a worshipper of his stomach, the Apostle calls him [cf. *Rom.* XVI:18, and D. L. *Socrates* II, 34]—said that he lived to eat, a temperate man, listening, did not tolerate it, but said, "Would it not be much better if you ate to live?" He spoke, surely, thinking of that same rule. For the first displeased the Apostle only because he so underestimated his life, in saying that he lived for his dinner, that he thought it cheaper than the pleasure of his palate. And the second found favor with him just because he understood which of these two acts was for the sake of and subject to the other, and he taught that we should eat to live rather than live to eat.

Similarly you, perhaps, and anyone else who values things rightly would answer some loquacious lover of words who might say, "I teach that I may talk," with "Fellow, why don't you talk instead that you may teach?" And if this is true, as you know it is, you surely see how much less valuable words must be considered than the purpose for which we use the words. For the actual use of words must be preferred to the words used, since the words exist that we use them, and we use them in order to teach. By as much as teaching is better than speaking, by so much is speech better than words. But tell me what you think might be said against this.

AD. I certainly agree that teaching is better than words, but I am not certain that nothing can be said against the proposition that everything which exists for the sake of something else is inferior to what it exists for.

AUG. We will deal with that another time more conveniently and carefully. What you have granted now is sufficient for my purposes. For you grant that knowledge of things is more to be cherished than their signs. Consequently, the knowledge of signified things must be preferred to knowledge of their signs. Does this seem right?

AD. I did not admit, did I, that the knowledge of things is above the knowledge of signs and not above just the signs themselves? For this reason I fear I do not agree with you here. Consider this case: As the noun *manure* is better than the substance it signifies, so must not knowledge of the noun also be preferred to the knowledge of the thing, although the noun itself is of less worth than that knowledge. There are evidently four items: noun, and thing, and knowledge of the noun, and of the thing. So why doesn't the third surpass the fourth as the first surpasses the second? But must it also be inferior if it is not to surpass it?

AUG. You hold your point and explain your opinion marvelously well. But you understand, I think, that the syllable we sound when we say "vice" is better than what it signifies, although knowledge of the noun itself is much less valuable than a knowledge of vices. And so, allowing those four terms you have set up and considered—name, and thing, and knowledge of the name, and of the thing—we rightly prefer the first to the second. For this noun, set in verse, as Persius has it, "But he is stupefied with vice" [*Sat.* 111:32] not only is no vice in the line, but is even something of an ornament. But the actual thing signified by this noun forces whatever it is in to be vice-ridden. Yet the third term does not also in this way surpass the fourth, but, we see, the fourth surpasses the third; for knowledge of the name is of little value compared to a knowledge of vices.

AD. And you think that such knowledge should be preferred even when it makes men wretched? For Persius also sets this punishment ahead of all those dreamed up and meted out by the cruelty and cupidity of tyrants: to force men to recognize the vices they cannot avoid.

AUG. By this reasoning you can also deny that it is necessary to prefer even the knowledge of virtues to knowledge of this noun "vice," because to see virtue without having it is the punishment our satirist wishes on tyrants.

AD. God forbid such madness. Now indeed I understand that we must not blame knowledge itself, which the best instruction of all inculcates, but that we must judge, as I think Persius has, the most wretched of all men to be those afflicted with a disease such as no medicine can help.

AUG. You understand it well; but what is Persius's opinion to us? For we are not subservient to the authority of such as he in such matters as these. If knowledge, then, in any way must be preferred to knowledge, it is not easy to explain it here. But I am satisfied if it has been established that a knowledge of signified things is to be preferred at least to the signs themselves, even if not to a knowledge of the signs.

Consequently, let us now discuss much more thoroughly the character of those things that we say can be demonstrated through themselves, without signs—for example, speaking, walking, sitting, lying, and others of that sort.

AD. I recall what you have already said.

X

AUG. Do all those things that we can do right after we have been asked about them seem to you to be demonstrable without a sign? Or do you make an exception?

AD. Indeed, reviewing the whole group again and again I can find nothing there that can be taught without a sign except perhaps speech and—if someone should ask about the process itself—teaching. For I see that no matter what action I go through after his question to teach him, he does not learn from the action itself what he wants to be shown. If while I am reading or doing something else someone should ask me what walking is and I should try to teach him what he asked at once, without a sign, but by walking, how would I warn him against thinking that walking was only as much as I had done? But if he thought that he would be misled; for he would think that anyone who walks more or less than I had was not walking. And what I have said about this one verb holds for all those acts which I had agreed could be shown without a sign, with those two exceptions.

AUG. I accept this. But don't speaking and teaching seem to you different things?

AD. Certainly, for if they were the same no one could teach without speaking, but since in fact we learn many things with other signs than words, who can doubt the difference?

AUG. What about teaching and signifying? Are they not at all different, or somewhat?

AD. I think they are the same.

AUG. Isn't it right to say that we signify in order to learn?

AD. Quite right.

AUG. And if someone should say that we teach in order to signify, won't he be easily refuted by our previous proposition?

AD. Yes.

AUG. Then if we signify to teach, we do not teach to signify; teaching is one thing, signifying another.

AD. What you say is true, and I was wrong to answer that they are both the same.

AUG. Does someone teach what teaching is by signifying or by some other means?

AD. I don't see how else he could do it.

AUG. Then what you said a little before is false, that the question, "What is teaching itself?" could be answered without signs, since we see that not even this can be answered without signification inasmuch as you granted that teaching is one thing and signifying another. For if they are different—as is the case—and if the first can not be demonstrated unless through the second, then assuredly it is not demonstrated through itself—as had seemed to you the case. Accordingly, nothing has yet been found that can be shown through itself except speech, which signifies, among other things, itself. However, since it is itself a sign, absolutely nothing exists that it seems possible to teach without signs.

AD. I have no reason not to agree.

AUG. It has been established, then, that nothing can be taught without signs and that we ought to cherish knowledge itself more than the signs by which we get knowledge, although not everything that can be signified is to be preferred to its sign.

AD. So it seems.

AUG. Do you remember by how long and roundabout a way so small a result has at last been reached? For we have been tossing words about for a long time and labored to discover three things: whether anything can be taught without signs, whether some signs must be preferred to the things that they signify, and whether the actual knowledge of things is better than their signs. But there is a fourth thing that I would like to learn briefly from you: whether you can have no doubts about what has been found out this way?

AD. I do indeed wish that after so many bends and windings we had reached certainty; but that question of yours somehow bothers me and restrains me from agreeing. For it seems to me that you would not have asked it unless you had something to say against them; and the very complexity of these matters does not allow me to see them as a whole and respond with assurance, for fear lest in so many windings something lies hid that the keenness of my mind cannot penetrate.

AUG. I gladly welcome your hesitation, for it is a sign of the least rash spirit, and that is the greatest preserver of peace of mind. For assuredly it is most difficult not to be disturbed when those ideas that we were quickly and easily convinced of are knocked over by contrary arguments and twisted from our hands. In consequence, just as it is right to yield to carefully deliberated and thoroughly examined arguments, it is dangerous to take what is unknown for known. We should certainly be afraid that the frequent overthrow of what we took to be most firmly and permanently established will lead us into so great a hatred or fear of reason that it no longer seems necessary to have faith in the clarity of truth itself.

But now let us consider again, more quickly, whether your doubts are right. Consider this case: A man ignorant of the use of twigs and lime in birdcatching meets a fowler, armed with his equipment, but on the road, not at work. He would stand still in astonishment at the sight and would ask himself what kind of man would deck himself out like that. The fowler, when he saw himself stared at, would prepare his reeds with a desire to display himself, and using his stick and falcon would fix, subdue, and capture some little bird noticed nearby. Would he not teach his spectator with no use of signification, but by the thing itself, what that one wanted to know?

AD. I am afraid he is like the one I mentioned before, who asked what walking is. I do not see in this case, either, that fowling has been totally demonstrated.

AUG. It is easy to free you from this worry. I can add the condition that the spectator is intelligent enough to infer the whole character of the art from what some he sees. For it is enough for our argument that some men can be taught some things, although not all, without a sign.

AD. I, too, can add this condition for the other situation: if the spectator is truly intelligent, from the few steps of the demonstration he will understand the whole of walking.

AUG. I will allow you to; I not only don't object, I applaud it. For, you see, we have each established that some things can be taught some men without signs, and that what seemed right to us before is wrong, namely, the existence of nothing at all that could be revealed without signs. Indeed, now not just one or two, but thousands of things spring to mind that, without the use of a sign, can be demonstrated through themselves.

Indeed, tell me why we should doubt it. Forget the countless spectacles in all the theaters where men produce exhibitions not by signs but by the thing itself; surely the sun up there, and the light flooding and clothing everything here, the moon and the other stars, the earth and the seas, and all that exists in them—do not God and nature show and display these through themselves to those who look?

But if we were to look into it more carefully, perhaps you would find nothing which is taught by its sign. For when I am given a sign, if I am ignorant of the thing it is a sign of, it cannot teach me anything; but if I already know, what do I learn through the sign? For example, when I read, "their *saraballae* were not altered" [*Dan.* III:27], the word there does not show me what it signifies. For if certain coverings for the head are meant by this noun, did I learn, at the sound of it, either what a head is, or what coverings are? I become acquainted with these things not when they are named by others, but when they are seen by me. In fact, when that syllable *head* first struck my ears I was as ignorant of what it signified as I was when I first heard or read *saraballae*. But after it had been spoken again and again, I discovered, by taking note of when it was said, that it was a word for a thing already well known to me by sight. Before I discovered this the word was only a sound to me. But I learned that it was a sign when I found out what it was a sign of. And I learned this, as I said, not through the process of signification but by sight. Thus, it is rather the case that we learn the sign when we know the thing than that we learn the thing when the sign is given.

To understand this more clearly, imagine that we are now hearing for the first time the word "head" and that, being ignorant whether that expression is just a sound or is also a sign, we ask "What is *head?*" (Remember, we wish to become acquainted not with the thing signified but with the sign itself. We completely lack acquaintance with the sign as long as we don't know what it is a sign of.) If someone then points to the thing itself with his finger, we learn at this sight the sign that we had only heard and not yet known. Yet although the two qualities of sound and signification are both in this sign, we certainly do not perceive the sound through the signification but rather because of its striking the ear; the signification, on the other hand, we perceive by the sight of what is signified. For the pointing of the finger can only signify that at which the finger points; moreover, it points not at a sign but at that part which is called "head." So from that pointing I cannot learn a thing I had already known, nor a sign which is not being pointed at.

But I am not very concerned with the pointing of the finger, since I think it is a sign of the demonstration rather than of the objects demonstrated, just like the interjection *"Look!"* For we usually say this as we point, in case just one sign of demonstration should not be enough. Most of all, I am anxious to persuade you—if I can—that we learn nothing through those signs which we call *words*. Instead we learn, as I have said, the force of the word, that is, the signification hid in the sound, from knowledge of the thing signified, and we do not perceive the thing from the signification.

And what I have said about the head I could also say about the coverings and countless other things. These, however, I already know, but those *saraballae* I still have no knowledge of. If someone should signify them to me with a gesture, or paint a picture of them, or show me something to which they are similar, I would not say then that he has not taught me what they are—although I easily could, if I spoke at greater length—but I would say what is very close to that: He has not taught it to me with words.

And if it should happen that just as I was looking at them he declared to me, "Look! *saraballae*," I would learn then something I had not known, not, however, through the words spoken but through the sight of it. And through the sight I could also learn and retain the value of that noun. For when I learned the actual thing I heeded not someone else's words but my own eyes; the words, perhaps, I heeded in order to direct my attention, so I might seek from the sight what I was to see.

XI

To give them the greatest credit possible, words have this power: they prompt us to look for objects, but they do not display them for us to learn. And the person who teaches me something supplies my eyes, or another of the bodily senses, or even my mind with whatever I want to know. From words, consequently, we learn only words, or rather the sound and noise of words; for if what is not a sign cannot be a word, then even once I have heard it I do not know that a word is a word until I know what it is a sign of.

With the knowledge of things, therefore, knowledge of words comes, too; but when words are heard, they are not learned. For we do not learn the ones we already know, and we cannot declare that we have learned the ones we did not know until we become aware of their signification; and that awareness comes not from hearing voices but with knowledge of the things signified.

Here indeed is the truest argument and the one most truly spoken: when words are expressed we either do or do not know what they signify. If we do know, we are remembering rather than learning them. But if we do not know, we certainly do not remember them but are perhaps prompted to seek for their meaning.

But what if you should say this: those head-coverings, to be sure, of which we grasp the name only by its sound, we cannot get to know except by sight, and we cannot know the name itself more fully except by acquaintance with the actual things; nonetheless, what we hear of the boys, how they overcame the king and the fire through faith and religion, what praises they sang to God, what esteem they won even from their enemy—do we learn this through anything but words?

I will answer that everything signified by those words was already in our knowledge. For the meanings of "three boys," "furnace," "fire," "king," even of "unharmed by the fire" and of everything else signified by those words were already in my comprehension. But Ananias and Azarias and Misael are as unknown to me as those *saraballae.* And these names have not and could not have in any way aided me in getting to know them.

Indeed, I confess that I believe rather than know that all the events to be read in that story took place at that time just as they are written. And the very authors we do believe were well aware of that difference. Thus the Prophet says: "If you should not believe you shall not understand" [*Is.* VII:9]. He certainly would not have said this if he did not deem them separate. As much as I understand, therefore, I also believe, but I do not also understand all that I believe. Furthermore, everything that I understand, I know, but I do not know everything that I believe. But I am not for this reason unaware how useful it is to believe many things still that I do not know. In this useful category I place the story of the three boys. Thus, although there are many things I cannot know, I know the usefulness of believing them.

Part two: The only teacher of truth is Christ

Now then, in regard to the classes of things we understand, we seek advice not from the speaker outside of ourselves but from the truth within that governs our mind, while the words, perhaps, prompt us to seek advice. And he to whom we go for aid is the teacher, Christ, who is said to dwell in the innermost man, the inalterable strength and eternal wisdom of God. Indeed, every rational soul consults this, but it is available to each only to the extent he can grasp it by virtue of his own good or bad will. If it is ever deceived, it is not the fault of the truth consulted, just as a mistake of the bodily eyes is not the fault of the exterior light. We admit that we seek help from the light to show us visible things to the extent that we have the strength to discern them.

XII

But if in regard to colors we seek aid from the light, and in regard to the other things that we sense through the body we consult the elements of this world, the very bodies that we sense, and the very senses that the mind uses as interpreters to learn such matters, and if in regard to matters that we understand we take counsel, by means of reason, from the truth within us, what, then, can be said to prove that we learn anything through words beyond the actual sound that strikes our ears?

For we perceive everything with either the physical senses or the mind. The former we label "sensible," the latter "intelligible," or, to speak as our authors do, the former are "carnal," the latter "spiritual."

When we are asked about the first, we answer, if the sensible objects are at hand—for example, if we are asked while we look at it about the nature and position of the new moon. The man who asked, if he does not see it, believes our words, or perhaps he does not. But in no way does he learn, if he does not also see what we are speaking of. In that case he has learned not from the sound of the words but from the subjects themselves and from his senses. For the words sound the same to one who sees as to one who doesn't.

When, however, the question concerns not our immediate sensations, but things we once sensed, we no longer speak of the actual things but of the images taken from them and committed to memory. I do not know at all how it is we say these to be real when what we contemplate is not, unless it is because we declare not that we see and feel them, but that we have seen and felt them. Thus, those images in the storehouse of our memory are treated by us as documents of what we previously felt. We contemplate these in the mind and with a good conscience we do not lie when we talk. To us they are documents. Now the man who hears me, if he sensed these things and was present does not learn them from my words but recognizes the images he himself carried away. But if he did not himself experience them, who would not suppose that he is believing my words rather than learning from them?

Yet when it is a question of what we contemplate with the mind, that is, by intellect and reason, we speak of those very things whose presence we see in that interior light of truth from which he whom we call the inner man derives light and enjoyment. But in that case, too, if our listener himself sees them with his hidden, open eye, he knows what I am saying from his own con-templation, not from my words.

Therefore I, who speak the truth, teach not even him, who regards the truth. For he learns not from my words but from the things themselves, which are made plain as God displays them within. And so, were he questioned about these he, too, could answer. So what is more absurd than to think that he was taught by my speech, since, if asked, he could, even before I spoke, explain these very things.

It often happens that someone will deny something he has been asked and then admit it after he has been pressed by other questions. This comes from his weakness in this kind of contemplation, inasmuch as he is unable to take the aid of that light on the whole matter. He is prompted to do this by parts when he is asked about those parts that make up a sum that he had not the ability to see as a whole. Similarly, if I asked you our present question, "Can nothing be taught with words?" at first you would think it absurd, being unable to see the whole. It would, therefore, be right for me to question you in accordance with your ability to hear that teacher within and say, "Where did you learn what you concede to be true in my speech, and what you are sure of, and what you assert that you know?" Perhaps you would answer what I have taught.

Then I might add, "What if I were to say that I saw a man flying? Would my words leave you as certain as you be if you heard that wise men are better than fools?" You would deny it at once and answer that you did not believe my first statement, or, even if you did believe it, you had no knowledge of it, but that my second statement you knew with assurance to be a fact. From this you would surely understand that neither in the first case, where you remained without knowledge of what I declared, nor in the second, where you knew it perfectly well, did you learn anything from my words. For asked about the in-dividual facts, you would certainly have sworn that one was unknown, one known to you.

Then indeed you would admit the whole idea that you had denied, when you realized that the pieces of which it was composed were clear and certain. Obviously our audience, in regard to everything that we say, either does not know if it is true, or is not ignorant than it is false, or knows that it is true. Of these three possibilities, the first is grounds for belief, opinion, or doubt; the second, for opposition and denial; the third, for affirmation. Nowhere, then, is learning. For the one who knows nothing of the subject after I have spoken, and the one who knows that what he heard was false, and the one who, if asked, could have given the same answer that I gave—all these are proven to have learned nothing from words.

XIII

For this reason, anyone unable to perceive subjects that are perceived by the mind listens in vain to the speeches of someone who can, and if not in vain, only because it is useful to believe such things as long as he is ignorant of them. But anyone who *can* see them is a student of the truth within and, in the outer world, a judge of the speaker or, rather, of the speech itself.

For most of the time he knows the things that are said, while the speaker himself is ignorant of what he says. For example, a follower of the Epicureans, who believed in the mortality of the soul, might make an oration in which he used the arguments put forth by wiser men to prove its immortality while one who could contemplate spiritual subjects listened. This man would judge that the orator does speak the truth, but the speaker does not know if he does, or, rather, he even thinks it entirely false. Must he, then, be thought to teach the things he doesn't know? Yet he uses the very words he could use if he did know. For this reason it is not even left to words to indicate the thoughts of the speaker, since it is uncertain if he knows what he is saying.

Add, too, liars and deceivers; they will easily make you understand that words not only don't open but even hide the mind. For in no way do I doubt that the words of truthful men attempt it, and to some extent do speak openly, so that the speaker's mind is seen. Everyone agrees that they would attain this if liars were not allowed to talk.

Nevertheless, we have often had the experience, both among ourselves and among others, of words being expressed that did not correspond to what was on the mind. I see two ways for this to happen: we recite automatically a speech that we have committed to memory, and frequently gone over, while thinking of other things (this often happens to us when we sing a hymn), or words other than those intended leap out against our will, by the tongue's own error—for in this case also the signs heard are not of what we have in mind. For liars too think about the things they are saying as well, so that even if we do not know if they are speaking the truth, we do know that they are saying what they have in mind as long as one of these two accidents doesn't befall them. And if someone should maintain that this happens only occasionally and that it is obvious when it does happen, I would not argue with him, although it is hidden and does deceive me, as a listener.

There is a kind of accident different from these that occurs very widely and is the source of countless arguments and disagreements: when the speaker signifies what he is in fact thinking, but for the most part only to himself and some others, while to the listener and many others as well he does not signify the same thing. For example, someone might say that man is surpassed in manliness [*virtus*] by some of the wild beasts. We would immediately find this unbearable and refute with great eagerness so false and dangerous an opinion. But perhaps he calls bodily strength "manliness," and so with this noun he is expressing what he thinks and is not lying, or confusing matters, or putting together memorized words while thinking about something else, or saying what he does not think through a slip of the tongue. It is only that he calls what he is thinking by a different name than we do. We would agree with him at once if we could look in and see the thought that he has not been able to open up to us even when the words have been expressed and his opinion set out.

Some say that definition is a remedy for this confusion. In this case the speaker could define "manliness." He would make it clear, they say, that the argument was about the word, not the proposition. Granting this, how many men skillful at defining can be found? Still, there are many things said against the science of definition that it is not convenient to discuss now and that I am not altogether satisfied with.

I am leaving out the fact that we do not hear many things correctly and argue long and loud about them as if they had been heard. Thus, recently, when I had said that a certain Punic word signified "pity," you said that you had heard from those who knew better that it meant "compassion." But I objected, maintaining that you had completely forgotten what you had heard, for it seemed to me that you had said not "compassion" but "faith," although you were sitting very close to me and there is no way the sounds of those two words might deceive the ear by their similarity. Nevertheless, for a long time I thought that you did not know what had been said to you, while I did not know what you had said. For if I had heard you right, I would have found it in no way absurd for one Punic word to indicate both pity and compassion.

This happens very often, but we leave this case out, as I said, lest I should seem to reproach words for the negligence of the listener or even for the deafness of men. The cases I enumerated before trouble us more, in which we are unable to become acquainted with the thoughts of the person speaking from words clearly heard and in Latin, our own language.

But look, I will relent and concede that when the words are heard by someone to whom they are known, it is possible for him to know what the speaker thought about those subjects signified by the words. He doesn't also, does he, learn for this reason what is now the question: if he speaks the truth?

XIV

Do teachers proclaim that what is perceived and retained are their thoughts and not the science that they think they hand on by speaking? For who is so foolishly curious that he sends his son to school to learn what the teacher thinks? But when they have explained, through words, all those sciences that they profess to teach, even the sciences of wisdom and virtue, then those called students consider within themselves whether the truth was spoken, looking, in fact, at that truth within them to the extent they are able. It is then that they learn, and when they find, within themselves, that the truth has been spoken, they give praise. They are unaware that they are not praising the teachers rather than the taught—if at least these teachers, too, know what they are saying.

Moreover, since most of the time there is no delay between the time of speech and of thought, men make the mistake of calling teachers those who are not. And since they learn, within, immediately after the prompting of the speaker, they think that they learn outside themselves from the one who prompted them.

But we will investigate elsewhere, if God allows, the whole utility of words; when well considered, it is not found small. But now, I urge you, let us not credit them with more than their due, so that we may not only believe but also begin to understand already how truly it has been written by divine order that we are not to call anyone on earth a teacher, because there is in heaven one teacher of all men [*Matt.* XXIII: 8–10].

What, moreover, He is in heaven, He himself will teach us; He by whom we are prompted, through men, with signs outside ourselves, to turn to him inside and be taught our lessons, He of whom knowledge and love make up the blessed life, a life which all proclaim that they seek, but which few rejoice to have truly found.

But now I would like you to tell me what you think of my whole discourse. For if you acknowledge that what has been said is true, when asked about the individual statements you would also have said that you knew these things. You see therefore from whom you learned all this, and that it was not from me, since you only answered my questions. But if you do not recognize them as true, neither I nor He taught you. Not I, because I can never teach; not He, because you still can not learn.

AD. I indeed have learned at the prompting of your words that words do nothing else than prompt men to learn and that it is a minor thing that some portion of the speaker's thought becomes evident through words. I have learned, moreover, that only He can teach us whether the truth is spoken, He who warns us when there is speech outside that He dwells within.

Nonetheless, I am most thankful for the uninterrupted discourse that you delivered, because it forestalled and defeated everything I had ready to say against it. And you have left aside absolutely nothing that was causing doubt for me, nothing about which that hidden oracle would not answer me just as your words asserted.

Gilbert Ryle, "Teaching and Training"

I have no teaching tricks or pedagogic maxims to impart to you, and I should not impart them to you if I had any. What I want to do is to sort out and locate a notion which is cardinal to the notions of teaching, training, education, etc. about which too little is ordinarily said. This notion is that of *teaching oneself* which goes hand in glove with the notion of *thinking for oneself.* You will all agree, I think, that teaching fails, that is, either the teacher is a failure or the pupil is a failure if the pupil does not sooner or later become able and apt to arrive at his own solutions to problems. But how, in logic, can anyone be taught to do untaught things? I repeat, how, in logic, can anyone be taught to do untaught things?

To clear the air, let me begin by quickly putting on one side an unimportant but familiar notion, that of the self-taught man. Normally when we describe someone as a self-taught man we think of a man who, having been deprived of tuition from other teachers, tries to make himself an historian, say, or a linguist or an astronomer, without criticism, advice or stimulation from anyone else, save from the authors of such textbooks, encyclopaedia articles and linguaphone records as he may happen to hit on. He hits on these, of course, randomly, without having anyone or anything to tell him whether they are good ones, silly ones, old-fashioned ones or cranky ones. We admire the devotion with which he studies, but, save for the rare exception, we pity him for having been the devoted pupil only of that solitary and untrained teacher, himself. However, I am not interested in him.

What I am interested in is this. Take the case of an ordinary unbrilliant, unstupid boy who is learning to read. He has learned to spell and read monosyllables like 'bat', 'bad', 'at', 'ring', 'sing', etc. and some two-syllable words like 'running', 'dagger' and a few others. We have never taught him, say, the word 'batting'. Yet we find him quite soon reading and spelling unhesitantly the word 'batting'. We ask him who taught him this word and, if he remembers, he says that he had found it out for himself. He has learned from himself how the word 'batting' looks in print, how to write it down on paper and how to spell it out aloud, so in a sense he has taught himself this word—taught it to himself without yet knowing it. How can this be? How can a boy who does not know what 'b-a-t-t-i-n-g' spells teach himself what it spells?

In real life we are not a bit puzzled. It is just what we expect of a not totally stupid child. Yet there is the semblance of a conceptual paradox here, for we seem to be describing him as at a certain stage being able to teach himself something new, which *ipso facto* was not yet in his repertoire to teach. Here his teacher was as ignorant as the pupil, for they were the same boy. So how can the one learn something from the other?

What should we say? Well, clearly we want to say that the prior things that we *had* taught him, namely words like 'bat', 'bad', 'rat' and longer words like 'butter', 'running' etc. enabled him and perhaps encouraged him to make a new bit of independent, uncoached progress on his own. We had taught him how to read some monosyllables, *how* to run some of them together in dissyllables, and so on. We had taught him a way or some ways of coping with combinations of printed letters, though not in their particular application to this new word 'batting'. He had made this particular application himself. So to speak, we had previously from the deck shown him the ropes and now he climbs one of them with his own hands and feet; that is to say, not being totally stupid, he was able and ready to employ this slightly general knowledge that we had given to him on a new concrete and particular problem that we had not solved for him. We had given him the wherewithal with which to think it out for himself—and this thinking out was his doing and not ours. I could just as well have taken an example from the much more sophisticated stratum where a brilliant undergraduate makes a good philosophical move that no one else has ever taught him, and maybe no one else has ever made.

Naturally, most often the boy or the undergraduate, if asked Who taught you that? would reply not that he had taught it to himself or that he had learned it from himself, but rather that he had found it out or thought it out or worked it out for himself. Just this brings out a big part of what interests me, namely, that though in one way it is obviously impossible for one person's own discovery, whether trivial or important, to be simply what someone else had previously taught him—since it would then not be his discovery—, yet in another way it is and ought to be one main business of a teacher precisely to get his pupils to advance beyond their instructions and to discover new things for themselves, that is, to get them to think things out for themselves. I teach Tommy to read a few words like 'bat', 'run' and 'running' in order that he may then, of his own motion, find out how to read lots and lots of other words, like 'batting', that we have not taught to him. Indeed we do not deem him really able to spell or read until he can spell and read things that he has not been introduced to. Nor, to leave the schoolroom for the moment, do I think that Tommy has learned to bicycle until he can do things on his bicycle far more elaborate, speedy, tricky and delicate than the things I drilled him in on the first morning. I taught him the few elements on the first morning just in order that he might then find out for himself how to cope with hosts of non-elementary tasks. I gave him a few stereotyped exercises, and, as I had hoped and expected, in a couple of days he had developed for himself on this basis a fair wealth of boyish skills and dexterities, though he acquired these while I was away in London.

However, there remains a slight feeling of a puzzle or paradox here, and it comes, I think, from this source. A familiar and indispensable part or sort of teaching consists in teaching by rote lists of truths or facts, for example the proposition that 7 × 7 is 49, etc., the proposition that Waterloo was fought in 1815, etc., and the proposition that Madrid is the capital of Spain, etc. That the pupil has learned a lesson of this propositional sort is shown, in the first instance, by his being able and reasonably ready to reproduce word-perfectly these pieces of information. He gets them by heart, and he can come out with them on demand. Now every teacher knows that only a vanishingly small fraction of his teaching-day really consists in simply reciting lists of such snippets of information to pupils, but very unfortunately, it happens to be the solitary part which unschooled parents, sergeant-majors, some silly publicists and some educationalists always think of when they think of teaching and learning. They think or half-think that the request 'Recite what you have learned in school today, Tommy' is a natural and proper one, as if all that Tommy could or should have learned is a number of memorizable propositions; or as if to have learned anything consisted simply in being able to echo it, like a gramophone. As you all know, most teaching has nothing whatsoever in common with this crude, semi-surgical picture of teaching as the forcible insertion into the pupil's memory of strings of officially approved propositions; and I hope to show before long that even that small and of course indispensable part of instruction which is the imparting of factual information is grossly mis-pictured when pictured as literal cramming. Yet, bad as the picture is, it has a powerful hold over people's general theorizings about teaching and learning. Even Tommy's father, after spending the morning in teaching Tommy to swim, to dribble the football or to diagnose and repair what is wrong with the kitchen clock, in the afternoon cheerfully writes to the newspapers letters which take it for granted that all lessons are strings of memorizable propositions. His practice is perfectly sensible, yet still his theory is as silly as it could be.

Perhaps the prevalence of this very thin and partial notion of teaching and learning inherits something from the teaching and learning that are done in the nursery, where things such as 'Hickory Dickory Dock' and simple tunes are learned by heart from that mere vocal repetition which enables the parrot to pick them up too.

Well, in opposition to this shibboleth, I want to switch the centre of gravity of the whole topic onto the notions of Teaching-to so and so, and Learning-to so and so, that is, on to the notion of the development of abilities and competences. Let us forget for a while the memorization of truths, and, of course, of rhymes and tunes, and attend, instead, to the acquisition of skills, knacks and efficiencies. Consider, for example, lessons in drawing, arithmetic and cricket and, if you like, in philosophy. These lessons cannot consist of and cannot even contain much of dictated propositions. However many true propositions the child has got by heart, he has not begun to learn to draw or play cricket until he has been given a pencil or a bat and a ball and has practised doing things with them; and even if he progresses magnificently in these arts, he will have little or nothing to reply to his parents if they ask him in the evening to recite to them the propositions that he has learned. He can *exhibit* what he has begun to master, but he cannot *quote* it. To avoid the ambiguity between 'teach' in the sense of 'teach that' and 'teach' in the sense of 'teach to' or 'teach how to', I shall now sometimes use the word 'train'. The drawing-master, the language-teacher or the cricket-coach *trains* his pupils in drawing or in French pronunciation or in batting or bowling, and this training incorporates only a few items of quotable information. The same is true of philosophy.

Part, but only part of this notion of training is the notion of drilling, i.e. putting the pupil through stereotyped exercises which he masters by sheer repetition. Thus the recruit learns to slope arms just by going through the same sequence of motions time after time, until he can, so to speak, perform them in his sleep. Circus dogs and circus seals are trained in the same way. At the start piano-playing, counting and gear-changing are also taught by simple habituation. But disciplines do not reduce to such sheer drills. Sheer drill, though it is the indispensable beginning of training, is, for most abilities, only their very beginning. Having become able to do certain low-level things automatically and without thinking, the pupil is expected to advance beyond this point and to employ his inculcated automatisms in higher-level tasks which are not automatic and cannot be done without thinking. Skills, tastes and scruples are more than mere habits, and the disciplines and the self-disciplines which develop them are more than mere rote-exercises.

His translators and commentators have been very unjust to Aristotle on this matter. Though he was the first thinker, and is still the best, systematically to study the notions of ability, skill, training, character, learning, discipline, self-discipline, etc., the translators of his works nearly always render his key-ideas by such terms as 'habit' and 'habituation'—as if, for example, a person who has been trained and self-trained to play the violin, or to behave scrupulously in his dealings with other people acts from sheer habit, in the way in which I do tie up my shoelaces quite automatically and without thinking what I am doing or how to do it. Of course Aristotle knew better than this, and the Greek words that he used are quite grossly mistranslated when rendered merely by such words as 'habit' and 'habituation'. The well-disciplined soldier, who does indeed slope arms automatically, does not also shoot automatically or scout by blind habit or read maps like a marionette.

Nor is Tommy's control of his bicycle merely a rote-performance, though he cannot begin to control his bicycle until he has got some movements by rote. Having learned through sheer habit-formation to keep his balance on his bicycle with both hands on the handlebars, Tommy can now try to ride with one hand off, and later still with both hands in his pockets and his feet off the pedals. He now progresses by experimentation. Or, having got by heart the run of the alphabet from ABC through to XYZ, he can now, but not without thinking, tell you what three letters run *backwards* from RQP, though he has never learned by heart this reversed sequence.

I suggest that our initial seeming paradox, that a learner can sometimes of himself, after a bit of instruction, better his instructions, is beginning to seem less formidable. The possibility of it is of the same pattern as the familiar fact that the toddler who has this morning taken a few aided steps tries this afternoon with or without success to take some unaided steps. The swimmer who can now keep himself up in salt water, comes by himself, at first with a bit of extra splashing, to keep himself up in fresh water. How do any formerly difficult things change into now easy things? Or any once untried things into now feasible ones? The answer is just in terms of the familiar notions of the development of abilities by practice, that is trying and failing and then trying again and not failing so often or so badly, and so on.

Notoriously a very few pupils are, over some tasks, so stupid, idle, scared, hostile, bored or defective that they make no efforts of their own beyond those imposed on them as drill by their trainer. But to be non-stupid, vigorous and interested *is* to be inclined to make, if only as a game, moves beyond the drilled moves, and to practice of oneself, e.g. to multiply beyond 12 × 12, to run through the alphabet backwards, to bicycle with one hand off the handlebar, or to slope arms in the dark with a walking-stick when no drill-sergeant is there. As Aristotle says, 'The things that we have got to do when we have learned to do them, we learn to do by doing them.' What I can do today I could not do easily or well or successfully yesterday; and the day before I could not even try to do them; and if I had not tried unsuccessfully yesterday, I should not be succeeding today.

Before returning to go further into some of these key notions of ability, practice, trying, learning to, teaching to, and so on, I want to look back for a moment to the two over-influential notions of teaching *that* so and so, i.e. telling or informing, and of learning *that* so and so, i.e. the old notion of propositional cramming. In a number of nursery, school and university subjects, there are necessarily some or many true propositions to be accumulated by the student. He must, for example, learn that Oslo is the capital of Norway, Stockholm is the capital of Sweden and Copenhagen is the capital of Denmark. Or he must learn that the Battle of Trafalgar was fought in 1805 and that of Waterloo in 1815. Or that $7 + 5 = 12$, $7 + 6 = 13$, $7 + 7 = 14$, etc.

At the very start, maybe, the child just memorizes these strings of propositions as he memorizes 'Hickory Dickory Dock', the alphabet or 'Thirty days hath September'. But so long as parroting is all he can do, he does not yet know the geographical fact, say, that Stockholm is the capital of Sweden, since if you ask him what Stockholm is the capital of, or whether Madrid is the capital of Sweden, he has no idea how to move. He can repeat, but he cannot yet use the memorized dictum. All he can do is to go through the memorized sequence of European capitals from start through to the required one. He does not qualify as knowing that Stockholm is the capital of Sweden until he can detach this proposition from the memorized rigmarole; and can, for example, answer new-type questions like 'Of which country out of the three, Italy, Spain and Sweden, is Stockholm the capital?' or 'Here is Stockholm on the globe—whereabouts is Sweden?' and so on. To know the geographical fact requires having taken it in, i.e. being able and ready to operate with it, from it, around it and upon it. To possess a piece of information is to be able to mobilize it apart from its rote-neighbours and out of its rote-formulation in unhackneyed and *ad hoc* tasks. Nor does the pupil know that $7 + 7 = 14$ while this is for him only a still undetachable bit of a memorized sing-song but only when, for example, he can find fault with someone's assertion that $7 + 8 = 14$, or can answer the new-type question How many 7s are there in 14? or the new-type question 'If there are seven boys and seven girls in a room, how many children are in the room?' etc. Only then has he taken it in.

In other words, even to have learned the piece of information *that something is so* is more than merely to be able to parrot the original telling of it—somewhat as to have digested a biscuit is more than merely to have had it popped into one's mouth. Can he or can he not infer from the information that Madrid is the capital of Spain that Madrid is not in Sweden? Can he or can he not tell us what sea-battle occurred ten years before Waterloo?

Notice that I am not in the least deprecating the inculcation of rotes like the alphabet, the figures of the syllogism, 'Hickory Dickory Dock', the dates of the Kings of England, or sloping arms. A person who has not acquired such rotes cannot progress from and beyond them. All that I am arguing is that he does not qualify as knowing even that Waterloo was fought in 1815 if all that he can do is to sing out this sentence inside the sing-song of a memorized string of such sentences. If he can only echo the syllables that he has heard, he has not yet taken in the information meant to be conveyed by them. He has not grasped it if he cannot handle it. But if he could not even echo things told to him, *a fortiori* he could not operate with, from or upon their informative content. One cannot digest a biscuit unless it is first popped into one's mouth. So we see that even to have learned a true proposition is to have learned *to do* things other than repeating the words in which the truth had been dictated. To have learned even a simple geographical fact is to have become able to cope with some unhabitual geographical tasks, however elementary.

We must now come back to our central question: How is it possible that a person should learn from himself something which he previously did not know, and had not, e.g. been taught by someone else? This question is or embodies the apparently perplexing question: How can one person teach another person to think things out for himself, since if he gives him, say, the new arithmetical thoughts, then they are not the pupil's own thoughts; or if they are his own thoughts, then he did not get them from his teacher? Having led the horse to the water, how can we make him drink? But I have, I hope, shifted the centre of gravity of this seeming puzzle, by making the notions of *learning-to* and *teaching-to* the primary notions. In its new form the question is: How, on the basis of some tuition, can a person today get himself to do something which he had not been able to do yesterday or last year? How can competences, abilities and skills develop? How can trying ever succeed? We are so familiar, in practice, with the fact that abilities do develop, and that trying can succeed that we find little to puzzle us in the idea that they do.

Looked at from the end of the teacher the question is: How can the teacher get his pupil to make independent moves of his own? If this question is tortured into the shape: How can the teacher make or force his pupil to do things which he is not made or forced to do? i.e. How can the teacher be the initiator of the pupil's initiatives? the answer is obvious. He cannot. I cannot compel the horse to drink thirstily. I cannot coerce Tommy into doing spontaneous things. Either he is not coerced, or they are not spontaneous.

As every teacher, like every drill-sergeant or animal trainer knows in his practice, teaching and training have virtually not yet begun so long as the pupil is too young, too stupid, too scared or too sulky to respond—and to respond is not just to yield. Where there is a modicum of alacrity, interest or anyhow docility in the pupil, where he tries, however faintheartedly, to get things right rather than wrong, fast rather than slow, neat rather than awkward, where, even, he registers even a slight contempt for the poor performances of others or chagrin at his own, pleasure at his own successes and envy of those of others, then he is, in however slight a degree, cooperating and so self-moving. He is doing something, though very likely not much, and is not merely having things done to him. He is, however unambitiously and however desultorily, attempting the still difficult. He has at least a little impetus of his own. A corner, however small a corner, of his heart is now in the task. The eager pupil is, of course, the one who, when taught, say, to read or spell a few words like 'at', 'bat' and 'mat' travels home on the bus trying out, just for fun, all the other mono-syllables that rhyme with 'at', to see which of them are words. When taught to read and spell a dissyllable or two, he tries his hand, just for fun and often but not always unsuccessfully, on the polysyllables on the advertisement hoardings; and just for fun he challenges his father to spell long words when he gets home. He does this for fun; but like much play it is spontaneous self-practising. When he returns to school after the holidays, although his spelling and reading are now far in advance of their peak of last term, he will stoutly deny that he has done any work during the holidays. It has not been work, it has been absorp-tion in a new hobby, like exercising a new limb.

His over-modest teacher may say that he has taught this boy next to nothing—nor has he, save for the very beginnings of everything.

However, we should remember that although a total absence of eagerness or even willingness spells total unteachability, the presence of energy, adven-turousness and self-motion is not by itself enough. The wild guesser and the haphazard plunger have freedom of movement of a sort, but not of the best sort. Learning how to do new and therefore more or less difficult things does indeed require trying things out for oneself, but if this trying-out is not con-trolled by any testing or making sure, then its adventurousness is recklessness and not enterprise. He is like the gambler, not like the investor. The moves made, though spontaneous, are irresponsible and they yield no dividends. Nothing can be learned by him from their unsuccesses or from their occasional fortuitous successes. He shoots away, but learns nothing from his misses—or from his fluke hits.

It is just here, with the notion of taking care when taking risks, that there enters on the scenes the cardinal notion of *method*, i.e. of techniques, *modi operandi*, rules, canons, procedures, knacks, and even tricks of the trade. In doing a thing that he has never done before, a person may, but need not, op-erate according to a method, sometimes even according to a sheer drill that he has adhered to before. If he does, then his action is still an innovation, al-though the pattern of his action is a familiar and inculcated one. The poet composes a sonnet, taking care to adhere to the regulation 14 lines, to the regu-lation rhyming scheme, to the regulation metrical pattern, or else perhaps to one of the several permitted patterns—yet, nonetheless, his sonnet is a new one. No one has ever composed *it* before. His teacher who taught him how to compose sonnets had not and could not have made him compose this sonnet, else it would be the teacher's and not the pupil's sonnet. Teaching people how to do things just *is* teaching them methods or *modi operandi*; and it is just be-cause it is one thing to have learned a method and another thing to essay a new application of it that we can say without paradox that the learner's new move is his own move and yet that he may have learned the *how* of making it from someone else. The cook's pudding is a new one and piping hot, but its recipe was known to Mrs. Beeton in the days of Queen Victoria.

Well, then, what sort of a thing is a method? First for what it is not. Despite what many folk would say, a method is not a stereotyped sequence-pattern or routine of actions, inculcatable by pure rote, like sloping arms or going through the alphabet. The parrot that can run through 'Hickory Dickory Dock' has not learned how to do anything or therefore how not to do it. There is nothing that he takes care not to do.

A method is a learnable way of doing something, where the word 'way' connotes more than mere rote or routine. A way of doing something, or a *modus operandi*, is something general, and general in at least two dimensions. First, the way in which you do a thing, say mount your bicycle, can be the way or a way in which some other people or perhaps most other people mount or try to mount their bicycles. Even if you happen to be the only person who yet does something in a certain way, it is possible that others should in future learn from you or find out for themselves the very same way of doing it. *Modi operandi* are, in principle, public property, though a particular action performed in this way is my action and not yours, or else it is your action and not mine. We mount our bicycles in the same way, but my bicycle-mounting is my action and not yours. You do not make my mince pies, even though we both follow the same Victorian recipe.

The second way in which a method is something general is the obvious one, that there is no limit to the number of actions that may be done in that way. The method is, roughly, applicable anywhere and anywhen, as well as by anyone. For, however many people are known by me to have mounted their bicycles in a certain way, I know that there could have been and there could be going to be any number of other bicycle-mountings performed by myself and others in the same way.

Next, methods can be helpfully, if apparently cynically, thought of as systems of avoidances or as patterns of *don'ts*. The rules, say, of English grammar do not tell us positively what to say or write; they tell us negatively not to say or write such things as 'A dog *are* . . .' and 'The dogs *is* . . .', and learning the art of rock-climbing or tree-climbing is, among hundreds of other things, learning never or hardly ever, to trust one's whole weight to an untried projection or to a branch that is leafless in summer time.

People sometimes grumble at the Ten Commandments on the score that most of them are prohibitions, and not positive injunctions. They have not realized that the notice 'Keep off the grass' licenses us to walk anywhere else we choose; where the notice 'Keep to the gravel' leaves us with almost no freedom of movement. Similarly to have learned a method is to have learned to take care against certain specified kinds of risk, muddle, blind alley, waste, etc. But carefully keeping away from this cliff and from that morass leaves the rest of the countryside open for us to walk lightheartedly in. If I teach you even twenty kinds of things that would make your sonnet a bad sonnet or your argument a bad argument, I have still left you an indefinite amount of elbowroom within which you can construct your own sonnet or argument, and this sonnet or argument of yours, whether brilliant or ordinary or weak, will at least be free of faults of those twenty kinds.

There exists in some quarters the sentimental idea that the teacher who teaches his pupils how to do things is hindering them, as if his apron-strings coerced their leg-movements. We should think of the inculcation of methods rather as training the pupils to avoid specified muddles, blockages, sidetracks and thin ice by training them to recognize these for what they are. Enabling them to avoid troubles, disasters, nuisances and wasted efforts is helping them to move where they want to move. Road signs are not, for the most part, impediments to the flow of traffic. They are preventives of impediments to the flow of traffic.

Of course we can easily think of silly ways of doing things which continue to be taught by grown-ups to children and adhered to by the grown-ups themselves. Not all methods are good methods, or all recipes good recipes. For example, the traditional ban on splitting the infinitive was a silly rule. But the gratuitous though trivial bother of conforming to this particular veto was negligible compared with the handicap that would be suffered by the child who had never been taught or had never picked up for himself any of the procedures for composing or construing sentences. He would have been kept back at the level of total infancy. He could not say or follow anything at all if, for example, he had not mastered conjunctions, or even verbs, and mastering them involves learning how *not* to make hashes of them.

How does one teach methods or ways of doing things? Well, there is no simple answer to this. Different arts and crafts require different kinds of disciplines; and in some one particular field, say drawing, one teacher works very differently from another. Sometimes a little, sometimes a lot can be told; there is much that cannot be told, but can be shown by example, by caricature and so on. But one thing is indispensable. The pupil himself must, whether under pressure or from interest or ambition or conscientiousness, practise doing what he is learning how to do. Whether in his exercises in the art he religiously models his strokes after Bradman, or whether he tries to win the praise or avoid the strictures or sarcasms of a feared, respected or loved coach, he learns by performing and improves by trying to better his own and his fellows' previous performances by eradicating their faults. The methods of operating taught to him become his personal methods of operating by his own criticized and self-criticized practice. Whether in spelling, in Latin grammar, fencing, arithmetic or philosophy, he learns the ropes, not much by gazing at them or hearing about them, but by trying to climb them—and by trying to climb them less awkwardly, slowly and riskily today than he did yesterday.

So far I have been, for simplicity, dividing the contributions of the teacher and the pupil by saying that the teacher in teaching how to so and so is teach- * ing a method or way of operating, while the pupil keeps his initiative by making his own, at the start somewhat arduous, because new, applications of that method. The teacher introduces the pupil to the ropes, but it is for the pupil to try to climb them.

But now we should pay some attention to the fact that pretty soon the pupil has become familiar with the quite general fact that for lots and lots of widely different kinds of operations—spelling, say, skating and bowling at cricket—there exist different *modi operandi*. There are spelling-mistakes and there are bowling-faults, and neither spelling nor bowling can go right unless these faults are systematically avoided. So now, when he undertakes an altogether new kind of operation, canoeing, say, he from the start expects there to be *modi operandi* here too. This too will be a thing that he will have to learn how to do, partly by learning how not to do it. But this time, it may be, there is no one to teach him, and not even any other canoeist to imitate. He has got to find out for himself the way, or anyhow a way, of balancing, propelling and steering his canoe. Well at first he tries a lot of random things, and nearly all of them end in immersion or collision; but he does after a time find out some ways of managing his craft. He may not achieve elegance or speed but he does find out how not to topple over and how not to run into obstacles. He is trained, this time purely self-trained, regularly to avoid some kinds of faulty watermanship. But it is because he had previously learned by practice, coaching and imitation the 'hows' of lots of other things such as tree-climbing, spelling and skating that he now takes it for granted that canoeing has its 'hows' as well which similarly can be learned by practice, trial and error, and looking for ways of avoiding the repetition of errors. Here, as elsewhere, he has to study in order to improve; but this time he has nothing to study save his own unsuccesses and successes.

His more reckless and impatient brother, though full of go, just makes a dash at it, and then another quite different dash at it, and learns nothing or almost nothing from the failures which generally result, or even from the successes which sometimes just happen to result. He is not a self-trainer.

The third brother is uninterested, slow in the uptake, scared or idle. He never chances his arm. He tries nothing, and so initiates nothing either successfully or unsuccessfully. So he never learns to canoe; never, perhaps, even regrets not having learned it or envies those who have. There is no question of his training himself in this particular art, or even, if he is a very bad case, of his being trained by anyone else; just as there was fifty years ago no real question of me training myself or of my being trained by anyone else in the arts of cricket or music.

The supreme reward of the teacher is to turn out from time to time the student who comes to be not merely abreast of his teacher but ahead of him, the student, namely, who advances his subject or his craft not just by adding to it further applications of the established ways of operating but by discovering new methods or procedures of types which no one could have taught to him. He has given to his subject or his craft a new idea or a battery of new ideas. He is original. He himself, if of a grateful nature, will say that his original idea just grew of itself out of what he had learned from his teachers, his competitors and his colleagues; while they, if of a grateful nature, will say that the new idea was his discovery. Both will be right. His new idea is the fruit of a tree that others had planted and pruned. It is really his own fruit and he is really their tree.

We started off with the apparent paradox that though the teacher in teaching is doing something to his pupil, yet the pupil has learned virtually nothing unless he becomes able and ready to do things of his own motion other than what the teacher exported to him. We asked: How in logic can the teacher dragoon his pupil into thinking for himself, impose initiative upon him, drive him into self-motion, conscript him into volunteering, enforce originality upon him, or make him operate spontaneously? The answer is that he cannot— and the reason why we half felt that he must do so was that we were unwittingly enslaved by the crude, semi-hydraulic idea that in essence to teach is to pump propositions, like 'Waterloo, 1815' into the pupils' ears, until they regurgitate them automatically.

When we switched from the notion of 'hydraulic injection' to the notion of 'teaching to' or 'teaching how to', the paradox began to disappear. I can introduce you to a way or the way of doing something, and still your actual essays in the exercise of this craft or competence are yours and not mine. I do not literally make you do them, but I do enable you to do them. I give you the *modus operandi* but your operatings or tryings to operate according to this *modus* are your own doings and not my inflictings and the practising by which you master the method is your exertion and not mine. I have given you some equipment against failing *if* you try. But that you try is not something that I can coerce. Teaching is not gate-shutting but gate-opening, yet still the dull or the scared or the lame calf does not walk out into the open field. All this does not imply the popular sentimental corollary that teachers should never be strict, demanding, peremptory or uncondoning. It is often the hard taskmaster who alone succeeds in instilling mistrust of primrose paths. The father may enlarge the child's freedom of movement by refusing to hold his hand, and the boxing-instructor or the philosophy-tutor may enlarge his pupil's powers of defence and attack by hitting him hard and often. It is not the chocolates and the sponge-cakes that strengthen the child's jaw-muscles. They have other virtues, but not this one.

Philip W. Jackson, "Real Teaching"

There used to be a game show on television some years back whose format was as simple and straightforward as it was entertaining. The show's panelists—four "TV personalities" as they are usually called—were introduced to successive trios of strangers, each made up of one person who worked at some unusual occupation such as taming lions or cutting diamonds, plus two others of the same sex and supposedly the same name who claimed to be similarly employed but were actually imposters. The point of the game was to identify the honest member of each trio by asking all three of them questions about the line of work in which they claimed to be engaged. When the time limit for questions had been reached and each of the contestants had made a guess as to which of the three was telling the truth, the show's announcer would call upon the real Mister or Miss So-and-So to stand and be identified. Cries of surprise, followed by laughter and applause, crowned the departure of each trio of contestants.

That once popular show, called "To Tell the Truth," invariably comes to mind whenever my thoughts turn to the question of what teaching is like as an occupation and how it might be defined. It does so because the show's format reminds me of an experience I had some time ago as a newly appointed principal of a nursery school. That experience is itself worth describing in some detail, for it introduces in a rather dramatic if lighthearted way the questions to be examined in this chapter.

I was a newcomer to both school administration and nursery schools at the time. Consequently, in order to familiarize myself with the institution and how its teachers behaved I spent as much time as I could during my first few weeks on the job poking about the school as a complete stranger might, watching what was going on and trying to get a feel for the place. The teachers, who wanted to get to know me as much as I did them, warmly welcomed me to their classrooms. Their doing so made the experience as enjoyable as it was informative.

As the days wore on I slowly became aware of certain things the teachers did that distinguished them from the kinds of teachers I had spent most time with in the past—those with much older pupils. For example, I noticed that when nursery school teachers spoke to individual children or listened to what they had to say, they first descended to the child's height by bending at the knees until their faces were on a level with the child's own. At the same time, I was bemused to note, when I myself spoke or listened to a child I tended to bend at the *waist* rather than the knees. As a result, I hovered above the tyke like some huge crane, causing him or her to gaze skyward and, if out of doors on a bright day, to shade the eyes while doing so.

I noticed also that when reading to pupils the nursery school teachers did something else both odd and amusing. They propped the books they were reading on their laps with the open pages facing the students. The reason for doing so was obviously to allow the children to see the book's illustrations. But what made such a natural thing so amusing to me was that it required the teachers to develop the knack of reading upside down!

These and other examples of what seemed to me to be characteristic behavior of nursery school teachers so intrigued me that I decided to share my discoveries with the teachers themselves. I thought it possible they might add to my store of examples. I also expected them to be mildly amused by my report on the outcome of my observations.

Broaching the topic over lunch one day, I rather casually announced that it seemed as though my observations around school were beginning to pay off. "I think I'm beginning to catch on to a few of the tricks of your trade," I began. "For example, I've noticed that when you teachers . . . " and then I described a few of the things I had seen, mimicking postures and gestures in a somewhat exaggerated way, just to add to the fun. I concluded by claiming that should the chance ever occur to pass myself off as a nursery school teacher, I now thought I knew enough to be easily mistaken for the real McCoy.

My mimicking of their behavior amused the teachers, as I had thought it would, and so did my boast at the end. But the latter, rather surprisingly, turned out to be more than simply amusing. It triggered a discussion that went on far past lunch, one that we returned to on several occasions in the ensuing months. The focus of that recurrent discussion was whether I or anyone else could indeed get away with impersonating a teacher without ever being found out and what it would mean, insofar as teaching is concerned, if that were to happen.

The teachers could easily imagine a person getting away with such a pretense for quite some time. They even conceded that I might succeed in doing it myself for a while. But the notion of someone pretending to be a nursery school teacher and *never* getting caught, was a condition they found puzzling. For if the person were never found out, they reasoned, shouldn't we at some point stop thinking of him or her as an imposter, even though this knowledge remains his or her own secret? Indeed, should the 'teacher' not at some point stop thinking of himself or herself that way? In short, when does the successful imposter actually become the real McCoy, or does that never happen? If not, why not?

A closely related question that we also discussed was whether the imposter had only to *behave* like a nursery school teacher in order to carry off the deception or whether there was more to it than that. Some of the teachers thought it would be necessary for the imposter to *think* like a nursery school teacher in order to *behave* like one. But that introduced the question of what it meant to think like a teacher. How does a nursery school teacher think?

The teachers and I went round and round in our discussions of these and other questions about teaching, all stimulated by my casual and, as I thought at the time, humorous observation that it might be possible to get by as a nursery school teacher without any formal training whatsoever. From that starting point, we soon discovered the paths of speculation fan out in many directions. Can one determine whether a teacher is genuine or a fake (or good rather than bad) simply by watching her or him? Can teaching be defined behaviorally? What does it mean to say that teaching in general or good teaching in particular can be defined in any way at all? Where might such a definition come from? Is it something discovered or decided upon? If the former, how is that accomplished? If the latter, who does the deciding? And so on.

As could be guessed, the teachers and I never did succeed in answering most of the questions we so enthusiastically and, I fear, naively wrestled with back then. Nor have I yet done so. But both individually and collectively we did develop some tentative notions about the directions in which a few of the answers might lie. For me at least, several of those tentative notions have since become convictions.

What are they? Insofar as they relate to the topic of this chapter, my convictions are three in number. The first says there is no such thing as a behavioral definition of teaching and there never can be. We can never simply watch a person in action and be sure that something called teaching is going on. The second, closely related to the first, says that our attempt to say when a person is or is not teaching is always an act of interpretation. We are forever "readers" of human action, seeking to determine which "reading" is correct from among those possible. The third conviction, one that follows on the heels of the first two, denies the possibility of our ever arriving upon an enduring definition of what it means to teach. In the remainder of this chapter each of those propositions will be treated in turn.

I.

To begin, let's return to my early days as a nursery school principal, wandering from class to class in order to learn what nursery school teaching was all about. Picture my going about that task. Do you imagine I was very puzzled about when a teacher was or was not teaching? I assure you I was not.

As I moved from one room to another I *saw* with my own eyes teachers teaching and I did not for a moment doubt my judgment. Teaching was what

I was witnessing, no doubt about it. One would have had to have been blind not to see it.

"But hold on now," as my conversations with the nursery school teachers later forced me to say to myself. "Is the observation of teaching really as simple and straightforward as that? What made me so confident that what I was witnessing every step of the way was something called teaching?"

Before answering those questions I must distinguish between two uses of the word "teaching." One treats it as an enterprise, the other as an activity.[1] When we speak of a person holding a job as a teacher we might describe him or her as now teaching in such-and-such a school or in such-and-such a city even though we know perfectly well that the person being talked about is at this moment home in bed (assuming it to be very late at night), or outside playing golf (if a Sunday afternoon). In other circumstances, however, when we say so-and-so is teaching, what we mean is that he or she is doing so at this very moment. In the first instance teaching is being treated as an enterprise, in the latter, an activity.

The former use of the term is obviously inclusive of the latter, for one would never describe a person as engaged in teaching as an enterprise if it were never true that he or she engaged in teaching as an activity. Nonetheless, the distinction is a useful one to keep in mind all the same.

Returning now to my feeling of confidence as I observed the nursery school teachers in action, we may ask again how I knew that what I was seeing were instances of teaching. Should someone have asked me that question at the time, I think I would have answered somewhat as follows:

> "Well, to start with, I know this is a school I'm in, right? I know these are class-rooms and I know the adults in these classrooms are either teachers or teachers' aids. (I also happen to know which are which.) I watch what the teachers are doing and I see that their doings are episodic in nature, which is to say, they do one thing for a while and then they do something else. These episodes are units—atoms, if you like—of teaching behavior. Seeing them, recording them, describing them to others (as I did over lunch), are easy enough to do. There is nothing difficult or mysterious about the process at all."

Most people would probably give such a common sense explanation or something very much like it in a similar circumstance. The notion that teach-

---

1. The distinction is more fully explicated in Paul Komisar's "Teaching: act and enterprise," C. J. B. Macmillan and Thomas W. Nelson (eds.), *Concepts of Teaching: Philosophical Essays* (Chicago: Rand McNally, 1968), 63–88.

ing is what teachers can be seen doing seems sensible enough as an observational guide. There are limits to such a principle, of course, but everyone seems to know what they are. For example, if the teacher stops to tie his shoes or take off his jacket, or if he steps out in the hall for a drink of water, most people would not think of describing such actions as instances of teaching behavior. Thus it is tacitly assumed by most observers that not *everything* a teacher does while on the job is classifiable as teaching, though *most* of it probably will be. Many of the actions to be excluded are easily agreed upon.

A somewhat more difficult distinction is called for by the teacher who is standing in front of the class with his or her arms folded, waiting for the noise to abate. Is she or he at that instant teaching or merely getting ready to teach? And what about the teacher who is monitoring seatwork or marking papers? Should those activities be counted as part of teaching as well?

Judgments about such matters seem to depend, in part, on why the teacher in question is being observed in the first place. A supervisor of student teachers, for example, might find it very important to comment on the way a trainee prepared the class for instruction. From his or her point of view, standing in front of the class with arms folded is very much part of a teacher's repertoire of attention-getting devices and therefore is definitely an aspect of teaching worthy of comment.

Contrast that situation with someone doing research on teaching via an observational device focusing exclusively on teacher-pupil interaction. Under those circumstances, coding would begin when instruction was actually underway. Until then, from the researcher's point of view, teaching had not yet begun.

These examples point to a well-known truth, that some of a teacher's actions are easier to classify as instances of teaching than are others. When a teacher is explaining something to students or demonstrating a skill that is later to be imitated, who can doubt that at that instant teaching is underway? Similarly, when teachers are listening to students or watching what they do, there seems little or no ambiguity about whether or not they are actually teaching.

It is when the interactions between teachers and students do not obviously bear upon what is to be learned that the greatest uncertainty arises. But even these ambiguous instances are often resolvable once the observer's purposes are known. What aspects of a teacher's behavior are to be counted as instances of teaching is a question whose answer depends on prior considerations having to do with the circumstances under which the question is raised in the first place.

An additional distinction related to how to talk about teaching introduces an argument with an interesting history in education and in philosophy as well. It has to do with whether we should keep separate the idea of teaching as an accomplishment from that of teaching as an effort, an attempt to do something.[2]

One way of managing this dispute would be to limit the use of the term "teaching" to its sense as something that has been accomplished. This would require that we insist on evidence that learning has occurred before we can acknowledge that teaching has occurred. John Dewey, for one, seems to have something like this in mind when he tells his readers that,

> Teaching may be compared to selling commodities. No one can sell unless someone else buys. We should ridicule a merchant who said that he had sold a great many of goods although no one had bought any. But perhaps there are teachers who think that they have done a good day's teaching irrespective of what pupils have learned. There is the same exact equation between teaching and learning that there is between selling and buying.[3]

Were we to take Dewey seriously on this point, it would affect the way we discussed what we saw when we observed teachers in action. The discovery that the students we had observed had learned nothing from their teacher would force us to acknowledge that the teacher had not been teaching, no matter what she might have appeared to be doing when we observed her. She may have been *trying* to teach, we might readily admit, but she wasn't actually teaching.

Under certain circumstances it makes good sense to restrict the use of the term in this way. It does so when it comes to what we would like to say about the activity, especially when we speak of teaching in the past tense. To say that Jones taught Smith how to swim but Smith learned nothing whatsoever about the sport does sound a bit peculiar, if not downright contradictory. It makes us want to counter with, "Well then, Jones didn't *really* teach Smith how to swim."

But note that if we insist upon this necessary connection between teaching and learning we then find it impossible to say with certainty that a person is teaching until after the fact—until evidence that learning has occurred is in hand. Lacking such evidence, all we can say as we watch teachers in action is

2. The distinction between words that describe our trying to do something and words covering our success in having done it was brought to the fore within philosophical circles by Gilbert Ryle in his influential book, *The Concept of Mind* (New York: Barnes and Noble, 1949). In that work Ryle distinguished between what he called "task verbs" and "achievement verbs." The former refer to things one is trying to do, the latter to things one has done. For example, "kicking" is a task verb, "scoring" an achievement verb. A similar distinction holds between treating and healing, hunting and finding, listening and hearing, and so forth. Teaching, as luck would have it, has come to be used in both senses, as something tried and as something accomplished, hence the confusion that plagues our understanding when it is not clear which of these senses applies.

3. John Dewey, *How We Think* (Lexington, Mass.: D.C. Heath and Co., 1933), 34–35.

that they *look* as though they are teaching, or perhaps, "They are definitely try-ing to teach." To put the matter somewhat differently, by too strict an insis-tence on the teaching-learning connection we automatically rule out the pos-sibility of unsuccessful teaching.

To qualify as an instance of teaching, if a teacher's actions *must* result in learning, then we are left with the question of what to call the same set of actions when such a result is not forthcoming. They can't be called instances of teaching that didn't work, for we have just ruled out that possibility. Treat-ing them as "tries," rather than "successes," allows us to declare that the teacher has tried to teach, which may be quite enough to say in many circumstances. Indeed, it could be that in everyday affairs that's what most people mean when they use the term. When we say, "Look, there's a person teaching," what we mean is, "There's a person trying to teach." The "trying to" is understood. Its omission is simply a kind of verbal shorthand.

To short-circuit an argument that seems to get more and more picayune as it goes along, most people would probably be content to have the phrase "trying to" tacked on to their descriptions of teachers in action wherever the word "teaching" appears. The cost of such a grammatical change seems a small price to pay for avoiding what could be an interminable debate. But note that by inserting such a qualifier in our speech we do not manage to sidestep the problem entirely. Indeed, we simply carry it with us. We may no longer face the question of how we know when a person is teaching, but we now must ask how we know when a person is *trying* to teach.

II.

We can answer that question with confidence, it would seem, in only one of two ways. Either we must have some prior knowledge of what trying to teach looks like, or we must trust the testimony of the person who says that is what he or she is doing. Let's look at the first possibility a little more carefully.

How did I know that the teachers I witnessed in the nursery school were trying to teach? Perhaps I possessed at the time some idea of what "trying to teach" looks like in general. The rest is simply a matter of matching the teach-ers observed with that prior conception. In other words, because those teachers were behaving in ways I recognized as being "teacherly," I confidently concluded that they were trying to teach. Is that the way my sense of recognition worked?

Something like that process must surely have been in operation, no doubt, but is it sufficient to explain my feeling of confidence? I think not. To under-stand why, consider the following situation.

A visitor to a school peeks through the window of a classroom door and sees a woman with chalk in hand standing before a group of approximately twenty-five young people seated at desks. The woman is gesturing toward a mathematical formula written on the blackboard. The visitor naturally concludes that he is witnessing a class in session; he is corrected by the principal, who happens by with the news that what is going on in that room is not a class at all but rather a rehearsal of a scene from the play, *The Prime of Miss Jean Brodie,* which the local drama society is putting on in a few days.

What does such an unlikely turn of events tell us about the problem of identifying an instance of someone trying to teach? Obviously, the observer who thinks he knows an act of teaching when he sees it can be fooled. People can pretend to teach. The whole scene can be make-believe. That rarely happens, of course, but it *could* happen and that's the important point. In other words, the identification of teaching can never be made on visual evidence alone. Something else is required, something having to do with the genuineness of the total situation.

Recall that when the hypothetical questioner asked why I was so confident in my judgment, I began by saying that I knew this was a school and these were classrooms and those people teachers and those students. I was confident, in other words, that I was not walking around a movie set, witnessing the filming of *Up the Down Staircase* or something like that.

There was even a touch of impatience in my answer, for my imaginary interrogator seemed to question the obvious. But my answer showed that my sense of confidence very much depended on a host of half-buried assumptions, beginning with the few I have mentioned and including many others as well.

Not only did I know what schools and classrooms and teachers were like, being able to recognize them on sight, and trusting my conviction that I was witnessing the real McCoy, but I also knew a reasonable amount about the ends those objects were designed to serve (or prepared to fulfill, as we would say of teachers themselves). I further knew something about their historical development, their political and social significance, and so on. In other words, the events I was witnessing were embedded within a cultural and historical context of which I was only partially conscious at the time, but one that infused them with meaning, all the same. That gave me confidence that I was witnessing an instance of teaching and not something else. Without that background of tacit understanding my feeling of confidence could never have arisen.

What I am saying here should remind us of the section of Chapter 1 that dealt with common sense and the role it plays in teaching. Here we seem to be saying that common sense (or "school sense," if that term is preferred) also plays an important role in our observations of teachers and in our talk about what they do. This extrapolation from what was said earlier should hardly come as a surprise, for there it was acknowledged that almost everything we do depends in large measure on common sense. But there is something additional being said here that is well worth highlighting.

The point to be noted is that teaching, like most other human actions, is not so much "seen" as it is "read." In other words, though we may feel that what we are witnessing in classrooms is as plain as the nose on our face (as I did during my wanderings about the nursery school), we feel that way thanks to the largely unconscious operation of a vast apparatus of understanding that we seldom bother to bring to the surface of awareness for close scrutiny.[4]

Here an illustration may help. Recall that I was impressed by the way the nursery school teachers lowered their whole upper torsos by bending at the knee when they wanted to speak to one of their pupils, whereas I bent over at the waist to achieve the same goal. The teachers' way seemed so much better than mine, so obviously superior as an adaptation to the difference in height between adult and child that I felt a little chagrined at not having thought of doing it that way myself. I "saw" immediately that it was a better way of doing things.

But was my sight as unaided by thought and reason as I felt it to be at the time? Did the superiority of the teachers' method require nothing but the naked eye to discern? Upon reflection, I realized that more than that was involved.

As a solution to the problem of how to move within speaking and hearing distance of a very small child, my way was just as good as the teachers', at least in physical terms. I could speak to the children and hear what they said just as well as they. What made their way superior was what the posture symbolized and what it might possibly communicate to the children.

Instead of the child having to crane his neck skyward, as he was forced to do when speaking to me, when his own teachers talked to him he was able to face them at eye level. That physical relationship was at once more intimate and less threatening than was my crane-like posture. It was also more egalitarian.

But why did I immediately see that as a better way of doing things? Who cares if a child has to crane her neck a little when talking to adults? Why should teachers worry about such things as creating an atmosphere of equality in the classroom?

The answers to such questions obviously call for more than meets the eye. They rest on assumptions built into my way of looking at what I saw in those classrooms. Alter those assumptions and my perception of the events alters with them.

---

4. A process similar to the one described here is treated in some detail by Michael Polanyi in his book, *Personal Knowledge* (Chicago: University of Chicago Press, 1958). Polanyi referred to these unarticulated forms of knowing as "tacit knowledge."

In other words, my response to what I saw was not nearly as automatic as I felt it to be at the time. What seemed blatant and obvious in the teachers' behavior was actually an interpretation of a fairly complicated sort. I not only saw what the teachers *did,* I also saw (or thought I saw) *why* they behaved as they did. In short, their actions made sense to me.

That sense was not a function of the stimulus properties of what I witnessed. Rather, it arose from prior understanding that I as an observer brought to the act of observing. Both the teachers and I knew the rules of the game, so to speak. That combination of tacit knowledge and *a priori* reasoning was what made possible my seemingly effortless "reading" of what appeared before my eyes in those nursery school classrooms.

This insight, which may not be much of a revelation to most people, is obviously not limited to what happens when we look at teachers. The same holds true when we observe anything in the world around us. In short, the meaning and significance of everything we see and hear is, in essence, an interpretation of the information provided by the senses.

Oddly enough, though the interpretative nature of our perceptual encounters with the world is clear enough when we pause to think about how we make sense of things, we tend to lose sight of it much of the time. We become so used to so many common sights and sounds that we no longer experience them as being in any way problematic. We know what they are and what they mean, just by looking at them—the way I looked and listened in those nursery school classrooms some years back. Once we are sufficiently familiar with an object or an event, its meaning becomes transparent, enabling us to short-circuit the initial phase of our puzzling encounter with what we now know. We forget, in other words, that meanings are achievements, partial creations rather than givens, and we also lose sight of the fact that they are vulnerable to change.[5]

It is well that our minds work this way most of the time, for if we had to ponder afresh each thing we saw and heard, life would be more of a puzzle than most of us could stand. At the same time, we also need to recognize the importance of questioning, now and again, our habitual way of interpreting the world. By so doing we make a wager in which there can be no loser.

Either such questioning will alter the way we see things, in a manner that is somehow more satisfying than our former view, or it will deepen our commitment to the interpretation we have already put upon reality. We stand to

5. The notion that our conception of reality is a "construction" rather than a "given" plays a large part in the branch of social science known as "the sociology of knowledge." For an influential statement of recent thinking in this field see Peter L. Burger and Thomas Luchmann, *The Social Construction of Reality* (Garden City, N.Y.: Doubleday, 1966). The classic statement of this position is to be found in the essays of Karl Mannheim. See Paul Kecskemeti, (ed.) *Essays on the Sociology of Knowledge* (New York: Oxford University Press, 1952).

win either way. The task of looking at the familiar as if it were once again strange is far from easy. Some would call it impossible.[6] But the potential benefits more than repay the effort involved.

To relate this to teachers and teaching we need only acknowledge that teachers are no less caught up in the task of interpreting what goes on around them than are any of the rest of us. They too are faced with the unending chore of attaching meaning and significance to what they see and hear as they go about their work as teachers. That acknowledgment may sound innocent enough perhaps, but its consequences are considerable, not only for the way we look at teachers but also for the way they look at themselves.[7]

The observation that teachers are caught up in interpreting what goes on around them does not distinguish them from anyone else. Moreover, even when we consider the content of what they are called upon to interpret, we find an enormous overlap between the experience of teachers and that of the rest of us. As we have already noted, at the simplest level teachers need to know what chairs and tables and doors and countless other objects are for, just as the rest of us do. They must also recognize the significance of innumerable social actions—gestures, speech, and the like—as must we all. Given this shared interpretive obligation, we may wonder whether there is anything at all distinctive or unique about the way teachers view their surroundings. In short, is there anything like a pedagogical outlook on things, a "teacherly" way of viewing the world?[8]

When we recognize the great variety of teachers the world over, it is hard to imagine that such a diverse group might be bound together by any single perspective on their work, an outlook that would characterize them all. At the same time, by staying at a rather low level of generalization and by focusing on perception alone, we can observe distinctions between the ways "experts" and "laymen" look at things that would seem to hold true for the difference between teachers and nonteachers as well.

For example, other things being equal, we might expect the expert's view to be more differentiated than that of the layman. We would expect him or her to have a "finer" than ordinary perception of the object of his expertise, to see it in greater detail. We would also expect such a person to have a "quicker"

---

6. The question of whether and how to recapture the freshness of vision we once had as children is a topic of great interest to many, from the Romantic poets of the nineteenth century to many of today's psychotherapists.

7. This point is made with considerable force in Elliot W. Eisner's *The Educational Imagination* (New York: Macmillan Publishing Co., 1979). See in particular Chapter 9, "On the Art of Teaching."

8. This question is treated in an intriguing manner in J. M. Stephens, *The Process of Schooling: A Psychological Examination* (New York: Holt, Rinehart and Winston, 1967). Stephens hypothesizes that people with certain proclivities and impulses, such as the proclivity to detect errors and the impulse to correct them, are naturally drawn to teaching.

vision as well, to be able to take in a lot of information at a glance, homing in quickly on features worthy of special attention. We would expect the expert to have an eye for irregularities and trouble spots. We would also expect him to see opportunities missed by others. He or she would be expected to be more "future-oriented," to see possibilities where others see none.

We would also expect the expert to see things in perspective, to know, for example, whether to treat something with perspective or more routinely. In other words, we would not expect the expert to get "rattled" by the unexpected quite as easily as might the layman. In sum, we normally expect the expert to be more thoughtful than the nonexpert about things, not in the sense of thinking *more*, but rather in the sense of thinking *differently*. Moreover, this thoughtfulness can be reflected in a variety of ways.

As applied to teachers and teaching, this set of expectations yields an image of the seasoned teacher that distinguishes him or her, at least in principle, from laymen in general and possibly even from novice teachers. Expert teachers "see more" than do nonexperts. They are alive to the latent pedagogical possibilities in the events they witness. Within a classroom setting, they anticipate what is going to happen. They can spot an inattentive student a mile off. They can detect signs of incipient difficulty. Their senses are fully tuned to what is going on around them. They are not easily rattled. As younger students sometimes swear is true, they behave as though they had eyes in the back of their heads.

Is this image of expert teaching accurate? Are all seasoned teachers really like that? Are any of them? In short, are we talking about what is or what ought to be?

The quick sketch given here admittedly comes closer to the "ought" than the "is" of teachers and teaching. At the same time, it is not entirely a fiction. It reminds me sufficiently of teachers I have known that I will defend it as a model realizable in the here and now.

But even more important than whether many or most teachers come to resemble our hypothetical expert, how does such a perspective on teaching address the array of questions treated in this chapter? Of special interest is what it seems to say about the relationship between what a teacher *does* and what he or she *thinks*.

I now return for a final time to the rather lighthearted discussions that took place in the nursery school, and readily admit, though it should be abundantly obvious, that I knew all along a person could not become a nursery school teacher simply by learning how to hold a book while reading a story to children or by bending this way or that while talking or listening to a small child. The teachers knew that as well, of course, which explains their willingness to go along with the fun. They knew, and I knew, that to be a real nursery school teacher one had to see and to react in a certain spirit or manner to a special portion of the world—rooms full of three- and four-year-olds. Specific skills, such as knowing how to make playdough or how to bandage a cut knee, had an important place in that world, as we might expect them to, but to mistake such skills for the heart of the matter, as my lunchtime boast seemed to do, was—well, just laughable, that's all.

Is the situation drastically different with other types of teaching? My own experience in colleges and universities leads me to say no. There too the difference between the novice (who for rhetorical purposes has been likened to an imposter) and his or her more experienced colleagues turns out to be less a matter of skill than one of feeling and acting at home within a particular instructional milieu.

This sense of "being at home" in the classroom is hard to specify, I admit, but as a psychological state it is quite genuine all the same. One of the nursery school teachers nearly referred to it directly when she said, "Well, even if the imposter never gives himself away, *he* knows he doesn't belong there."

III.

The final question to be raised in this chapter is the one toward which my discussion with the nursery school teachers pointed but never reached: Is there some ultimate, non-modifiable definition of teaching (*true* teaching, let's call it) that we can discover through empirical and / or logical maneuvering?

We need first to acknowledge that the question is academic, in the sense that teachers themselves seem not to worry about it very much. Except when prodded by one of their instructors while in training or by a school administrator with nothing better to do, most teachers I have known seldom wonder aloud about the *true* meaning of teaching. Like other kinds of practitioners the world over, they usually are too busy doing what they have to do to worry about formal definitions of their practice.

Yet there are groups of people—educational philosophers among them— who do have time for such matters and who look upon it as part of their professional responsibility to answer the definitional question, whether practicing teachers are interested or not. Moreover, the answers they offer are more than academic exercises. These answers appear in textbooks and other "official" documents where they may potentially influence how teachers and others think about teaching.

This is hardly the place to examine all such efforts in detail. However, I would like to touch upon three different approaches to the task of determining once and for all what teaching is or should be. In my judgment, each of the three is seriously flawed, yet each builds from a foundational premise that in certain respects is quite appealing. Each strikes me as contributing to an understanding of why the search for a final logically airtight definition of teaching is not only a futile undertaking but may even be harmful if allowed to legislate what teachers themselves must believe about their work.

I will call these three approaches to the definition of teaching the *generic*, the *epistemic*, and the *consensual*. The meaning of those terms will become clear in the exposition to follow.

What I call a *generic* approach to the definition of teaching works like this: It begins by insisting that there be an important difference between a definition of teaching, on the one hand, and the performance of teaching on the other. This distinction is important, for it divides the labor of speaking authoritatively about teaching between two groups of professionals—educational philosophers and educational researchers. From this point of view it is the job of the philosophers to propose a definition of teaching that is sufficiently general to cover whatever future research might discover about the right *way* to teach. The job of researchers, in turn, is to discover answers to questions about how teaching should proceed. The result of the former effort will be singular and universal; that of the latter, plural and particular. Here is the way one well-known educational philosopher, B. O. Smith, poses the problem and then goes on to solve it.

> "The way in which teaching is or can be performed," Smith tells us, "is mistaken for teaching itself. In its generic sense, teaching is a system of actions intended to induce learning. So defined, teaching is everywhere the same, irrespective of the cultural context in which it occurs. But these actions may be performed differently from culture to culture or from one individual to another within the same culture, depending on the state of knowledge about teaching and the teacher's pedagogical knowledge and skill. Didactics, or the science and art of teaching, are not the same as the actions which they treat. A definition of teaching as such, which packs a set of biases about how these actions are to be conducted, confuses teaching with its science and its art."[9]

This approach has a degree of common sense about it that must be acknowledged at the start. Teaching may be variably performed, that much is certainly true. Thus it makes good sense to seek a definition of teaching that is flexible but not so broad that it embraces everything under the rubric of "teaching." The question is whether Smith's definition of teaching as a system of actions intended to induce learning fits the bill. I fear it does not.

Consider, for instance, the giving of medicine to a hyperactive child in order to calm him or her down so that she or he might benefit from instruction.

9. B. Othanel Smith, "A concept of teaching," in B. Othanel Smith and Robert H. Ennis (eds.), *Language and Concepts in Education* (Chicago: Rand McNally, 1961), 87–88.

This certainly must be acknowledged as a system of actions intended to induce learning, must it not? But is it an instance of teaching? I suspect few would be willing to consider it so.

And what of the work of school administrators? Much of what they do would certainly conform to Smith's generic definition of teaching. But, again, who would want to call most principals or superintendents teachers? I for one would not, and once again, I suspect most people would agree.

So Smith's generic definition of teaching, if I understand it correctly, is far too broad to be of much use. All of teaching fits within it, sure enough, but so do many other activities that we do not want to confuse with teaching.

And even if the definition could be tightened to exclude those activities we do not want,[10] it is still hard to imagine that such a definition might be useful in practice. Suppose we could define teaching generically—that is, say nothing about how teaching should be done but differentiate between teaching and all other activities. What would we do with such a definition once we had it? What questions of consequence would it help to answer? That I can think of none may reflect nothing more than my lack of imagination, but it is enough to leave me dubious about the promise of a *generic* approach to the definition of teaching.

An *epistemic*, as contrasted with a *generic*, definition of teaching links the activity to the concept of knowledge propounded by most modern epistemologists. In this view, knowledge is understood to be "evidentially supported belief." If we add to that understanding the corollary that teaching is primarily concerned with the transmission of such knowledge, we can begin to see that it *logically entails* certain kinds of actions and not others.

For example, it obliges teachers to provide grounds or reasons for the beliefs they seek to inculcate in their students. It requires them to be respectful of the truth and to be prepared at all times to reevaluate their own beliefs in the light of new evidence and in the face of fresh argument. It also demands that they seek to develop in each student his or her own capacity to test the worthiness of everything taught.

These obligations have nothing to do with personal choice or preference. Like a geometer's proof, they flow naturally from the starting premises of the argument, which say that teaching has to do with the spread of knowledge as contemporaneously defined and with the conditions conducive to that end.

From those same premises there follows a list of "don'ts" as well as "dos." Teachers committed to viewing knowledge as "evidentially supported belief"

---

10. One way to do so would be to restrict the meaning of the verb "induce" to that of "moving by persuasion or influence." But even this narrowing of normal usage seems to leave the definitional door too far ajar.

are also obliged not to intimidate, or threaten, or lie, or propagandize. They are sworn to avoid at all costs anything known to be inimical to the conduct of human inquiry and to the motivational spirit which animates it. Should they violate either set of these obligations, the positive or the negative, they step beyond the parameters of teaching as circumscribed by an epistemic definition.

This approach to a definition of teaching is attractive in several ways. To begin with, it is more philosophically sophisticated than is the generic approach. It does not so readily embrace features that teaching shares with many other activities. Instead, it tries to identify what is unique to teaching, what distinguishes it from all or almost all other activities. Also, it speaks out on behalf of a conception of teaching that has many supporters, both within the profession and outside of it. The teacher as a purveyor of knowledge, in the sense explicated, is an ancient and honored image of what teachers and teaching are all about.

At the same time, the epistemic view is not without difficulties of its own. For one thing, it does not address educational goals that are only indirectly associated with the transmission of knowledge. It may well be that the development of attitudes, interests, values, and the like can be reduced to knowledge of one sort or another, but I doubt that many teachers regard those goals in that way.

Finally, the epistemic approach to a definition of teaching leaves us in an awkward position with respect to teachers, past and present, who did and do indeed indoctrinate, intimidate, propagandize, and goodness knows what else, thinking it quite proper to do so.[11] What shall we say of them? Here is an answer given by Thomas Green, another educational philosopher, who is at the same time a strong advocate of an epistemic approach to the definition of teaching.

> Lying, propagandizing, slander and threat of physical violence are not teaching activities, although they may be ways of influencing persons' beliefs or shaping their behavior. We know *in fact* that these activities are excluded from the concept of teaching with as much certainty as we know that training and instruction are included. [Emphasis added][12]

> It is a matter of no consequence that there have been societies which have extended the concept of teaching . . . [to include such practices] . . . That propaganda, lies, threats, and intimidation have been used as methods of education is

---

11. For a powerful statement on behalf of teachers as indoctrinators and propagandizers, see George C. Counts, *Dare the Schools Build a New Social Order?* (New York: John Day Co., 1932).

12. Thomas F. Green, "A typology of the teaching concept." In Macmillan and Nelson, *Concepts of Teaching*, 36–37. (Italics added.)

not doubted. But the conclusion warranted by this fact is not that teaching includes such practices, but that education may. Propaganda, lies, threats are more or less effective means of influencing and shaping beliefs and patterns of behavior. It follows that teaching is not the only method of education. It does not follow that the use of propaganda, lies and threats are methods of teaching.[13]

We can treat undesirable actions on the part of teachers as instances of nonteaching, but one wonders what we gain by such a move. What it does, so far as I can tell, is sweep an interesting question under the rug, that question being: Why might teachers, past and present, have put such tactics to use in the first place? To imply that they did so out of ignorance, that they lacked knowledge of the true meaning of teaching, seems a bit condescending, to say the least. It also begs the question of how or whether we can have a "true" definition of the term.

The third approach (I call it *consensual*) to the question of how to define teaching is close in spirit to the second, but more accommodating in tone and less rigidly tied to epistemological claims. It allows for many ways of teaching, but it seeks to distinguish between those that are *standard* and those that are *nonstandard*. Israel Scheffler, yet another educational philosopher, is an articulate spokesman for this point of view. "Teaching may, to be sure, proceed by various methods," Scheffler begins,

> but some ways of getting people to do things are excluded from the *standard range* of the term 'teaching.' To teach, *in the standard sense,* is at some points at least to subject oneself to the understanding and independent judgment of the pupil, to his demand for reasons, to his sense of what constitutes an adequate explanation. To teach someone that such and such is the case is not merely to try to get him to believe it: deception for example, is not a method or mode of teaching . . . To teach is thus, *in the standard use of the term,* to acknowledge the 'reason' of the pupil, i.e. his demand for and judgment of reasons, even though such demands are not uniformly appropriate at every phase of the teaching interval. [Emphasis added][14]

In what kind of society would Scheffler's version of teaching flourish? "It would be a place," he tells us,

> where the culture itself institutionalizes reasoned procedures in its basic spheres, where it welcomes the exercise of criticism and judgment, where, that is to say, it

13. Ibid., 37.
14. Israel Scheffler, *The Language of Teaching* (Springfield, Ill.: Charles C. Thomas, 1960), 57–58. (Italics added.)

is a democratic culture in the strongest sense. To support the widest diffusion of teaching as a model of cultural renewal is, in effect, to support something peculiarly consonant with the democratization of culture and something that poses a threat to cultures whose basic social norms are institutionally protected from criticism.[15]

So in the final analysis it is only in a democratic society, or one in the process of becoming so, that teaching in Scheffler's sense of the term can be carried on. His standard use of the term is consensual in the dictionary sense of "existing or made by mutual consent without the intervention of any act of writing." But the consenting parties, in Scheffler's view, must be like-minded in broad political terms.

The notion that teaching in its "truest" sense can be carried on only in a democratic society may be comforting to those of us who believe we live in such a society. But how fair is it to restrict by definition the idea of teaching to a particular political context? Is there not something a trifle chauvinistic about such a move?

Of course we should feel free to criticize the way teaching is carried out in societies other than our own, just as we should here at home. But I fail to see how it helps to approach this job of criticism armed with a definition that to start with rules out the possibility of our calling what goes on in nondemocratic countries "teaching." Scheffler dodges this question, at least in part, by his willingness to speak of *non-standard* teaching. Yet, reading his words carefully, I must conclude that what he means by the *non-standard* form of the activity is almost not teaching at all.[16]

There is much to be said for both the epistemic and the consensual approaches to the definition of teaching, as this brief exposition sought to make clear. Each rests on a premise that many of today's teachers are almost certain to find attractive. It makes good sense to think that teaching is centrally concerned with the transmission of knowledge, as the epistemic approach insists we do. It is also appealing to think that teaching is a kind of emancipatory activity, either sustaining a democratic society or paving the way for its emergence, as the consensual approach requires.

But in the final analysis both views turn out to be more limiting than edifying. We must ask, why should teaching be perceived solely in terms of its

15. Ibid., 59.
16. There is a real question whether it is possible to define teaching ontologically—in a way that speaks of its true meaning or essence—without also getting entangled with a definition that is axiological—one that involves the meaning of "good" teaching. For a discussion of this issue see W. A. Hart, "Is teaching what the philosophers understand by it?" *British Journal of Educational Studies* 24, number 2 (June 1976): 155–170.

contribution to the transmission of knowledge? And why must it be confined to the kind of teaching that typifies democratic societies (if any kind actually does)? But if we reject such limitations are we not forced back to a generic definition of the kind Smith proposed, one so general as to be useless? Not necessarily.

There is, I would suggest, a fourth approach to the question of how teaching is defined, an approach that I call *evolutionary*. The term comes from Stephen Toulmin, who describes such a view in the following way.

> A properly evolutionary way of dealing with experience obliges us to recognize that no event or process has any single unambiguous description: we describe any event in different terms, and view it as an element in a different network of relations, depending on the standpoint from which—and the purposes for which—we are considering it.[17]

What would be the consequences of looking upon teaching in this way? We begin by conceding that there is no unequivocal definition of teaching that holds for all time and all places. What we accept as a satisfactory view of the process today within our society may not be the definition agreed upon in another time or another culture. But that does not mean that everyone holding different views, whether in the past or the present, can now be called wrong. What such an evolutionary view commits us to is neither the truth nor the falsity of any single definition; rather, it is an attempt to locate teaching within what Toulmin calls "a network of relations." Its place within that network is its ultimate source of meaning and significance.

Lest this sound far too abstract to be of practical help, let us move closer to the everyday world of teaching to see what the possible consequences of such a view might be. First of all, it would put to rest all ontological questions of the kind I discussed with teachers during my early days as a nursery school principal—questions of who is real and who is fake, whether one is really teaching as opposed to doing something else that might resemble teaching but is not the genuine article, and so forth.

This does not mean that people could no longer lie about their teaching abilities or falsify their credentials to make people believe they have had training when they have not. In short, it does not eliminate the possibility of frauds and fakes within the ranks of teachers. It does help us see that what is fraudulent in such situations is not teaching *per se* but the claim to competence.

To put the argument in a nutshell, there is no such thing as "genuine" teaching. There is only an activity that people call teaching, which can be

17. Stephen Toulmin, "The charm of the scout," *New York Review of Books*, April 3, 1980, 38.

viewed from a variety of critical perspectives. Sometimes the criticism that teaching can undergo leads us to conclude that the person performing the activity, or claiming to be able to perform it, has deceived us in some way. Such deceptions are rare, we would hope, but they have been known to happen.

Of far more practical importance than anything involving "genuine" teaching are questions of "good" and "poor" teaching. What does an "evolutionary" view of the process enable us to say about that? It leads to the understanding that we can make few if any judgments about the quality of teaching without reference to the context in which the action takes place; "context" is understood to cover far more than the physical setting of the action. The phrase "cultural context" comes closer to the meaning being sought here. It includes the awarenesses, presuppositions, expectations, and everything else that impinges upon the action or that contributes to its interpretation by the actors themselves and by outsiders as well.

Consider this example. Teachers of approximately a hundred years ago routinely applied hickory sticks to the backsides of recalcitrant or misbehaving students, or so we are told. What shall we, today, make of that fact? Shall we think of our colleagues of years ago as having been poor teachers for behaving as they did?

I find that too hasty and harsh a judgment. Moreover, I see nothing to be gained by it. To learn something from the past it seems to me far more fruitful to ask why that particular practice (and others like it) have gradually died out. Such a question is also much more in keeping with what I am calling an "evolutionary" point of view. An understanding of the demise of the hickory stick yields a correlative understanding of why many related practices have disappeared as well.

But what about contemporary practice? Does an evolutionary and contextual outlook leave us powerless to criticize what goes on today? Does it get stalled at the level of "mere understanding," leaving the tough job of being critical and of taking a stand on issues to someone else?

Not at all. There is no incompatibility between understanding an activity and either approving or disapproving it. Here an example might help. Suppose we learn of a teacher who seeks to win a student over to his or her own point of view through deception of one kind or another. Does not such a practice surpass understanding and call for immediate censure? Scheffler, for one, would say so, for he explicitly tells us that "deception . . . is not a method or mode of teaching." But what if we learn that the teacher in question is none other than Jean Jacques Rousseau and the student his famous fictional creation, Emile?[18]

---

18. *Emile* is full of instances in which the teacher seeks to deceive his pupil in some way, to achieve what he alleges to be a pedagogical end.

In such an instance would we not be better advised to try to understand what Rousseau was up to and why he did what he did *before* we conclude that censure is in order? What applies to fiction holds in real life as well. Confronted with any instance of teaching we might either praise or blame, we must always ask: What are the circumstances of the case? Why were these actions undertaken?[19]

Our answers to such questions no more prevent us from censuring any particular teacher (or a whole nation full of them, if need be) than does an investigation of an alleged crime prevent us from punishing the criminal. Indeed, the process of deliberating on such matters resembles that of case law more closely than it does that of establishing the proof of a theorem in geometry or mathematics. What grows out of such a procedure is not a definition that will stand forever. Rather, it is an argument and its defense.[20]

Who are real teachers and what is real teaching? There are no such things, says the person who has adopted an evolutionary point of view. There are interpretations of events, including those in which teachers are the central actors. There are arguments that can be made on behalf of this or that teaching practice. Some arguments are better than others. Doubtless there are some practices that most of us teaching today would defend. Part of our professional responsibility is to get on with that defense. If we are lucky, as I was during my fledgling days as a nursery school principal, the task of deciding who is and who is not a teacher, though serious enough in the long run, will have its lighter moments as well.

19. For an interesting discussion of how the case study point of view has moved from medicine to ethical theory and has rejuvenated the latter, see Stephen Toulmin, "How medicine saved the life of ethics," *Perspectives in Biology and Medicine* 25, number 4 (Summer 1982): 736–750.

20. For an insightful treatment of the distinction between logical reasoning and the kind of reasoning employed in everyday argumentation, see Stephen Toulmin, *The Uses Of Argument* (Cambridge: Cambridge University Press, 1958).

Part III

FORMS AND WAYS OF TEACHING

If all of us teach, if teaching has many purposes, and if the nature and the meaning of teaching are very hard to specify exactly, we should expect that the forms and the ways of teaching are various. And indeed they are. They are nevertheless surprisingly few. When my children go off to school to inform their fellow classmates about something of importance to them, the class session reserved for this activity is called "show and tell," a pair of terms we have used in Part II to distinguish between certain aspects of ancient and modern understandings of teaching and learning. When my students in the interdisciplinary honors college where I teach interrogate one another about the courses they are taking, one of the first things they want to know is whether a given class is mostly lecture—a form of telling—or "discussion."

These three gerunds—showing, telling, and discussing—capture among them a huge number of the ways that we apparently teach in everyday life and of the literary forms that written representations of these ways of apparent teaching might assume. "Showing," for example, would surely include scientific experiments and demonstrations; illustrations, computer simulations, and schematic diagrams of the sort that often accompany instruction booklets; dramatizations, gesturings, and even "setting examples," both in the sense of setting out a concrete instance of a class of objects or abstract ideas, and in the sense of behaving in a manner that would and should inspire emulation. "Telling," in addition to lecturing, would surely include storytelling and the offering of advice and wise counsel, sometimes in the form of "sayings" or proverbs or aphorisms. Finally, "discussion" would include the kind of dialogues that we have already seen in the works of Plato and St. Augustine, interrogations that sometimes might be more aptly called examinations, and several other forms of carefully guided collective inquiries.

Under each heading, we can think of common activities that seem like forms of teaching but that might more appropriately be called "training" in Gilbert Ryle's sense of the word (Part II). For example, does so-called "programmed learning," an increasingly familiar process whereby a computerized program leads a "student" through a set of questions whose sequence varies in response to the student's own answers, also involve teaching in any sense of the word? Where is the teacher? Is the "program" the teacher? Or is the teacher the person who designed the program? And can such programs and their "questions" be said to have the same kind of depth that Eva Brann finds in the texts that she speaks about in the essay "Depth and Desire" that concludes Part IV? In an age in which "distance learning" is becoming increasingly popular at leading colleges and universities across the country, questions such as these are vitally important.

The readings in this section have been selected and arranged to raise again some of the questions we encountered in Part II about the nature of teaching by expanding our ideas of the ways and the forms of teaching. So, for example, Part III includes one sermon and three public orations. We encounter preaching and public speaking frequently in everyday life: here we consider these speeches as instances of teaching. We also witness and participate in many "discussions," though most of these do not involve teaching in any sense of the word. Several examples of "discussions" that do involve teaching appear in other parts of this book, ranging from Plato's *Meno* (Part II) at one extreme to the kindergarten conversations recounted by Vivian Paley (Part IV) at the other. This part offers two very different cases of question-and-answer discourse: the Reformer Martin Luther's catechetical instruction, and a Zen koan along with discourse and commentary.

Many of us spend a good deal of our time telling stories or listening to them. As with discussions, most stories that we hear in everyday life do not have much value as forms of teaching. Some stories, however, are designed to reveal truths that perhaps could not be revealed in any other way. As such, they are "teachings" in the highest and best sense of that word. Accordingly, Part III offers two kinds of such stories: parables and Hasidic tales.

Many of the Hasidic tales are stories of wise men offering advice and counsel to people in need or perplexity. We today, along with all human beings throughout the centuries, still long for memorable words of wisdom and good counsel about those things that matter to us. Most of us are not, however, members of religious communities that are as closely knit as those of Hasidic Judaism. By contrast to the Hasidic tales, our own culture offers us ready-made "teachings" about any and every subject or difficulty in the form of what might be the most popular genre of "teaching" in contemporary everyday life, the advice column. Accordingly, the last readings in Part III are a miscellaneous collection of proverbs and wise sayings from ancient religious traditions, together with some samples drawn from one of the best of the advice columns our culture has to offer.

We have selected most of our examples of forms and ways of teaching from materials that are part of religious traditions—Judaism, Christianity, and Zen Buddhism. This is not simply or even mainly because most forms of teaching were historically bound up with religious traditions, though we could construe many if not most of our secularized forms of teaching as variations upon one or another of those pedagogical practices that were originally religious in both substance and inspiration. Nor are our selections based simply upon the classical status of many of the readings. Rather, the texts offered here as examples of the various ways and forms of teaching have been selected primarily from religious traditions in order to provoke reflection upon a particular question about the nature of teaching.

We were left at the end of the last section wondering about how to distinguish genuine teaching from a number of activities that are akin to it, like those that Gilbert Ryle discusses as part of training. In the same section, Philip Jackson led us to wonder how to distinguish genuine teaching from a wide range of activities that are or might be a part of teaching but that are just as often not instances of teaching at all. The readings in this part of the book should lead us to consider once again what both Plato and St. Augustine have already invited us to ponder. Does all genuine teaching finally address and awaken the human spirit—that part of our souls that is in some sense in touch with those ultimate and possibly transcendent dimensions that give meaning to our lives? We need not be theists in order to answer that question in the affirmative. We need only believe that all acts of genuine pedagogy are parts of a larger whole, of a process that enables us to become what we most truly and finally are as human beings.

The first reading, the sermon from James Joyce's *A Portrait of the Artist as A Young Man*, gives us a vivid "portrait" of the human spirit that emerges directly from a powerful and elaborate religious tradition. We should notice as we read this engaging address the ways in which it instructs its audience about very complex theological matters in the course of moving the same audience toward repentance. It is designed to engage the heart, the soul, and the mind, largely through a series of startling images. It offers what one writer has called "education for salvation."

If the sermon is designed to prepare human souls for citizenship in the heavenly city, the next three speeches are designed to shape human beings for responsible membership in earthly ones. Both Pericles in the "Funeral Oration" and Lincoln in the "Gettysburg Address" stir the hearts even as they instruct the minds of their listeners in order to move them to deeds that are worthy of the fallen soldiers and of the ideals for which they fought. But both of these orations achieve something far more important: they actually transform human beings into citizens of a new and exalted city, for Pericles, and of a new nation, for Lincoln. Similarly, in his second inaugural address, Lincoln manages to accomplish in speech the very reconciliation between the North and the South that he is seeking to inspire in action. We should ask ourselves whether these speeches show us a kind of teaching that can transform the quality of civic life itself, not just the character of the individuals who constitute it.

The next two readings offer two strikingly different deployments of question-and-answer discourse. In the *Small Catechism,* both the questions and the answers have been composed by Martin Luther for the purposes of instruction in Christian doctrine. Many young people who are preparing themselves for the rite of confirmation of their Christian faith, a renewal of their baptism, memorize substantial portions of Luther's small catechism. Indeed, many religious "teachings" cast in question-and-answer form were designed originally with this express purpose in mind, namely, that learning would proceed largely through a process of "memory work." The practice of memorization as a part of learning has almost totally disappeared from contemporary culture, and many think it is educationally retrograde. Its proponents throughout the ages, however, have believed that truths first committed to memory will later blossom into "lived" truths and that they will in the meantime serve as a kind of spiritual treasure trove to be drawn upon in times of trouble or doubt. The philosopher William James, among several of his contemporaries, claimed that he was saved from suicidal despair in part by recalling certain Bible passages that he had once memorized.

The Zen koan and the question-and-answer discourse that follows it serve very different purposes. 'Koan' translated literally means "a record of a public discussion," and koans probably developed out of stories that praised the wisdom of various Zen masters. Many koans, like the one selected here, were designed to challenge and to break down accepted patterns of rationality through a process of extended meditation upon them. Since many readers may find this form of teaching very difficult to comprehend, the selection includes a commentary by the translator on the text of the koan and the discourse that follows upon it.

Of those ways of teaching that are familiar to most readers, the one most similar to the koan, at least in intention, is the parable. Jesus's parables were told in order to reveal things "hidden since the foundation of the world" by upsetting established understandings of basic ideas of justice and rationality.

These little stories are just as difficult to interpret with certainty as the koans, and they typically give us images of the shape of God's kingdom, a realm that is not only often at odds with our own but that is impossible to grasp in our world's terms. The parables recorded in the selection from Matthew 13 are less bewildering taken one at a time than they are taken together. And like koans, they seem fully comprehensible only to those who have undergone a long process of initiation or discipleship.

The several Hasidic tales included here are relatively more accessible, and as forms of teaching, they serve multiple purposes. These tales are legends that honor the great teachers and leaders (the zaddikim, the "proven ones") of communities of Hasidic Jews (Hasidism being a movement within orthodox Judaism that is exceptionally intense and devout). These tales serve as guides for conduct, they entertain, they attest to the righteousness and the wisdom of the zaddikim, and they help to initiate the young into a special way of life. Many of them contain a marvelous admixture of historical fact and "legendary reality."

The last three selections offer different forms and kinds of advice and counsel. The selection from the book of Proverbs contains several different forms of teaching: lyric poetry, allegory, and admonitory discourses. Much of the "proverbial" wisdom that is contained in the selection is phrased for purposes of memorization. The sayings of the desert fathers come from the early history of Christian monasticism and so from a way of life that will seem strange and even repugnant to many readers. Nevertheless, as the sayings themselves reveal, the advice that emerges from them is more often than not the outcome of fierce and protracted spiritual struggle. The last selection is taken from one of the best of our contemporary advice columnists, Judith Martin, better known as Miss Manners. Though the tone and the substance of her counsel seem initially far removed from the worlds of Proverbs and the desert fathers, Miss Manners regularly offers "teachings" about many of the same moral issues that bedeviled the monks of North Africa—matters of hospitality, friendship, restraint, and charity.

Do these several disparate ways and forms of teaching have anything at all in common? Most of them share what we might call "embeddedness," in that their full meaning and purpose can be fully comprehended only within a network of practices and beliefs that gives them both their strength and their validity. They are small parts of a way of life. The koan is part of an exceptionally disciplined set of monastic practices including meditation and obedience to a set of rules. The catechism is only one part of a whole set of church practices, including worship and schooling, that lead, in many Lutheran churches, to the rite of confirmation. Jesus told his parables to disciples most of whom never fully grasped either the shape of the kingdom that Jesus proclaimed or what it meant to be followers of his way. We can certainly make the same claim of embeddedness for the Hasidic tales, the sayings of the desert fathers, and the proverbs. Even the speeches of Pericles and Lincoln depend for their rhetorical force to some extent upon their social locations as parts of civic or religious practices like funeral services, cemetery dedications, penitential rituals, or inaugural ceremonies.

Judith Martin's advice column provides something of an exception to this shared quality of embeddedness. For we might ask by what authority, apart from her own considerable wit, wisdom, and good sense, she speaks in her teaching, and which set of practices or rituals or communities gives her teaching its ground and its meaning. Our best answer to this latter question would be to invoke the whole fabric of social practices called manners or etiquette. But having said this, we realize at once how shredded this fabric has become. Miss Manners' tone is so often one of outraged astonishment precisely because of the disappearance of manners and the absence of common standards of behavior. She offers her advice and counsel in newspapers. If there is a ritual involved, it is the daily one of reading the morning paper, perhaps one of the few remaining civic disciplines.

These similarities and differences among the several ways and forms of teaching suggest yet another possible characteristic of all genuine teaching—its integrity. By this we mean only to reformulate the social fact of embeddedness in moral and spiritual terms and thereby to clarify the earlier suggestion that all genuine teaching is part of a larger whole. Too often today there are almost no connections in human lives among work, home, school, and synagogue. And this means that there are no connections between on-the-job instruction, bedtime stories, classroom lectures and discussions, and ritual practices. For many people, there simply is no ultimate horizon that gives these several activities their sense and their purpose, just as there is no major community to which they finally belong. Instruction, training, questioning, and advising go on more than ever before, but an increasingly lower percentage of these activities can rightly be construed as genuine teaching.

In the wonderful story by Mark Twain (Part I) about the apprenticeship of the cub pilot, the boy's soul grew progressively divided against itself as the result of his education. He gained technical knowledge of the river at the expense of the awe and wonder he once felt for its beauty. A great separation grew up between the practical and the aesthetic, the material and the spiritual. Such division could not arise as the result of initiation into Zen Buddhism or into any number of religious communities that cultivate a sacramental understanding of the world. Whatever their several problems and difficulties, most religious traditions strive to see life whole. Might all genuine teaching, religious or not, strive mediately or immediately for this kind of spiritual integrity?

Readings in Part III

1. James Joyce, *A Portrait of the Artist as a Young Man* (New York: Viking Press, 1982), pp. 127–135. This is one of a series of sermons preached to a group of college boys who are on a spiritual retreat in honor of the patron saint of their college, Francis Xavier. Though fictional, the account is based very closely upon Joyce's own experience among the Jesuits. According to the story, after the sermon many of the boys went immediately to the college chapel in order to make their confessions.

2. Thucydides, *The Peloponnesian War,* translated by Rex Warner (New York: Penguin Books, 1982), pp. 143–151. This selection from Thucydides' history is his own rendition of Pericles' "Funeral Oration," delivered at the end of the first year of what became for Athens a protracted and finally devastating military conflict. It has long been regarded as among the four or five most exemplary pieces of political rhetoric in the West.

3. Abraham Lincoln, "Gettysburg Address." This speech delivered on November 19, 1863, at the dedication of the cemetery at Gettysburg accomplishes many of the same aims of Pericles in his funeral oration, but far more briefly and hence more memorably. One recent student of the address has suggested that those Americans who heard the speech became, by virtue of hearing it, citizens of a new nation.

4. Abraham Lincoln, "Second Inaugural Address." Lincoln delivered his second inaugural on March 4, 1865, a few weeks before he was assassinated. The words in the closing paragraph were hung out on banners and other signs of mourning throughout the Union.

5. Martin Luther, *Luther's Small Catechism* (St. Louis, Mo.: Concordia Publishing House, 1943), 39–43. Luther thought of his catechism as a handbook of Christian doctrine in question and answer form. This edition also contains Luther's instructions for heads of households as to how they should teach their families the six chief parts of Christian doctrine, which are listed in the selection that follows.

6. *The Sound of the One Hand: 281 Zen Koans with Answers,* translated with a commentary by Yoel Hoffmann (New York: Basic Books, 1975), pp. 47–51, 219–223. The Japanese edition of this book was first published in 1916. At the time, it created a considerable controversy, since it made public for the first time hundreds of koans and their answers that had been secretly transmitted

from masters to their pupils in the Rinzai sect since the origination of the koan-teaching system in Japan by Zen Master Hakuin during the early eighteenth century.

7. Matthew 13. This chapter of Matthew's gospel contains the most familiar and extended of Jesus' discourses in parables and about parables in the New Testament.

8. Martin Buber, *Tales of the Hasidim: the Early Masters,* translated by Olga Marx (New York: Schocken Books, 1947), pp. 50–55, 66, 90, 103, 127, 144, 146–147, 300–301. These tales were collected, retold, and edited by Martin Buber, who was himself one of the most eminent Jewish teachers of the twentieth century. Buber's own *Between Man and Man* contains some fine essays on the subject of education.

9. Proverbs 1–9. The book of Proverbs is a compendium of moral and religious teachings that were given to Jewish youth during the period after the Babylonian exile. The several forms of teaching contained in the selection include allegory, parables, maxims, and aphorisms.

10. Helen Waddell, editor and translator, *The Desert Fathers* (Ann Arbor: University of Michigan Press, 1947), pp. 76–77, 123–124. The sayings of the desert fathers have been reclaimed over the course of the last decade as sources of contemporary religious thought and piety. Readers may wish to consult, for example, the works of Roberta Bondi, especially *To Love as God Loves* and *To Love and to Pray.*

11. Judith Martin, *Miss Manners' Guide to Excruciatingly Correct Behavior* (New York: Warner Books, 1983), pp. 299–302. Miss Manners' advice has been widely syndicated for many years. She is known not only for her wisdom, but also for her wit and her often scornful observations about the state of manners and morals today.

James Joyce, *A Portrait of the Artist as a Young Man*

—This morning we endeavoured, in our reflection upon hell, to make what our holy founder calls in his book of spiritual exercises, the composition of place. We endeavoured, that is, to imagine with the senses of the mind, in our imagination, the material character of that awful place and of the physical torments which all who are in hell endure. This evening we shall consider for a few moments the nature of the spiritual torments of hell.

—Sin, remember, is a twofold enormity. It is a base consent to the promptings of our corrupt nature to the lower instincts, to that which is gross and beastlike; and it is also a turning away from the counsel of our higher nature, from all that is pure and holy, from the Holy God Himself. For this reason mortal sin is punished in hell by two different forms of punishment, physical and spiritual.

—Now of all these spiritual pains by far the greatest is the pain of loss, so great, in fact, that in itself it is a torment greater than all the others. Saint Thomas, the greatest doctor of the church, the angelic doctor, as he is called, says that the worst damnation consists in this that the understanding of man is totally deprived of divine light and his affection obstinately turned away from the goodness of God. God, remember, is a being infinitely good and therefore the loss of such a being must be a loss infinitely painful. In this life we have not a very clear idea of what such a loss must be but the damned in hell, for their greater torment, have a full understanding of that which they have lost and understand that they have lost it through their own sins and have lost it for ever. At the very instant of death the bonds of the flesh are broken asunder and the soul at once flies towards God. The soul tends towards God as towards the centre of her existence. Remember, my dear little boys, our souls long to be with God. We come from God, we live by God, we belong to God: we are His, inalienably His. God loves with a divine love every human soul and every human soul lives in that love. How could it be otherwise? Every breath that we draw, every thought of our brain, every instant of life proceed from God's inexhaustible goodness. And if it be pain for a mother to be parted from her child, for a man to be exiled from hearth and home, for friend to be sundered from friend, O think what pain, what anguish, it must be for the poor soul to be spurned from the presence of the supremely good and loving Creator Who has called that soul into existence from nothingness and sustained it in life and loved it with an immeasurable love. This, then, to be separated for ever from its greatest good, from God, and to feel the anguish of that separation, knowing full well that it is unchangeable, this is the greatest torment which the created soul is capable of bearing, *poena damni*, the pain of loss.

—The second pain which will afflict the souls of the damned in hell is the pain of conscience. Just as in dead bodies worms are engendered by putrefaction so in the souls of the lost there arises a perpetual remorse from the putrefaction of sin, the sting of conscience, the worm, as Pope Innocent the Third calls it, of the triple sting. The first sting inflicted by this cruel worm will be the memory of past pleasures. O what a dreadful memory will that be! In the lake of alldevouring flame the proud king will remember the pomps of his court, the wise but wicked man his libraries and instruments of research, the lover of artistic pleasures his marbles and pictures and other art treasures, he who delighted in the pleasures of the table his gorgeous feasts, his dishes prepared with such delicacy, his choice wines; the miser will remember his hoard of gold, the robber his illgotten wealth, the angry and revengeful and merciless murderers their deeds of blood and violence in which they revelled, the impure and adulterous the unspeakable and filthy pleasures in which they delighted. They will remember all this and loathe themselves and their sins. For how miserable will all those pleasures seem to the soul condemned to suffer in hellfire for ages and ages. How they will rage and fume to think that they have lost the bliss of heaven for the dross of earth, for a few pieces of metal, for vain honours, for bodily comforts, for a tingling of the nerves. They will repent indeed: and this is the second sting of the worm of conscience, a late and fruitless sorrow for sins committed. Divine justice insists that the understanding of those miserable wretches be fixed continually on the sins of which they were guilty and moreover, as saint Augustine points out, God will impart to them His own knowledge of sin so that sin will appear to them in all its hideous malice as it appears to the eyes of God Himself. They will behold their sins in all their foulness and repent but it will be too late and then they will bewail the good occasions which they neglected. This is the last and deepest and most cruel sting of the worm of conscience. The conscience will say: You had time and opportunity to repent and would not. You were brought up religiously by your parents. You had the sacraments and graces and indulgences of the church to aid you. You had the minister of God to preach to you, to call you back when you had strayed, to forgive you your sins, no matter how many, how abominable, if only you had confessed and repented. No. You would not. You flouted the ministers of holy religion, you turned your back on the confessional, you wallowed deeper and deeper in the mire of sin. God appealed to you, threatened you, entreated you to return to Him. O what shame, what misery! The Ruler of the universe entreated you, a creature of clay, to love Him Who made you and to keep His law. No. You would not. And now, though you were to flood all hell with your tears if you could still weep, all that sea of repentance would not gain for you what a single tear of true repentance shed during your mortal life would have gained for you. You implore now a moment of earthly life wherein to repent: in vain. That time is gone: gone for ever.

—Such is the threefold sting of conscience, the viper which gnaws the very heart's core of the wretches in hell so that filled with hellish fury they curse themselves for their folly and curse the evil companions who have brought them to such ruin and curse the devils who tempted them in life and now mock them and torture them in eternity and even revile and curse the Supreme Being Whose goodness and patience they scorned and slighted but Whose justice and power they cannot evade.

—The next spiritual pain to which the damned are subjected is the pain of extension. Man, in this earthly life, though he be capable of many evils, is not capable of them all at once inasmuch as one evil corrects and counteracts another just as one poison frequently corrects another. In hell on the contrary one torment, instead of counteracting another, lends it still greater force: and moreover as the internal faculties are more perfect than the external senses, so are they more capable of suffering. Just as every sense is afflicted with a fitting torment so is every spiritual faculty; the fancy with horrible images, the sensitive faculty with alternate longing and rage, the mind and understanding with an interior darkness more terrible even than the exterior darkness which reigns in that dreadful prison. The malice, impotent though it be, which possesses these demon souls is an evil of boundless extension, of limitless duration, a frightful state of wickedness which we can scarcely realise unless we bear in mind the enormity of sin and the hatred God bears to it.

—Opposed to this pain of extension and yet coexistent with it we have the pain of intensity. Hell is the centre of evils and, as you know, things are more intense at their centres than at their remotest points. There are no contraries or admixtures of any kind to temper or soften in the least the pains of hell. Nay, things which are good in themselves become evil in hell. Company, elsewhere a source of comfort to the afflicted, will be there a continual torment: knowledge, so much longed for as the chief good of the intellect, will there be hated worse than ignorance: light, so much coveted by all creatures from the lord of creation down to the humblest plant in the forest, will be loathed intensely. In this life our sorrows are either not very long or not very great because nature either overcomes them by habits or puts an end to them by sinking under their weight. But in hell the torments cannot be overcome by habit. For while they are of terrible intensity they are at the same time of continual variety, each pain, so to speak, taking fire from another and reendowing that which has enkindled it with a still fiercer flame. Nor can nature escape from these intense and various tortures by succumbing to them for the soul is sustained and maintained in evil so that its suffering may be the greater. Boundless extension of torment, incredible intensity of suffering, unceasing variety of torture—this is what the divine majesty, so outraged by sinners, demands, this is what the holiness of heaven, slighted and set aside for the lustful and low pleasures of the corrupt flesh, requires, this is what the blood of the innocent Lamb of God, shed for the redemption of sinners, trampled upon by the vilest of the vile, insists upon.

—Last and crowning torture of all the tortures of that awful place is the eternity of hell. Eternity! O, dread and dire word. Eternity! What mind of man can understand it? And, remember, it is an eternity of pain. Even though the pains of hell were not so terrible as they are yet they would become infinite as they are destined to last for ever. But while they are everlasting they are at the same time, as you know, intolerably intense, unbearably extensive. To bear even the sting of an insect for all eternity would be a dreadful torment. What must it be, then, to bear the manifold tortures of hell for ever? For ever! For all eternity! Not for a year or for an age but for ever. Try to imagine the awful meaning of this. You have often seen the sand on the seashore. How fine are its tiny grains! And how many of those tiny little grains go to make up the small handful which a child grasps in its play. Now imagine a mountain of that sand, a million miles high, reaching from the earth to the farthest heavens, and a million miles broad, extending to remotest space, and a million miles in thickness: and imagine such an enormous mass of countless particles of sand multiplied as often as there are leaves in the forest, drops of water in the mighty ocean, feathers on birds, scales on fish, hairs on animals, atoms in the vast expanse of the air: and imagine that at the end of every million years a little bird came to that mountain and carried away in its beak a tiny grain of that sand. How many millions upon millions of centuries would pass before that bird had carried away even a square foot of that mountain, how many eons upon eons of ages before it had carried away all. Yet at the end of that immense stretch of time not even one instant of eternity could be said to have ended. At the end of all those billions and trillions of years eternity would have scarcely begun. And if that mountain rose again after it had been all carried away and if the bird came again and carried it all away again grain by grain: and if it so rose and sank as many times as there are stars in the sky, atoms in the air, drops of water in the sea, leaves on the trees, feathers upon birds, scales upon fish, hairs upon animals, at the end of all those innumerable risings and sinkings of that immeasurably vast mountain not one single instant of eternity could be said to have ended; even then, at the end of such a period, after that eon of time the mere thought of which makes our very brain reel dizzily, eternity would have scarcely begun.

—A holy saint (one of our own fathers I believe it was) was once vouch-safed a vision of hell. It seemed to him that he stood in the midst of a great hall, dark and silent save for the ticking of a great clock. The ticking went on unceasingly; and it seemed to this saint that the sound of the ticking was the ceaseless repetition of the words: ever, never; ever, never. Ever to be in hell, never to be in heaven; ever to be shut off from the presence of God, never to enjoy the beatific vision; ever to be eaten with flames, gnawed by vermin, goaded with burning spikes, never to be free from those pains; ever to have the conscience upbraid one, the memory enrage, the mind filled with darkness and despair, never to escape; ever to curse and revile the foul demons who gloat fiendishly over the misery of their dupes, never to behold the shining raiment of the blessed spirits; ever to cry out of the abyss of fire to God for an instant, a single instant, of respite from such awful agony, never to receive, even for an instant, God's pardon; ever to suffer, never to enjoy; ever to be damned, never to be saved; ever, never; ever, never. O what a dreadful punishment! An eternity of endless agony, of endless bodily and spiritual torment, without one ray of hope, without one moment of cessation, of agony limitless in extent, limit-less in intensity, of torment infinitely lasting, infinitely varied, of torture that sustains eternally that which it eternally devours, of anguish that everlastingly preys upon the spirit while it racks the flesh, an eternity, every instant of which is itself an eternity, and that eternity an eternity of woe. Such is the terrible pun-ishment decreed for those who die in mortal sin by an almighty and a just God.

—Yes, a just God! Men, reasoning always as men, are astonished that God should mete out an everlasting and infinite punishment in the fires of hell for a single grievous sin. They reason thus because, blinded by the gross illusion of the flesh and the darkness of human understanding, they are unable to com-prehend the hideous malice of mortal sin. They reason thus because they are unable to comprehend that even venial sin is of such a foul and hideous nature that even if the omnipotent Creator could end all the evil and misery in the world, the wars, the diseases, the robberies, the crimes, the deaths, the murders, on condition that He allowed a single venial sin to pass unpunished, a single venial sin, a lie, an angry look, a moment of wilful sloth, He, the great om-nipotent God, could not do so because sin, be it in thought or deed, is a trans-gression of His law and God would not be God if He did not punish the trans-gressor.

—A sin, an instant of rebellious pride of the intellect, made Lucifer and a third part of the cohorts of angels fall from their glory. A sin, an instant of folly and weakness, drove Adam and Eve out of Eden and brought death and suffering into the world. To retrieve the consequences of that sin the Only Begotten Son of God came down to earth, lived and suffered and died a most painful death, hanging for three hours on the cross.

—O, my dear little brethren in Christ Jesus, will we then offend that good Redeemer and provoke His anger? Will we trample again upon that torn and mangled corpse? Will we spit upon that face so full of sorrow and love? Will we too, like the cruel jews and the brutal soldiers, mock that gentle and compassionate Saviour Who trod alone for our sake the awful winepress of sorrow? Every word of sin is a wound in His tender side. Every sinful act is a thorn piercing His head. Every impure thought, deliberately yielded to, is a keen lance transfixing that sacred and loving heart. No, no. It is impossible for any human being to do that which offends so deeply the divine majesty, that which is punished by an eternity of agony, that which crucifies again the Son of God and makes a mockery of Him.

—I pray to God that my poor words may have availed today to confirm in holiness those who are in a state of grace, to strengthen the wavering, to lead back to the state of grace the poor soul that has strayed if any such be among you. I pray to God, and do you pray with me, that we may repent of our sins. I will ask you now, all of you, to repeat after me the act of contrition, kneeling here in this humble chapel in the presence of God. He is there in the tabernacle burning with love for mankind, ready to comfort the afflicted. Be not afraid. No matter how many or how foul the sins if only you repent of them they will be forgiven you. Let no worldly shame hold you back. God is still the merciful Lord Who wishes not the eternal death of the sinner but rather that he be converted and live.

—He calls you to Him. You are His. He made you out of nothing. He loved you as only a God can love. His arms are open to receive you even though you have sinned against Him. Come to Him, poor sinner, poor vain and erring sinner. Now is the acceptable time. Now is the hour.

Pericles, "Funeral Oration"

In the same winter the Athenians, following their annual custom, gave a public funeral for those who had been the first to die in the war. These funerals are held in the following way: two days before the ceremony the bones of the fallen are brought and put in a tent which has been erected, and people make whatever offerings they wish to their own dead. Then there is a funeral procession in which coffins of cypress wood are carried on wagons. There is one coffin for each tribe, which contains the bones of members of that tribe. One empty bier is decorated and carried in the procession: this is for the missing, whose bodies could not be recovered. Everyone who wishes to, both citizens and foreigners, can join in the procession, and the women who are related to the dead are there to make their laments at the tomb. The bones are laid in the public burial-place, which is in the most beautiful quarter outside the city walls. Here the Athenians always bury those who have fallen in war. The only exception is those who died at Marathon, who, because their achievement was considered absolutely outstanding, were buried on the battlefield itself.

When the bones have been laid in the earth, a man chosen by the city for his intellectual gifts and for his general reputation makes an appropriate speech in praise of the dead, and after the speech all depart. This is the procedure at these burials, and all through the war, when the time came to do so, the Athenians followed this ancient custom. Now, at the burial of those who were the first to fall in the war Pericles, the son of Xanthippus, was chosen to make the speech. When the moment arrived, he came forward from the tomb and, standing on a high platform, so that he might be heard by as many people as possible in the crowd, he spoke as follows:

'Many of those who have spoken here in the past have praised the institution of this speech at the close of our ceremony. It seemed to them a mark of honour to our soldiers who have fallen in war that a speech should be made over them. I do not agree. These men have shown themselves valiant in action, and it would be enough, I think, for their glories to be proclaimed in action, as you have just seen it done at this funeral organized by the state. Our belief in the courage and manliness of so many should not be hazarded on the goodness or badness of one man's speech. Then it is not easy to speak with a proper sense of balance, when a man's listeners find it difficult to believe in the truth of what one is saying. The man who knows the facts and loves the dead may well think that an oration tells less than what he knows and what he would like to hear: others who do not know so much may feel envy for the dead, and think the orator over-praises them, when he speaks of exploits that are beyond their own capacities. Praise of other people is tolerable only up to a certain point, the point where one still believes that one could do oneself some of the things one is hearing about. Once you get beyond this point, you will find people becoming jealous and incredulous. However, the fact is that this institution was set up and approved by our forefathers, and it is my duty to follow the tradition and do my best to meet the wishes and the expectations of every one of you.

'I shall begin by speaking about our ancestors, since it is only right and proper on such an occasion to pay them the honour of recalling what they did. In this land of ours there have always been the same people living from generation to generation up till now, and they, by their courage and their virtues, have handed it on to us, a free country. They certainly deserve our praise. Even more so do our fathers deserve it. For to the inheritance they had received they added all the empire we have now, and it was not without blood and toil that they handed it down to us of the present generation. And then we ourselves, assembled here today, who are mostly in the prime of life, have, in most directions, added to the power of our empire and have organized our State in such a way that it is perfectly well able to look after itself both in peace and in war.

'I have no wish to make a long speech on subjects familiar to you all: so I shall say nothing about the warlike deeds by which we acquired our power or the battles in which we or our fathers gallantly resisted our enemies, Greek or foreign. What I want to do is, in the first place, to discuss the spirit in which we faced our trials and also our constitution and the way of life which has made us great. After that I shall speak in praise of the dead, believing that this kind of speech is not inappropriate to the present occasion, and that this whole assembly, of citizens and foreigners, may listen to it with advantage.

'Let me say that our system of government does not copy the institutions of our neighbours. It is more the case of our being a model to others, than of our imitating anyone else. Our constitution is called a democracy because power is in the hands not of a minority but of the whole people. When it is a question of settling private disputes, everyone is equal before the law; when it is a question of putting one person before another in positions of public responsibility, what counts is not membership of a particular class, but the actual ability which the man possesses. No one, so long as he has it in him to be of service to the state, is kept in political obscurity because of poverty. And, just as our political life is free and open, so is our day-to-day life in our relations with each other. We do not get into a state with our next-door neighbour if he enjoys himself in his own way, nor do we give him the kind of black looks which, though they do no real harm, still do hurt people's feelings. We are free and tolerant in our private lives; but in public affairs we keep to the law. This is because it commands our deep respect.

'We give our obedience to those whom we put in positions of authority, and we obey the laws themselves, especially those which are for the protection of the oppressed, and those unwritten laws which it is an acknowledged shame to break.

'And here is another point. When our work is over, we are in a position to enjoy all kinds of recreation for our spirits. There are various kinds of contests and sacrifices regularly throughout the year; in our own homes we find a beauty and a good taste which delight us every day and which drive away our cares. Then the greatness of our city brings it about that all the good things from all over the world flow in to us, so that to us it seems just as natural to enjoy foreign goods as our own local products.

'Then there is a great difference between us and our opponents, in our attitude towards military security. Here are some examples: Our city is open to the world, and we have no periodical deportations in order to prevent people observing or finding out secrets which might be of military advantage to the enemy. This is because we rely, not on secret weapons, but on our own real courage and loyalty. There is a difference, too, in our educational systems. The Spartans, from their earliest boyhood, are submitted to the most laborious training in courage; we pass our lives without all these restrictions, and yet are just as ready to face the same dangers as they are. Here is a proof of this: When the Spartans invade our land, they do not come by themselves, but bring all their allies with them; whereas we, when we launch an attack abroad, do the job by ourselves, and, though fighting on foreign soil, do not often fail to defeat opponents who are fighting for their own hearths and homes. As a matter of fact none of our enemies has ever yet been confronted with our total strength, because we have to divide our attention between our navy and the many missions on which our troops are sent on land. Yet, if our enemies engage a detachment of our forces and defeat it, they give themselves credit for having thrown back our entire army; or, if they lose, they claim that they were beaten by us in full strength. There are certain advantages, I think, in our way of meeting danger voluntarily, with an easy mind, instead of with a laborious training, with natural rather than with state-induced courage. We do not have to spend our time practising to meet sufferings which are still in the future; and when they are actually upon us we show ourselves just as brave as these others who are always in strict training. This is one point in which, I think, our city deserves to be admired. There are also others:

'Our love of what is beautiful does not lead to extravagance; our love of the things of the mind does not make us soft. We regard wealth as something to be properly used, rather than as something to boast about. As for poverty, no one need be ashamed to admit it: the real shame is in not taking practical measures to escape from it. Here each individual is interested not only in his own affairs but in the affairs of the state as well: even those who are mostly occupied with their own business are extremely well-informed on general politics—this is a peculiarity of ours: we do not say that a man who takes no interest in politics is a man who minds his own business; we say that he has no business here at all. We Athenians, in our own persons, take our decisions on policy or submit them to proper discussions: for we do not think that there is an incompatibility between words and deeds; the worst thing is to rush into action before the consequences have been properly debated. And this is another point where we differ from other people. We are capable at the same time of taking risks and of estimating them beforehand. Others are brave out of ignorance; and, when they stop to think, they begin to fear. But the man who can most truly be accounted brave is he who best knows the meaning of what is sweet in life and of what is terrible, and then goes out undeterred to meet what is to come.

'Again, in questions of general good feeling there is a great contrast between us and most other people. We make friends by doing good to others, not by receiving good from them, This makes our friendship all the more reliable, since we want to keep alive the gratitude of those who are in our debt by showing continued goodwill to them: whereas the feelings of one who owes us something lack the same enthusiasm, since he knows that, when he repays our kindness, it will be more like paying back a debt than giving something spontaneously. We are unique in this. When we do kindnesses to others, we do not do them out of any calculations of profit or loss: we do them without afterthought, relying on our free liberality. Taking everything together then, I declare that our city is an education to Greece, and I declare that in my opinion each single one of our citizens, in all the manifold aspects of life, is able to show himself the rightful lord and owner of his own person, and do this, moreover, with exceptional grace and exceptional versatility. And to show that this is no empty boasting for the present occasion, but real tangible fact, you have only to consider the power which our city possesses and which has been won by those very qualities which I have mentioned. Athens, alone of the states we know, comes to her testing time in a greatness that surpasses what was imagined of her. In her case, and in her case alone, no invading enemy is ashamed at being defeated, and no subject can complain of being governed by people unfit for their responsibilities. Mighty indeed are the marks and monuments of our empire which we have left. Future ages will wonder at us, as the present age wonders at us now. We do not need the praises of a Homer, or of anyone else whose words may delight us for the moment, but whose estimation of facts will fall short of what is really true. For our adventurous spirit has forced an entry into every sea and into every land; and everywhere we have left behind us everlasting memorials of good done to our friends or suffering inflicted on our enemies.

'This, then, is the kind of city for which these men, who could not bear the thought of losing her, nobly fought and nobly died. It is only natural that every one of us who survive them should be willing to undergo hardships in her service. And it was for this reason that I have spoken at such length about our city, because I wanted to make it clear that for us there is more at stake than there is for others who lack our advantages; also I wanted my words of praise for the dead to be set in the bright light of evidence. And now the most important of these words has been spoken. I have sung the praises of our city; but it was the courage and gallantry of these men, and of people like them, which made her splendid. Nor would you find it true in the case of many of the Greeks, as it is true of them, that no words can do more than justice to their deeds.

'To me it seems that the consummation which has overtaken these men shows us the meaning of manliness in its first revelation and in its final proof. Some of them, no doubt, had their faults; but what we ought to remember first is their gallant conduct against the enemy in defence of their native land. They have blotted out evil with good, and done more service to the commonwealth than they ever did harm in their private lives. No one of these men weakened because he wanted to go on enjoying his wealth: no one put off the awful day in the hope that he might live to escape his poverty and grow rich. More to be desired than such things, they chose to check the enemy's pride. This, to them, was a risk most glorious, and they accepted it, willing to strike down the enemy and relinquish everything else. As for success or failure, they left that in the doubtful hands of Hope, and when the reality of battle was before their faces, they put their trust in their own selves. In the fighting, they thought it more honourable to stand their ground and suffer death than to give in and save their lives. So they fled from the reproaches of men, abiding with life and limb the brunt of battle; and, in a small moment of time, the climax of their lives, a culmination of glory, not of fear, were swept away from us.

'So and such they were, these men—worthy of their city. We who remain behind may hope to be spared their fate, but must resolve to keep the same daring spirit against the foe. It is not simply a question of estimating the advantages in theory. I could tell you a long story (and you know it as well as I do) about what is to be gained by beating the enemy back. What I would prefer is that you should fix your eyes every day on the greatness of Athens as she really is, and should fall in love with her. When you realize her greatness, then reflect that what made her great was men with a spirit of adventure, men who knew their duty, men who were ashamed to fall below a certain standard. If they ever failed in an enterprise, they made up their minds that at any rate the city should not find their courage lacking to her, and they gave to her the best contribution that they could. They gave her their lives, to her and to all of us, and for their own selves they won praises that never grow old, the most splendid of sepulchres—not the sepulchre in which their bodies are laid, but where their glory remains eternal in men's minds, always there on the right occasion to stir others to speech or to action. For famous men have the whole earth as their memorial: it is not only the inscriptions on their graves in their own country that mark them out; no, in foreign lands also, not in any visible form but in people's hearts, their memory abides and grows. It is for you to try to be like them. Make up your minds that happiness depends on being free, and freedom depends on being courageous. Let there be no relaxation in face of the perils of the war. The people who have most excuse for despising death are not the wretched and unfortunate, who have no hope of doing well for themselves, but those who run the risk of a complete reversal in their lives, and who would feel the difference most intensely, if things went wrong for them. Any intelligent man would find a humiliation caused by his own slackness more painful to bear than death, when death comes to him unperceived, in battle, and in the confidence of his patriotism.

'For these reasons I shall not commiserate with those parents of the dead, who are present here. Instead I shall try to comfort them. They are well aware that they have grown up in a world where there are many changes and chances. But this is good fortune—for men to end their lives with honour, as these have done, and for you honourably to lament them: their life was set to a measure where death and happiness went hand in hand. I know that it is difficult to convince you of this. When you see other people happy you will often be reminded of what used to make you happy too. One does not feel sad at not having some good thing which is outside one's experience: real grief is felt at the loss of something which one is used to. All the same, those of you who are of the right age must bear up and take comfort in the thought of having more children. In your own homes these new children will prevent you from brooding over those who are no more, and they will be a help to the city, too, both in filling the empty places, and in assuring her security. For it is impossible for a man to put forward fair and honest views about our affairs if he has not, like everyone else, children whose lives may be at stake. As for those of you who are now too old to have children, I would ask you to count as gain the greater part of your life, in which you have been happy, and remember that what remains is not long, and let your hearts be lifted up at the thought of the fair fame of the dead. One's sense of honour is the only thing that does not grow old, and the last pleasure, when one is worn out with age, is not, as the poet said, making money, but having the respect of one's fellow men.

'As for those of you here who are sons or brothers of the dead, I can see a hard struggle in front of you. Everyone always speaks well of the dead, and, even if you rise to the greatest heights of heroism, it will be a hard thing for you to get the reputation of having come near, let alone equalled, their standard. When one is alive, one is always liable to the jealousy of one's competitors, but when one is out of the way, the honour one receives is sincere and unchallenged.

'Perhaps I should say a word or two on the duties of women to those among you who are now widowed. I can say all I have to say in a short word of advice. Your great glory is not to be inferior to what God has made you, and the greatest glory of a woman is to be least talked about by men, whether they are praising you or criticizing you. I have now, as the law demanded, said what I had to say. For the time being our offerings to the dead have been made, and for the future their children will be supported at the public expense by the city, until they come of age. This is the crown and prize which she offers, both to the dead and to their children, for the ordeals which they have faced. Where the rewards of valour are the greatest, there you will find also the best and bravest spirits among the people. And now, when you have mourned for your dear ones, you must depart.'

Abraham Lincoln, "Gettysburg Address"

Four score and seven years ago our fathers brought forth on this continent, a new nation, conceived in Liberty, and dedicated to the proposition that all men are created equal.

Now we are engaged in a great civil war, testing whether that nation, or any nation so conceived and so dedicated, can long endure. We are met on a great battle-field of that war. We have come to dedicate a portion of that field, as a final resting place for those who here gave their lives that that nation might live. It is altogether fitting and proper that we should do this.

But, in a larger sense, we can not dedicate—we can not consecrate—we can not hallow—this ground. The brave men, living and dead, who struggled here, have consecrated it, far above our poor power to add or detract. The world will little note, nor long remember what we say here, but it can never forget what they did here. It is for us the living, rather, to be dedicated here to the unfinished work which they who fought here have thus far so nobly advanced. It is rather for us to be here dedicated to the great task remaining before us—that from these honored dead we take increased devotion to that cause for which they gave the last full measure of devotion—that we here highly resolve that these dead shall not have died in vain—that this nation, under God, shall have a new birth of freedom—and that government of the people, by the people, for the people, shall not perish from the earth.

November 19, 1863

Abraham Lincoln, "Second Inaugural Address"

Fellow Countrymen:

At this second appearing to take the oath of the presidential office, there is less occasion for an extended address than there was at the first. Then a statement, somewhat in detail, of a course to be pursued, seemed fitting and proper. Now, at the expiration of four years, during which public declarations have been constantly called forth on every point and phase of the great contest which still absorbs the attention, and engrosses the energies of the nation, little that is new could be presented. The progress of our arms, upon which all else chiefly depends, is as well known to the public as to myself; and it is, I trust, reasonably satisfactory and encouraging to all. With high hope for the future no prediction in regard to it is ventured.

On the occasion corresponding to this four years ago, all thoughts were anxiously directed to an impending civil-war. All dreaded it—all sought to avert it. While the inaugeral address was being delivered from this place, devoted altogether to *saving* the Union without war, insurgent agents were in the city seeking to *destroy* it without war—seeking to dissolve the Union, and divide effects, by negotiation. Both parties deprecated war; but one of them would *make* war rather than let the nation survive; and the other would *accept* war rather than let it perish. And the war came.

One eighth of the whole population were colored slaves, not distributed generally over the Union, but localized in the Southern part of it. These slaves constituted a peculiar and powerful interest. All knew that this interest was, somehow, the cause of the war. To strengthen, perpetuate, and extend this interest was the object for which the insurgents would rend the Union, even by war; while the government claimed no right to do more than to restrict the territorial enlargement of it. Neither party expected for the war, the magnitude, or the duration, which it has already attained. Neither anticipated that the *cause* of the conflict might cease with, or even before, the conflict itself should cease. Each looked for an easier triumph, and a result less fundamental and astounding. Both read the same Bible, and pray to the same God; and each invokes His aid against the other. It may seem strange that any men should dare to ask a just God's assistance in wringing their bread from the sweat of other men's faces; but let us judge not that we be not judged. The prayers of both could not be answered; that of neither has been answered fully. The Almighty has His own purposes. "Woe unto the world because of offences! for it must needs be that offences come; but woe to that man by whom the offence cometh!" If we shall suppose that American Slavery is one of those offences which, in the providence of God, must needs come, but which, having continued through His appointed time, He now wills to remove, and that He gives to both North and South, this terrible war, as the woe due to those by whom the offence came, shall we discern therein any departure from those divine attributes which the believers in a Living God always ascribe to Him? Fondly do we hope—fervently do we pray—that this mighty scourge of war may speedily pass away. Yet, if God wills that it continue, until all the wealth piled by the bond-man's two hundred and fifty years of unrequited toil shall be sunk, and until every drop of blood drawn with the lash, shall be paid by another drawn with the sword, as was said three thousand years ago, so still it must be said "the judgments of the Lord, are true and righteous altogether."

With malice toward none; with charity for all; with firmness in the right, as God gives us to see the right, let us strive on to finish the work we are in; to bind up the nation's wounds; to care for him who shall have borne the battle, and for his widow, and his orphan—to do all which may achieve and cherish a just, and a lasting peace, among ourselves, and with all nations.

March 4, 1865

Martin Luther, *Small Catechism*

Introduction

1. **What do we call the book which we are about to study?**
   We call this book "The Catechism."

2. **What is a catechism?**
   A catechism is a book of instruction in the form of questions and answers.

3. **Who wrote our Small Catechism?**
   Doctor Martin Luther wrote our Small Catechism. (1529 A.D.)

4. **What does Luther's Small Catechism contain?**
   Luther's Small Catechism contains *the chief parts of Christian doctrine.*

5. **Which are the chief parts of Christian doctrine?**
   1. The Ten Commandments.
   2. The Apostles' Creed.
   3. The Lord's Prayer.
   4. The Sacrament of Holy Baptism.
   5. The Office of the Keys and Confession.
   6. The Sacrament of the Altar.

6. **From which book did Luther take these chief parts of Christian doctrine?**
   Luther took the chief parts of Christian doctrine *from the Bible.*

The Bible

7. **What is the Bible?**
   The Bible is the *Word of God.*

   NOTE.—Other names for the Bible are: Holy Scripture, The Scriptures, Holy Writ, The Book of Books, The Word of God.

8. **Who wrote the Bible?**
   Holy men of God wrote the Bible. The *Prophets* wrote the books of the Old Testament, and the *Evangelists* and the *Apostles* wrote the books of the New Testament.

NOTE.—For the books of the Bible see page 209.

[1] *Holy men of God* spake as they were moved by the Holy Ghost. *2 Peter 1:21.*

9. Why is the Bible the Word of God although it was written by men?

The Bible is the Word of God because these men wrote it by *inspiration of God.*

[2] All Scripture is given by *inspiration of God. 2 Tim. 3:16.*

10. What does "by inspiration of God" mean?

"By inspiration of God" means that God the Holy Ghost *moved* the holy men *to write,* and *put into their minds,* the very *thoughts* which they expressed and the very words which they wrote. (Verbal Inspiration.)

[3] Holy men of God spake as they were *moved by the Holy Ghost. 2 Peter 1:21.*

[4] We speak, not in *the words* which man's wisdom teacheth, but *which the Holy Ghost teacheth. 1 Cor. 2:13.*

11. Whose word, then, is every word of the Bible?

Every word of the Bible is *God's word,* and therefore the Bible is without error.

[5] Thy Word is *truth. John 17:17.*

[6] *All Scripture* is given by inspiration of God. *2 Tim. 3:16.*

[7] The Scripture *cannot be broken. John 10:35.*

12. For what purpose did God give us the Bible?

God gave us the Bible to make us "*wise unto salvation* through faith which is in Christ Jesus," and to *train us in holy living.*

[8] From a child thou hast known the Holy Scriptures, which are able to *make thee wise unto salvation through faith which is in Christ Jesus.* All Scripture is given by inspiration of God and is profitable *for doctrine, for reproof, for correction, for instruction in righteousness,* that the man of God may be perfect, thoroughly furnished *unto all good works. 2 Tim. 3:15–17.*

[9] Thy Word is a *lamp unto my feet* and a *light unto my path. Ps. 119:105.*

13. What use should we make of the Bible?

We should diligently and reverently *read and study* the Bible, *listen* attentively when it is read and explained, *believe* it, and *live* according to it.

[10] *Search the Scriptures,* for in them ye think ye have eternal life; and they are they which testify of Me. *John 5:39.*

[11] Blessed are they that *hear* the Word of God and *keep* it. *Luke 11:28.*

[12] Mary *kept* all these things and *pondered* them in her heart. *Luke 2:19.*

[13] If a man love Me, he will *keep My words. John 14:23.*

Law and Gospel

14. What are the two great doctrines of the Bible?

Law and Gospel are the two great doctrines of the Bible.

15. What is the Law?

The Law is that doctrine of the Bible in which God tells us how we *are to be* and what we *are to do* and *not to do.*

[14] Ye shall *be holy;* for I, the Lord, your God, am holy. *Lev.19:2.*

[15] *Observe* thou that which I command thee. *Ex. 34:11.*

[16] These words which *I command thee* this day shall be in thine heart; and *thou shalt* teach them diligently unto thy children. *Deut. 6:6, 7.*

16. What is the Gospel?

The Gospel is that doctrine of the Bible in which God tells us the good news of our salvation in Jesus Christ.

[17] In this was manifested the *love of God* toward us, because that God *sent His only-begotten Son* into the world that we might *live through Him. 1 John 4:9.*

[18] God so loved the world that He *gave His only-begotten Son,* that *whosoever believeth in Him* should not perish, but *have everlasting life. John 3:16.*

[19] I am not ashamed of the *Gospel of Christ;* for it is the *power of God unto salvation. Rom. 1:16.*

17. What is the difference between the Law and the Gospel?

1. The Law teaches what *we* are to do and not to do; the Gospel teaches what *God* has done, and still does, for our salvation.
2. The Law shows us *our sin* and the *wrath* of God; the Gospel shows us *our Savior* and the *grace of God.*
3. The Law must be preached to all men, but especially to *impenitent* sinners; the Gospel must be preached to sinners who are *troubled* in their minds because of their sins.

Yoel Hoffmann, *The Sound of the One Hand: 281 Zen Koans with Answers*

I. The Way of the Inzan School

A. The Koan on the Sound of the One Hand

In clapping both hands a sound is heard; what is the sound of the one hand?

ANSWER

The pupil faces his master, takes a correct posture, and without a word, thrusts one hand forward.

DISCOURSE

1   MASTER

If you've heard the sound of the one hand, prove it.

ANSWER

Without a word, the pupil thrusts one hand forward.

2   MASTER

It's said that if one hears the sound of the one hand, one becomes a Buddha [i.e., becomes enlightened]. Well then, how will you do it?

ANSWER

Without a word, the pupil thrusts one hand forward.

3   MASTER

After you've become ashes, how will you hear it?

ANSWER

Without a word, the pupil thrusts one hand forward.

4   MASTER

What if the one hand is cut by the Suimo Sword?

ANSWER

"It can't be."

Or:

"If it can, let me see you do it." So saying, the pupil extends his hand forward.

Or:

Without a word, the pupil thrusts one hand forward.

5   MASTER

Why can't it cut the one hand?

ANSWER

"Because the one hand pervades the universe."

6   MASTER

Then show me something that contains the universe.

ANSWER

Without a word, the pupil thrusts one hand forward.

7   MASTER

The before-birth-one-hand, what is it like?

ANSWER

Without a word, the pupil thrusts one hand forward.

8   MASTER

The Mt.-Fuji-summit-one-hand, what is it like?

ANSWER

The pupil, shading his eyes with one hand, takes the pose of looking down from the summit of Mt. Fuji and says, "What a splendid view!" naming several places to be seen from Mt. Fuji—or others would name places visible from where they happen to be.

9   MASTER

Attach a quote to the-Mt.-Fuji-summit-one-hand.

ANSWER

(Quote)

> Floating clouds connected the sea and the
> mountain,
> And white flat plains spread into the states of
> Sei and Jo.

10   MASTER

Did you hear the sound of the one hand from the back or from the front?

ANSWER

Extending one hand, the pupil repeatedly says, "Whether it's from the front or from the back, you can hear it as you please."

Or:

"From the back it's caw! caw! [the sound of a crow]. From the front it's chirp, chirp [the sound of a sparrow]."

11   MASTER
Now that you've heard the sound of the one hand, what are you going to do?

ANSWER
"I'll pull weeds, scrub the floor, and if you're tired, give you a massage."

12   MASTER
If it's that convenient a thing, let me hear it too!

ANSWER
Without a word, the pupil slaps his master's face.

13   MASTER
The one hand—how far will it reach?

ANSWER
The pupil places his hand on the floor and says, "This is how far it goes."

14   MASTER
The before-the-fifteenth-day-one-hand, the after-the-fifteenth-day-one-hand, the fifteenth-day-one-hand, what's it like?

ANSWER
The pupil extends his right hand and says, "This is the before-the-fifteenth-day-one-hand." Extending his left hand he says, "This is the after-the-fifteenth-day-one-hand." Bringing his hands together he says, "This is the fifteenth-day-one-hand."

15   MASTER
The sublime-sound-of-the-one-hand, what is it like?

ANSWER
The pupil immediately imitates the sound he happens to hear when sitting in front of his master. That is, if it happens to be raining outside, he imitates the sound of rain, "Pitter-patter"; if at that moment a bird happens to call, he says, "Caw! Caw!' imitating the bird's call.

16   MASTER
The soundless-voice-of-the-one-hand, what is it like?

ANSWER
Without a word, the pupil abruptly stands up, then sits down again, bowing in front of his master.

17   MASTER

The true-[mental]-sphere-of-the-one-hand, what's it like?

ANSWER

"I take it to be as fleeting as a dream or phantom, or as something like an illusory flower. That's how I think of it."

18   MASTER

The source-of-the-one-hand, what is it?

ANSWER

"On the plain there is not the slightest breeze that stirs the smallest grain of sand."

(Quote)

> All communication with places north of the
>   White Wolf River is disconnected,
> And south to the Red Phoenix City,
>   autumn nights have grown so long.

Or:

"It is from the place where there is not even one rabbit's hair that I have struck the sound of the one hand."

(Quote.)

> The wind blows and clears the sky of all
>   floating clouds,
> And the moon rises above those green hills
>   like a piece of round white jade.

Or:

> Arriving at the river, the territories of the
>   state of Go seem to come to an end,
> Yet on the other bank, the mountains of the
>   state of Etsu look so far away.

Notes to Part One
The Koan on the Sound of the One Hand
The Way of the Inzan School

A: The Koan on the Sound of the One Hand

This koan was composed by the Japanese Zen Master Hokuin (1686–1769). It is either this koan or the koan on "mu" which the novice receives as his first koan upon entering the monastery. The pupil is usually expected to "contemplate" his first koan for a long time. It may take him up to three years to reach the answer. In the meantime, the master rejects all the answers that do not correspond to the answer of "thrusting one hand forward." However, the master may guide the pupil in various ways. For instance, if the pupil comes up with an answer such as, "It is half" (namely, half the sound of clapping both hands), the master may reject the answer, explaining that the pupil is taken in by "two" (i.e., dualistic thinking). The master may also hint at the answer in a more concrete way. He may say, for instance, "Think of handing over your ticket upon entering the train" (i.e., extending one hand forward). In this case however, there is the danger that the pupil, through guessing, reaches only the correct *form* of the answer without really realizing its "meaning."

It will not be of much use trying to "explain" the koan. The state of mind which it embodies is not fully understood if we take into consideration only its philosophical, or rather anti-philosophical (anti-rational) aspect. The formation of the koan and its answer are to be viewed in relation to *zazen* (Zen meditation).

In the "clapping of both hands" the phenomenon ("sound") is the outcome of the interaction between two (or more) factors. It is thus possible, through distinction and differentiation, to trace its "reason" in other phenomena. In rational thinking we are always concerned with the *relation* of one "thing" with the "other." When "the sound of the one hand" is "heard," not a thing has been excluded. Every thing is ("u") in as far as it cannot be denied. However, its raison d'être does not lie in any "other" thing, nor does it lie in some principle or truth beyond the thing itself. The essence of a thing is no-thing or nothing ("mu"). Thus the one who has heard "the sound of the one hand" has realized "mu" without denying "u."

ANSWER

The seemingly paradoxical requirement to hear the sound of the one hand is answered through an act of extreme simplicity. To reach this height of simplicity, the pupil's mind undergoes a process of ever-growing sophistication. Yet however sophisticated rational thinking may be, its basic function is still that of adding one to one. Through seeing each one in itself and all as one, the pupil abandons rational thinking as a mode of being. This does not of necessity imply that logical thinking can no longer be employed for pragmatic purposes.

The pattern of response in the answer may be expressed in the following way:
Question: "What is the sound of *two* hands?"
Answer: Clapping *both* hands.
Question: "What is the sound of the *one* hand?"
Answer: Extending *one* hand forward.

Or to give another example—no one in the usual state of mind would ever answer three successive calls in the same manner. Now imagine the following exchange:

Hey you.	Yes.	
Hey you.	Yes.	Same intonation, same pitch
Hey you.	Yes.	

In this manner of response, there is such an extreme immediacy between every call and its answer that it is impossible to describe the situation as a process developing according to normal "reason." (It may start anywhere and it may end anywhere.) If we apply the above to the koan, we get the following pattern:

Question: "Two hands!"

Answer: Extending (or clapping) *two* hands.

Question: "One hand!"

Answer: Extending *one* hand.

DISCOURSE

1. The pupil is not taken in by "prove it." He evades explanations by simply implying "that's it."

2. The pupil is not taken in by "enlightenment-non-enlightenment." The answer implies "here, now."

3. The pupil is not taken in by "existence-non-existence." Through the immediacy of his response, the pupil implies "here, now." The "after death" notion exists only while one is alive.

4. Suimo sword—the sharpest of all swords. "Suimo" is composed of the characters meaning "blow" and "hair"; namely, the sword that is so sharp that it cuts a hair that is blown against it.

There is nothing to be cut. Cut (or divide) no-thing and you still have nothing ("mu"). The third answer, because of its immediacy, is the best.

5. Surprisingly enough, the pupil responds to the "why" with a "philosophical" answer. However, it should be assumed that the response (if genuine) is of a more immediate nature than in the usual process of philosophical reasoning. The answer implies "non-distinction."

6. No comment necessary.

7. Similar to note 3. The pupil is not taken in by "life-death." The notion of "before life" is artificial and can be entertained only while alive (i.e., here, now).

8. The "essence" of a situation is the situation itself and nothing beyond it. When asked, "What is actually happening now?" there is no way of answering the "what is actually" phrase. All that can be said is to repeat the "happening now." Thus the pupil responds to "summit" in a natural way by describing the view from the summit.

9. There is no need to speculate too much about the "meaning" of quotes. The pupil simply responds to "summit" and quotes a Chinese poem on a landscape viewed from a summit.

10. This question is a trap. The master tests whether the pupil is taken in by distinction or not. The "sound of the one hand" is not to be located spatially. Nevertheless it is not unrelated to space. Both answers imply that whether from the back or from the front it is just the same. However, it seems that through the second answer the pupil also implies that he has seen through the master's trap.

11. The pupil answers according to his own situation. As for the reader, the answer would be, "I'll go on reading" (or anything else he intends to do).

12. The pupil answers the challenge of the trap-question by slapping his master. By slapping he also implies that the master should not underestimate his understanding of the koan.

13. Again, a simple trap-question. The "one hand" is not to be located in space, but the pupil naively responds to the question within the frame of common sense.

14. This trap-question is intended to test if the pupil is taken in by distinctions of time or phase (beginning, middle, end) as to the "sound of the one hand." The answer implies "there is not much difference," no more than the simple difference of before a certain fixed limit and after that limit. More concretely, in terms of "beginning, middle, end," the answer is a simple response showing "this end" (right hand), "that end" (left hand), and "middle" (both hands together).

"Before-the-fifteenth-day" and "after-the-fifteenth-day" is sometimes also used as a set phrase for "before enlightenment" and "after enlightenment." This question may also be interpreted in such a way which does not differ much from the above interpretation. In such a case however, the reader should not read into the bringing of the hands together on the "fifteenth day" (the time of enlightenment) as an overtly abstract philosophical meaning (such as "unity" or "non-distinction"). The question is of the same pattern as question 10. Thus, instead of the answer in the book (extending right hand, then left hand, then bringing hands together), the pupil may, as in question 10, answer through sound imitations of three animals, or through the enumeration of three examples of any other phenomena of the same category.

15. The trap lies in the notion of "sublime." The expectation of a supermundane experience is perhaps the greatest obstacle in the way of Zen enlightenment. Through his answer, the pupil implies that he is not taken in by the distinction of "sublime-mundane."

16. The pupil's action is an imitation of the Japanese style of greeting. Through the omission of the words which usually accompany the greeting

ceremony, the pupil simply responds only to the word "soundless" in the master's question.

17. In the demand to explain what it is "truly" like, the question entails a trap. Asked what it is "truly" like (i.e., its "essence"), the pupil has to answer that it is "truly" nothing ("mu"), for to define "truth" in positive terms is mere illusion. In his answer, the pupil rejects the master's demand to define the "ultimate truth" as something of illusory nature. If the pupil responded philosophically—for example, "everything exists, yet ultimately it is nothing"— he would be ridiculed by the master for the denial of existence.

18. To define the "source" of things is similar to the definition of their "ultimate truth." The answer suggests that the emptiness (or void) of "mu" is the "source." The answer and the attached quotes express the mood of "mu" by using the symbols of far-extended time and space, serenity, and evenness.

The Gospel of Matthew, Chapter 13

13 That same day Jesus went out of the house and sat beside the sea. [2]And great crowds gathered about him, so that he got into a boat and sat there; and the whole crowd stood on the beach. [3]And he told them many things in parables, saying: "A sower went out to sow. [4]And as he sowed, some seeds fell along the path, and the birds came and devoured them. [5]Other seeds fell on rocky ground, where they had not much soil, and immediately they sprang up, since they had no depth of soil, [6]but when the sun rose they were scorched; and since they had no root they withered away. [7]Other seeds fell upon thorns, and the thorns grew up and choked them. [8]Other seeds fell on good soil and brought forth grain, some a hundredfold, some sixty, some thirty. [9]He who has ears, let him hear."

[10]Then the disciples came and said to him, "Why do you speak to them in parables?" [11]And he answered them, "To you it has been given to know the secrets of the kingdom of heaven, but to them it has not been given. [12]For to him who has will more be given, and he will have abundance; but from him who has not, even what he has will be taken away. [13]This is why I speak to them in parables, because seeing they do not see, and hearing they do not hear, nor do they understand. [14]With them indeed is fulfilled the prophecy of Isaiah which says:

'You shall indeed hear but never understand,
and you shall indeed see but never perceive.
[15]For this people's heart has grown dull,
and their ears are heavy of hearing,
and their eyes they have closed,
lest they should perceive with their eyes,
and hear with their ears,
and understand with their heart, and turn for me to heal them.'

[16]But blessed are your eyes, for they see, and your ears, for they hear. [17]Truly, I say to you, many prophets and righteous men longed to see what you see, and did not see it, and to hear what you hear, and did not hear it.

[18]"Hear then the parable of the sower. [19]When any one hears the word of the kingdom and does not understand it, the evil one comes and snatches away what is sown in his heart; this is what was sown along the path. [20]As for what was sown on rocky ground, this is he who hears the word and immediately receives it with joy; [21]yet he has no root in himself, but endures for a while,

and when tribulation or persecution arises on account of the word, immediately he falls away. [22]As for what was sown among thorns, this is he who hears the word, but the cares of the world and the delight in riches choke the word, and it proves unfruitful. [23]As for what was sown on good soil, this is he who hears the word and understands it; he indeed bears fruit, and yields, in one case a hundredfold, in another sixty, and in another thirty."

[24]Another parable he put before them, saying, "The kingdom of heaven may be compared to a man who sowed good seed in his field; [25]but while men were sleeping, his enemy came and sowed weeds among the wheat, and went away. [26]So when the plants came up and bore grain, then the weeds appeared also. [27]And the servants of the householder came and said to him, 'Sir, did you not sow good seed in your field? How then has it weeds?' [28]He said to them, 'An enemy has done this.' The servants said to him, 'Then do you want us to go and gather them?' [29]But he said, 'No; lest in gathering the weeds you root up the wheat along with them. [30]Let both grow together until the harvest; and at harvest time I will tell the reapers, Gather the weeds first and bind them in bundles to be burned, but gather the wheat into my barn.'"

[31]Another parable he put before them, saying, "The kingdom of heaven is like a grain of mustard seed which a man took and sowed in his field; [32]it is the smallest of all seeds, but when it has grown it is the greatest of shrubs and becomes a tree, so that the birds of the air come and make nests in its branches."

[33]He told them another parable. "The kingdom of heaven is like leaven which a woman took and hid in three measures of meal, till it was all leavened."

[34]All this Jesus said to the crowds in parables; indeed he said nothing to them without a parable. [35]This was to fulfil what was spoken by the prophet:

"I will open my mouth in parables,
I will utter what has been hidden since the foundation of the world."

[36]Then he left the crowds and went into the house. And his disciples came to him, saying, "Explain to us the parable of the weeds of the field." [37]He answered, "He who sows the good seed is the Son of man; [38]the field is the world, and the good seed means the sons of the kingdom; the weeds are the sons of the evil one, [39]and the enemy who sowed them is the devil; the harvest is the close of the age, and the reapers are angels. [40]Just as the weeds are gathered and burned with fire, so will it be at the close of the age. [41]The Son of man will send his angels, and they will gather out of his kingdom all causes of sin and all evildoers, [42]and throw them into the furnace of fire; there men will weep and gnash their teeth. [43]Then the righteous will shine like the sun in the kingdom of their Father. He who has ears, let him hear.

[44] "The kingdom of heaven is like treasure hidden in a field, which a man found and covered up; then in his joy he goes and sells all that he has and buys that field.

[45] "Again, the kingdom of heaven is like a merchant in search of fine pearls, [46] who, on finding one pearl of great value, went and sold all that he had and bought it.

[47] "Again, the kingdom of heaven is like a net which was thrown into the sea and gathered fish of every kind; [48] when it was full, men drew it ashore and sat down and sorted the good into vessels but threw away the bad. [49] So it will be at the close of the age. The angels will come out and separate the evil from the righteous, [50] and throw them into the furnace of fire; there men will weep and gnash their teeth.

[51] "Have you understood all this?" They said to him, "Yes." [52] And be said to them, "Therefore every scribe who has been trained for the kingdom of heaven is like a householder who brings out of his treasure what is new and what is old."

[53] And when Jesus had finished these parables, he went away from there, [54] and coming to his own country he taught them in their synagogue, so that they were astonished, and said, "Where did this man get this wisdom and these mighty works? [55] Is not this the carpenter's son? Is not his mother called Mary? And are not his brothers James and Joseph and Simon and Judas? [56] And are not all his sisters with us? Where then did this man get all this?" [57] And they took offense at him. But Jesus said to them, "A prophet is not without honor except in his own country and in his own house." [58] And he did not do many mighty works there, because of their unbelief.

Martin Buber, *Tales of the Hasidim:*
The Early Masters

When the Sabbath Drew Near

The disciples of a zaddik who had been a disciple of the Baal Shem Tov, were sitting together at noon, before the sabbath, and telling one another about the miraculous deeds of the Baal Shem. The zaddik, who was seated in his room which adjoined theirs, heard them. He opened the door and said: "What is the sense of telling miracle tales! Tell one another of his fear of God! Every week, on the day before the sabbath, around the hour of noon, his heart began to beat so loudly that all of us who were with him could hear it."

The Money That Stayed in the House

Never did the Baal Shem keep money in his house overnight. When he returned from a journey, he paid all the debts which had accumulated in his absence and distributed whatever he had left, among the needy.

Once he brought a large amount of money back from a journey, paid his debts, and gave the rest away. But in the meantime, his wife had taken a little of the money so that she might not have to buy on credit for a few days. In the evening, the Baal Shem felt something impeding his prayer. He went home and said: "Who took of the money?" His wife confessed it was she who had done so. He took the money from her and had it distributed among the poor that very evening.

Without the Coming World

Once the spirit of the Baal Shem was so oppressed that it seemed to him he would have no part in the coming world. Then he said to himself: "If I love God, what need have I of a coming world!"

The Master Dances Too

One Simhat Torah evening, the Baal Shem himself danced together with his congregation. He took the scroll of the Torah in his hand and danced with it. Then he laid the scroll aside and danced without it. At this moment, one of his disciples who was intimately acquainted with his gestures, said to his companions: "Now our master has laid aside the visible, dimensional teachings, and has taken the spiritual teachings unto himself."

The Address

Every evening after prayer, the Baal Shem went to his room. Two candles were set in front of him and the mysterious Book of Creation put on the table among other books. Then all those who needed his counsel were admitted in a body, and he spoke with them until the eleventh hour.

One evening, when the people left, one of them said to the man beside him how much good the words the Baal Shem had directed to him, had done him. But the other told him not to talk such nonsense, that they had entered the room together and from that moment on the master had spoken to no one except himself. A third, who heard this, joined in the conversation with a smile, saying how curious that both were mistaken, for the rabbi had carried on an intimate conversation with him the entire evening. Then a fourth and a fifth made the same claim, and finally all began to talk at once and tell what they had experienced. But the next instant they all fell silent.

The Limits of Advice

The disciples of the Baal Shem heard that a certain man had a great reputation for learning. Some of them wanted to go to him and find out what he had to teach. The master gave them permission to go, but first they asked him: "And how shall we be able to tell whether he is a true zaddik?"

The Baal Shem replied. "Ask him to advise you what to do to keep unholy thoughts from disturbing you in your prayers and studies. If he gives you advice, then you will know that he belongs to those who are of no account. For this is the service of men in the world to the very hour of their death; to struggle time after time with the extraneous, and time after time to uplift and fit it into the nature of the Divine Name."

Gifts

When, in saying grace, Rabbi Barukh came to the passage: "Let us not require gifts of flesh and blood and not the loan of them, but only your full, open, and holy hand," he repeated these words three times and with great fervor. When he had ended, his daughter asked him: "Father, why did you pray so fervently that you might be able to do without the gifts of man? Your only means of subsistence is that the people who come to you give you things of their own accord, to show their gratitude."

"My daughter," he replied, "you must know that there are three ways of bringing money to the zaddik. Some say to themselves: 'I'll give him something. I am the kind of man who brings gifts to the zaddik.' The words: 'Let us not require gifts . . . ' refers to these. Others think: 'If I give something to this devout man, it will profit me hereafter.' These want heaven to pay them interest. That is the 'loan.' But there are some who know: 'God has put this money in my hand for the zaddik, and I am his messenger.' These serve the 'full and open hand.'"

Teaching

In a certain year, on the eve of Shavuot, the feast of the Revelation, the rabbi of Rizhyn sat at his table and said no word of the teachings to his disciples, as he usually did at this hour. He was silent and wept. It was the same the second evening of the feast. But after grace he said: "Many a time, when my ancestor, the holy maggid, taught at table, his disciples discussed what their teacher had said, on the way home, and each quoted him differently, and each was positive he had heard it in this, and no other way, and what they said was quite contradictory. There was no possibility of clearing up the matter because when they went to the maggid and asked him, he only repeated the traditional saying: 'Both, these and those are words of the living God.' But when the disciples thought it over, they understood the meaning of the contradiction. For at the source, the Torah is one; in the worlds her face is seventyfold. If, however, a man looks intently at one of these faces, he no longer has need of words or of teachings, for the features of that eternal face speak to him."

Country Houses

Rabbi Pinhas said: "God's relationship to the wicked may be compared to that of a prince who, besides his magnificent palaces, owns all manner of little houses hidden away in the woods and in villages, and visits them occasionally to hunt or to rest. The dignity of a palace is no greater than that of such a temporary abode, for the two are not alike, and what the lesser accomplishes, the greater cannot. It is the same with the righteous man. Though his value and service be great, he cannot accomplish what the wicked man accomplishes in the hour he prays, or does something to honor God, and God who is watching the worlds of confusion, rejoices in him. That is why the righteous man should not consider himself better than the wicked."

Humility No Commandment

They asked the maggid of Zlotchov: "All the commandments are written in the Torah. But humility, which is worth all the other virtues put together, is not stated in it as a commandment. All we read about it is the words in praise of Moses, saying that he was more humble than all other people. What is the significance of this silence concerning humility?"

The rabbi replied: "If anyone were humble in order to keep a commandment, he would never attain to true humility. To think humility is a commandment is the prompting of Satan. He bloats a man's heart telling him he is learned and righteous and devout, a master in all good works, and worthy to think himself better than the general run of people; but that this would be proud and impious since it is a commandment that he must be humble and put himself on a par with others. And a man who interprets this as a commandment and does it, only feeds his pride the more in doing so."

Learn from All

They asked Rabbi Mikhal: "In the Sayings of the Fathers we read: 'Who is wise?' He who learns from all men, as it is said, 'From all my teachers I have gotten understanding.' Then why does it not say: 'He who learns from every teacher'?"

Rabbi Mikhal explained: "The master who pronounced these words, is intent on having it clear that we can learn not only from those whose occupation is to teach, but from every man. Even from one who is ignorant, or from one who is wicked, you can gain understanding as to how to conduct your life."

Imitation of the Fathers

The maggid of Zlotchov was asked by one of his disciples: "In the book of Elijah we read: 'Everyone in Israel is in duty bound to say: When will my work approach the works of my fathers, Abraham, Isaac and Jacob.' How are we to understand this? How could we ever venture to think that we could do what our fathers could?"

The rabbi expounded: "Just as our fathers invented new ways of serving, each a new service according to his own character: one the service of love, the other that of stern justice, the third that of beauty, so each one of us in his own way shall devise something new in the light of the teachings and of service, and do what has not yet been done."

Jacob Yitzhak of Lublin ("The Seer")
His Old Teacher

Rabbi Jacob Yitzhak once journeyed to a distant city in the company of some of his friends and disciples. It was Friday afternoon and they must have been quite close to their destination when they came to a crossroads. The coachman asked which road he was to take. The rabbi did not know and so he said: "Give the horses their head and let them go where they want." After a time they saw the houses of a town. Soon, however, they discovered that it was not the one they were bound for. "Well, after that, better not call me rabbi any more," said the Seer of Lublin.

"But how are we going to get food and shelter for the sabbath," his disciples asked, "if we are not allowed to say who you are?" Now the reason for this question was this: the zaddik never kept overnight even the smallest coins of the gifts of money he had received during the day, but gave everything to the poor.

"Let us go to the House of Prayer," he said. "There some burgher or other will take each of us home with him as his sabbath guest." And that was what happened, only that the rabbi himself took so long over his prayers that the House of Prayer was all but empty when he had done. Looking up, he saw that one man alone, a man of eighty or thereabouts, was still there. This old man asked the stranger: "Where are you going for the consecration of the sabbath?"

"I don't know," said the zaddik.

"Just go to the inn," said the old man, "and when the day of rest is over, I'll take up a collection to settle your bill."

"I cannot keep the sabbath at the inn," said Rabbi Jacob Yitzhak, "because there they do not say the blessing over the lights."

The old man hesitated. Then he said: "In my house I have only a little bread and wine for my wife and myself."

"I am not a big eater," the rabbi of Lublin assured him, and they went off together.

First the old man said the blessing over the wine, and then the rabbi. After the blessing over the bread, the old man asked: "Where do you come from?"

"From Lublin."

"And do you know *him?*"

"I am always in his company."

Then the old man begged his guest in a voice that trembled: "Tell me something about him!"

"Why are you so eager to know?"

"When I was young," said the old man, "I was an assistant at the school and he was one of the children assigned to my care. He did not seem especially gifted. But then I heard that he became a very great man. Since that time I fast one day every week, that I may be found worthy to see him. For I am too poor to ride to Lublin and too weak to walk there."

"Do you remember anything at all about him?" the rabbi inquired.

"Day after day," said the old man, "I had to look for him when the time to study the prayer-book had come, and I never found him. After a fairly long time he came of his own accord, and then I smacked him. Once I watched where he was going and followed. There he sat on an ant-hill in the woods and cried aloud: 'Hear, O Israel, the Lord our God, the Lord is one.' After that I never smacked him any more."

Now Rabbi Jacob Yitzhak knew why his horses had taken him to this town. "I am he," he said. When the old man heard this, he fainted and it took a long time to revive him.

At the end of the sabbath, the zaddik left the city with his disciples, and the old man accompanied him until he grew tired and had to turn back. He reached home, lay down, and died. While this was happening, the rabbi and his companions were having the post-sabbath meal at a village inn. When they had finished eating, he rose, and said: "Now let us return to the city and bury my old teacher."

The Book of Proverbs, Chapters 1–9

1   The Proverbs of Solomon, son of David, king of Israel:
² That men may know wisdom and instruction, understand words of insight,
³ receive instruction in wise dealing, righteousness, justice, and equity;
⁴ that prudence may be given to the simple, knowledge and discretion to the youth—
⁵ the wise man also may hear and increase in learning, and the man of understanding acquire skill,
⁶ to understand a proverb and a figure, the words of the wise and their riddles.
⁷ The fear of the LORD is the beginning of knowledge; fools despise wisdom and instruction.
⁸ Hear, my son, your father's instruction, and reject not your mother's teaching;
⁹ for they are a fair garland for your head, and pendants for your neck.
¹⁰ My son, if sinners entice you, do not consent.
¹¹ If they say, "Come with us, let us lie in wait for blood, let us wantonly ambush the innocent;
¹² like Sheol let us swallow them alive and whole, like those who go down to the Pit;
¹³ we shall find all precious goods, we shall fill our houses with spoil;
¹⁴ throw in your lot among us, we will all have one purse"—
¹⁵ my son, do not walk in the way with them, hold back your foot from their paths;
¹⁶ for their feet run to evil, and they make haste to shed blood.
¹⁷ For in vain is a net spread in the sight of any bird;
¹⁸ but these men lie in wait for their own blood, they set an ambush for their own lives.
¹⁹ Such are the ways of all who get gain by violence; it takes away the life of its possessors.
²⁰ Wisdom cries aloud in the street; in the markets she raises her voice;
²¹ on the top of the walls she cries out; at the entrance of the city gates she speaks
²² "How long, O simple ones, will you love being simple? How long will scoffers delight in their scoffing and fools hate knowledge?
²³ Give heed to my reproof; behold, I will pour out my thoughts to you; I will make my words known to you.
²⁴ Because I have called and you refused to listen, have stretched out my hand and no one has heeded,
²⁵ and you have ignored all my counsel and would have none of my reproof,

[26] I also will laugh at your calamity; I will mock when panic strikes you,

[27] when panic strikes you like a storm, and your calamity comes like a whirlwind, when distress and anguish come upon you.

[28] Then they will call upon me, but I will not answer; they will seek me diligently but will not find me.

[29] Because they hated knowledge and did not choose the fear of the LORD,

[30] would have none of my counsel, and despised all my reproof,

[31] therefore they shall eat the fruit of their way and be sated with their own devices.

[32] For the simple are killed by their turning away, and the complacence of fools destroys them;

[33] but he who listens to me will dwell secure and will be at ease, without dread of evil."

2   My son, if you receive my words and treasure up my commandments with you,

[2] making your ear attentive to wisdom and inclining your heart to understanding;

[3] yes, if you cry out for insight and raise your voice for understanding,

[4] if you seek it like silver and search for it as for hidden treasures;

[5] then you will understand the fear of the Lord and find the knowledge of God.

[6] For the LORD gives wisdom; from his mouth come knowledge and understanding;

[7] he stores up sound wisdom for the upright; he is a shield to those who walk in integrity,

[8] guarding the paths of justice and preserving the way of his saints.

[9] Then you will understand righteousness and justice and equity, every good path;

[10] for wisdom will come into your heart, and knowledge will be pleasant to your soul;

[11] discretion will watch over you; understanding will guard you;

[12] delivering you from the way of evil, from men of perverted speech,

[13] who forsake the paths of uprightness to walk in the ways of darkness,

[14] who rejoice in doing evil and delight in the perverseness of evil;

[15] men whose paths are crooked, and who are devious in their ways.

[16] You will be saved from the loose woman, from the adventuress with her smooth words,

[17] who forsakes the companion of her youth and forgets the covenant of her God;

[18] for her house sinks down to death, and her paths to the shades;

[19] none who go to her come back nor do they regain the paths of life.

[20] So you will walk in the way of good men and keep to the paths of the righteous.

[21] For the upright will inhabit the land, and men of integrity will remain in it;

[22] but the wicked will be cut off from the land, and the treacherous will be rooted out of it.

3 My son, do not forget my teaching, but let your heart keep my commandments;

[2] for length of days and years of life and abundant welfare will they give you.

[3] Let not loyalty and faithfulness forsake you; bind them about your neck, write them on the tablet of your heart.

[4] So you will find favor and good repute in the sight of God and man.

[5] Trust in the LORD with all your heart, and do not rely on your own insight.

[6] In all your ways acknowledge him, and he will make straight your paths.

[7] Be not wise in your own eyes; fear the LORD, and turn away from evil.

[8] It will be healing to your flesh and refreshment to your bones.

[9] Honor the LORD with your substance and with the first fruits of all your produce;

[10] then your barns will be filled with plenty, and your vats will be bursting with wine.

[11] My son, do not despise the LORD's discipline or be weary of his reproof,

[12] for the LORD reproves him whom he loves, as a father the son in whom he delights.

[13] Happy is the man who finds wisdom, and the man who gets understanding,

[14] for the gain from it is better than gain from silver and its profit better than gold.

[15] She is more precious than jewels, and nothing you desire can compare with her.

[16] Long life is in her right hand; in her left hand are riches and honor.

[17] Her ways are ways of pleasantness, and all her paths are peace.

[18] She is a tree of life to those who lay hold of her; those who hold her fast are called happy.

[19] The LORD by wisdom founded the earth; by understanding he established the heavens;

[20] by his knowledge the deeps broke forth, and the clouds drop down the dew.

[21] My son, keep sound wisdom and discretion; let them not escape from your sight,

[22] and they will be life for your soul and adornment for your neck.

[23] Then you will walk on your way securely and your foot will not stumble.

[24] If you sit down, you will not be afraid; when you lie down, your sleep will be sweet.

[25] Do not be afraid of sudden panic, or of the ruin of the wicked, when it comes;

[26] for the LORD will be your confidence and will keep your foot from being caught.

[27] Do not withhold good from those to whom it is due, when it is in your power to do it.

[28] Do not say to your neighbor, "Go, and come again, tomorrow I will give it"—when you have it with you.

[29] Do not plan evil against your neighbor who dwells trustingly beside you.

[30] Do not contend with a man for no reason, when he has done you no harm.

[31] Do not envy a man of violence and do not choose any of his ways;

[32] for the perverse man is an abomination to the LORD, but the upright are in his confidence.

[33] The LORD's curse is on the house of the wicked, but he blesses the abode of the righteous.

[34] Toward the scorners he is scornful, but to the humble he shows favor.

[35] The wise will inherit honor, but fools get disgrace.

4 Hear, O sons, a father's instruction, and be attentive, that you may gain insight;

[2] for I give you good precepts: do not forsake my teaching.

[3] When I was a son with my father, tender, the only one in the sight of my mother,

[4] he taught me, and said to me, "Let your heart hold fast my words; keep my commandments, and live;

[5] do not forget, and do not turn away from the words of my mouth. Get wisdom; get insight.

[6] Do not forsake her, and she will keep you; love her, and she will guard you.

[7] The beginning of wisdom is this: Get wisdom, and whatever you get, get insight.

[8] Prize her highly, and she will exalt you; she will honor you if you embrace her.

[9] She will place on your head a fair garland; she will bestow on you a beautiful crown."

[10] Hear, my son, and accept my words, that the years of your life may be many.

[11] I have taught you the way of wisdom; I have led you in the paths of uprightness.

[12] When you walk, your step will not be hampered; and if you run, you will not stumble.

[13] Keep hold of instruction, do not let go; guard her, for she is your life.

[14] Do not enter the path of the wicked, and do not walk in the way of evil men.

[15] Avoid it; do not go on it; turn away from it and pass on.

[16] For they cannot sleep unless they have done wrong; they are robbed of sleep unless they have made some one stumble.

[17] For they eat the bread of wickedness and drink the wine of violence.

[18] But the path of the righteous is like the light of dawn, which shines brighter and brighter until full day.

[19] The way of the wicked is like deep darkness; they do not know over what they stumble.

[20] My son, be attentive to my words; incline your ear to my sayings.

[21] Let them not escape from your sight; keep them within your heart.

[22] For they are life to him who finds them, and healing to all his flesh.

[23] Keep your heart with all vigilance; for from it flow the springs of life.

[24] Put away from you crooked speech, and put devious talk far from you.

[25] Let your eyes look directly forward, and your gaze be straight before you.

²⁶ Take heed to the path of your feet, then all your ways will be sure.
²⁷ Do not swerve to the right or to the left; turn your foot away from evil.

5 My son, be attentive to my wisdom, incline your ear to my understanding;
² that you may keep discretion, and your lips may guard knowledge.
³ For the lips of a loose woman drip honey, and her speech is smoother than oil;
⁴ but in the end she is bitter as wormwood, sharp as a two-edged sword.
⁵ Her feet go down to death; her steps follow the path to Sheol;
⁶ she does not take heed to the path of life; her ways wander, and she does not know it.
⁷ And now, O sons, listen to me, and do not depart from the words of my mouth.
⁸ Keep your way far from her, and do not go near the door of her house;
⁹ lest you give your honor to others and your years to the merciless;
¹⁰ lest strangers take their fill of your strength, and your labors go to the house of an alien;
¹¹ and at the end of your life you groan, when your flesh and body are consumed,
¹² and you say, "How I hated discipline, and my heart despised reproof!
¹³ I did not listen to the voice of my teachers or incline my ear to my instructors.
¹⁴ I was at the point of utter ruin in the assembled congregation."
¹⁵ Drink water from your own cistern, flowing water from your own well.
¹⁶ Should your springs be scattered abroad, streams of water in the streets?
¹⁷ Let them be for yourself alone, and not for strangers with you.
¹⁸ Let your fountain be blessed, and rejoice in the wife of your youth,
¹⁹ a lovely hind, a graceful doe. Let her affection fill you at all times with delight, be infatuated always with her love.
²⁰ Why should you be infatuated, my son, with a loose woman and embrace the bosom of an adventuress?
²¹ For a man's ways are before the eyes of the Lord, and he watches all his paths.
²² The iniquities of the wicked ensnare him, and he is caught in the toils of his sin.
²³ He dies for lack of discipline, and because of his great folly he is lost.

6 My son, if you have become surety for your neighbor, have given your pledge for a stranger;
² if you are snared in the utterance of your lips, caught in the words of your mouth;
³ then do this, my son, and save yourself, for you have come into your neighbor's power: go, hasten, and importune your neighbor.
⁴ Give your eyes no sleep and your eyelids no slumber;

[5] save yourself like a gazelle from the hunter, like a bird from the hand of the fowler.

[6] Go to the ant, O sluggard; consider her ways, and be wise.

[7] Without having any chief, officer or ruler,

[8] she prepares her food in summer, and gathers her sustenance in harvest.

[9] How long will you lie there, O sluggard? When will you arise from your sleep?

[10] A little sleep, a little slumber, a little folding of the hands to rest,

[11] and poverty will come upon you like a vagabond, and want like an armed man.

[12] A worthless person, a wicked man, goes about with crooked speech,

[13] winks with his eyes, scrapes with his feet, points with his finger,

[14] with perverted heart devises evil, continually sowing discord;

[15] therefore calamity will come upon him suddenly; in a moment he will be broken beyond healing.

[16] There are six things which the LORD hates, seven which are an abomination to him:

[17] haughty eyes, a lying tongue, and hands that shed innocent blood,

[18] a heart that devises wicked plans, feet that make haste to run to evil,

[19] a false witness who breathes out lies, and a man who sows discord among brothers.

[20] My son, keep your father's commandment, and forsake not your mother's teaching.

[21] Bind them upon your heart always; tie them about your neck.

[22] When you walk, they will lead you; when you lie down, they will watch over you; and when you awake, they will talk with you.

[23] For the commandment is a lamp and the teaching a light, and the reproofs of discipline are the way of life,

[24] to preserve you from the evil woman, from the smooth tongue of the adventuress.

[25] Do not desire her beauty in your heart, and do not let her capture you with her eyelashes;

[26] for a harlot may be hired for a loaf of bread, but an adulteress stalks a man's very life.

[27] Can a man carry fire in his bosom and his clothes not be burned?

[28] Or can one walk upon hot coals and his feet not be scorched?

[29] So is he who goes in to his neighbor's wife; none who touches her will go unpunished.

[30] Do not men despise a thief if he steals to satisfy his appetite when he is hungry?

[31] And if he is caught, he will pay sevenfold; he will give all the goods of his house.

[32] He who commits adultery has no sense; he who does it destroys himself.

[33] Wounds and dishonor will he get, and his disgrace will not be wiped away.

³⁴ For jealousy makes a man furious, and he will not spare when he takes revenge.
³⁵ He will accept no compensation, nor be appeased though you multiply gifts.

7 My son, keep my words and treasure up my commandments with you;
² keep my commandments and live, keep my teachings as the apple of your eye;
³ bind them on your fingers, write them on the tablet of your heart.
⁴ Say to wisdom, "You are my sister," and call insight your intimate friend;
⁵ to preserve you from the loose woman, from the adventuress with her smooth words.
⁶ For at the window of my house I have looked out through my lattice,
⁷ and I have seen among the simple, I have perceived among the youths, a young man without sense,
⁸ passing along the street near her corner, taking the road to her house
⁹ in the twilight, in the evening, at the time of night and darkness.
¹⁰ And lo, a woman meets him, dressed as a harlot, wily of heart.
¹¹ She is loud and wayward, her feet do not stay at home;
¹² now in the street, now in the market, and at every corner she lies in wait.
¹³ She seizes him and kisses him, and with impudent face she says to him:
¹⁴ "I had to offer sacrifices, and today I have paid my vows;
¹⁵ so now I have come out to meet you, to seek you eagerly, and I have found you.
¹⁶ I have decked my couch with coverings, colored spreads of Egyptian linen;
¹⁷ I have perfumed my bed with myrrh, aloes, and cinnamon.
¹⁸ Come, let us take our fill of love till morning; let us delight ourselves with love.
¹⁹ For my husband is not at home; he has gone on a long journey;
²⁰ he took a bag of money with him; at full moon he will come home."
²¹ With much seductive speech she persuades him; with her smooth talk she compels him.
²² All at once he follows her, as an ox goes to the slaughter, or as a stag is caught fast
²³ till an arrow pierces its entrails; as a bird rushes into a snare; he does not know that it will cost him his life.
²⁴ And now, O sons, listen to me, and be attentive to the words of my mouth.
²⁵ Let not your heart turn aside to her ways, do not stray into her paths;
²⁶ for many a victim has she laid low; yea, all her slain are a mighty host.
²⁷ Her house is the way to Sheol, going down to the chambers of death.

8 Does not wisdom call, does not understanding raise her voice?
² On the heights beside the way, in the paths she takes her stand;
³ beside the gates in front of the town, at the entrance of the portals she cries aloud:

[4] "To you, O men, I call, and my cry is to the sons of men.

[5] O simple ones, learn prudence; O foolish men, pay attention.

[6] Hear, for I will speak noble things, and from my lips will come what is right;

[7] for my mouth will utter truth; wickedness is an abomination to my lips.

[8] All the words of my mouth are righteous; there is nothing twisted or crooked in them.

[9] They are all straight to him who understands and right to those who find knowledge.

[10] Take my instruction instead of silver, and knowledge rather than choice gold;

[11] for wisdom is better than jewels, and all that you may desire cannot compare with her.

[12] I, wisdom, dwell in prudence, and I find knowledge and discretion.

[13] The fear of the LORD is hatred of evil. Pride and arrogance and the way of evil and perverted speech I hate.

[14] I have counsel and sound wisdom, I have insight, I have strength.

[15] By me kings reign, and rulers decree what is just;

[16] by me princes rule, and nobles govern the earth.

[17] I love those who love me, and those who seek me diligently find me.

[18] Riches and honor are with me, enduring wealth and prosperity.

[19] My fruit is better than gold, even fine gold, and my yield than choice silver.

[20] I walk in the way of righteousness, in the paths of justice,

[21] endowing with wealth those who love me, and filling their treasuries.

[22] The LORD created me at the beginning of his work, the first of his acts of old.

[23] Ages ago I was set up, at the first, before the beginning of the earth.

[24] When there were no depths I was brought forth, when there were no springs abounding with water.

[25] Before the mountains had been shaped, before the hills, I was brought forth;

[26] before he had made the earth with its fields, or the first of the dust of the world.

[27] When he established the heavens, I was there, when he drew a circle on the face of the deep,

[28] when he made firm the skies above, when he established the fountains of the deep,

[29] when he assigned to the sea its limit, so that the waters might not transgress his command, when he marked out the foundations of the earth,

[30] then I was beside him, like a master workman; and I was daily his delight, rejoicing before him always,

[31] rejoicing in his inhabited world and delighting in the sons of men.

[32] And now, my sons, listen to me: happy are those who keep my ways.

[33] Hear instruction and be wise, and do not neglect it.

[34] Happy is the man who listens to me, watching daily at my gates, waiting beside my doors.

35 For he who finds me finds life and obtains favor from the LORD;

36 but he who misses me injures himself; all who hate me love death."

9   Wisdom has built her house, she has set up her seven pillars.

2 She has slaughtered her beasts, she has mixed her wine, she has also set her table.

3 She has sent out her maids to call from the highest places in the town,

4 "Whoever is simple, let him turn in here!" To him who is without sense she says,

5 "Come, eat of my bread and drink of the wine I have mixed.

6 Leave simpleness, and live, and walk in the way of insight."

7 He who corrects a scoffer gets himself abuse, and he who reproves a wicked man incurs injury.

8 Do not reprove a scoffer, or he will hate you; reprove a wise man, and he will love you.

9 Give instruction to a wise man, and he will be still wiser; teach a righteous man and he will increase in learning.

10 The fear of the LORD is the beginning of wisdom, and the knowledge of the Holy One is insight.

11 For by me your days will be multiplied, and years will be added to your life.

12 If you are wise, you are wise for yourself; if you scoff, you alone will bear it.

13 A foolish woman is noisy; she is wanton and knows no shame.

14 She sits at the door of her house, she takes a seat on the high places of the town,

15 calling to those who pass by, who are going straight on their way,

16 "Whoever is simple, let him turn in here!" And to him who is without sense, she says,

17 "Stolen water is sweet, and bread eaten in secret is pleasant."

18 But he does not know that the dead, are there, that her guests are in the depths of Sheol.

Helen Waddell,
The Desert Fathers

v. The abbot Cyrus of Alexandria, questioned as to the imagination of lust, made answer: "If thou hast not these imaginings, thou art without hope: for if thou hast not the imagination thereof, thou hast the deed itself. For he who fights not in his mind against sin, nor gainsays it, sins in the flesh. And he who sins in the flesh, hath no trouble from the imagination thereof."

vi. An old man questioned a brother, saying, "Is it not thy wont to have speech with women?" And the brother said, "Nay. But my imagination and certain memories I have are painters old and new, disquieting me with images of women." And the old man said to him, "Fear not the dead, but flee the living: that is to say, the consenting to, and the act of, sin: and give thyself longer to prayer."

ix. At one time a brother came to the abbot Pastor, and said to him, "What am I to do, Father? For I am harried with lust. And I sought out the abbot Hybistion, and he said to me, 'Thou oughtst not to allow it to tarry long in thee.'" And the abbot Pastor said to him, "The deeds of the abbot Hybistion are above with the angels in heaven: but thou and I are in fleshly lust. But if a monk keep his belly and his tongue and stay in solitude, he may have confidence that he will not die."

Of Love

i. Said the abbot Antony: "I do not now fear God, but I love Him, for love casteth fear out of doors."

ii. Again he said, That with our neighbour there is life and death: for if we do good to our brother, we shall do good to God: but if we scandalise our brother, we sin against Christ.

v. The abbot Marcus said to the abbot Arsenius, "Wherefore dost thou flee from us?" And the old man said, "God knows that I love you: but I cannot be with God and with men. A thousand and a thousand thousand of the angelic powers have one will: and men have many. Wherefore I cannot send God from me, and come and be with men."

vii. At one time the abbot John was climbing up from Scete with other brethren: and he who was by way of guiding them mistook the way: for it was night. And the brethren said to the abbot John, "What shall we do, Father, for the brother has missed the way, and we may lose ourselves and die?" And the old man said, "If we say aught to him, he will be cast down. But I shall make a show of being worn out and say that I cannot walk, but must lie here till morning." And he did so. And the others said, "Neither shall we go on, but shall sit down beside thee." And they sat down until morning, so as not to discountenance their brother.

xviii. A brother asked a certain old man, saying, "There be two brothers, and one of them is quiet in his cell, and prolongs his fast for six days, and lays much travail on himself but the other tends the sick. Whose work is the more acceptable to God?" And the old man answered, "If that brother who carries his fast for six days were to hang himself up by the nostrils, he could not equal the other, who does service to the sick."

xix. A certain brother asked an old man saying, "Tell me, Father, wherefore is it that the monks travail in discipline and yet receive not such grace as the ancient Fathers had?" And the old man said to him, "Then was love so great that each man set his neighbour on high: but now hath love grown cold and the whole world is set in malice, and each doth pull down his neighbour to the lower room, and for this reason we come short of grace."

Judith Martin, *Miss Manners' Guide to Excruciatingly Correct Behavior*

The Bonds of Friendship

Dear Miss Manners:

I am separated from my husband, and my gentleman friend has, so far, escaped the bonds of matrimony. Our problem is that we do not know how to refer to one another on those rare occasions when first names of the standard terms of endearment just won't do. Am I his mistress (he insists I am, but I thought that referred to the female friend of a married man; besides, it sounds too tacky for my taste). Is he my lover? Personally, I am quite satisfied with "friend," on the premise that the rest of it is nobody's business but our own, but in the interest of domestic tranquillity, I promised him I'd check.

Gentle Reader:

There are several accurate ways in which you and your gentleman friend could explain your relationship to casual acquaintances. "Pamela is Buster McClintock's wife, but she showed up at my place once at two AM and has been there ever since," or "Eldred and I have been together for three years now, but so far he has escaped the bonds of matrimony." Miss Manners does not see how either of these explanations would add to your domestic tranquillity, although they certainly would liven up the lives of others. The beauty of the term "friend" is that it is ambiguous.

Ceremony and "Congruence"

Dear Miss Manners:

I received a troublesome invitation last week, and I need your advice. Two former college friends sent a silk-screened card inviting me to "partake in a ritual celebrating the congruence of their lives." Knowing the couple makes me doubt very much that this is a wedding, yet I think it is something more than the exchange of friendship rings. Just what are my social duties in this case? Do I congratulate them, and if so, on what? What sort of gift does one send for a congruence, and how should one dress for the occasion?

Gentle Reader:

Miss Manners had hoped that the plague of social originality among lovers had been stamped out, but here it is flaring up again. If it were Miss Manners who had been invited, she would go in a chiffon pastel dress and garden hat and send them a silver chafing dish. The other dignified approach is to play tourist and write, "I am afraid that I am not familiar with the customs of your faith. Would you be kind enough to explain to me exactly what you are doing?"

Extended Nonfamily

Dear Miss Manners:
How do you like this one: my daughter is twenty-six, and lives with a divorced man exactly my age and his twenty-two-year-old daughter who has an adorable eight-month-old baby girl. At this stage in my life, I can't think of anything I want more than a grandchild—I baby-sit this "semi-step-great-grandaughter" (or whatever she is besides being simply darling), but this isn't exactly what I've had in mind. And talk about making introductions when my daughter and I are out to lunch or shopping with the baby—whew! It's one of the few times I'm almost rendered speechless. Any suggestions?

Gentle Reader:
Whew! is right. If you attempt to explain this relationship to people you meet while out lunching or shopping, the baby will probably grow up and move away before you finish talking. Miss Manners suggests you curtail the introduction to merely, "And this is Baby Snooks," or whatever. People will naturally assume that you have kidnapped this child for complex psychological reasons or hope of financial gain, or that she has selected you for her nursery Adopt-a-Grandparent work project. But so what! She will grow up learning that you can't explain everything to everyone, which is a valuable lesson in life.

Pieces of Paper

Dear Miss Manners:
It will soon be exactly a year since my lover and I moved in together, Neither she nor I ever has any intention of getting married, which we consider unnecessary for many reasons, but we will probably be together a long time, maybe even permanently. I would like to surprise her by celebrating our first anniversary. What would be appropriate to get her? I looked up wedding anniversary suggestions and found that the first is considered the "paper anniversary." Would this apply to our situation?

Gentle Reader:
No, no, no. That is for married people only! Don't even think of it! *Stop that.* (Wait. Miss Manners is sorry she got hysterical. You know how tolerant

Miss Manners usually is about young love, or old love, for that matter. It's just that you unmarried people have bored her to death talking all the time about how you "don't need a piece of paper to love each other," so don't expect her to let you have any paper now. Besides, there ought to be some thrills attached to marriage only.)

Correcting Mistaken Assumptions

Dear Miss Manners:
How does one handle possibly disapproving visitors to a nonmarital household? Such visitors as poll takers, charity collectors, and friendly neighbors, etc., may initiate a conversation; and, in the course of the talking they begin to refer to the household sharer as "your husband" or "your wife."

Such a reference puts the sharer in an awkward position. Should a reply like "Mr. Jones and I are not married" be given? Is it polite to include any further explanation, like "We've known each other for eleven months" or "We are waiting for his divorce to become final" or "We live together but we don't share the same bed"?

Gentle Reader:
The greatest benefit of civilized society is that respect for others also relieves people of the responsibility for the habits, morals, or errors of others. Thus, a poll taker, friendly-or-otherwise neighbor, or Girl Scout cookie vendor has no occasion to approve or disapprove of your living arrangements. Similarly, you have no responsibility for that person's assumptions about you. The explanation that you and Mr. Jones are not married because you are already a bigamist, your grandchildren disapprove, or you don't know each other well enough is superfluous. Explaining your bedding habits to whoever rings the doorbell is gratuitous, to say the least. If you should encounter this person later and he says, "But I thought you and Mr. Jones were married," you may then say, "I am afraid you were mistaken," or, if you prefer, "You thought wrong, buddy."

Delicacy

Dear Miss Manners:
My boyfriend will be moving into my apartment as soon as his lease is up. We will be sharing everything, and I want to do what is proper. I have been accustomed, when living alone, to hanging up my things that I wash out every night on the shower curtain. I don't know if it's right, though, to have my lingerie all over what will, after all, be his bathroom, too. Not that he hasn't seen it before, but my mother says it isn't right. I said I'd ask Miss Manners.

Gentle Reader:

Miss Manners says you should ask your gentleman friend. Miss Manners never interferes with intimate actions performed in private by consenting adults.

Sharing a Guest Room

Dear Miss Manners:

When my son and his girl friend come home to visit, they expect to share his bedroom. I know they are living together at college, but I don't feel right about it in my house. My son says I'm being Victorian.

Gentle Reader:

No, you're not. The Victorian solution, employed with great success at English house parties, was to put illicit couples in separate rooms, but to ignore nocturnal traffic in the hallway.

Part IV

TEACHING AT HOME; AT HOME TEACHING

In the last reading selection of Part II, "Real Teaching," Philip Jackson observes that the difference between novice teachers and more seasoned ones "turns out to be less a matter of skill than one of feeling and acting at home within a particular instructional milieu." We might wonder how far Jackson wants to push this metaphorical description of experienced teaching. Does he mean only to suggest, in describing veteran teachers as "feeling and acting at home," that they are more comfortable and secure in their roles and places? Or does he mean to say that seasoned teachers have learned to mobilize feelings and energies appropriate to hearth and home in order to domesticate other teaching places and so render them more accommodating and hospitable to the activities of teaching and learning? Are good teachers more "maternal" or "paternal" in the treatment of their students than bad ones? What exactly does Jackson mean here?

Indeed, just what is or should be the relationship between home and school, parenting and teaching? The United States today abounds with practices and controversies that impinge upon this issue. We see a steady and impressive growth in "home schooling." We observe that many colleges and universities are revisiting a question they thought they had settled in the 1960s, namely, the question of whether or not the college should stand *in loco parentis*, in the place of the parent. Just how far should schools try to live up to their designation in the hearts of many alumni of *alma mater?* To what extent should parents control the curriculum at local schools? To what extent should teachers be allowed to "discipline" children? The social, legal, moral, political, and religious dimensions of these related matters have made them some of the most urgent questions in our public life today. It is therefore fitting that we should conclude this anthology with a series of readings that traverse the troubled terrain between the home and the school. It is equally fitting that we should offer here a somewhat different "take" on the problem of the relationship between home and school, treating it as a matter having to do with teaching and learning. We seek thereby to sharpen and sometimes to modify the questions.

The readings from James Agee's *A Death in the Family* take us quickly into the soul of a small child fearful of the night, longing for consolation and reassurance. How does such a child regard his parents? What does the child need to learn in such a situation, and how does his father teach him? Which arts, skills, virtues, affections, and judgments are involved in this "teaching"? What does the father learn in the course of this teaching of the child? What is involved in fathering, and what is the relationship in this scene between fathering and teaching?

Both the father and the mother sing to the boy. The boy notes the differences in their singing in the same way that he feels the differences in their parenting. What are these differences? The boy senses a change in his mother and guesses in confused and sometimes wordless ways about the reasons for the change. This confusion leads to questions. What should we think about the father and the mother as "teachers" in their responses to the boy's questions? Later, in the absence of the father, and after she has been through a long meditation on her own parents and on her own duties as a wife and mother, the mother is faced with a barrage of questions. Does she practice good teaching in answering these questions? Does her practice successfully carry out her resolution to "bring up her children thoroughly and devoutly in the faith?" Or does her practice better carry out her other resolution at the end of the preceding chapter 4, to see to it "that the family remain one"?

In Agee's work we are perhaps more "at home" than in any other we might have selected. And we witness many activities like asking questions and answering them that seem to be instances of teaching but that seem also to extend far beyond teaching in both intention and significance. Conversely, we witness many acts, like those of comfort and assurance, that do not seem like teaching but that most certainly result in learning for both the young boy and his parents. When the mother sends Rufus off to school, away from the questions at home, this seems somehow appropriate, for there, we think, at school, the point and the purpose of the questions and the answers will be more safely, more properly, and more appropriately circumscribed.

It is tempting to say that the Agee reading shows more powerfully than most anything else could, the strong differences between home and school. Could we ever expect or want such intimacy at school as we find among the

parents and the children in the Agee text? And could we ever expect or want
a child to come to feel about a professional teacher the way Rufus feels about
his own parents? No, we are tempted to say, the transactions that we witness
among parents and children here are so moving, so tender, so powerful, so
poignant, and so formative that it would be almost sacrilegious to characterize
them as mere teaching and even more troublesome to suggest that they should
take place anywhere other than the home. We might also be tempted to say
that these matters of birth and death, sexuality and mortality, are best restricted to domestic life, not to the larger world of public education. Rufus
goes off to school precisely to engage other questions that are less basic and to
learn his lessons in reading, writing, and arithmetic, most definitely not in
sexuality and mortality.

Should we resist the temptations to think these things or succumb to
them? The readings that follow may help us make up our minds. The next
reading contains an example of teaching without words as a retired President
of the United States, John Quincy Adams, gives his grandson Henry Adams a
lesson about school and schooling. In the central episode of the chapter, we
move, with Henry, from the home to the school. The last three readings are
set for the most part within classrooms. Vivian Paley, a MacArthur Award–
winning preschool teacher at the Chicago Laboratory School, follows a group
of kindergartners through a year in *Wally's Stories,* Robert Inchausti takes us
into his classroom of unruly ninth-graders in *Spitwad Sutras.* Finally, Eva Brann,
who has taught for many years at St. John's College in Annapolis, Maryland,
addresses all of us who remain beginning teachers and beginning students, as
she once spoke to the "freshmen" at St. John's at the beginning of their school
year in 1990. She concludes this section and this entire collection by exploring
that which most fundamentally motivates the best teaching and the best learning, the depth of our desire to know. And she leaves all of us, appropriately
enough, with an invitation to ask questions. We might begin by asking ourselves how the worlds of home in Agee and of school in these last three readings differ from one another.

The answers will not come easily. Paley's kindergarten is a world filled
with play, story-telling, questions about anything and everything, wonder,
frustration, love, fear, and anger—all of the activities and emotions that Agee
dramatizes. Paley variously describes her own role as stage manager, as Greek
chorus, as listener, and as teacher. But never as parent. We might ask ourselves,
as we, like Meno watching Socrates teach the slave boy, watch Vivian Paley teach
and attend to her own interventions, what her aims might be. She tells us in
the appendix exactly what she has been trying to do over the course of the year
and exactly how she has been trying to do it. Did we discern this on our own?
Have we become, during the course of these many readings, better observers

of good teaching? Once we know the aims and methods behind Paley's actions, can we say how her work differs from the work of a mother, how her classroom differs from Agee's kitchen in chapter 5 of *A Death in the Family?*

And what about the world of *Spitwad Sutras?* Its author tells us that he never wanted to be a schoolteacher, so that it came as a great surprise to him when, five years after graduation from college, he found himself interviewing "for a job to teach ninth grade English at St. Vincent Boy's Preparatory Academy, an orderly little school tucked inside a disintegrating lower-middle-class neighborhood in central California." *Spitwad Sutras* is largely the story of how Inchausti learned how to teach. It is appropriate that we should approach the end of this long effort of our own to become better teachers by watching someone else try to do the same thing.

To what extent, we might ask, does Inchausti have to become something of a father to the boys before he can become an effective teacher? Does his departure from lesson plans and established methods make him a better or worse teacher? Can his definition of teaching as "attempting the impossible" also serve as a useful definition of parenting? And does his notion of teaching as a form of prayer make sense, or is it too exalted, even pretentious, to help us along our own way toward better teaching?

We may and should ask some of these same questions of Eva Brann. In particular, we should notice a contrast between Paley on the one hand and Inchausti and Brann on the other. In the last words of her book, Paley tells us that she strives in her teaching to show students how to think about "the problems they need to solve." But neither Inchausti nor Brann construe human learning or human life primarily in terms of problem-solving. They are more inclined to speak, in the context of teaching and learning, of depth, mystery, prayer, and understanding than to speak of problems and solutions, or of techniques and skills. They are not so much opposed to the kind of closure that "solving" suggests as they are comparatively less interested in things that have solutions. They prefer questions to problems.

Whatever we think of someone like Inchausti and his teaching, his work reviews for us in the conventional context of the classroom many of the themes that we have set forth to inform our presentation of teaching in everyday life. Like Plato and Augustine, Inchausti presents teaching within a religious framework, and he construes teaching as a "sublime vocation." Part of his own development as a teacher involved his thinking about the aims of education critically in terms of many of the motives and reasons for teaching that we encountered in Part I. Perhaps most important, he learned to teach by finding a brother to teach him.

We can compare Brother Blake to Mr. Bixby in Twain's *Old Times on the Mississippi* (Part I), to Socrates in *Meno* (Part II), to the prophet Nathan (Part I), and to all of the teachers we have met during the course of these readings. The word 'brother' suggests both family ties and religious obligations. And this brings to mind all of the times we have seen family members haunt and invade the classroom—the *oma* or grandmother in the poem "Dream of the School" in Part I, John Quincy Adams in the reading from *The Education of Henry Adams*, the maternal figure of Madame Guérin in the life of *The Wild Boy of Aveyron* (Part I), and the grandmother and grandfather who appear in the very first story that Vivian Paley recounts in the prologue to *Wally's Stories*. However much we may try to keep the home out of the classroom, however much modern culture has tended to separate the components of human growth and development into separate functions and domains, we have found it difficult to keep these realms altogether apart and distinct. Indeed, the major premise of this collection is that teaching is a part of the ethics of everyday life for all of us, not simply the business of a professional group.

Perhaps we should conclude by revisiting that premise. On the one hand, we have learned much to suggest that human beings in all domains of life have much to teach one another about teaching. On the other hand, we have come to experience the sudden appearances of parents or grandparents in classrooms as intrusions. The walk from home to school is something of a forced march, as it was for the young Henry Adams, and something of an escape from the messier emotional terrain of domesticity, as it was for the young Rufus in Agee's *A Death in the Family*. Many of us have probably felt similar misgivings about the place of religion in teaching. On the one hand, we may be inclined to agree with writers as different as St. Augustine and Robert Inchausti that all teaching is a kind of religious exercise, depending in part for its efficacy on processes and powers beyond our control, and requiring of the teacher the exercise of virtues that are as much moral and spiritual as they are intellectual. On the other hand, we may conclude that religious faith is a private matter, not a public one, that many good teachers are not at all religious, and that the idea that education is finally spiritual formation belongs to a vanished world.

The difficulties peculiar to our own time and place have given to some of these questions their own distinctive urgencies. If all families or even most of them were like the family portrayed in Agee's book, it would be easier, more cogent, and more plausible to argue for fairly rigorous and rigid boundaries between what is appropriate at home and what is appropriate at school. But we know that in our own time we have found "wild boys" like the one found at Aveyron in the midst of our own major cities: savagery in the midst of civilization. None of us, therefore, can be completely confident about the answers we might give to the larger public questions about the relationships between home, school, and church. Nor can a book like this one address successfully questions of that magnitude. It can recognize, however, that in confusing times like these we need more than ever to learn about how to teach well from whatever sources of wisdom we can find, and to uphold one another in these everyday ventures of faith and hope. We hope that this collection of readings furthers these modest endeavors. And we join in concluding with Eva Brann that now is the time for questions.

Readings in Part IV

1. James Agee, *A Death in the Family* (New York: Bantam Books, 1969), pp. 53–62, 80–103. This tenderly eloquent portrayal of a family shows the father and mother shaping the world of the young boy Rufus in countless ways, showing, as well as any work I know, the deep connections between love and human understanding. The film version of this book, *All the Way Home*, directed by David Susskind and starring Robert Preston and Jean Simmons, superbly explores these issues as well. It is a great film for the entire family.

2. Henry Adams, *The Education of Henry Adams*, edited by Ernest Samuels (Boston: Houghton/Mifflin, 1973), pp. 3–22. Henry Adams was the grandson of President John Quincy Adams and the great-grandson of John Adams, the second president of the United States. This opening chapter of Henry's famous autobiography captures masterfully the way in which pressures of cultural environment and family tradition shape character and supply education. The central episode of the chapter is a splendid example of teaching without words, and it describes quite literally a movement from the home to the school that Henry Adams never forgot.

3. Vivian Gussin Paley, *Wally's Stories: Conversations in the Kindergarten* (Cambridge: Harvard University Press, 1981), pp. 1–31, 194–223. This selection lets us listen to the imaginative play and the conversations among a group of kindergarten children. Vivian Paley, the MacArthur Award–winning teacher at the Lab School at the University of Chicago, has written several books based upon her observations of children. I feel personally indebted to "Mrs. Paley," as she was once known to me, since she was my oldest daughter Kaethe's first teacher, and Kaethe has remained ever since alive to the pleasures of learning.

4. Robert Inchausti, *Spitwad Sutras: Classroom Teaching as Sublime Vocation* (Westport, Conn.: Bergin and Garvey, 1993), pp. 23–70, 153–168. This reading invites all of us to think of teaching as a "calling" and to think of the whole process of education in religious terms. It also gives us the opportunity to watch Inchausti's teacher, Brother Blake, teach him how to teach. The selection

concludes with Brother Blake's own "Maxims and Aphorisms" and with a list of recommended readings on teaching, some of which are included in the present volume.

5. Eva Brann, *Depth and Desire* (Annapolis, Md.: St. John's University Press, 1990), pp. 1–11. This concluding reading completes our journey in this last section from home to kindergarten to middle school and finally to college. It ends where we began, by pondering some of the most fundamental questions about teaching and learning.

James Agee, *A Death in the Family*

Waking in darkness, he saw the window. Curtains, a tall, cloven wave, towered almost to the floor. Transparent, manifold, scalloped along their inward edges like the valves of a sea creature, they moved delectably on the air of the open window.

Where they were touched by the carbon light of the street lamp, they were as white as sugar. The extravagant foliage which had been wrought into them by machinery showed even more sharply white where the light touched, and elsewhere was black in the limp cloth.

The light put the shadows of moving leaves against the curtains, which moved with the moving curtains and upon the bare glass between the curtains.

Where the light touched the leaves they seemed to burn, a bitter green. Elsewhere they were darkest gray and darker. Beneath each of these thousands of closely assembled leaves dwelt either no natural light or richest darkness. Without touching each other these leaves were stirred as, silently, the whole tree moved in its sleep.

Directly opposite his window was another. Behind this open window, too, were curtains which moved and against them moved the scattered shadows of other leaves. Beyond these curtains and beyond the bare glass between, the room was as dark as his own.

He heard the summer night.

All the air vibrated like a fading bell with the latest exhausted screaming of locusts. Couplings clashed and conjoined; a switch engine breathed heavily. An auto engine bore beyond the edge of audibility the furious expletives of its incompetence. Hooves broached, along the hollow street, the lackadaisical rhythms of the weariest of clog dancers, and endless in circles, narrow iron tires grinced continuously after. Along the sidewalks, with incisive heels and leathery shuffle, young men and women advanced, retreated.

A rocking chair betrayed reiterant strain, as of a defective lung; like a single note from a stupendous jew's-harp, the chain of a porch swing twanged.

Somewhere very near, intimate to some damp inch of the grass between these homes, a cricket peeped, and was answered as if by his echo.

Humbled beneath the triumphant cries of children, which tore the whole darkness like streams of fire, the voices of men and women on their porches rubbed cheerfully against each other, and in the room next his own, like the laboring upward of laden windlasses and the mildest pouring out of fresh water, he heard the voices of men and women who were familiar to him. They groaned, rewarded;

lifted, and spilled out: and watching the windows, listening at the heart of the proud bell of darkness, he lay in perfect peace.

Gentle, gentle dark.
My darkness. Do you listen? Oh, are you hollowed, all one taking ear?
My darkness. Do you watch me? Oh, are you rounded, all one guardian eye?
Oh gentlest dark. Gentlest, gentlest night. My darkness. My dear darkness.

Under your shelter all things come and go.
Children are violent and valiant, they run and they shout like the winners of impossible victories, but before long now, even like me, they will be brought into their sleep.
Those who are grown great talk with confidence and are at all times skillful to serve and to protect, but before long now they too, before long, even like me, will be taken in and put to bed.
Soon come those hours when no one wakes. Even the locusts, even the crickets, silent shall be, as frozen brooks
In Your great sheltering.

I hear my father; I need never fear.
I hear my mother; I shall never be lonely, or want for love.
When I am hungry it is they who provide for me; when I am in dismay, it is they who fill me with comfort.
When I am astonished or bewildered, it is they who make the weak ground firm beneath my soul: it is in them that I put my trust.
When I am sick it is they who send for the doctor; when I am well and happy, it is in their eyes that I know best that I am loved; and it is towards the shining of their smiles that I lift up my heart and in their laughter that I know my best delight.
I hear my father and my mother and they are my giants, my king and my queen, beside whom there are no others so wise or worthy or honorable or brave or beautiful in this world.
I need never fear: nor ever shall I lack for loving kindness.

And those also who talk with them in that room beneath whose door the light lies like a guardian slave, a bar of gold, my witty uncle, and my girlish aunt: I have yet to know them well, but they and my father and my mother are all fond of each other, and I like them, and I know that they like me.
I hear the easy chiming of their talk and their laughter.

*But before long now they too will leave and the house will become al-
most silent and before long the darkness, for all its leniency, will take my father
and my mother and will bring them, even as I have been brought, to bed and
to sleep.*

*You come to us once each day and never a day rises into brightness but you
stand behind it; you are upon us, you overwhelm us, all of each night. It is you
who release from work, who bring parted families and friends together, and people
for a little while are calm and free, and all at ease together; but before long, before
long, all are brought down silent and motionless*
     Under your sheltering, your great sheltering, darkness.
     *And all through that silence you walk as if none but you had ever breathed,
had ever dreamed, had ever been.*

My darkness, are you lonely?

Only listen, and I will listen to you.
Only watch me, and I will watch into your eyes.
*Only know that I am awake and aware of you, only be my friend, and I will
be your friend.*
     You need not ever fear; or ever be lonely; or want for love.
     Tell me your secrets; you can trust me.
     Come near. Come very near.

*Darkness indeed came near. It buried its eye against the eye of the child's own
soul, saying:*
     Had ever breathed, had ever dreamed, had ever been.
     *And somewhat as in blind night, on a mild sea, a sailor may be made aware
of an iceberg, fanged and mortal, bearing invisibly near, by the unwarned charm
of its breath, nothingness now revealed itself: that permanent night upon which
the stars in their expiring generations are less than the glinting of gnats, and nebu-
lae, more trivial than winter breath; that darkness in which eternity lies bent and
pale, a dead snake in a jar, and infinity is the sparkling of a wren blown out to
sea; that inconceivable chasm of invulnerable silence in which cataclysms of gal-
axies rave mute as amber.*
     Darkness said:
     *When is this meeting, child, where are we, who are you, child, who are you,
do you know who you are, do you know who you are, child; are you?*
     *He knew that he would never know, though memory, almost captured, un-
recapturable, unbearably tormented him. That this little boy whom he inhabited
was only the cruelest of deceits. That he was but the nothingness of nothingness,*

condemned by some betrayal, condemned to be aware of nothingness. That yet in that desolation, he was not without companions. For featureless on the abyss, invincible, moved monstrous intuitions. And from the depth and wide throat of eternity burned the cold, delirious chuckle of rare monsters beyond rare monsters, cruelty beyond cruelty.

Darkness said:

Under my sheltering: in my great sheltering.

In the corner, not quite possible to detach from the darkness, a creature increased, which watched him.

Darkness said:

You hear the man you call your father: how can you ever fear?

Under the washstand, carefully, something moved.

You hear the woman who thinks you are her child.

Beneath his prostrate head, eternity opened.

Hear how he laughs at you; in what amusement she agrees.

The curtain sighed as powers unspeakable passed through it.

Darkness purred with delight and said:

What is this change your eye betrays?

Only a moment ago, I was your friend, or so you claimed; why this sudden loss of love?

Only a moment ago you were all eagerness to know my secrets; where is your hunger now?

Only be steadfast: for now, my dear, my darling, the moment comes when hunger and love will be forever satisfied.

And darkness, smiling, leaned ever more intimately inward upon him, laid open the huge, ragged mouth ———

Ahhhhh . . . !

Child, child, why do you betray me so?

Come near. Come very near.

Ohhhhhh . . . !

Must you be naughty? It would grieve me terribly to have to force you.

You know that you can never get away: you don't even want to get away.

But with that, the child was torn into two creatures, of whom one cried out for his father.

The shadows lay where they belonged, and he lay shaken in his tears. He saw the window; waited.

Still the cricket struck his chisel; the voices persisted, placid as bran.

But behind his head, in that tall shadow which his eyes could never reach, who could dare dream what abode its moment?

The voices chafed, untroubled: grumble and babble.

He cried out again more fiercely for his father.

There seemed a hollowing in the voices, as if they crossed a high trestle.

Serenely the curtain dilated, serenely failed.

The shadows lay where they belonged, but strain as he might, he could not descry what lay in the darkest of them.

The voices relaxed into their original heartlessness.

He swiftly turned his head and stared through the bars at the head of the crib. He could not see what stood there. He swiftly turned again. Whatever it might be had dodged, yet more swiftly: stood once more, still, forever, beyond and behind his hope of seeing.

He saw the basin and that it was only itself; but its eye was wicked ice.

Even the sugar curtains were evil, a senselessly fumbling mouth; and the leaves, wavering, stifled their tree like an infestation.

Near the window, a stain on the wallpaper, pale brown, a serpent shape.

Deadly, the opposite window returned his staring.

The cricket cherished what avaricious secret: patiently sculptured what effigy of dread?

The voices buzzed, pleased and oblivious as locusts. They cared nothing for him.

He screamed for his father.

And now the voices changed. He heard his father draw a deep breath and lock it against his palate, then let it out harshly against the bones of his nose in a long snort of annoyance. He heard the Morris chair creak as his father stood up and he heard sounds from his mother which meant that she was disturbed by his annoyance and that she would see to him, Jay; his uncle and his aunt made quick, small, attendant noises and took no further part in the discussion and his father's voice, somewhat less unkind than the snort and the way he had gotten from his chair but still annoyed, saying, "No, he hollered for me, I'll see to him"; and heard his mastering, tired approach. He was afraid, for he was no longer deeply frightened; he was grateful for the evidence of tears.

The room opened full of gold, his father stooped through the door and closed it quietly; came quietly to the crib. His face was kind.

"Wuzza matter?" he asked, teasing gently, his voice at its deepest.

"Daddy," the child said thinly. He sucked the phlegm from his nose and swallowed it.

His voice raised a little. "Why, what's *the* trouble *with my* little boy," he said, and fumbled and got out his handkerchief. "What's *the* trouble! What's *he* crine *about!*" The harsh cloth smelt of tobacco; with his fingertips, his father removed crumbs of tobacco from the child's damp face.

"Blow," he said. "You know your mamma don't like you to swallah that stuff." He felt the hand strong beneath his head and a sob overtook him as he blew.

"Why, what's wrong?" his father exclaimed; and now his voice was entirely kind. He lifted the child's head a little more, knelt and looked carefully into his eyes; the child felt the strength of the other hand, covering his chest, patting gently. He endeavored to make a little more of his sobbing than came out, but the moment had departed.

"Bad dream?"

He shook his head, no.

"Then what's the trouble?"

He looked at his father.

"Feared a—fraid of the dark?"

He nodded; he felt tears on his eyes.

"Noooooooooo," his father said, pronouncing it like do. "You're a big *boy* now. Big *boys* don't get skeered of a little dark. Big *boys* don't cry. Where's the dark that skeered you? Is it over here?" With his head he indicated the darkest corner. The child nodded. He strode over, struck a match on the seat of his pants.

Nothing there.

"Nothing there that oughtn't to be. . . . Under here?" He indicated the bureau. The child nodded, and began to suck at his lower lip. He struck another match, and held it under the bureau, then under the washstand.

Nothing there. There either.

"Nothing there but an old piece a baby-soap. See?" He held the soap close where the child could smell it; it made him feel much younger. He nodded. "Any place else?"

The child turned and looked through the head of the crib; his father struck a match. "Why, there's poor ole Jackie," he said. And sure enough, there he was, deep in the corner.

He blew dust from the cloth dog and offered it to the child. "You want Jackie?"

He shook his head.

"You don't want poor little ole Jackie? So lonesome? Alayin back there in the corner all this time?"

He shook his head.

"Gettin too big for Jackie?"

He nodded, uncertain that his father would believe him. "Then you're gettin too big to cry."

Poor ole Jackie.

"Pore ole Jackie."

"Pore little ole Jackie, so lonesome."

He reached up for him and took him, and faintly recalled, as he gave him comfort, a multitude of fire-tipped candles (and bristling needles) and a strong green smell, a dog more gaily colored and much larger, over which he puzzled, and his father's huge face, smiling, saying, "It's a dog." His father too remembered how he had picked out the dog with great pleasure and had given it too soon, and here it was now too late. Comforting gave him comfort and a deep yawn, taking him by surprise, was half out of him before he could try to hide it. He glanced anxiously at his father.

"Gettin sleepy, uh?" his father said; it was hardly even a question.

He shook his head.

"Time you did. Time we all got to sleep."

He shook his head.

"You're not skeered any more are you?"

He considered lying, and shook his head.

"Boogee man, all gone, scared away, huh?"

He nodded.

"Now go on to sleep then, son," his father said. He saw that the child very badly did not want him to go away, and realized suddenly that he might have lied about being scared, and he was touched, and put his hand on his son's forehead. "You just don't want to be lonesome," he said tenderly; "just like little ole Jackie. You just don't want to be left alone." The child lay still.

"Tell you what I'll do," his father said, "I'll sing you one song, and then you be a good boy and go on to sleep. Will you do that?" The child pressed his forehead upward against the strong warm hand and nodded.

"What'll we sing?" his father asked.

"Froggy would a wooin go," said the child; it was the longest.

"At's a long one," his father said, "at's a long old song. You won't ever be awake that long, will you?"

He nodded.

"Ah right," said his father; and the child took a fresh hold on Jackie and settled back looking up at him. He sang very low and very quietly: Frog he would a wooin' go uhhooooo!, Frog he would a wooin' go uh-hooooo, uh-hoooooo, and all about the courting-clothes the frog wore, and about the difficulties and ultimate success of the courtship and what several of the neighbors said and who the preacher would be and what he said about the match, uh-hoooo, and finally, what will the weddin supper be uhooooo, catfish balls and sassafras tea uh-hoooo, while he gazed at the wall and the child gazed up into the eyes which did not look at him and into the singing face in the dark. Every couple of verses or so the father glanced down, but the child's eyes were as darkly and steadfastly open at the end of the long song as at the beginning, though it was beginning to be an effort for him.

He was amused and pleased. Once he got started singing, he always loved to sing. There were ever so many of the old songs that he knew, which he liked best, and also some of the popular songs; and although he would have been embarrassed if he had been made conscious of it, he also enjoyed the sound of his own voice. "Ain't you asleep yet?" he said, but even the child felt there was no danger of his leaving, and shook his head quite frankly.

"Sing gallon," he said, for he liked the amusement he knew would come into his father's face, though he did not understand it. It came, and he struck up the song, still more quietly because it was a fast, sassy tune that would be likely to wake you up. He was amused because his son had always mistaken the words "gal and" for "gallon," and because his wife and to a less extent her relatives were not entirely amused by his amusement. They felt, he knew, that he was not a man to take the word "gallon" so purely as a joke; not that the drinking had been any sort of problem, for a long time now. He sang:

I got a gallon an a sugarbabe too, my honey, my baby,
I got a gallon an a sugarbabe too, my honey, my sweet thing.
I got a gallon an a sugarbabe too,
Gal don't love me but my sugarbabe do
    This mornin,
    This evenin,
      So soon.

When they kill a chicken, she saves me the wing, my honey, my baby,
When they kill a chicken, she saves me the wing, my honey, my sweet thing,
When they kill a chicken, she saves me the wing, my honey
Think I'm aworkin ain't adoin a thing
    This mornin,
    This evenin,
      So soon.

Every night about a half past eight, my honey, my baby,
Every night about a half past eight, my honey, my sweet thing
Every night about a half past eight, my honey
Ya find me awaitin at the white folks' gate
    This mornin,
    This evenin,
      So soon.

The child still stared up at him; because there was so little light or perhaps because he was so sleepy, his eyes seemed very dark, although the father knew they *were nearly as light as his own. He took his hand away and blew the moisture dry on the child's forehead, smoothed his hair away, and put his hand back:*

What in the world you doin, Google Eyes? he sang, very slowly, while he and the child looked at each other,
> *What in the world you doin, Google Eyes?*
> *What in the world you doin, Google Eyes?*
> *What in the world you doin, Google Eyes?*

His eyes slowly closed, sprang open, almost in alarm, closed again.

> *Where did you get them great big Google Eyes?*
> *Where did you get them great big Google Eyes?*
> *You're the best there is and I need you in my biz,*
> *Where in the world did you get them Google Eyes?*

He waited. He took his hand away. The child's eyes opened and he felt as if he had been caught at something. He touched the forehead again, more lightly. "Go to sleep, honey," he said. "Go on to sleep now." The child continued to look up at him and a tune came unexpectedly into his head, and lifting his voice almost to tenor he sang, almost inaudibly:

> *Oh, I hear them train car wheels arumblin,*
> *Ann, they're mighty near at hand,*
> *I hear that train come arumblin,*
> *Come arumblin through the land.*
> > *Git on board, little children,*
> > *Git on board, little children,*
> > *Git on board, little children,*
> > *There's room for many and more.*

To the child it looked as if his father were gazing off into a great distance and, looking up into these eyes which looked so far away, he too looked far away:

> *Oh, I look a way down yonder,*
> *Ann, uh what dyou reckon I see,*
> *A band of shinin angels,*
> *A comin' after me.*
> > *Git on board, little children,*
> > *Git on board, little children,*

> Git on board, little children,
> There's room for many and more.

He did not look down but looked straight on into the wall in silence for a good while, and sang:

> Oh, every time the sun goes down,
> There's a dollar saved for Betsy Brown,
> Sugar Babe.

He looked down. He was almost certain now that the child was asleep. So much more quietly that he could scarcely hear himself, and that the sound stole upon the child's near sleep like a band of shining angels, he went on:

> There's a good old sayin, as you all know,
> That you can't track a rabbit when there ain't no snow
> Sugar Babe.

Here again he waited, his hand listening against the child, for he was so fond of the last verse that he always hated to have to come to it and end it; but it came into his mind and became so desirable to sing that he could resist it no longer:

> Oh, tain't agoin to rain on, tain't agoin to snow:

He felt a strange coldness on his spine, and saw the glistening as a great cedar moved and tears came into his eyes:

> But the sun's agoin to shine, an the wind's agoin to blow
> Sugar Babe.

A great cedar, and the colors of limestone and of clay; the smell of wood smoke and, in the deep orange light of the lamp, the silent logs of the walls, his mother's face, her ridged hand mild on his forehead: Don't you fret, Jay, don't you fret. And before his time, before even he was dreamed of in this world, she must have lain under the hand of her mother or her father and they in their childhood under other hands, away on back through the mountains, away on back through the years, it took you right on back as far as you could ever imagine, right on back to Adam, only no one did it for him; or maybe did God?

How far we all come. How far we all come away from ourselves. So far, so much between, you can never go home again. You can go home, it's good to go *home, but you never really get all the way home again in your life. And what's it all for? All I tried to be, all I ever wanted and went away for, what's it all for?*

Just one way, you do get back home. You have a boy or a girl of your own and now and then you remember, and you know how they feel, and it's almost the same as if you were your own self again, as young as you could remember.

And God knows he was lucky, so many ways, and God knows he was thankful. Everything was good and better than he could have hoped for, better than he ever deserved; only, whatever it was and however good it was, it wasn't what you once had been, and had lost, and could never have again, and once in a while, once in a long time, you remembered, and knew how far you were away, and it hit you hard enough, that little while it lasted, to break your heart.

He felt thirsty, and images of stealthiness and deceit, of openness, anger and pride, immediately possessed him, and immediately he fought them off. *If ever I get drunk again,* he told himself proudly, *I'll kill myself. And there are plenty good reasons why I won't kill myself. So I won't even get drunk again.*

He felt consciously strong, competent both for himself and against himself, and this pleasurable sense of firmness contended against the perfect and limpid remembrance he had for a moment experienced, and he tried sadly, vainly, to re-capture it. But now all that he remembered, clear as it was to him, and dear to him, no longer moved his heart, and he was in this sadness, almost without thought, staring at the wall, when the door opened softly behind him and he was caught by a spasm of rage and alarm, then of shame for these emotions.

"Jay," his wife called softly. "Isn't he asleep yet?"

"Yeah, he's asleep," he said, getting up and dusting his knees. "Reckon it's later than I knew."

"Andrew and Amelia had to go," she whispered, coming over. She leaned past him and straightened the sheet. "They said tell you good night." She lifted the child's head with one hand, while her husband, frowning, vigorously shook his head; "It's all right, Jay, he's sound asleep;" she smoothed the pillow, and drew away: "They were afraid if they disturbed you they might wake Rufus."

"Gee. I'm sorry not to see them. Is it so late?"

"You must have been in here nearly an hour! What was the matter with him?"

"Bad dream, I reckon; fraid of the dark."

"He's all right? Before he went to sleep, I mean?"

"Sure; he's all right." He pointed at the dog. "Look what I found."

"Goodness sake, where was it?"

"Back in the corner, under the crib."

"Well shame on me! But Jay, it must be awfully dirty!"

"Naww; I dusted it off."

She said, shyly, "I'll be glad when I can stoop again."

He put his hand on her shoulder. "So will I."

"Jay!" she drew away, really offended.

"Honey!" he said, amused and flabbergasted. He put his arm around her. "I only meant the baby! I'll be glad when the baby's here!"

She looked at him intently (she did not yet realize that she was near-sighted), understood him, and smiled and then laughed softly in her embarrassment. He put his finger to her lips, jerking his head towards the crib. They turned and looked down at their son.

"So will I, Jay darling," she whispered. "So will I."

His mother sang to him too. Her voice was soft and shining gray like her dear gray eyes. She sang, "Sleep baby sleep, Thy father watches the sheep," and he could see his father sitting on a hillside looking at a lot of white sheep in the darkness but why; "thy mother shakes the dreamland tree and down fall little dreams on thee," and he could see the little dreams floating down easily like huge flakes of snow at night and covering him in the darkness like babes in the wood with wide quiet leaves of softly shining light. She sang, "Go tell Aunt Rhoda," three times over, and then, "The old gray goose is dead," and then "She's worth the saving," three times over, and then "To make a featherbed," and then again. Three times over. Go tell Aunt Rhoda; and then again the old gray goose is dead. He did not know what "she's worth the saving" meant, and it was one of the things he always took care not to ask, because although it sounded so gentle he was also sure that somewhere inside it there was something terrible to be afraid of exactly because it sounded so gently, and he would become very much afraid instead of only a little afraid if he asked and learned what it meant. All the more, because when his mother sang this song he could always see Aunt Rhoda, and she wasn't at all like anybody else, she was like her name, mysterious and gray. She was very tall, as tall even as his father. She stood near a well on a big flat open place of hard bare ground, quite a way from where he saw her from, and even so he could see how very tall she was. Far back behind her there were dark trees without any leaves. She just stood there very quiet and straight as if she were waiting to be gone and told that the old gray goose is dead. She wore a long gray dress with a skirt that touched the ground and her hands were hidden in the great falling folds of the skirt. He could never see her face because it was too darkly within the shadow of the sunbonnet she wore, but from within that shadow he could always just discern the shining of her eyes, and they were looking straight at him, not angrily, and not kindly either, just looking and waiting. She is worth the saving.

She sang, "Swing low, sweet cherryut," and that was the best song of all. "Comin for to care me home." So glad and willing and peaceful. A cherryut was a sort of a beautiful wagon because home was too far to walk, a long, long way, but of course it was like a cherry, too, only he could not understand how a beautiful wagon and a cherry could be like each other, but they were. Home was a long,

long way. Much too far to walk and you can only come home when God sends the cherryut for you. And it would care him home. He did not even try to imagine *what home was like except of course it was even nicer than home where he lived, but he always knew it was home.* He always especially knew how happy he was *in his own home when he heard about the other home because then he always felt he knew exactly where he was and that made it good to be exactly there.* His father *loved to sing this song too and sometimes in the dark, on the porch, or lying out all together on a quilt in the back yard, they would sing it together. They would not be talking, just listening to the little sounds, and looking up at the stars, and feeling ever so quiet and happy and sad at the same time, and all of a sudden in a very quiet voice his father sang out, almost as if he were singing to himself,* "Swing low," *and by the time he got to* "cherryut" *his mother was singing too, just as softly, and then their voices went up higher, singing* "comin for to carry me home," *and looking up between their heads from where he lay he looked right into the stars, so near and friendly, with a great drift of dust like flour across the tip of the sky. His father sang it differently from his mother. When she sang the second* "Swing" *she just sang* "swing low," *on two notes, in a simple, clear voice, but he sang* "swing" *on two notes, sliding from the note above to the one she sang, and blurring his voice and making it more forceful on the first note, and springing it, dark and blurry, off the* "l" *in* "low," *with a rhythm that made his son's body stir. And when he came to* "Tell all my friends I'm comin too," *he started four full notes above her, and slowed up a little, and sort of dreamed his way down among several extra notes she didn't sing, and some of these notes were a kind of blur, like hitting a black note and the next white one at the same time on Grandma's piano, and he didn't sing* "I'm comin'" *but* "I'm uh-comin," *and there too, and all through his singing, there was that excitement of rhythm that often made him close his eyes and move his head in contentment. But his mother sang the same thing clear and true in a sweet, calm voice, fewer and simpler notes. Sometimes she would try to sing it his way and he would try to sing it hers, but they always went back pretty soon to their own way, though he always felt they each liked the other's way very much. He liked both ways very much and best of all when they sang together and he was there with them, touching them on both sides, and even better, from when they sang* "I look over Jordan what do I see," *for then it was so good to look up into the stars, and then they sang* "A band of angels comin after me" *and it seemed as if all the stars came at him like a great shining brass band so far away you weren't quite sure you could even hear the music but so near he could almost see their faces and they all but leaned down deep enough to pick him up in their arms.* Come for to care me home.

They sang it a little slower towards the end as if they hated to come to the finish of it and then they didn't talk at all and after a minute their hands took each other across their child, and things were even quieter, so that all the little noises of the city night raised up again in the quietness, locusts, crickets, foot-steps, hoofs, faint voices, the shufflings of a switch engine, and after awhile, while they all looked into the sky, his father, in a strange and distant, sighing voice, said "Well . . . " and after a little his mother answered, with a quiet and strange happy sadness, "Yes . . . " and they waited a good little bit longer, not saying anything, and then his father took him up into his arms and his mother rolled up the quilt and they went in and he was put to bed.

He came right up to her hip bone; not so high on his father.

She wore dresses, his father wore pants. Pants were what he wore too, but they were short and soft. His father's were hard and rough and went right down to his shoes. The cloths of his mother's clothes were soft like his.

His father wore hard coats too and a hard celluloid collar and sometimes a vest with hard buttons. Mostly his clothes were scratchy except the striped shirts and the shirts with little dots or diamonds on them. But not as scratchy as his cheeks.

His cheeks were warm and cool at the same time and they scratched a little even when he had just shaved. It always tickled, on his cheek or still more on his neck, and sometimes hurt a little, too, but it was always fun because he was so strong.

He smelled like dry grass, leather and tobacco, and sometimes a different smell, full of great energy and a fierce kind of fun, but also a feeling that things might go wrong. He knew what that was because he overheard them arguing. Whiskey.

For awhile he had a big mustache and then he took it off and his mother said, "Oh Jay, you look just worlds *nicer, you have such a* nice *mouth, it's a* shame *to hide it." After awhile he grew the mustache again. It made him look much older, taller and stronger, and when he frowned the mustache frowned too and it was very frightening. Then he took it off again and she was pleased all over again and after that he kept it off.*

She called it mustásh. He called it must'ash and sometimes mush'tash but then he was joking, talking like a darky. He liked to talk darky talk and the way he sang was like a darky too, only when he sang he wasn't joking.

His neck was dark tan and there were deep crisscross cracks all over the back of it.

His hands were so big he could cover him from the chin to his bath-thing. There were big blue strings under the skin on the backs of them. Veins, those were. Black hair even on the backs of the fingers and ever so much hair on the wrists; big veins in his arms, like ropes.

For some time now his mother had seemed different. Almost always when she spoke to him it was as if she had something else very much on her mind, and so was making a special effort to be gentle and attentive to him. And it was as if whatever it was that was on her mind was very momentous. Sometimes she looked at him in such a way that he felt that she was very much amused about something. He did not know how to ask her what she was amused by and as he watched her, wondering what it was, and she watched his puzzlement, she sometimes looked more amused than ever, and once when she looked particularly amused, and he looked particularly bewildered, her smile became shaky and turned into laughter and, quickly taking his face between her hands, she exclaimed, "I'm not laughing at you, darling!" and for the first time he felt that perhaps she was.

There were other times when she seemed to have almost no interest in him, but only to be doing things for him because they had to be done. He felt subtly lonely and watched her carefully. He saw that his father's manner had changed towards her ever so little; he treated her as if she were very valuable and he seemed to be conscious of the tones of his voice. Sometimes in the mornings Grandma would come in and if he was around he was told to go away for a little while. Grandma did not hear well and carried a black ear trumpet which was sticky and sour on the end that she put in her ear; but try as he would they talked so quietly that he could hear very little, and none of it enlightened him. There were special words which were said with a special kind of hesitancy or shyness, such as "pregnancy" and "kicking" and "discharge," but others, which seemed fully as strange, such as "layette" and "basinette" and "bellyband," seemed to inspire no such fear. Grandma also treated him as if something strange was going on, but whatever it was, it was evidently not dangerous, for she was always quite merry with him. His father and his Uncle Andrew and Grandpa seemed to treat him as they always had, though there seemed to be some hidden kind of strain in Uncle Andrew's feeling for his mother. And Aunt Hannah was the same as ever with him, except that she paid more attention to his mother, now. Aunt Amelia looked at his mother a good deal when she thought nobody else was watching, and once when she saw him watching her she looked quickly away and turned red.

Everyone seemed either to look at his mother with ill-concealed curiosity or to be taking special pains not to look anywhere except, rather fixedly and cheerfully, into her eyes. For now she was swollen up like a vase, and there was a peculiar lethargic lightness in her face and in her voice. He had a distinct feeling that he should not ask what was happening to her. At last he asked Uncle Andrew, "Uncle Andrew, why is Mama so fat?" and his uncle replied, with such apparent anger or alarm that he was frightened, "Why, don't you know?" and abruptly walked out of the room.

Next day his mother told him that soon he was going to have a very wonderful surprise. When he asked what a surprise was she said it was like being given things for Christmas only ever so much nicer. When he asked what he was going to be given she said that she did not mean it was a present, specially for him, or for him to have, or keep, but something for everybody, and especially for them. When he asked what it was, she said that if she told him it wouldn't be a surprise any more, would it? When he said that he wanted to know anyway, she said that she would tell him, only it would be so hard for him to imagine what it was before it came that she thought it was better for him to see it first. When he asked when it was coming she said that she didn't know exactly but very soon now, in only a week or two, perhaps sooner, and she promised him that he would know right away when it did come.

He was aflame with curiosity. He had been too young, the Christmas before, to think of looking for hidden presents, but now he looked everywhere that he could imagine to look until his mother understood what he was doing and told him there was no use looking for it because the surprise wouldn't be here until exactly when it came. He asked where was it, then, and heard his father's sudden laugh; his mother looked panicky and cried, "Jay!" all at once, and quickly informed him, "In heaven; still up in heaven."

He looked quickly to his father for corroboration and his father, who appeared to be embarrassed, did not look at him. He knew about heaven because that was where Our Father was, but that was all he knew about it, and he was not satisfied. Again, however, he had a feeling that he would be unwise to ask more.

"Why don't you tell him, Mary?" his father said.

"Oh, Jay," she said in alarm; then said, by moving her lips, "Don't talk of it in front of him!"

"Oh, I'm sorry," and he, too, said with his lips—only a whisper leaked around the silence, "but what's the good? Why not get it over with?"

She decided that it was best to speak openly. "As you know, Jay, I've told Rufus about our surprise that's coming. I told him I'd be glad to tell him what it was, except that it would be so very hard for him to imagine it and such a lovely surprise when he first sees it. Besides, I just have a feeling he might m-make see-oh-en-en-ee-see-tee-eye-oh-en-ess, between—between one thing and another."

"Going to make them, going to make em anyhow," his father said.

"But Jay, there's no use simply forcing it on his att-eighteen-ten, his attention, now, is there? Is there, Jay!"

She seemed really quite agitated, he could not understand why.

"You're right, Mary, and don't you get excited about it. I was all wrong about it. Of course I was." And he got up and came over to her and took her in his arms, and patted her on the back.

"I'm probably just silly about it," she said.

"No, you're not one bit silly. Besides, if you're silly about that, so am I, some way. That just sort of caught me off my guard, that about heaven, that's all."

"Well what can you say?"

"I'm Godd—I can't imagine, sweetheart, and I better just keep my mouth shut."

She frowned, smiled, laughed through her nose and urgently shook her head at him, all at once.

Chapter 4

During the rest of the night, Mary lay in a "white" sleep. She felt as odd, alone in the bed, as if a jaw-tooth had just been pulled, and the whole house seemed larger than it really was, hollow and resonant. The coming of daylight did not bring things back to normal, as she had hoped; the bed and the house, in this silence and pallor, seemed even emptier. She would doze a little, wake and listen to the dry silence, doze, wake again sharply, to the thing that troubled her. She thought of her husband, driving down on one of the most solemn errands of his life, and of his father, lying fatally sick, perhaps dying, perhaps dead at this moment (she crossed herself), and she could not bring herself to feel as deeply about it as she felt that she should, for her husband's sake. She realized that if the situation were reversed, and it was her own father who was dying, Jay would feel much as she felt now, and that she could not blame either him or herself, but that did her no good. For she knew that at the bottom of it the trouble was, simply, that she had never really liked the old man.

She was sure that she didn't look down on him, as many of Jay's relatives all but said to her face and as she feared that Jay himself occasionally believed; certainly not; but she could not like him, as almost everyone else liked him. She knew that if it was Jay's mother who lay dying, there would be no question of her grief, or inadequacy to her husband; and that was a fair measure of how little she really cared for his father. She wondered why she liked him so little (for to say that she actually disliked him, she earnestly assured herself, would be putting it falsely). She realized that it was mainly because everyone forgave him so much, and liked him so well in spite of his shortcomings, and because he accepted their forgiveness and liking so casually, as if this were his natural due or, worse, as if he didn't even realize anything about it. And the worst of this, the thing she resented with enduring anger and distaste, was the burden he had constantly imposed on his wife, and her perfect patience with him, as if she didn't even know it was a burden or that he was taking advantage. It was this unconsciousness in both of them that she could not abide, and if only once Jay's mother had shown one spark of anger, of realization, Mary felt she might have begun to be able to like him. But this brought her into a resentment, almost a dislike, of Jay's mother, which she knew was both unjust and untrue to her actual feelings, and which made her uncomfortable; she was shocked also to realize that she was lying awake in the hour which might well be his last, to think ill of him. *Shame on you,* she said to herself, and thought earnestly of all that she knew was good about him.

He was generous, for one thing. Generous to a fault. And she remembered how, time and again, he had given away, "loaned," to the first person who asked him the favor, money or food or things which were desperately needed home to keep body and soul together. Fault, indeed. Yet it was a good fault. It was no wonder people loved him—or pretended to—and took every possible advantage of him. And he was very genuinely kind-hearted. A wonderful virtue. And tolerant. She had never heard him say an unkind or a bitter word of anybody, not even of people who had outrageously abused his generosity—he could not, she realized, bear to believe that they really meant to; and he had never once, of that she was sure, joined with most of the others in their envious, hostile, contemptuous talking about her.

On the other hand she could be equally sure that he had never really stood up for her strongly and bravely, and angrily, against everyone, as his wife had, for he disliked arguments as much as he did unkindness; but she put that out of her mind. He had never, so far as she knew, complained, about his sickness or pain, or his poverty, and chronically, insanely, as he made excuses for others, he had never made excuses for himself. And certainly he had precious little right to complain, or make excuses; but that too she hastened to put out of her mind. She reproached herself by remembering how thoroughly nice and friendly he had always been to her; and if she had to realize that that was not at all for herself but purely because she was "Jay's woman," as he'd probably say, she certainly couldn't hold that against him; her own best feelings towards him came out of her recognition of him as Jay's father. You couldn't like anyone more than you happened to like them; you simply couldn't. And you couldn't feel more about them than that amount of liking made possible to you. There was a special kind of basic weakness about him; that was what she could not like, or respect, or even forgive, or resign herself to accepting, for it was a kind of weakness which took advantage, and heaped disadvantage and burden on others, and it was not even ashamed for itself, not even aware. And worse, at the bottom of it all, maybe, Jay's father was the one barrier between them, the one stubborn, unresolved, avoided thing, in their complete mutual understanding of Jay's people, his "background." Even now she could not really like him much, or feel deep concern. Her thoughts for him were grave and sad, but only as they would be for any old, tired, suffering human being who had lived long and whose end, it appeared, had come. And even while she thought of him her real mind was on his son's grief and her inadequacy to it. She had not even until this moment, she realized with dismay, given Jay's mother a thought; she had been absorbed wholly in Jay. I must write her, she thought. But of course, perhaps, I'll see her soon.

And yet, clearly as she felt that she realized what the bereavement would mean to Jay's mother, and wrong as she was even to entertain such an idea, she could not help feeling that even more, his death would mean great relief and release. And, it occurred to her, he'll no longer stand between me and Jay.

At this, her soul stopped in utter coldness. God forgive me, she thought, amazed; I almost *wished* for his death!

She clasped her hands and stared at a stain on the ceiling.

O Lord, she prayed; forgive me my unspeakable sinful thought. Lord, cleanse my soul of such abominations. Lord, if it be Thy will, spare him long that I may learn to understand and care for him more, with Thy merciful help. Spare him not for me but for himself, Lord.

She closed her eyes.

Lord, open my heart that I may be worthy in realization of this sorrowful thing, if it must happen, and worthy and of use and comfort to others in their sorrow. Lord God, Lord Jesus, melt away my coldness and apathy of heart, descend and fill my emptiness of heart. And Lord, if it be Thy will, preserve him yet a while, and let me learn to bear my burden more lightly, or to know this burden is a blessing. And if he must be taken, if he is already with Thee now (she crossed herself), may he rest in Thy peace (again she crossed herself).

And Lord, if it be Thy will, that this sorrow must come upon my husband, then I most humbly beseech Thee in Thy mercy that through this tribulation Thou openest my husband's heart, and awake his dear soul, that he may find comfort in Thee that the world cannot give, and see Thee more clearly, and come to Thee. For there, Lord, as Thou knowest, and not in his poor father or my unworthy feelings, is the true, widening gulf between us.

Lord, in Thy mercy, Who can do all things, close this gulf. Make us one in Thee as we are one in earthly wedlock. For Jesus' sake, Amen.

She lay somewhat comforted, but more profoundly disturbed than comforted. For she had never before so clearly put into words, into visible recognition, their religious difference, or the importance of the difference to her. And how important is it to him, she wondered. And haven't I terribly exaggerated my feeling of it? A "gulf"? And "widening"? Was it really? Certainly he never said anything that justified her in such a feeling; nor did she feel anything of that largeness. It really was only that both of them said so very little, as if both took care to say very little. But that was just it. That a thing which meant so much to her, so much more, all the time, should be a thing that they could not share, or could not be open about. Where her only close, true intimate was Aunt Hannah, and her chief love and hope had to rest in the children. That was it. That was the way it seemed bound to widen (she folded her hands, and shook her head, frowning): it was the children. She felt sure that he felt none of Andrew's anger and contempt, and none of her father's irony, but it was very clear by his special quietness, when instances of it came up, that he was very far away from it and from her, that he did not like it. He kept his distance, that was it. His distance, and some kind of dignity, which she respected in him, much as it hurt her, by this silence and withdrawal. And it would widen, oh, inevitably, because quiet and gentle as she would certainly try to be about it, they were going to be brought up as she knew she must bring them up, as Christian, Catholic children. And this was bound to come into the home, quite as much as in church. It was bound in some ways, unless he changed; it was bound in some important ways, try as hard and be as good about it as she was sure they both would, to set his children apart from him, to set his own wife apart from him. And not by any action or wish of his, but by her own deliberate will. Lord God, she prayed, in anguish. Am I wrong? Show me if I am wrong, I beseech Thee. Show me what I am to do.

But God showed her only what she knew already: that come what might she must, as a Christian woman, as a Catholic, bring up her children thoroughly and devoutly in the Faith, and that it was also her task, more than her husband's, that the family remain one, that the gulf be closed.

But if I do this, nothing else that I can do will close it, she reflected. Nothing, nothing will avail.

But I must.

I must just: trust in God, she said, almost aloud. Just: do His will, and put all my trust in Him.

A streetcar passed; Catherine cried.

Chapter 5

"Daddy had to go up to see Grandfather Follet," their mother explained. "He says to kiss both of you for him and he'll probably see you before you're asleep tonight."

"When?" Rufus asked.

"Way, early this morning, before it was light."

"Why?"

"Grampa Follet is very sick. Uncle Ralph phoned up very late last night, when all of us were asleep. Grampa has had one of his attacks."

"What's attack?"

"Eat your cereal, Catherine. Rufus, eat yours. His heart. Like the one he had that time last fall. Only worse, Uncle Ralph says. He wanted very much to see Daddy, just as quick as Daddy could come."

"Why?"

"Because he loves Daddy and if . . . *Eat,* wicker, or it'll all be nasty and cold, and *then* you know how you hate to eat it. Because if Daddy didn't see him soon, Grampa might not get to see Daddy again."

"Why not?"

"Because Grampa is getting old, and when you get old, you can be sick and not get well again. And if you can't get well again, then God lets you go to sleep and you can't see people any more."

"Don't you ever wake up again?"

"You wake up right away, in heaven, but people on earth can't see you any more, and you can't see them."

"Oh."

"*Eat,*" their mother whispered, making a big, nodding mouth and chewing vigorously on air. They ate.

"Mama," Rufus said, "when Oliver went to sleep did he wake up in heaven too?"

"I don't know. I imagine he woke up in a part of heaven God keeps specially for cats."

"Did the rabbits wake up?"

"I'm sure they did if Oliver did."

"All bloody like they were?"

"No, Rufus, that was only their poor little bodies. God wouldn't let them wake up all hurt and bloody, poor things."

"Why did God let the dogs get in?"

"We don't know, Rufus, but it must be a part of His plan we will understand someday."

"What good would it do *Him?*"

"Children, don't dawdle. It's almost school time."

"What good would it do *Him,* Mama, to let the dogs in?"

"I don't know, but someday we'll understand, Rufus, if we're very patient. We mustn't trouble ourselves with these things we can't understand. We just have to be sure that God knows best."

"I bet they sneaked in when He wasn't looking," Rufus said eagerly. "Cause He sure wouldn't have let them if He'd been there. Didn't they, Mama? Didn't they?"

Their mother hesitated, and then said carefully, "No, Rufus, we believe that God is everywhere and knows everything and nothing can happen without His knowing. But the Devil is everywhere too—everywhere except heaven, that is—and he is always tempting us. When we do what he tempts us to do, then God lets us do it."

"What's tempt?"

"Tempt is, well, the Devil tempts us when there is something we want to do, but we know it is bad."

"Why does God let us do bad things?"

"Because He wants us to make up our own minds."

"Even to do bad things, right under His nose?"

"He doesn't *want* us to do bad things, but to know good from bad and be good of our own free choice."

"Why?"

"Because He loves us and wants us to love Him, but if He just *made* us be good, we couldn't really love Him enough. You can't love to do what you are *made* to do, and you couldn't love God if He *made* you."

"But if God can do anything, why can't He do that?"

"Because He doesn't *want* to," their mother said, rather impatiently.

"Why *doesn't* He want to?" Rufus said. "It would be so much easier for Him."

"*God—doesn't—believe—in—the—easy—way,*" she said, with a certain triumph, spacing the words and giving them full emphasis. "Not for us, not for anything or anybody, not even for Himself. God wants us to *come* to Him, to *find* Him, the best we can."

"Like hide-and-go-seek," said Catherine.

"What was that?" their mother asked rather anxiously.

"Like hide . . . "

"Aw, it isn't a *bit* like hide-and-seek, *is* it Mama?" Rufus cut in. "Hidenseek's just a *game*, just a *game*. God doesn't fool around playing *games, does* He, Mama! *Does* He! *Does* He!"

"*Shame on* you, Rufus," his mother said warmly, and not without relief. "Why, *shame on* you!" For Catherine's face had swollen and her mouth had bunched tight, and she glared from her brother to her mother and back again with scalding hot eyes.

"Well He *does*n't," Rufus insisted, angry and bewildered at the turn the discussion had taken.

"That's *enough*, Rufus," his mother whipped out sternly, and leaned across and patted Catherine's hand, which made Catherine's chin tremble and her tears overflow. "That's *all right*, little wicker! That's *all right*! He doesn't play games. Rufus is right about that, but it *is*, someways it *is* like hide-and-seek. You're ab-so-lootly *right!*"

But with this, Catherine was dissolved, and Rufus sat aghast, less at her crying, which made him angry and jealous, than at his sudden solitude. But her crying was so miserable that, angry and jealous as he was, he became ashamed, then sorry for her, and was trying, helplessly, to find a way of showing that he was sorry when his mother glanced up at him fiercely and said, "*Now you march* and get ready for school. I ought to tell Daddy, you're a *bad boy!*"

At the door, a few minutes later, when she leaned to kiss him good-bye and saw his face, she mistook the cause of it and said, more gently but very earnestly: "Rufus, I can see you're sorry, but you mustn't be mean to Catherine. She's just a little *girl*, your *little sister*, and you mustn't ever be unkind to her and hurt her feelings. Do you understand? *Do* you, Rufus?"

He nodded, and felt terribly sorry for his sister and for himself because of the gentleness in his mother's voice.

"Now you come back and tell her how sorry you are, and *hurry*, or you'll be late for school."

He came in shyly with his mother and came up to Catherine; her face was swollen and red and she looked at him bleakly.

"Rufus wants to tell you how sorry he is, Catherine, he hurt your feelings," their mother said.

Catherine looked at him, brutally and doubtfully.

"I *am* sorry, Catherine," he said. "Honest to goodness I am. Because you're a little, *little girl*, and . . ."

But with this Catherine exploded into a roar of angry tears, and brought both fists down into her plate, and Rufus, dumfounded, was hustled brusquely off to school.

Henry Adams, *The Education of Henry Adams*

Chapter I
Quincy (1838–1848)

UNDER the shadow of Boston State House, turning its back on the house of John Hancock, the little passage called Hancock Avenue runs, or ran, from Beacon Street, skirting the State House grounds, to Mount Vernon Street, on the summit of Beacon Hill; and there, in the third house below Mount Vernon Place, February 16, 1838, a child was born, and christened later by his uncle, the minister of the First Church after the tenets of Boston Unitarianism, as Henry Brooks Adams.

Had he been born in Jerusalem under the shadow of the Temple and circumcised in the Synagogue by his uncle the high priest, under the name of Israel Cohen, he would scarcely have been more distinctly branded, and not much more heavily handicapped in the races of the coming century, in running for such stakes as the century was to offer; but, on the other hand, the ordinary traveller, who does not enter the field of racing, finds advantage in being, so to speak, ticketed through life, with the safeguards of an old, established traffic. Safeguards are often irksome, but some times convenient, and if one needs them at all, one is apt to need them badly. A hundred years earlier, such safeguards as his would have secured any young man's success; and although in 1838 their value was not very great compared with what they would have had in 1738, yet the mere accident of starting a twentieth-century career from a nest of associations so colonial—so troglodytic—the First Church, the Boston State House, Beacon Hill, John Hancock and John Adams, Mount Vernon Street and Quincy, all crowding on ten pounds of unconscious babyhood, was so queer as to offer a subject of curious speculation to the baby long after he had witnessed the solution. What could become of such a child of the seventeenth and eighteenth centuries, when he should wake up to find himself required to play the game of the twentieth? Had he been consulted, would he have cared to play the game at all, holding such cards as he held, and suspecting that the game was to be one of which neither he nor anyone else back to the beginning of time knew the rules or the risks or the stakes? He was not consulted and was not responsible, but had he been taken into the confidence of his parents, he would certainly have told them to change nothing as far as concerned him. He would have been astounded by his own luck. Probably no child, born in the year, held better cards than he. Whether life was an honest game of chance, or whether the cards were marked and forced, he could not refuse to play his excellent hand. He could never make the usual plea of irresponsibility. He accepted the situation as though he had been a party to it, and under the same circumstances would do it again, the more readily for knowing the exact values. To his life as a whole he was a consenting, contracting party and partner from the moment he was born to the moment he died. Only with that understanding—as a consciously assenting member in full partnership with the society of his age—had his education an interest to himself or to others.

As it happened, he never got to the point of playing the game at all; he lost himself in the study of it, watching the errors of the players; but this is the only interest in the story, which otherwise has no moral and little incident. A story of education—seventy years of it—the practical value remains to the end in doubt, like other values about which men have disputed since the birth of Cain and Abel; but the practical value of the universe has never been stated in dollars. Although everyone cannot be a Gargantua-Napoleon-Bismarck and walk off with the great bells of Notre Dame, everyone must bear his own universe, and most persons are moderately interested in learning how their neighbors have managed to carry theirs.

This problem of education, started in 1838, went on for three years, while the baby grew, like other babies, unconsciously, as a vegetable, the outside world working as it never had worked before, to get his new universe ready for him. Often in old age he puzzled over the question whether, on the doctrine of chances, he was at liberty to accept himself or his world as an accident. No such accident had ever happened before in human experience. For him, alone, the old universe was thrown into the ash-heap and a new one created. He and his eighteenth-century, troglodytic Boston were suddenly cut apart—separated forever—in act if not in sentiment, by the opening of the Boston and Albany Railroad; the appearance of the first Cunard steamers in the bay; and the telegraphic messages which carried from Baltimore to Washington the news that Henry Clay and James K. Polk were nominated for the Presidency. This was in May, 1844; he was six years old; his new world was ready for use, and only fragments of the old met his eyes.

Of all this that was being done to complicate his education, he knew only the color of yellow. He first found himself sitting on a yellow kitchen floor in strong sunlight. He was three years old when he took this earliest step in education; a lesson of color. The second followed soon; a lesson of taste. On December 3, 1841, he developed scarlet fever. For several days he was as good as dead, reviving only under the careful nursing of his family. When he began to recover strength, about January 1, 1842, his hunger must have been stronger than any other pleasure or pain, for while in after life he retained not the faintest recollection of his illness, he remembered quite clearly his aunt entering the sickroom bearing in her hand a saucer with a baked apple.

The order of impressions retained by memory might naturally be that of color and taste, although one would rather suppose that the sense of pain would be first to educate. In fact, the third recollection of the child was that of discomfort. The moment he could be removed, he was bundled up in blankets and carried from the little house in Hancock Avenue to a larger one which his parents were to occupy for the rest of their lives in the neighboring Mount Vernon Street. The season was midwinter, January 10, 1842, and he never forgot his acute distress for want of air under his blankets, or the noises of moving furniture.

As a means of variation from a normal type, sickness in childhood ought to have a certain value not to be classed under any fitness or unfitness of natural selection; and especially scarlet fever affected boys seriously, both physically and in character, though they might through life puzzle themselves to decide whether it had fitted or unfitted them for success; but this fever of Henry Adams took greater and greater importance in his eyes, from the point of view of education, the longer he lived. At first, the effect was physical. He fell behind his brothers two or three inches in height, and proportionally in bone and weight. His character and processes of mind seemed to share in this fining-down process of scale. He was not good in a fight, and his nerves were more delicate than boys' nerves ought to be. He exaggerated these weaknesses as he grew older. The habit of doubt; of distrusting his own judgment and of totally rejecting the judgment of the world; the tendency to regard every question as open; the hesitation to act except as a choice of evils; the shirking of responsibility; the love of line, form, quality; the horror of ennui; the passion for companionship and the antipathy to society—these are well-known qualities of New England character in no way peculiar to individuals but in this instance they seemed to be stimulated by the fever, and Henry Adams could never make up his mind whether, on the whole, the change of character was morbid or healthy, good or bad for his purpose. His brothers were the type; he was the variation.

As far as the boy knew, the sickness did not affect him at all, and he grew up in excellent health, bodily and mental, taking life as it was given; accepting its local standards without a difficulty, and enjoying much of it as keenly as any other boy of his age. He seemed to himself quite normal, and his companions seemed always to think him so. Whatever was peculiar about him was education, not character, and came to him, directly and indirectly, as the result of that eighteenth-century inheritance which he took with his name.

The atmosphere of education in which he lived was colonial, revolutionary, almost Cromwellian, as though he were steeped, from his greatest grandmother's birth, in the odor of political crime. Resistance to something was the law of New England nature; the boy looked out on the world with the instinct of resistance; for numberless generations his predecessors had viewed the world chiefly as a thing to be reformed, filled with evil forces to be abolished, and they saw no reason to suppose that they had wholly succeeded in the abolition; the duty was unchanged. That duty implied not only resistance to evil, but hatred of it. Boys naturally look on all force as an enemy, and generally find it so, but the New Englander, whether boy or man, in his long struggle with a stingy or hostile universe, had learned also to love the pleasure of hating; his joys were few.

Politics, as a practice, whatever its professions, had always been the systematic organization of hatreds, and Massachusetts politics had been as harsh as the climate. The chief charm of New England was harshness of contrasts and extremes of sensibility—a cold that froze the blood, and a heat that boiled it—so that the pleasure of hating—oneself if no better victim offered—was not its rarest amusement; but the charm was a true and natural child of the soil, not a cultivated weed of the ancients. The violence of the contrast was real and made the strongest motive of education. The double exterior nature gave life its relative values. Winter and summer, cold and heat, town and country, force and freedom, marked two modes of life and thought, balanced like lobes of the brain. Town was winter confinement, school, rule, discipline; straight, gloomy streets, piled with six feet of snow in the middle; frosts that made the snow sing under wheels or runners; thaws when the streets became dangerous to cross; society of uncles, aunts, and cousins who expected children to behave themselves, and who were not always gratified; above all else, winter represented the desire to escape and go free. Town was restraint, law, unity. Country, only seven miles away, was liberty, diversity, outlawry, the endless delight of mere sense impressions given by nature for nothing, and breathed by boys without knowing it.

Boys are wild animals, rich in the treasures of sense, but the New England boy had a wider range of emotions than boys of more equable climates. He felt his nature crudely, as it was meant. To the boy Henry Adams, summer was drunken. Among senses, smell was the strongest—smell of hot pine-woods and sweet-fern in the scorching summer noon; of new-mown hay; of ploughed earth; of box hedges; of peaches, lilacs, syringas; of stables, barns, cow-yards; of salt water and low tide on the marshes; nothing came amiss. Next to smell came taste, and the children knew the taste of everything they saw or touched, from pennyroyal and flagroot to the shell of a pignut and the letters of a spelling-book—the taste of A-B, AB, suddenly revived on the boy's tongue sixty years afterwards. Light, line, and color as sensual pleasures, came later and were as crude as the rest. The New England light is glare, and the atmosphere harshens color. The boy was a full man before he ever knew what was meant by atmosphere; his idea of pleasure in light was the blaze of a New England sun. His idea of color was a peony, with the dew of early morning on its petals. The intense blue of the sea, as he saw it a mile or two away, from the Quincy hills; the cumuli in a June afternoon sky; the strong reds and greens and purples of colored prints and children's picture-books, as the American colors then ran; these were ideals. The opposites or antipathies, were the cold grays of November evenings, and the thick, muddy thaws of Boston winter. With such standards, the Bostonian could not but develop a double nature. Life was a double thing. After a January blizzard, the boy who could look with pleasure into the violent snow-glare of the cold white sunshine, with its intense light and shade, scarcely knew what was meant by tone. He could reach it only by education.

Winter and summer, then, were two hostile lives, and bred two separate natures. Winter was always the effort to live; summer was tropical license. Whether the children rolled in the grass, or waded in the brook, or swam in the salt ocean, or sailed in the bay, or fished for smelts in the creeks, or netted minnows in the salt-marshes, or took to the pine-woods and the granite quarries, or chased muskrats and hunted snapping-turtles in the swamps, or mushrooms or nuts on the autumn hills, summer and country were always sensual living, while winter was always compulsory learning. Summer was the multiplicity of nature; winter was school.

The bearing of the two seasons on the education of Henry Adams was no fancy; it was the most decisive force he ever knew; it ran through life, and made the division between its perplexing, warring, irreconcilable problems, irreducible opposites, with growing emphasis to the last year of study. From earliest childhood the boy was accustomed to feel that, for him, life was double. Winter and summer, town and country, law and liberty, were hostile, and the man who pretended they were not, was in his eyes a schoolmaster—that is, a man employed to tell lies to little boys. Though Quincy was but two hours' walk from Beacon Hill, it belonged in a different world. For two hundred years, every Adams, from father to son, had lived within sight of State Street; and sometimes had lived in it, yet none had ever taken kindly to the town, or been taken kindly by it. The boy inherited his double nature. He knew as yet nothing about his great-grandfather, who had died a dozen years before his own birth: he took for granted that any great-grandfather of his must have always been good, and his enemies wicked; but he divined his great-grandfather's character from his own. Never for a moment did he connect the two ideas of Boston and John Adams; they were separate and antagonistic; the idea of John Adams went with Quincy. He knew his grandfather John Quincy Adams only as an old man of seventy-five or eighty who was friendly and gentle with him, but except that he heard his grandfather always called "the President," and his grandmother "the Madam," he had no reason to suppose that his Adams grandfather differed in character from his Brooks grandfather who was equally kind and benevolent.

He liked the Adams side best, but for no other reason than that it reminded him of the country, the summer, and the absence of restraint. Yet he felt also that Quincy was in a way inferior to Boston, and that socially Boston looked down on Quincy. The reason was clear enough even to a five-year-old child. Quincy had no Boston style. Little enough style had either; a simpler manner of life and thought could hardly exist, short of cave-dwelling. The flint-and-steel with which his grandfather Adams used to light his own fires in the early morning was still on the mantelpiece of his study. The idea of a livery or even a dress for servants, or of an evening toilette, was next to blasphemy. Bathrooms, water-supplies, lighting, heating, and the whole array of domestic comforts, were unknown at Quincy. Boston had already a bathroom, a water-supply, a furnace, and gas. The superiority of Boston was evident, but a child liked it no better for that.

The magnificence of his grandfather Brooks's house in Pearl Street or South Street has long ago disappeared, but perhaps his country house at Medford may still remain to show what impressed the mind of a boy in 1845 with the idea of city splendor. The President's place at Quincy was the larger and older and far the more interesting of the two; but a boy felt at once its inferiority in fashion. It showed plainly enough its want of wealth. It smacked of colonial age, but not of Boston style or plush curtains. To the end of his life he never quite overcame the prejudice thus drawn in with his childish breath. He never could compel himself to care for nineteenth-century style. He was never able to adopt it, any more than his father or grandfather or great-grandfather had done. Not that he felt it as particularly hostile, for he reconciled himself to much that was worse; but because, for some remote reason, he was born an eighteenth-century child. The old house at Quincy was eighteenth century. What style it had was in its Queen Anne mahogany panels and its Louis Seize chairs and sofas. The panels belonged to an old colonial Vassall who built the house; the furniture had been brought back from Paris in 1789 or 1801 or 1817, along with porcelain and books and much else of old diplomatic remnants; and neither of the two eighteenth-century styles—neither English Queen Anne nor French Louis Seize—was comfortable for a boy, or for anyone else. The dark mahogany had been painted white to suit daily life in winter gloom. Nothing seemed to favor, for a child's objects, the older forms. On the contrary, most boys, as well as grown-up people, preferred the new, with good reason, and the child felt himself distinctly at a disadvantage for the taste.

Nor had personal preference any share in his bias. The Brooks grandfather was as amiable and as sympathetic as the Adams grandfather. Both were born in 1767, and both died in 1848. Both were kind to children, and both belonged rather to the eighteenth than to the nineteenth centuries. The child knew no difference between them except that one was associated with winter and the other with summer; one with Boston, the other with Quincy. Even with Medford, the association was hardly easier. Once as a very young boy he was taken to pass a few days with his grandfather Brooks under charge of his aunt, but became so violently homesick that within twenty-four hours he was brought back in disgrace. Yet he could not remember ever being seriously homesick again.

The attachment to Quincy was not altogether sentimental or wholly sympathetic. Quincy was not a bed of thornless roses. Even there the curse of Cain set its mark. There as elsewhere a cruel universe combined to crush a child. As though three or four vigorous brothers and sisters, with the best will, were not enough to crush any child, everyone else conspired towards an education which he hated. From cradle to grave this problem of running order through chaos, direction through space, discipline through freedom, unity through multiplicity, has always been, and must always be, the task of education, as it is the moral of religion, philosophy, science, art, politics, and economy; but a boy's will is his life, and he dies when it is broken, as the colt dies in harness, taking a new nature in becoming tame. Rarely has the boy felt kindly towards his tamers. Between him and his master has always been war. Henry Adams never knew a boy of his generation to like a master, and the task of remaining on friendly terms with one's own family, in such a relation, was never easy.

All the more singular it seemed afterwards to him that his first serious contact with the President should have been a struggle of will, in which the old man almost necessarily defeated the boy, but instead of leaving, as usual in such defeats, a lifelong sting, left rather an impression of as fair treatment as could be expected from a natural enemy. The boy met seldom with such restraint. He could not have been much more than six years old at the time—seven at the utmost—and his mother had taken him to Quincy for a long stay with the President during the summer. What became of the rest of the family he quite forgot; but he distinctly remembered standing at the house door one summer morning in a passionate outburst of rebellion against going to school. Naturally his mother was the immediate victim of his rage; that is what mothers are for, and boys also; but in this case the boy had his mother at unfair disadvantage, for she was a guest, and had no means of enforcing obedience. Henry showed a certain tactical ability by refusing to start, and he met all efforts at compulsion by successful, though too vehement protest. He was in fair way to win, and was holding his own, with sufficient energy, at the bottom of the long staircase which led up to the door of the President's library, when the door opened, and the old man slowly came down. Putting on his hat, he took the boy's hand without a word, and walked with him, paralyzed by awe, up the road to the town. After the first moments of consternation at this interference in a domestic dispute, the boy reflected that an old gentleman close on eighty would never trouble himself to walk near a mile on a hot summer morning over a shadeless road to take a boy to school, and that it would be strange if a lad imbued with the passion of freedom could not find a corner to dodge around, somewhere before reaching the school door. Then and always, the boy insisted that this reasoning justified his apparent submission; but the old man did not stop, and the boy saw all his strategical points turned, one after another, until he found himself seated inside the school, and obviously the centre of curious if not malevolent criticism. Not till then did the President release his hand and depart.

The point was that this act, contrary to the inalienable rights of boys, and nullifying the social compact, ought to have made him dislike his grandfather for life. He could not recall that it had this effect even for a moment. With a certain maturity of mind, the child must have recognized that the President, though a tool of tyranny, had done his disreputable work with a certain intelligence. He had shown no temper, no irritation, no personal feeling, and had made no display of force. Above all, he had held his tongue. During their long walk he had said nothing; he had uttered no syllable of revolting cant about the duty of obedience and the wickedness of resistance to law; he had shown no concern in the matter; hardly even a consciousness of the boy's existence. Probably his mind at that moment was actually troubling itself little about his grandson's iniquities, and much about the iniquities of President Polk, but the boy could scarcely at that age feel the whole satisfaction of thinking that President Polk was to be the vicarious victim of his own sins, and he gave his grandfather credit for intelligent silence. For this forbearance he felt instinctive respect. He admitted force as a form of right; he admitted even temper, under protest; but the seeds of a moral education would at that moment have fallen on the stoniest soil in Quincy, which is, as everyone knows, the stoniest glacial and tidal drift known in any Puritan land.

Neither party to this momentary disagreement can have felt rancor, for during these three or four summers the old President's relations with the boy were friendly and almost intimate. Whether his older brothers and sisters were still more favored he failed to remember, but he was himself admitted to a sort of familiarity which, when in his turn he had reached old age, rather shocked him, for it must have sometimes tried the President's patience. He hung about the library; handled the books; deranged the papers; ransacked the drawers; searched the old purses and pocket-books for foreign coins; drew the sword-cane; snapped the travelling-pistols; upset everything in the corners, and penetrated the President's dressing-closet where a row of tumblers, inverted on the shelf, covered caterpillars which were supposed to become moths or butterflies, but never did. The Madam bore with fortitude the loss of the tumblers which her husband purloined for these hatcheries; but she made protest when he carried off her best cut-glass bowls to plant with acorns or peachstones that he might see the roots grow, but which, she said, he commonly forgot like the caterpillars.

At that time the President rode the hobby of tree-culture, and some fine old trees should still remain to witness it, unless they have been improved off the ground; but his was a restless mind, and although he took his hobbies seriously and would have been annoyed had his grandchild asked whether he was bored like an English duke, he probably cared more for the processes than for the results, so that his grandson was saddened by the sight and smell of peaches and pears, the best of their kind, which he brought up from the garden to rot on his shelves for seed. With the inherited virtues of his Puritan ancestors, the little boy Henry conscientiously brought up to him in his study the finest peaches be found in the garden, and ate only the less perfect. Naturally he ate more by way of compensation, but the act showed that he bore no grudge. As for his grandfather, it is even possible that he may have felt a certain self-reproach for his temporary role of schoolmaster—seeing that his own career did not offer proof of the worldly advantages of docile obedience—for there still exists somewhere a little volume of critically edited Nursery Rhymes with the boy's name in full written in the President's trembling hand on the fly-leaf. Of course there was also the Bible, given to each child at birth, with the proper inscription in the President's hand on the fly-leaf; while their grandfather Brooks supplied the silver mugs.

So many Bibles and silver mugs had to be supplied, that a new house, or cottage, was built to hold them. It was "on the hill," five minutes' walk above "the old house," with a far view eastward over Quincy Bay, and northward over Boston. Till his twelfth year, the child passed his summers there, and his pleasures of childhood mostly centred in it. Of education he had as yet little to complain. Country schools were not very serious. Nothing stuck to the mind except home impressions, and the sharpest were those of kindred children; but as influences that warped a mind, none compared with the mere effect of the back of the President's bald head, as he sat in his pew on Sundays, in line with that of President Quincy, who, though some ten years younger, seemed to children about the same age. Before railways entered the New England town, every parish church showed half-a-dozen of these leading citizens, with gray hair, who sat on the main aisle in the best pews, and had sat there, or in some equivalent dignity, since the time of St. Augustine, if not since the glacial epoch. It was unusual for boys to sit behind a President grandfather, and to read over his head the tablet in memory of a President great-grandfather, who had "pledged his life, his fortune, and his sacred honor" to secure the independence of his country and so forth; but boys naturally supposed, without much reasoning, that other boys had the equivalent of President grandfathers, and that churches would always go on, with the bald-headed leading citizens on the main aisle, and Presidents or their equivalents on the walls. The Irish gardener once said to the child: "You'll be thinkin' you'll be President too!" The casuality of the remark made so strong an impression on his mind that he never forgot it. He could not remember ever to have thought on the subject; to him, that there should be a doubt of his being President was a new idea. What had been would continue to be. He doubted neither about Presidents nor about Churches, and no one suggested at that time a doubt whether a system of society which had lasted since Adam would outlast one Adams more.

The Madam was a little more remote than the President, but more decorative. She stayed much in her own room with the Dutch tiles, looking out on her garden with the box walks, and seemed a fragile creature to a boy who sometimes brought her a note or a message, and took distinct pleasure in looking at her delicate face under what seemed to him very becoming caps. He liked her refined figure; her gentle voice and manner; her vague effect of not belonging there, but to Washington or to Europe, like her furniture, and writing-desk with little glass doors above and little eighteenth-century volumes in old binding, labelled "Peregrine Pickle" or "Tom Jones" or "Hannah More." Try as she might, the Madam could never be Bostonian, and it was her cross in life, but to the boy it was her charm. Even at that age, he felt drawn to it. The Madam's life had been in truth far from Boston. She was born in London in 1775, daughter of Joshua Johnson, an American merchant, brother of Governor Thomas Johnson of Maryland; and Catherine Nuth, of an English family in London. Driven from England by the Revolutionary War, Joshua Johnson took his family to Nantes, where they remained till the peace. The girl Louisa Catherine was nearly ten years old when brought back to London, and her sense of nationality must have been confused; but the influence of the Johnsons and the services of Joshua obtained for him from President Washington the appointment of Consul in London on the organization of the Government in 1790. In 1794 President Washington appointed John Quincy Adams Minister to The Hague. He was twenty-seven years old when he returned to London, and found the Consul's house a very agreeable haunt. Louisa was then twenty.

At that time, and long afterwards, the Consul's house, far more than the Minister's, was the centre of contact for travelling Americans, either official or other. The Legation was a shifting point, between 1785 and 1815; but the Consulate, far down in the City, near the Tower, was convenient and inviting; so inviting that it proved fatal to young Adams. Louisa was charming, like a Romney portrait, but among her many charms that of being a New England woman was not one. The defect was serious. Her future mother-in-law, Abigail, a famous New England woman whose authority over her turbulent husband, the second President, was hardly so great as that which she exercised over her son, the sixth to be, was troubled by the fear that Louisa might not be made of stuff stern enough, or brought up in conditions severe enough, to suit a New England climate, or to make an efficient wife for her paragon son, and Abigail was right on that point, as on most others where sound judgment was involved;

but sound judgment is sometimes a source of weakness rather than of force, and John Quincy already had reason to think that his mother held sound judgments on the subject of daughters-in-law which human nature, since the fall of Eve, made Adams helpless to realize. Being three thousand miles away from his mother, and equally far in love, he married Louisa in London, July 26, 1797, and took her to Berlin to be the head of the United States Legation. During three or four exciting years, the young bride lived in Berlin; whether she was happy or not, whether she was content or not, whether she was socially successful or not, her descendants did not surely know; but in any case she could by no chance have become educated there for a life in Quincy or Boston. In 1801 the overthrow of the Federalist Party drove her and her husband to America, and she became at last a member of the Quincy household, but by that time her children needed all her attention, and she remained there with occasional winters in Boston and Washington, till 1809. Her husband was made Senator in 1803, and in 1809 was appointed Minister to Russia. She went with him to St. Petersburg, taking her baby, Charles Francis, born in 1807; but brokenhearted at having to leave her two older boys behind. The life at St. Petersburg was hardly gay for her; they were far too poor to shine in that extravagant society; but she survived it, though her little girl baby did not, and in the winter of 1814–15, alone with the boy of seven years old, crossed Europe from St. Petersburg to Paris, in her travelling-carriage, passing through the armies, and reaching Paris in the *Cent Jours* after Napoleon's return from Elba. Her husband next went to England as Minister, and she was for two years at the Court of the Regent. In 1817 her husband came home to be Secretary of State, and she lived for eight years in F Street, doing her work of entertainer for President Monroe's administration. Next she lived four miserable years in the White House. When that chapter was closed in 1829, she had earned the right to be tired and delicate, but she still had fifteen years to serve as wife of a Member of the House, after her husband went back to Congress in 1833. Then it was that the little Henry, her grandson, first remembered her, from 1843 to 1848, sitting in her panelled room, at breakfast, with her heavy silver teapot and sugar-bowl and cream-jug, which still exist somewhere as an heirloom of the modern safety-vault. By that time she was seventy years old or more, and thoroughly weary of being beaten about a stormy world. To the boy she seemed singularly peaceful, a vision of silver gray, presiding over her old President and her Queen Anne mahogany; an exotic, like her Sèvres china; an object of deference to everyone, and of great affection to her son Charles; but hardly more Bostonian than she had been fifty years before, on her wedding-day, in the shadow of the Tower of London.

Such a figure was even less fitted than that of her old husband, the President, to impress on a boy's mind the standards of the coming century. She was Louis Seize, like the furniture. The boy knew nothing of her interior life, which had been, as the venerable Abigail, long since at peace, foresaw, one of severe stress and little pure satisfaction. He never dreamed that from her might come some of those doubts and self-questionings, those hesitations, those rebellions against law and discipline, which marked more than one of her descendants; but he might even then have felt some vague instinctive suspicion that he was to inherit from her the seeds of the primal sin, the fall from grace, the curse of Abel, that he was not of pure New England stock, but half exotic. As a child of Quincy he was not a true Bostonian, but even as a child of Quincy he inherited a quarter taint of Maryland blood. Charles Francis, half Marylander by birth, had hardly seen Boston till he was ten years old, when his parents left him there at school in 1817, and he never forgot the experience. He was to be nearly as old as his mother had been in 1845, before he quite accepted Boston, or Boston quite accepted him.

A boy who began his education in these surroundings, with physical strength inferior to that of his brothers, and with a certain delicacy of mind and bone, ought rightly to have felt at home in the eighteenth century and should, in proper self-respect, have rebelled against the standards of the nineteenth. The atmosphere of his first ten years must have been very like that of his grandfather at the same age, from 1767 till 1776, barring the battle of Bunker Hill, and even as late as 1846, the battle of Bunker Hill remained actual. The tone of Boston society was colonial. The true Bostonian always knelt in self-abasement before the majesty of English standards; far from concealing it as a weakness, he was proud of it as his strength. The eighteenth century ruled society long after 1850. Perhaps the boy began to shake it off rather earlier than most of his mates.

Indeed this prehistoric stage of education ended rather abruptly with his tenth year. One winter morning he was conscious of a certain confusion in the house in Mount Vernon Street, and gathered, from such words as he could catch, that the President, who happened to be then staying there, on his way to Washington, had fallen and hurt himself. Then he heard the word paralysis. After that day he came to associate the word with the figure of his grandfather, in a tall-backed, invalid armchair, on one side of the spare bedroom fireplace, and one of his old friends, Dr. Parkman or P. P. F. Degrand on the other side, both dozing.

The end of this first, or ancestral and Revolutionary, chapter came on February 21, 1848—and the month of February brought life and death as a family habit—when the eighteenth century, as an actual and living companion, vanished. If the scene on the floor of the House, when the old President fell, struck the still simple-minded American public with a sensation unusually dramatic, its effect on a ten-year-old boy, whose boy-life was fading away with the life of his grandfather, could not be slight. One had to pay for Revolutionary patriots; grandfathers and grandmothers; Presidents; diplomats; Queen Anne mahogany and Louis Seize chairs, as well as for Stuart portraits. Such things warp young life. Americans commonly believed that they ruined it, and perhaps the practical common-sense of the American mind judged right. Many a boy might be ruined by much less than the emotions of the funeral service in the Quincy church, with its surroundings of national respect and family pride. By another dramatic chance it happened that the clergyman of the parish, Dr. Lunt, was an unusual pulpit orator, the ideal of a somewhat austere intellectual type, such as the school of Buckminster and Channing inherited from the old Congregational clergy. His extraordinarily refined appearance, his dignity of manner, his deeply cadenced voice, his remarkable English and his fine appreciation, gave to the funeral service a character that left an overwhelming impression on the boy's mind. He was to see many great functions—funerals and festivals—in after-life, till his only thought was to see no more, but he never again witnessed anything nearly so impressive to him as the last services at Quincy over the body of one President and the ashes of another.

The effect of the Quincy service was deepened by the official ceremony which afterwards took place in Faneuil Hall, when the boy was taken to hear his uncle, Edward Everett, deliver a Eulogy. Like all Mr. Everett's orations, it was an admirable piece of oratory, such as only an admirable orator and scholar could create; too good for a ten-year-old boy to appreciate at its value; but already the boy knew that the dead President could not be in it, and had even learned why he would have been out of place there; for knowledge was beginning to come fast. The shadow of the War of 1812 still hung over State Street; the shadow of the Civil War to come had already begun to darken Faneuil Hall. No rhetoric could have reconciled Mr. Everett's audience to his subject. How could he say there, to an assemblage of Bostonians in the heart of mercantile Boston, that the only distinctive mark of all the Adamses, since old Sam Adams's father a hundred and fifty years before, had been their inherited quarrel with State Street, which had again and again broken out into riot, bloodshed, personal feuds, foreign and civil war, wholesale banishments and confiscations, until the history of Florence was hardly more turbulent than that of Boston? How could he whisper the word Hartford Convention before the men who had made it? What would have been said had he suggested the chance of Secession and Civil War?

Thus already, at ten years old, the boy found himself standing face to face with a dilemma that might have puzzled an early Christian. What was he?— where was he going? Even then he felt that something was wrong, but he concluded that it must be Boston. Quincy had always been right, for Quincy represented a moral principle—the principle of resistance to Boston. His Adams ancestors must have been right, since they were always hostile to State Street. If State Street was wrong, Quincy must be right! Turn the dilemma as he pleased, he still came back on the eighteenth century and the law of Resistance; of Truth; of Duty, and of Freedom. He was a ten-year-old priest and politician. He could under no circumstances have guessed what the next fifty years had in store, and no one could teach him; but sometimes, in his old age, he wondered—and could never decide—whether the most clear and certain knowledge would have helped him. Supposing he had seen a New York stock-list of 1900 and had studied the statistics of railways, telegraphs, coal, and steel— would he have quitted his eighteenth-century, his ancestral prejudices, his abstract ideals, his semi-clerical training, and the rest, in order to perform an expiatory pilgrimage to State Street, and ask for the fatted calf of his grandfather Brooks and a clerkship in the Suffolk Bank?

Sixty years afterwards he was still unable to make up his mind. Each course had its advantages, but the material advantages, looking back, seemed to lie wholly in State Street.

Vivian Gussin Paley, *Wally's Stories: Conversations in the Kindergarten*

Prologue

Imagine an enormous turnip in a row of ordinary turnips. Grandfather tries but fails to pull it up. Grandmother comes to help, but together they cannot do it. First a grandchild and then a black cat join the others, but the turnip stays firm. Only when a brown mouse adds his effort does it come up.

How can a tiny mouse make such a difference? Common sense insists that the turnip is ready to come up, and the mouse only appears to make the big difference. But in a kindergarten classroom the appearance is as good as the deed.

No—better than the deed. When a magical idea is presented, the common-sense approach is looked at but then discarded. Hear five-year-olds who have just entered kindergarten as they discuss *The Tale of the Turnip.*

Teacher:	Why did the turnip come up when the little brown mouse pulled?
Warren:	Because the grandfather and grandmother couldn't pull it up.
Teacher:	They couldn't. You're right. Then the mouse helped and it came up. Why?
Warren:	He was stronger.
Deana:	If all of them pulled, the enormous turnip *would* come up.
Wally:	That was only the strength they needed.
Eddie:	If just some pulled it wouldn't. But they needed all to pull.
Wally:	Maybe the mouse lived down there.
Jill:	Under the turnip? Is that where he lives at night?
Wally:	Maybe he pushed it up when it was coming out.
Jill:	Maybe he was stronger than they were.
Eddie:	Animals could be stronger than people.
Deana:	Maybe the roots got stuck to the bottom of the ground and when the mouse came he could pull the roots up.
Fred:	If the cat and mouse pulled theirselves it comes up.
Teacher:	Why?
Fred:	They're stronger. But if the roots stuck they might need help.
Wally:	Maybe someone was inside the dirt and he saw the roots and he pulled it so they couldn't pull the turnip.
Tanya:	If the mouse pulled it up by himself it would work.

Wally: What if two people were underneath pulling?
Teacher: How would they happen to be under the ground?
Eddie: They dug a hole.
Tanya: But the mouse has the most power. Right? *(Everyone agrees.)*

The mouse's size is not important. A mouse can push up a huge turnip because the child can see him do it in his mind. The child can also see the other story characters pulling on the turnip, but he would rather think about the mouse. Fine. Unless you are a teacher determined to teach the concepts that are in *your* mind. How does one approach a lesson on the wheel, for example, when children prefer to believe that it is easier to move an entire basket of wood than to move a small piece?

Teacher: Watch me try to move this heavy basket. Uh . . . this is really heavy. I'm getting out of breath.
Eddie: I can do it easy. *(Straining and tugging he moves it an inch.)* I can do it easy.
Teacher: You did get red in the face. Does anyone think that looked so easy?
Everyone: Yes.
Teacher: Okay. Look, here's the problem. Can anyone figure out an easy way to move the basket over to the woodbench?
Deana: With my feet. *(She pushes her feet against the basket but it does not move.)* These are the wrong shoes. I can do it easy with my other shoes.
Wally: I can pick it up. *(He winces as he scrapes his nails on the rough wood but lifts part of the basket perhaps half an inch.)* There! That was easy.
Teacher: Wally, could you bring me a piece of wood from the woodbox? *(He runs over and returns with a small piece.)* Was that easy or hard?
Wally: Easy.
Teacher: If *that* was easy, would you say moving the basket is easy or hard?
Wally: Easy. Real easy. I could do it with my head too. You want to see?

Months will pass before we "invent" the wheel. Meanwhile there are other questions: Can Wally become a mother lion? Who stole the lima beans that did not come up? Can a witch be invisible? Is there a black Santa? Does Tanya have the right to disturb the Ella Jenkins record? This is high drama in the kindergarten. The children care enough about these subjects to tell us what they really think. My purpose is to uncover and describe this remarkable point of view.

Wally: People don't feel the same as grown-ups.
Teacher: Do you mean "Children don't"?
Wally: Because grown-ups don't remember when they were little. They're already an old person. Only if you have a picture of you doing that. Then you could remember.
Eddie: But not thinking.
Wally: You never can take a picture of thinking. Of course not.

You can, however, write a book about thinking—by recording the conversations, stories, and playacting that take place as events and problems are encountered. A wide variety of thinking emerges, as morality, science, and society share the stage with fantasy. If magical thinking seems most conspicuous, it is because it is the common footpath from which new trails are explored. I have learned not to resist this magic but to seek it out as a legitimate part of "real" school.

Wally's Stories follows a group of five-year-olds through their kindergarten year. The scene is the classroom, and the teacher is the stage manager (additional stage directions are in the appendix). The children are scriptwriters and actors who know what kindergartners want to say.

Wally

"He did that on purpose! You knocked my tower down on purpose!" Fred grabs Wally's leg and begins to cry.

Wally pushes Fred away. "I'm a dinosaur. I'm smashing the city."

"You didn't ask me. You have to ask." The tears have stopped.

"Dinosaurs don't ask."

I swoop down, dinosaurlike, and order Wally to the time-out chair. This will give me a ten-minute respite from his fantasies. His quick smile that is a silent laugh and his laugh that is a lion's roar are gone. He stares past me at the window, hunched over on the chair. Wally has come to our school after two and a half years in a day-care center. Nothing in the school report suggests the scope of his imagination. It is a customary "bad boy" report: restless, hyperactive, noisy, uncooperative. Tonght the children will give their mothers a similar description: there's a boy Wally who growls like a lion; the teacher yells at him but not at me.

"Are you being bad, Wally?" asks Rose. Rose is from the same day-care center as Wally, and she once told me that he got spanked there every day.

"Were you bad, Wally?" she asks again.

"I was a dinosaur."

"Oh."

Wally cannot understand why I don't admire him when he is a dinosaur. Before he goes home he'll ask me if he was good. He has to tell his mother, and he is never sure. The time-out chair is not connected to his perception of events.

"Was I good today?" he asks. I am tying his shoes at the top of the outside steps.

"You were okay except for the playground."

"What did I do?"

"You knocked down that first-grade boy."

"The black boy? Jason? We were superheroes."

"You were too rough."

"He's still my friend."

Fred is still his friend, too. As Wally changes from dinosaur to superhero to lion, Fred keeps an eye on him. He examines Wally's behavior and then watches my reaction. Wally, however, never watches me. He seldom takes his cues from adults, bringing forth his own script for being a five-year-old. He is never bored, except when he's on the time-out chair, and even then his head dances with images and stories.

"Whoever sits in the time-out chair will die for six years until the magic spell is broken," he says one day after a session on the chair.

"They turn into a chair," Eddie decides, "and then God breaks the spell."

"Not God," corrects Wally. "God is for harder things."

"Fairies could do it," says Lisa. "Not the tooth kind."

"It *is* a fairy," Wally agrees. "The one for magic spells."

The children like Wally's explanations for events better than mine, so I give fewer and fewer interpretations each day and instead listen to Wally's. The familiar chord he strikes stimulates others to speak with candor, and I am the beneficiary. However, Wally does not always teach me what I want to learn. He is a lightning rod, attracting the teacher's negative sparks, keeping them from landing on others. It is a role that receives little credit.

"You're riding too fast, Wally," I caution.

"Okay."

"Don't crash into the wall."

"Okay."

"Do *not* slam into things, Wally!"

"I didn't see it."

When I begin to play the piano, he leaps over Lisa and Rose to get to the piano first, but before the song is finished he is on the outer edge of the rug, growling.

"Don't make that noise, Wally," I say.

"It's a warning growl."

"Not at piano time."

"I'm guarding the lions," he whispers. "The growl means I hear a suspicious noise." The children stop squirming and watch Wally as he crouches in concentration. Several boys copy his pose and give low growls.

One day at lunch Wally says, "I'm going to be a mother lion when I grow up."

"A mother lion?" I ask. "Can you become a mother lion?"

"Sure. The library has everything. Even magic. When I'm eight I can learn magic. That's how."

"Why a mother lion?"

"Because I would have babies and do the mommy work. They stay home and take care of babies. Daddy lions go to work and have to walk fast."

Deana has been listening. "People can't turn into animals."

"That's true," Wally says.

"You changed your mind, Wally?" I ask.

"It *is* true, what she said. But I'm going to use magic."

"Oh, I didn't hear him say that." Deana leans forward. "If he uses magic he might. Maybe. It's very hard to do."

Fred joins in. "I might become a daddy crocodile. Every time a person tries to kill them they can swat at their guns."

"Fred," I ask, "do you believe Wally can become a mother lion?"

"No. Only if he practices very hard."

Eddie and Lisa are in the doll corner when I bring up the subject. "Wally has decided to become a lion when he grows up." They look up and laugh hesitantly. "He intends to learn magic," I add.

"Oh, that way," says Eddie. "It depends how hard he studies. That's the hardest thing to do."

"It's impossible," Lisa argues. "You can't turn into a lion. That's too big. Maybe a mouse or a cat." She pauses. "But he can dress up to look like a lion."

I turn to Earl. "Do you suppose a boy could become a mother?"

"He can put on a dress and a wig," Earl answers.

"And a mask," says Lisa.

"How about a lion? Can Wally become a lion?"

"No," answers Earl. "He has to be a huge man with sideburns."

"What if he uses magic?"

"Oh, I thought you meant ordinary. He could do it with magic," says Earl.

"But it *would* be very hard," says Lisa.

The next day I ask Andy, "Do you think it's interesting to be a father?"

"Sure. If a robber comes, the father punches him in the nose."

"Wally wants to become a lion, Andy. What do you think?"

Andy is quiet for a moment. "He can't. Unless he becomes an actress. Or he can wish for it, and if God wants you to become that then you can do it. Wait. I'm not too sure about lions. I know he could become a smaller thing. But he could dress up like a lion."

"Would he *be* a lion if he dressed up like a lion?"

"I mean just until he learns to do that trick."

Wally frowns and squirms beside me on the playground bench. A hot flush gives his brown skin a reddish tone. His black curly hair is coated with sand, sweat, and dirt.

"You get into fights out here every day," I say. "You keep making me punish you."

"I don't care," he shrugs.

"I know you care. You'd rather be running around."

"I don't care."

Later he dictates a story.

Once upon a time there was a little lion and he lived alone because his mother and father was dead and one day he went hunting and he saw two lions and they were his mother and father so he took his blanket to their den because it was bigger.

"But weren't the mother and father dead?" I ask. He has a quick answer. "They came alive again because he only thought they were dead. They really went out shopping and he didn't recognize them because they were wearing different clothes."

"Can I be the father in your story?" Fred asks. We usually acted out stories as soon as they were written and books as soon as they were read.

"Okay," says Wally. "Fred will be the father, Rose is the mother, I'm the little brother, and Eddie is the magician."

"There's no magician in your story," I remind Wally, who doesn't read yet.

"Yes, there is, I just didn't tell you about him."

A few days later a first-grade teacher complains about Wally.

"This is embarrassing," I tell Wally and the whole class. "I don't know what else to do about you, Wally."

"Just keep reminding him," says Lisa.

"But I continually warn him," I tell her.

"Remind him nicely."

"Lisa, he made you cry today."

"Keep telling Wally not to be rough," she says.

Eddie agrees. "Say to him, 'Be good, Wally, will you?'"

I turn to Wally. "Your classmates don't want you to be punished."

He smiles shyly. "That's because we're friends."

Stories

"Once there was a man and a mother and two sisters and a brother."

We are acting out Wally's newest story. He dictates three or four a week, never repeating a plot.

Story dictation had been a minor activity in my previous kindergartens, even though books and dramatics had been high-priority activities. Few children chose to tell a story if they could do something else instead. For years I accepted the "fact" that no more than four or five children out of twenty-five enjoyed dictating stories, and most often they were girls.

I had asked last year's class about this.

Teacher: Why do girls choose story dictating more than boys?

Sam: Boys like to do Star Wars things—stuff like that. Girls like writing and listening to the teacher.

Robbie: Boys like blocks and woodwork and superheroes.

Tom: And guns and cars and tough things.

Sandy: I was making a motorcycle. That's why I didn't come.

Della: They think it's dull, sitting and coloring and telling things. Boys are rougher.

Teacher: But boys like to listen to stories and act them out. Then why not dictate stories?

Robbie: It's very hard to explain. I'm storing up energy because I have a cold. So I don't want to use up my energy writing stories.

The first time I asked Wally if he wanted to write a story he looked surprised. "You didn't teach me how to write yet," he said.

"You just tell *me* the story, Wally. I'll write the words."

"What should I tell about?"

"You like dinosaurs. You could tell about dinosaurs."

He dictated this story.

The dinosaur smashed down the city and the people got mad and put him in jail.

"Is that the end?" I asked. "Did he get out?"

He promised he would be good so they let him go home and his mother was waiting.

We acted out the story immediately for one reason—I felt sorry for Wally. He had been on the time-out chair twice that day, and his sadness stayed with me. I wanted to do something nice for him, and I was sure it would please him if we acted out his story.

It made Wally very happy, and a flurry of story writing began that continued and grew all year. The boys dictated as many stories as the girls, and we acted out each story the day it was written if we could.

Before, we had never acted out these stories. We had dramatized every other kind of printed word—fairy tales, story books, poems, songs—but it had always seemed enough just to write the children's words. Obviously it was not; the words did not sufficiently represent the action, which needed to be shared. For this alone, the children would give up play time, as it was a true extension of play.

To return to Wally's latest story.

Once there was a man and a mother and two sisters and a brother. First the oldest sister ran away. Then the second sister decided to stay home with the father but he ran away too. So the little brother and the sister were left and she learned how to cook. One day a lion came because she wished for a lion and also they lived in the jungle. He said, "Can I be your pet?" She said, "I was just wishing for a lion pet. You can carry us wherever you want." So they lived happily ever after.

Rulers

Rulers were another example of the wide gulf separating my beliefs from those the children demonstrated whenever they were allowed to follow their ideas to logical conclusions. I had not realized that "rulers are not really real." We were about to act out "Jack and the Beanstalk" when Wally and Eddie disagreed about the relative size of our two rugs.

Wally: The big rug is the giant's castle. The small one is Jack's house.
Eddie: Both rugs are the same.
Wally: They can't be the same. Watch me. I'll walk around the rug. Now watch—walk, walk, walk, walk, walk, walk, walk, walk,

walk—count all these walks. Okay. Now count the other rug.
Walk, walk, walk, walk, walk. See? That one has more walks.

Eddie: No fair. You cheated. You walked faster.

Wally: I don't have to walk. I can just look.

Eddie: I can look too. But you have to measure it. You need a ruler.
About six hundred inches or feet.

Wally: We have a ruler.

Eddie: Not that one. Not the short kind. You have to use the long
kind that gets curled up in a box.

Wally: Use people. People's bodies. Lying down in a row.

Eddie: That's a great idea. I never even thought of that.

Wally announces a try-out for "rug measurers." He adds one child at a
time until both rugs are covered—four children end to end on one rug and
three on the other. Everyone is satisfied, and the play continues with Wally as
the giant on the rug henceforth known as the four-person rug. The next day
Eddie measures the rugs again. He uses himself, Wally, and two other childen.
But this time they do not cover the rug.

Wally: You're too short. I mean someone is too short. We need
Warren. Where's Warren?

Teacher: He's not here today.

Eddie: Then we can't measure the rug.

Teacher: You can only measure the rug when Warren is here?

Jill: Because he's longer.

Deana: Turn everyone around. Then it will fit.

*(Eddie rearranges the measurers so that each is now in a different position. Their
total length is the same.)*

Eddie: No, it won't work. We have to wait for Warren.

Deana: Let me have a turn. I can do it.

Jill: You're too big, Deana. Look at your feet sticking out. Here's a
rule. Nobody bigger than Warren can measure the rug.

Fred: Wait. Just change Ellen and Deana because Ellen is shorter.

Jill: She sticks out just the same. Wait for Warren.

Fred: Now she's longer than before, that's why.

Teacher: Is there a way to measure the rug so we don't have to worry
about people's sizes?

Kenny: Use short people.

Teacher: And if the short people aren't in school?

Rose: Use big people.

Eddie: Some people are too big.
Teacher: Maybe using people is a problem.
Fred: Use three-year-olds.
Teacher: There aren't any three-year-olds in our class.
Deana: Use rulers. Get all the rulers in the room. I'll get the box of
             rulers.
Eddie: That was *my* idea, you know.
Deana: This isn't enough rulers.
Eddie: Put a short, short person after the rulers—Andy.
Andy: I'm not short, short. And I'm not playing this game.
Wally: Use the dolls.
Teacher: So this rug is ten rulers and two dolls long? (*Silence.*) Here's
             something we can do. We can use one of the rulers over
             again, this way.
Eddie: Now you made *another* empty space.
Teacher: Eddie, you mentioned a tape measure before. I have one here.
(*We stretch the tape along the edge of the rug, and I show the children that the
rug is 156 inches long. The lesson is done. The next day Warren is back in school.*)
Wally: Here's Warren. Now we can really measure the rug.
Teacher: Didn't we really measure the rug with the ruler?
Wally: Well, rulers aren't really real, are they?

Rulers are not real, but rug measurers are. Dressing up to look like a mother
and using magic to become a lion is real, but having parents die is not real.
Does "real" mean that which can be imagined and acted out? Does Wally *see*
himself as a mother lion rather than expect to *be* one? Wally once told Eddie
he was going to grow up and become Superman. "You can't do that, Wally,"
Eddie said. Whereupon Wally altered his statement to "I mean *look* like Superman," and Eddie approved.

I discovered that the scale I had just paid twenty dollars for was no more
real than the tape measure. We were about to act out *Stone Soup,* by Marcia
Brown, a story about three hungry soldiers who trick some selfish peasants into
giving them food by pretending to make soup out of three stones. As part of
the play, the children brought vegetables to cook.

"Do stones melt?" Rose suddenly asked. "Do we eat the stones?"

"Do you think they melt, Rose?"

"Yes."

I looked around at serious faces. "Does anyone agree with Rose?"

"They *will* melt if you cook them," said Lisa.

"If you *boil* them," Eddie added.

No one doubted that the stones in the story had melted and that ours too would melt.

"We can cook them and find out," I said. "How will we be able to tell if they've melted?"

"They'll be smaller," said Deana.

I lower three stones into boiling water. "How long shall they boil?" I ask. The suggestions range from a few minutes to ten hours. We decide on one hour and finish the story while the stones cook. Just before lunch we remove the stones and place them on a table.

Ellen:	They're much smaller.
Fred:	Much, much. Almost melted.
Rose:	I can't eat melted stones.
Teacher:	Don't worry, Rose. You won't. But I'm not convinced they've melted. Can we prove it?
Mickey:	Draw a picture of them.
Teacher:	And cook them again? All right.

(Mickey and Earl trace the stones on a piece of paper, and I put them back in the water to cook some more. Thirty minutes later the stones do look smaller.)

Teacher:	I know they seem smaller, but it's very hard to match stones and patterns. Is there another way to prove whether the stones have melted?

(There is no response. Clearly I am after the "right" answer, but the children have enough proof that the stones have melted.)

Teacher:	Let's weigh them on this scale. How much do they weigh?
Everyone:	Two.
Teacher:	Two pounds.
Lisa:	Do we have to cook them again? They'll just keep melting.
Teacher:	Maybe not.

(After a short period we weigh the stones again.)

Eddie:	Still two. But they *are* smaller.
Wally:	Much smaller.
Teacher:	They weigh the same. Two pounds before and two pounds now. That means they didn't lose weight.
Eddie:	They only got a *little* bit smaller.
Wally:	The scale can't *see* the stones. Hey, once in Michigan there were three stones in a fire and they melted away. They were gone. We saw it.
Deana:	Maybe the stones in the story are magic.
Wally:	But not these.

The endless contradictions did not offend them; the children did not demand consistency. Once Lisa told us that she and her family did not believe in the tooth fairy. Her mother gave her a quarter for her tooth. I asked what her mother would do with the tooth and why it was worth a quarter to her. "She can sell it to the tooth fairy and get real gold for it." Lisa saw nothing inconsistent about combining both ideas.

Nor did anyone at Lisa's table think it strange when she asked me if I were really Mrs. Paley. I had spoken of Mr. Paley during lunch and Lisa was surprised. "Then are you really Mrs. Paley?"

"Lisa, you know that's my name," I said.

"Yes," she replied, "but I thought you just called yourself that."

Jealousy

Scales do not see what they measure, and teachers' names are merely labels, but melted stones and tooth fairies are believable. Was the time-out chair real to them—or did it measure behavior as mysteriously as the ruler measured the rug? Even worse, did my punishment carry a message of fairy-tale retribution rather than the sensible lesson I envisioned?

Shortly after we read "The Three Pigs," this conversation took place.

Andy: There's a boy Jeffrey on the other block from me. I went to his house once and he wouldn't let me in.

Lisa: Why?

Andy: Someone else was there.

Wally: You should have gone down the chimney.

Lisa: You shouldn't sneak into someone's house.

Eddie: He should shape his hair in a different way and then come back and Jeffrey'll say "Come in" and tell the other boy to go home.

Fred: If he went down the chimney he might get boiled.

Wally: He could come down with a gun.

Eddie: Just to scare him. If he puts a boiling pot there, just jump over it.

Lisa: Not a gun.

Eddie: Here's a great idea. Get bullets and put it in the gun and aim it at Jeffrey.

Teacher: That's a great idea?

Eddie: No, I mean it's a bad idea.

Lisa: Well, let him come down the chimney but not with a gun.

Wally:	Let's all go to Jeffrey's house and climb down his chimney and make him let Andy come in.
Andy:	I'll find out if he has a chimney.
Wally	I'll get a time-out chimney and he has to stay in there until he lets you come in.

I was not surprised by Wally's fantasy solution to Andy's problem, because the image of not being allowed into the house recalled the chimney from "The Three Pigs." But his use of a time-out contrivance was interesting. In classroom conflicts, such as the following one in the record corner, the children did not seek to resolve the problem by isolating their classmates.

Jill:	Every time I listen to the Ella Jenkins record, you know it's supposed to say "Yes ma'am," but Tanya says "No ma'am" louder and louder.
Tanya:	So does Wally.
Wally:	I only did it once.
Jill:	Tanya *keeps keeps* doing it.
Teacher:	You told her to stop?
Jill:	I *keep keep* telling her. The next time she comes in and I put on that record I'm going to just take it off.
Teacher:	Why do that? There should be a rule about bothering people when they're listening to records.
Jill:	Next time Tanya comes in I'm going to leave.
Teacher:	Why should you be the one to leave?
Jill:	So she won't bother me.
Deana:	Here's a good rule: if you want to fool around, don't sing with a record.
Wally:	Whoever says "No ma'am" has to say "Yes ma'am."
Mickey:	Keep changing the record until you find one Tanya likes.
Teacher:	Is that fair to Jill?
Mickey:	Sure. Jill could listen to the different record too.
Teacher:	Tanya, it seems to me *you* should leave if you spoil the record, but they don't agree with me.
Tanya:	If I do it again I'll just take a book until I stop saying "No ma'am."
Jill:	Or maybe I'll just put on a record you like.

The previous day I had made Tanya leave the art table after she splattered paint on Ellen's picture. Tanya shouted, "I'm never going to paint again!" After lunch she returned to the painting table and repeated her mischief. Lisa looked up and said, "Tanya's just jealous."

In the record corner the childen said: we like you, Tanya, and you can stay. They did not withhold friendship or impose hardships, and Tanya stopped teasing. I had excluded Tanya from the art table and achieved little besides temporary peace and quiet.

Left to themselves, the children recognized and attended to the real issue: jealousy. They seemed to judge social behavior by two sets of rules: acts that deliberately provoked jealousy were "no fair" and not excused; other conduct was tolerated.

Eddie: My father brought me this from his trip. It's much bigger than my other Spiderman. This part moves.

Wally: Hey, can I play with that?

Eddie: Just wait.

Andy: I'm next.

Eddie: I can't give so many turns.

Andy: You're not coming to my birthday.

Eddie: Okay, you can be after Wally.

Fred: I'm next after him then.

Eddie: That's too many. My mother said only two people.

Fred: Who cares! Don't play with him, Wally! *(He pushes the doll and starts to cry.)* C'mon, let's not be his friend. He has to put it away.

Eddie: Oh yeah? You didn't that other time. That Superman doll? And I didn't get a turn.

Fred: You did too!

Eddie: Not so many turns.

Fred: You're not supposed to bring it to school.

Eddie: So what? Anyway, I changed my mind. I don't want to play with it. I'm not supposed to get it dirty anyway.

Eddie puts the doll in his cubby and the boys are instantly amiable. Later, however, Eddie breaks a clay house made by Earl. It is obvious he has done it on purpose.

Teacher: Why did you do that, Eddie? That was not nice!

Lisa: He has to make Earl another house.

Warren: Don't let him play with clay for two days.

Wally: Let him pick his own punishment. Okay, Eddie?

Eddie: I'm not picking a punishment and I don't care if I ever play with clay. And I didn't know it was Earl's house.

Teacher: Well, it had to be someone's house, didn't it?

Tanya: Let Eddie invite Earl to his house and Earl can decide everything they do all day long.

Fred: Let Earl break something of Eddie's.

Teacher: Which idea sounds fair, Earl?

Earl: That Eddie makes me a new house.

Eddie: I don't want to.

Wally: Okay. Let someone else do it.

Fred: I'll do it!

Earl: Fred can do it.

Teacher: How about Eddie?

Earl: He'll do it some other time.

Eddie's right to be difficult was respected, but not his right to bring the Spiderman doll. This view of the social contract was quite different from my own. I discriminated far less among different kinds of aggressive behavior; the child clearly defined "bad" as an action that made him jealous.

Wally: Here's something really not fair. Deana and Jill always pick the very same people to act in their stories. They never pick me.

Teacher: But they write the story. Can't they pick the actors?

Everyone: No!

Ellen: Then people just feel bad. You have to pick someone who didn't have a turn.

Wally: I only got one turn. In my own story.

Deana: I only got four turns.

Andy: I *never* had a turn!

Tanya: Yes, you did too. You were the lion in my story.

Wally: He was a wolf. I was the lion.

Teacher: How can we remember who had turns?

Deana: Go cubby by cubby—like for leaders.

Wally: Start with my cubby because I'm down by the door.

Deana: Start with Rose because she never writes a story.

Wally: Okay, start with Rose.

They worry about Rose, who never writes stories and therefore gets first choice of roles. Tanya feels left out in the record corner, so they look for a record she will like. Eddie can make up for his transgressions at another time when he's in a better mood. Fairness is given a high priority in the kindergarten.

Fairness

These kindergarten children are finding out they can make significant, lasting changes in their own social organization, and they are certain that absolute safety lies in absolute fairness. It is a heady feeling, encouraging the most advanced thinking and speaking skills in the cause of establishing rules of fairness.

When we read stories, for example, the children pay close attention to the issue of justice. At such times my ideas about fairness may be as far from the children's as is my faith in the scale.

"There was a bird named Tico and he didn't have any friends because all his friends had black wings and they didn't like him anymore because he asked the wishingbird for golden wings."

Lisa is telling us the story of *Tico and the Golden Wings* by Leo Lionni. The children and I do not agree about Tico; I applaud him as a nonconformist while they see him as a threat to the community.

This is the story: Tico, a wingless bird, is cared for by his bird friends. One night a wishingbird grants Tico his wish for golden wings. This angers his black-winged peers who abandon him, saying, "You wanted to be different." Perplexed and hurt, Tico discovers he can exchange his golden feathers for black ones by performing good deeds. When at last his wings are black, Tico is welcomed back to the flock, who observe, "Now you are just like us."

Teacher:	I don't think it's fair that Tico has to give up his golden wings.
Lisa:	It *is* fair. See, he was nicer when he didn't have any wings. They didn't like him when he had gold.
Wally:	He thinks he's better if he has golden wings.
Eddie:	He *is* better.
Jill:	But he's not supposed to be better. The wishingbird was wrong to give him those wings.
Deana:	She *has* to give him his wish. He's the one who shouldn't have asked for golden wings.
Wally:	He could put black wings on top of the golden wings and try to trick them.
Deana:	They'd sneak up and see the gold. He should just give every bird one golden feather and keep one for himself.
Teacher:	Why can't he decide for himself what kind of wings he wants?
Wally:	He *has* to decide to have black wings.

The author upholds the peer-group point of view. It is the same judgment Eddie received when he displayed his new giant Spiderman doll: do not make your friends jealous.

But what happens when your friends make you jealous? There is a story for this too, and again I support the opposite side. In the story, a Japanese folk-tale called A *Blue Seed* by Rieko Nakagawa, a fox gives a little boy a blue seed in exchange for a toy airplane. The seed sprouts a tiny blue house, which grows bigger and bigger as a happy group of animals and children join the boy in the house. Suddenly the fox returns, demands the house, and orders everyone out. Whereupon the house increases in size until it reaches the sun and explodes.

Teacher: Was it fair for the fox to chase every one out of the house?

Eddie: He wanted the seed back.

Deana: He needed his own house back. Maybe he never had his own house. Maybe he always had to share.

Ellen: He shouldn't have traded the blue seed.

Wally: But he didn't know it was going to grow into a house. See, the house wanted to be shared but it really belonged to the fox because it was his seed and he didn't have to share it if he wanted it for himself.

Eddie: Wally's right. Those other people had their own house. They didn't need to live in the fox's house.

No wonder punishment doesn't work. I would have punished the fox, and the children think the fox is right. I defend Tico, but the children say Tico is wrong. Now I understand why Wally has to ask me every day if he is good. Our definitions of goodness do not always match.

A week later Wally dictates a new script for Tico.

There was a bird named Tico and his fairy godmother said, "I'll give you golden wings if you kill the giant." And then he waited until the giant was sleeping and then he chopped off his head and then he took the chicken that laid golden eggs and then the fairy gave him golden wings.

"This is a different Tico story," Wally says as I write down his words. "When can we act it out? I'll be Tico."

"We can do it now, but first I have a question, Wally. How about Tico's friends? Do they fly away when they see his golden wings?"

"Of course not! His wish *has* to come true. He killed the giant!"

Wally has transformed Tico into a hero who is no longer at the mercy of the group's mundane demands. Tico has performed a daring feat and can keep the prize.

When we acted the original story, Wally did not want to be Tico, preferring instead to be one of the bossy friends. Now that Tico is a hero, Wally will play the role. The bird friends don't even get a part—fantasies do not have to be democratic.

Magic

Families were often the subject of Wally's stories; he explored various combinations and possibilities in family life. His own family consisted of his mother, his grandmother, and himself, but his stories included fathers, brothers, sisters, and lions.

Once upon a time a man went out to hunt and his son went with him. He found a lion and the lion killed the boy but the man had two sons and one was still at home. So he shot the lion and he and the other brother ate it for supper and then they went to bed.

Wally's lions were usually aggressive beasts, but in one story he turned a girl lion into a sister.

Once there was a boy hunter. His little sister didn't like him so he ran away. So he found a baby girl lion. Then he found a girl. "You can both be my sisters," he said. Then they met a good fairy and she turned the girl lion into a girl person so he had two real sisters. They lived happily ever after.

"Wally," I asked, "could the girl lion really turn into a girl person?"

"If God wanted that. First He finds out if the girl lion wants to become a girl person and then He tells a fairy to do it because He's busy."

"Could a magician do it?"

"God likes fairies better."

The real power then is in the wish. Even a girl lion is given the option to remain herself if she wishes. God must observe the rules by which wishes are carried out, and it is the children who invent the rules. If fairness insures safety in the present, wishing guarantees it for the future.

Magic weaves in and out of everything the children say and do. The boundaries between what the child thinks and what the adult sees are never clear to the adult, but the child does not expect compatibility. The child himself is the ultimate magician. He credits God and lesser powers, but it is the child who confirms the probability of events. If he can imagine something, it exists.

Wally: I know all about Jonas. He got swallowed by the whale.

Fred: How?

Wally: God sent him. But the whale was asleep so he just walked out.

Fred: How did he fly up to God? I mean how did he get back to shore if it was so deep?

Wally: He didn't come from the sky. But he could have because there's an ocean in the sky. For the rain to come down.

Fred: Oh yeah. That's for the gods. When they go deep they never drown, do they?

Wally: Of course not. They're just going nearer to Earth.

Jill: How does the ocean stay up?

Fred: They patch it up. They . . .

Wally: They take a big, big, big bag and put it around the ocean.

Fred: It's a very, very, very big bag.

Eddie: Which reminds me. Do you know how many Christmas trees God gets? Infinity.

Teacher: Who gives Him Christmas trees?

Eddie: He makes them.

Wally: When people burn them . . . You see He's invisible. He takes up the burned parts and puts them together.

Rose: Are there decorations?

Wally: Invisible decorations. He can see them because He's invisible. If you tell Him there's an invisible person here, He believes it.

Eddie: You can't fool God.

Wally: Sure you can. It's a good trick. You can say, "I'm here," and you're really not, but He can't see you. He can only see invisible things. You can fool Him.

Eddie: But He hears you.

Wally: Right. He hears you talk. He talks, too. But you have to ask Him. He talks very soft. I heard Him.

Eddie: You know, 353 years ago everyone could see God. He wasn't invisible then. He was young so He could stay down on Earth. He's so old now He floats up in the sky. He lived in Uganda and Egypt.

Fred: That's good, because everyone in Egypt keeps. They turn into mummies.

How does the child think of such things, the adult wonders. The child reasons that if a big bag in the sky or invisible decorations on heavenly Christmas trees were not possible, he could not have thought of them. As soon as he learns a language well enough, and *before* he is told he cannot invent the world, he will explain everything. This ability to imagine the beginnings and ends of events is most highly developed during the kindergarten year.

Carrots

Another pair of discussions resulted from a story written by Wally to celebrate the climbing ladder.

A little boy planted a carrot seed but he didn't know it was magic. So the next day there was a huge carrot growing up to the sky. And it had little bumpity places so you could climb up. Then he saw a giant. But the giant didn't see him. When the giant fell asleep he stoled a magic tinder box that gave you food if you were hungry. Which was a very good thing because his family was poor and didn't have any food. When he climbed down they had a party because it was also his birthday but he didn't know it.

"Wally, is that the same little boy from the carrot seed story?" Rose asked. "No, it's a different boy."

"Remember everyone kept telling the other little boy it wouldn't come up? They shouldn't do that. They have to say it will come up or it's not polite. And remember the giant carrot?"

Rose ran over to the bookcase and found *The Carrot Seed*. She held up the book. "Now we can have a discussion."

The book by Ruth Krauss had been read on the first day of school. It is the briefest of stories, about a little boy who plants a carrot seed. Everyone tells him it won't come up, but the boy waters it and pulls the weeds daily until one day a giant carrot comes up.

Our discussion in September had dealt with the points Rose referred to in May: the response of the family and the size of the carrot.

Teacher: Why do you think the family tells the boy it won't come up?
Eddie: Because he plants it in the sand.
Wally: He can't wait so long. He waited too long. So it *would* come up.
Earl: Because if they were saying it so long he'll keep pulling up the weeds.
Warren: They didn't have to tell him because I knew it would come up.

Jill:	He planted it in dried-out dirt.
Rose:	Boys don't even come there.
Wally:	She means to plant things there.
Jill:	If he keeps watering, it will come up.
Warren:	If they keep *telling* him, it will come up.
Deanna:	Why is the carrot bigger than the boy?
Eddie:	Because they weren't looking.
Warren:	He watered it too much. He didn't know how.
Jill:	Some carrots grow this big.
Teacher:	Bigger than a boy?
Eddie:	He planted too many seeds.
Wally:	Or he watered it too much. *And* he put in too much seeds and they got stuck together. Or maybe it's a giant's carrot.
Lisa:	An underground giant.
Wally:	Giants are in the sky. Only they grow their carrots in the ground.

By the spring I had forgotten how much younger the children had sounded in September. In May they seemed more mature in every way, as the Friday lunch project showed. Yet in literary matters, magic still prevailed.

Teacher:	Why is the carrot so big when it comes up?
Warren:	It was in the ground too long.
Rose:	What if the seed was too big?
Eddie:	Like if it had some small pieces of plant food in it.
Wally:	They put many seeds together to make the carrot bigger.
Fred:	Maybe he had a lot of carrot seeds and he wanted a big carrot.
Wally:	It could be a magic carrot.
Eddie:	A plastic carrot.
Teacher:	How could a plastic carrot have gotten into the ground?
Deana:	He just dug it in and it grew because it was magic. Maybe someone stoled the small carrot and put a big one in instead.
Teacher:	Who?
Rose:	When he was sleeping.
Kim:	How could the robber find a big carrot if they grew a small one?
Eddie:	Maybe someone put a plastic carrot in the ground for the one that was stolen.
Deana:	How did they find the place where the little carrot was so they could dig it up?
Eddie:	The robber found the sign with the carrot on it and he had his flashlight and he dug around.

Fred:	How could he see? He can't hold the flashlight while he's digging.
Eddie:	He puts it down while he digs. Then he puts a big carrot in and takes out the small one. Then he puts the sign back.
Deana:	And he smooths down the ground.
Wally:	Wait. Here's a good thing. The robber could go underground himself in the hole and then he could feel the roots and pull them out. See, he digs a tunnel from his house to the carrot and pushes the carrot over. He takes the real carrot and puts in a plastic one.
Tanya:	The boy will know it's plastic.
Wally:	Not if it's a magic seed. As soon as the boy picks it up, it turns into a real carrot.
Rose:	Why is the giant carrot red?
Teacher:	Oh. I can tell you that. You see, the book only uses three colors brown, tan, and red. So they make the carrot red. The more colors you use when you print a book the more it costs.
Eddie:	If it's a magic seed, then it *would* be a red carrot. Red is a magic color.
Lisa:	Unless it's food coloring.

Magical solutions were still acceptable; the children were more inventive and carried ideas further, but the direction was unchanged. My brief allusion to the economics of printing was washed away by the image of red as a magic color. I had never heard that red was a magic color—perhaps no one else had either—but Eddie's statement was accepted as a fact.

Earl's second-grade brother Harry visited us just after the *Carrot Seed* discussion, and Earl told him about the magic seed and the clever substitution of carrots by a robber. Harry said, "That's really weird. Boy, Earl, you're really weird."

After Harry left, I said, "Earl, your brother doesn't agree with you about the giant carrot."

"That's because he doesn't like carrots," Earl explained.

I was not surprised by Harry's disdain for magic seeds and robbers who steal carrots. I would not have expected a second-grader to think along those lines. Yet I wondered whether other kinds of magical thinking persisted in the second grade. Harry seemed so grown-up when he visited us—until he began to play. Then he entered the world of Star Wars and Superman as if he had never left kindergarten. Similarly, Lisa's sister, also a second-grader, could barely wait to get into our doll corner before saying, "I'll be the mother."

Suddenly I had a great urge to ask Harry's class about mother lions and magical powers. I talked it over with Harry's teacher, who offered to read to my class while I taped a discussion with hers.

Teacher: A kindergarten boy once told the class he intended to become a mother lion when he grew up. He said he would do this by practicing magic.

Thalia: Magic doesn't make things that people want to be.

Teacher: Is there any use for magic at all?

Thalia: There are magic tricks. You can learn tricks.

Harry: Well, he could put on a disguise and then there could be a tape recorder beside him of a lion and people would think that's a real lion.

Thalia: But that would still be a trick.

Stuart: Like the magic set my sister gave me. The balls don't really disappear. They're in the cups all the time.

Harry: The only kind of magic there really is is superhuman strength. Now *that* really is true.

Allan: If you know how to do a magician's things, you do have to keep practicing until you know how to do it real good.

Thalia: But it's still just tricks, Allan.

Allan: Everything isn't tricks, Thalia.

Teacher: Even if you practiced for years, could you learn to become an animal?

Allan: No. But maybe something else.

Stuart: My friend does this—it's not magic but it's like magic. Like once he believed so hard his father would give him something and when that day came his father really gave him what he believed.

Teacher: Is that like wishing?

Stuart: No. He was just believing in his mind that his father would give him something.

John: That boy in your class. It was just something he really wanted it to happen but it couldn't happen. It was a fantasy.

Harry: Scientists could work hard and make up a formula to make someone into a lion.

Thalia: The only kind of magic I've heard of are miracles.

Teacher: Is that something like Stuart's friend believing in something real hard?

Thalia: A little different. Like you're wishing something will happen but you know it won't and all of a sudden it happens.

Sally: I think there might be a potion some day. I don't think it could happen, I mean a potion to make someone a lion. But it might happen.

Harry: They might be able to not make him into a lion but make him look like a lion with all the doctors working hard to do it.

Sally: You mean to look like a lion but not talking like a lion. Not
             roaring or anything. But it wouldn't be magic. It'd be some-
             thing to do with science.

These doctors and scientists sounded a bit like the kindergarten magician who stands outside windows changing ordinary pennies into magic ones.
Harry and his friends spoke of fantasies, miracles, and potions, keeping a
safe analytical distance. But between the lines there was the possibility that
changed appearances constituted some kind of reality, that wishing might still
guarantee an outcome, and perhaps above all, that superhuman power was at-
tainable.

One day while trying to move the piano, I was reminded of another illusion of superior power.

"I can't seem to move it," I complained. Wally, Earl, and Deana began to
push with me, but the wheels refused to turn. We called Jill to join us, and this
time the piano inched away from the wall.

"This is like *The Tale of the Turnip*," I said. "Do you remember?"

Everyone remembered the story of the grandfather, grandmother, grandchild and black cat who cannot pull up an enormous turnip until a little brown
mouse comes to help. I wondered if the children still credited the mouse as the
chief agent of the move.

Teacher: Why did the turnip come up?
Tanya: The mouse is so strong.
Deana: All those people were there. So the brown mouse came and
             there were more people.
Jill: There were more people so it was too hard to keep it in.
Earl: I think they're all pretty strong so if they all pull it out it'll
             come out fast.
Rose: The mouse was holding on to it. He was holding the roots.
Wally: He must of seen the roots underground and he climbed up to
             see what it was so he tried to push it out because he's stronger.
Kim: The mouse's place was under the turnip. So first he pushed it
             up. Then he crawled around and pulled the cat's tail.
Tanya: Children aren't so strong as parents, and old people aren't
             strong because they're too old. The cat wasn't that strong but
             the mouse was stronger than the cat.
Eddie: But there were too many people pulling it so when the mouse
             came it might have just slipped out.

Warren: The mouse and cat are stronger because they're younger.

Wally: He could of been right under the turnip in a secret place and then he could of chewed it and pushed it a little and also when the people kept pulling and pulling it got looser and looser.

Wally teetered between the practical reality of people pulling together and the vision of a powerful mouse. Later I asked, "Remember before, when we tried to push the piano and it wouldn't budge? Then Jill came to help us and it moved. Is she stronger?"

"We only just needed a little extra help," Wally answered.

"Everyone helped the same," Jill said modestly. They knew it took our combined efforts to move the piano, but they were not quite sure about the turnip and the mouse.

"Did everyone help the same in pulling up the turnip?" I asked.

"Yes," said Fred. "But not if the mouse has superpower."

"Does he?"

"Maybe he does." Fred tried to read my face. "Maybe not the one in the book. Maybe a different one."

Jill came to his assistance. "He means like if there was a real giant turnip and a real supermouse—not in a book."

They were telling me that they knew the author did not intend the mouse to be a supermouse, but that such a phenomenon could exist. An idea could be examined on two levels: the obvious fact seen by the adult and the possibilities seen by the child.

Girls and Boys

Besides elevating children's moods and expectations, the superhero theme declares their differences as boys and girls. Nowhere is this separation of interests more clearly maintained than in their stories. Many family and magical themes are used by both girls and boys, but the most obvious differences lie in the boys' overt use of physical force, contrasted with the girls' emphasis on family serenity. Boys exult in superhuman strength, girls seek gentle relationships. Boys talk of blood and mayhem, girls avoid the subject; a character in a girl's story simply dies, no details given. Boys fly, leap, crash, and dive. Girls have picnics and brush their teeth; the meanest, ugliest character in a girl's story goes on picnics and keeps his teeth clean.

Boys narrate superhero adventures filled with dangerous monsters, while girls place sisters and brothers, mothers and fathers in relatively safe roles. If lost, they are quickly found, if harmed they are healed or replaced. Boys tell of animals who kill or are killed; girls seldom involve animals in violence. A bear or lion encountered in the forest is likely to lead a girl home and will not be shot and eaten for supper.

The plot of a girl's story often revolves around the friendship of two little girls who play and sleep together; I find no examples of little boys who are friends and do nothing but play. A friend is a superfriend, and the proper activity for superfriends is making trouble for bad guys. The most ordinary little boy kills lions and does not visit the playground. Certainly he will have nothing to do with the queens and princesses who inhabit the girl's forest.

Girls tell of beauty, love, and marriage, as in the fairy tales. Boys enjoy the same fairy tales but will not include such material in their stories. Phrases such as "fell in love" or "got married" embarrass them. They are more comfortable with "put him in jail" and "broke through the bars."

I had continual opportunities to observe these characteristics, for storytelling became the central activity of each day, taking up so much of my time—as well as the time of student teachers, aides, and visitors—that I tried to call a temporary halt.

"I have an idea and I think it's a good one," I told the children one day in early spring. "There are a number of games you would all enjoy, but I haven't had time to show them to you because of the stories. So, starting with next activity period, let's stop the stories for about a week. Okay?"

There was a general nodding of heads while the children looked at each other. Then suddenly there was a stampede to the story table—crayons, paper, and pencils flying.

"I was first!"

"I got here before you."

"That's my seat."

"You didn't take a number."

"Because your hand was on it!"

"Hold it!" I shouted. "I changed my mind. I didn't realize so many of you were about to do a story. Let's just keep going the way we were." In a day or two we were back to the normal rate of four to six stories a day. I did not again suggest a hiatus. It was as if I had said, "Tomorrow I'm closing the block and doll corners. Finish up all your play now."

During the last week of school, there was a flurry of superhero stories. Even Wally, who seldom mixed superhero play with story writing, dictated a series of Spiderman adventures, all variations of his first.

Captain America and Spiderman were in jail. Captain America broke the bars. Then Spiderman and Captain America got out. Then the other superheroes came. Then there was a boat. All the superheroes got on. Then a wave came with a shark. Then the shark tried to bite Captain America but it missed. Then the shark tried to bite Superman. Then Captain America beat up the shark. He said, "Watch out. Stay back." Then there was a sign in the water: "Don't pass." They passed to see what it was. A water devil was in it. All the other superheroes wanted to go home because they were scared but not Captain America and Spiderman.

For Eddie the theme remained constant.

There was once some superheroes. And there was Spiderman and Batman. All the other superheroes were dead. Spiderman and Batman got on their motorcycles. And Spiderman saw them dead on the ground. He got them all alive. Then he said, "All superheroes go away except Batman and me will stay here." The lions came to bite them. Spiderman and Batman beat them up. Then they went home. They slept until next morning. Next morning there was no trouble.

Earl introduced a new character into our cast of monsters.

The Creature of the Black Magoo

Once upon a time there was a ship. It was night time. Everybody was sleeping inside the ship. There was a princess there. Then two ugly hands came on the boat. It was the Creature of the Black Magoo. He took the princess underwater into a cave. Then it was morning. Then the people in the ship woke up. They saw the princess was all gone. A man on the ship got in a diver's suit to go find the princess. He went underwater in a cave where the princess was. While he was looking around, the Creature of the Black Magoo grabbed his neck and choked him. He died. Then the Creature of the Black Magoo broke the ship all up. He ate up the princess. A policeman shot him but it didn't hurt him. A policeman came and took him to jail. Then he broke out of jail. He bit the policeman and he died.

"Why do only boys do superhero stories?" I asked.
"I'm going to do a superhero story," said Jill.
"Me, too," Lisa added.
"Girls don't," Wally told them.

"Girls can if they want," asserted Lisa.

Lisa and Wally were both right. Girls can but they don't. They watched the same programs as the boys and seldom refused a part in the boy's stories, but they did not initiate superhero play or stories. Nor did they behave in these stories as the boys did. An all-boy cast choreographed a ballet in continuous motion. The presence of girls slowed down the physical activity and decreased the sound effects, for the girls used none of the code words or ritualized movements.

Jill and Lisa, determined to tell superhero stories, gave us two doll-corner stories in disguise.

Once upon a time Princess Leia, Stormtrooper, Darth Vader, R2-D2, Obi-wan Kenobi, C-3PO went for a picnic. They went back home. Then they went out for lunch. They ate supper, went to sleep, got up, brushed their teeth, and went for another picnic.

Once upon a time there lived a rocket ship in space. All the little kids used to have fun on the rocket ship. There were Martians there who were bad and the little children rescued them and put them in jail. Then they had more fun on the rocket ship.

"There are so many superhero stories lately," I said during lunch.

Deana knew why. "They just love them to pieces. The boys want to think about them all the time. They don't ever want to be daddies."

"It's better than daddies," said Eddie. "You can think you're a real superhero. Then you can be strong. Daddies can't be so strong."

"Don't girls want to be strong?" I asked.

"Girls want to be mothers and sisters," said Fred. "They do house stories."

Deana objected. "Mine are palace stories. Not house stories. Princesses and queens live in magic palaces."

"Are superheroes magical?" I asked.

"Some know magic and some don't," Wally said. "Joker does and Spiderman does."

"All the ones that fly do," Eddie decided. "Other people can't fly except in a plane."

"They can break through walls," Warren reminded him. "That's magic too."

"My dad says those walls are cardboard," said Eddie.

"I know," Warren agreed. "I'm talking about when it's real walls."

Deana was firm. "They're not magic because they're not real. They're on television."

"We're talking about real superheroes," argued Eddie. "With superhuman strength."

As if to prove that she did not tell house stories, Deana dictated a story with themes from at least six different fairy tales.

Once upon a time there lived a princess with her mother and father. They lived in the forest. Then one day the mother said, "Go into the forest." And so she went into the forest. She picked some strawberries and blueberries until she came to a little house. She knocked on the door. Nobody answered. So she opened the door. She was so tired that she lay down on one of the beds and fell asleep.

When the old lady come home and saw the pretty girl fast asleep she decided to take her for a walk. So when she woke up they went for a walk. When they came home the old lady was jealous because she thought the princess was much prettier than her. So she said, "Go out in the forest and get me some shiny red apples." So she went into the forest and she looked but she couldn't find any shiny red apples. She was lost.

Then she saw a hollow tree. She went into it. She was so tired she went to sleep. When she woke she fixed up the house and when it was all finished she got a basket and went out looking for something to eat. Then on the way she met a prince. They decided to get married. And they did. And they went to the king's palace and lived happily ever after.

Then the queen had a baby. The baby was a girl and that was the princess's sister. Then the mother needed a babysitter. The babysitter was jealous because the princess was prettier so she put the princess to do all the work. Then when the mother caught the princess doing all the work she said, "You'd better not make her do all the work." But the babysitter did not listen. One day when the princess was sleeping she woke her up to do the work. The princess ran away to a new palace and became the queen and married another prince.

I had a few questions for Deana:
"What happened to her mother?"
"She died."
"What happened to the first prince?"
"He died."
"And the sister?"
"She died—also the babysitter."

"Why does everyone die?"

"It's a magical story. They don't have to stay dead. Except bad people have to. Everything with a princess and queen is magical."

"Boys feel that way about superheroes," I said.

"No. Superheroes are pretend—not magic. They're just saying that. Magic is really alive. I mean it's invisible. Superheroes are like putting on a costume and thinking you're one.

I asked Wally if he agreed with Deana.

"She's right," he conceded. "Only God decides about magic. Superheroes don't have to do with God. Unless He wants it."

Even without their names at the top, I would have known that all the stories told on the last day were by girls. Ellen's could never have been dictated by a boy.

> Once upon a time there was a beautiful fairy. Her name was Jennifer. She had a father and it was a king. They loved each other very much. Then the fairy made her father the king into a beautiful prince. The prince and the fairy loved each other too. They decided to have a celebration and they got married.

Nor could Fred's story, a week earlier, have been a girl's.

> Speed Racer crashed into the wall but he still keeps going. Then he explodes Racer X and he catches Racer X on fire and he explodes Fire Fox and he wins the race.

Tanya and Jill dictated our final stories. In each one a parent is in need and a child goes out into the world to bring back a treasure. Having made the brother her hero, Tanya decided to take that part instead of the customary sister's role. Even in this respect girls were different. On occasion a girl would give herself a boy's part, but boys avoided female roles in their own or anyone else's story.

> Once upon a time there was a little girl. She lived with her mother and brother and they had no money so the mother said to the little boy, "Go out and find some money." He went. Then he said goodbye to the little girl and his mother. He found some money in a wallet in the woods. He ran home. He told his mother, "I found some money in the woods." They were all glad. The sister danced around for joy.

Jill listened carefully to Tanya's story and decided to give the little girl a stronger role.

Once upon a time there was a little girl. She lived in a cottage with her daddy. Her daddy said one day to go out and find some fruit and bring it home and we would be able to eat. And so the little girl did it. When she came home she brought a whole basket of fruit. And he loved her best of all because she brought him a whole basket of fruit and never asked for any money.

"Can I do a story?" Wally asked.
"I'm sorry, Wally. There's no time left." I pointed to the clock.
"I'll do it tomorrow."
"This is the last day, Wally."
It was suddenly very quiet around the circle.
"You'll start writing your own stories in first grade, you know," I said.
The children looked surprised and then pleased. But I felt lonely.

Appendix

Each year I come closer to understanding how logical thinking and precise speech can be taught in the classroom. These skills are, I believe, the important precursors to formal schooling and the main business of the kindergarten teacher. The book describes my search for the child's point of view with which I can help him take a step further. In this appendix I upstage the child and talk about the teacher.

The skills involved in rational discourse require much practice. The teacher, therefore, must use material that children want to discuss and dramatize. Fortunately, such topics are easy to come by, for anything that affects the child's status in the classroom, with particular emphasis on friendship and fantasy, will receive his attention. But that attention can be fleeting, appearance and form changing with the twirl of a Superman cape. The teacher must help the child see how one thing he knows relates to other things he knows.

In the following discussion the children are willing to concentrate on a problem because they want to affect its outcome. My task is to keep the inquiry open long enough for the consequences of their ideas to become apparent to them.

Teacher: Yesterday I asked Warren and Earl to share a cubby so we
            could get rid of the old section of cubbies. You know Earl is

the only one still using it, and we need the space to store our wood supply. But then Eddie and Wally said *they* wanted to share a cubby. And Deanna got upset because she asked Lisa but Lisa had already asked Jill. It's becoming a big problem.

Eddie: I think we should do it because last night I couldn't sleep. Just because it's not fair about Warren and Earl.

Lisa: It is a little bit fair because we need more room.

Deana: What if *I* can't sleep?

Lisa: Why doesn't everyone share?

Mickey: I don't want to. It's too crowded.

The cubbies will certainly be too crowded, but that is of little importance to most of the children—or to me. I would not have created such a problem, but it is real and it touches on many deep concerns: friendship, security, fairness. In the discussion I act as the ancient Greek chorus, seeking connections and keeping track of events, but the decisions must come from the children. This is not to be merely an academic exercise.

Teacher: We have at least three problems here. First, should I have asked Warren and Earl to share a cubby just because we need more space? Second, can others decide to share even if it hurts some one's feelings? Third, what if some people don't want to share at all?

Eddie: If a person says to share my cubby and if the other one doesn't want to, he doesn't have to. Or if the first one doesn't want to.

Tanya: Maybe you can't find someone to share.

Lisa: I would be a good sport and share with you.

Jill: That's not a good sport. You said I'm your partner.

Wally: It is fair because you just say she promised you first.

Rose: No one promised me.

Teacher: Mickey doesn't want to share and Rose thinks she won't have a partner. How can we tell if she'll be left out?

Eddie: Let everyone sit by the one they want.

Teacher: Okay. We'll see if anyone is left out. *(There is a noisy scramble but soon everyone is seated.)* I count four groups of three, four groups of two, and Kim and Mickey are alone. So that's three, six, nine, twelve who don't agree on partners.

Warren: The extras can go with the extras.

Deana: Jill can go with Tanya.

Jill: I'm not extra. You're extra.

Teacher: How do we know who is extra in a group of three?

Tanya: It could be who is the shortest one.

Jill: No! That hasn't got to do with cubbies! "Shortest" is when someone has to crawl through the window to get the key.

Teacher: What *does* have to do with cubbies?

Lisa: Whoever asks first.

Fred: Best friends.

Deana: But how about if three people are best friends? That reminds me. Why can't we pick our own actors to be in our own stories?

Any sudden switch in topics is a challenge for the teacher, who must try to find a common element between the new idea and the ongoing discussion. This is done not to soften the children's non sequiturs but to demonstrate logical connections. In Deana's case the connection is fairly obvious, but even when the teacher's reasoning is incorrect, the children witness the process by which such inferences are made. To dismiss a statement as being "off the subject" forfeits a valuable teaching moment.

Teacher: I think I know what reminded you of that, Deana. Choosing your own actors is a bit like picking a cubby partner. Let's talk about that after lunch. Right now we must decide about the cubbies. How about the children who will be disappointed? How many people can we allow to be sad before we say it's no fair?

Deana: One person.

Jill: No. That's not enough. Because you could only just be in a bad mood from something else.

Deana: All right. Half the class.

Teacher: How many is that?

Wally: When you say, "Half the class goes to music," is that the same as half the class?

Teacher: Yes.

Wally: Then that's eleven because Red group has eleven.

This is a good place to mention the tape recorder. I missed the implications of Wally's "Is that the same as half the class?" until I transcribed his comment from the tape later in the day. Then I was reminded of Lisa's, "Are you really Mrs. Paley?" Is "half the class" an arbitrary label, Wally wondered, or is it the same "half" he already knows? The class was divided into two groups, Red and Blue, because only half of the children could attend music at one time. My occasional references to "half the class" came across to Wally as code for "group." He knew that each group had eleven members and was called "half the class"; I had been satisfied with this reasoning until I heard the tape. His asking if "half the class" meant *half* the class showed that he did not visualize a numerical meaning for half of twenty-two children. He could break a cookie in half, draw a line through a circle, and divide six blocks at a glance, but he could not *see* half of a large number.

Subsequent activities revealed that others were also uncertain about this concept. Lisa, for example, told us that if you don't know a group of people you could ask them their names and divide them into half and put half on each half of the circle and then count up to eleven and that would be "half the class."

Lisa's complicated statement tells something about what she knows and doesn't know. However, before I can weigh this information, four hands are waving, Tanya is fussing with Rose, and Earl's brother comes in with a message from their mother. Luckily the tape recorder preserves everything.

It has become for me an essential tool for capturing the sudden insight, the misunderstood concept, the puzzling juxtaposition of words and ideas. I began to tape several years ago in an effort to determine why some discussions zoomed ahead in an easy flow of ideas and others plodded to a halt, and I was continually surprised by what I was missing in all discussions.

I now maintain a running dialogue with each tape as I transcribe its contents into a series of dated notebooks. The margins fill with unasked questions. "Does Lisa mean that half of any class is automatically eleven, or does 'count up to eleven' describe the *process* by which a group is divided equally?" reads one marginal note. Another states, "Her 'ask them their names' refers to my question: how can you tell what *half* is if you don't know the class or how many children it has?"

The tape recorder trains the teacher, not the child, who never listens to the tapes and who is curious about the machine only the first time. The teacher learns to watch for inexactness in her questions, to repeat a child's inaudible comments, to ask for clarifications and additions. The initial incentive for these changes in style may be her desire for a more useful tape, but she soon realizes that whatever produces a better tape also achieves a more articulate discussion.

"Mickey, when you say 'Put a block in the middle and then you'll know which is half,' what do you mean 'in the middle'?"

"Like ten over here and ten over there and then a block in the middle."

The continuity a teacher looks for in her curriculum can often be found on the tape. For this reason I own only one cassette, which forces me to transcribe material the same day it is produced. Many a new discussion begins with a statement like this:

> *Teacher:* I was thinking about what Tanya said yesterday: "You put one on one side and say 'one.' Then one on the other side and say 'two.' Then one on the other side and say 'three.'" Tanya, could you show me how that's done?

Step by step, the children and I can follow a train of thought, giving those who need more time the opportunity to reflect. And the teacher is there to make connections.

> *Teacher:* So, if eleven children are disappointed, we forget about sharing cubbies. Okay. I'll sit way over here. When I call you, come and whisper the name of the partner you want. Don't tell anyone else the name and I won't either, so no one is hurt.

Concentration is intense. The discussion is now thirty minutes old, but there is no sign of restlessness, although a few children have gone over to take something out of or put something into their cubbies, as if to reassure themselves that nothing has changed.

The children are silent as I tally the results of the whispered choices. I put X's on the board under two labels—a smiling face and a sad face. There are twelve in the sad column. I cannot assume, however, that everyone understands the meaning of the two groups of X's. The sudden appearance of an abstract symbol can be a distraction.

> *Teacher:* Why am I using X's instead of your names?
>
> *Rose:* X's and O's.
>
> *Teacher:* The X is like the one in the game. There it tells which box you picked. What does this X tell?
>
> *Kim:* Who you picked for a partner.
>
> *Teacher:* It tells something about who you picked.
>
> *Jill:* If you picked someone and she picked you then your face is happy. But it has to be a secret.
>
> *Teacher:* Right. So we use X's instead of names. Are there too many sad faces? *(Everyone agrees.)* Then we all keep our own cubbies.
>
> *Rose:* Even Earl?
>
> *Teacher:* Are they sharing because they're friends?
>
> *Lisa:* They *have* to share. That's not for being friends. That's for doing a favor to the workbench.

During the activity period that follows, Deana is the first to dictate a story, one whose origin is clearly the cubby in incident. My role as scribe is never passive; wherever possible, I enlarge the scope of the story, looking for points that need clarification and asking questions that might lead to new twists in the plot. My goal, however, is as much to give children practice in exposition as to improve their stories.

Once there was three children. They were princesses and one of them was a queen.

"You said 'three children.' Was the queen a child?"

Deana looks surprised. "No. I mean the children are acting out a story. Me and Lisa and Jill. Jill is the queen and she sleeps alone. Me and Lisa are the sisters and we sleep in the same bed."

"That sounds like sharing the same cubby."

"It is. No one else can ever come in our bed because we're the only two sisters."

"All right. So there are two princesses and a queen."

And then the first princess met a prince who was magical. He turned into a funny dragon because he wanted to get married to a princess. She said, "No." She went back to Strawberry Hill where she lived. The end.

"Did she know the dragon was a prince?"

"Of course."

"Why did he change himself into a funny dragon?"

"Because he wanted to make her laugh. But she wasn't marrying someone just because he made her laugh."

"That would be good in the story."

"Okay."

So when she went back to Strawberry Hill her sister asked her if she met someone in the forest and she said she met a dragon that was really a magic prince and he wanted to marry her but she told him, "No." So she said, "What else can you be?" And he said, "A handsome prince." So he did.

"Wasn't he already a prince?"

"Oh, yeah. I forgot."

Now the sister was happy because before the magic prince was so ugly. That was why he changed to a funny dragon. So then she said, "Can you become two handsome princes?" So he did and the two princesses got married and went to get a bridal shower.

"What's a bridal shower?"
"I don't remember."
"It's a party for someone who's getting married. Everyone gives her presents."

Then the magic prince gave them a baby called Princess Small One and they didn't have to make a wish and wait for the baby because it was a present.

When Deana is finished, I ask, "Shall we do the story after the discussion?"
"Yes. Because then I can pick Lisa to be my sister."
In the afternoon we take up Deana's objection.

Teacher: Deana wants story writers to choose their own actors. Who remembers why we started using the class list to give our parts?

Earl: Some people didn't get a turn too much.

Tanya: Then everyone is in a big fuss and they'll always be saying I didn't get picked neither and then it'll never stop and nobody'll ever get picked the whole time they're in school.

Teacher: Tanya thinks people will be jealous and keep arguing. That's why we began using the lists.

Deana: Let people always pick different people. Not the teacher. A child has to do it.

Eddie: Or if you don't get picked write your own story.

Warren: But if people aren't fair let everyone tell them to be more fair. Tell them who didn't get picked yet and they have to pick that one.

As the discussion continues, more children go over to Deana's side, which is seen as the one opposite to the teacher's position. The vote is unanimous in favor of the rights of authors. I am not surprised. The morning's decision left a number of children feeling dissatisfied and as Deana knew, there *is* a connection between sharing a cubby and sharing a story-play.

The hours of this day were tied together by a continuity of mutual purposes that transcended play, but wandered not far from it. For play is the natural response of children, with its own logic and consequences, and deals often with the same problems of possessiveness the class struggled with today.

I do not ask the children to stop thinking about play. Our contract reads more like this: if you will keep trying to explain yourselves I will keep showing you how to think about the problems you need to solve.

Robert Inchausti, *Spitwad Sutras: Classroom Teaching as Sublime Vocation*

3. Breakthrough

God instructs the heart—not by means of new ideas but by pains and contradictions.

—Father J. P. deCaussade, S. J.,
Self-Abandonment to Divine Providence

October

I gave up trying to solve my discipline problem. It was just too much for me. I simply accepted a degree of chaos in my classes, plodded along from day to day, and starting looking for other work.

At this time, my class took up the study of the New Testament parables. And although I tried to convince my students—when they were paying attention—that these stories possessed rich and complex teachings, they insisted upon seeing them as expressing only the most tired moral platitudes.

"No, no," I insisted. "There is nothing in these stories telling us to *be good!* The point seems to be exactly the opposite; God does what he pleases!"

But they were not intrigued by what they took to be my feigned heresy and considered my questions merely as some sort of trick to get them to do more work.

When I asked Jim Bailey to read the parable of the sower, he read with exaggerated religiosity in a voice like Billy Graham. This brought laughter from the back of the class, and I found myself strangely relieved to find that someone was paying *that* much attention. I knew I wasn't teaching them anything, so I was grateful for the good humor.

Every day, I would go home and replay classroom incidents over and over again in my mind. There was something in the complacent way Marty Shuster had interpreted the parable of the sower as indicating that we should all "love God" that struck me as the very thing I was put on earth to eliminate. It was not my students' ignorance that was so exasperating, nor was it their rowdy behavior; it was the audacity of their small minds and the power their pettiness possessed to undermine everything in life that I valued. Why were these kids so certain that there was nothing important they could learn *from me,* when one look *at them,* one walk down the damn school hallway, provoked so many revelations in my mind that I could barely process them all?

Each night, I would talk myself into new resolves by planning innovative lessons and novel approaches. But the next day, my enthusiasm would dry up when I saw their tired expressions. Sometimes, when I talked to that wall of disengaged faces, I would end up listening to myself and forgetting why I was talking. It was as if my mind was floating about three feet to the side of my body, unable to get back inside my head. It was an awful feeling, and when it happened I would often just stop talking and sit down while the students would talk to one another about nothing.

One day, I read aloud to them from Matthew 13: the passage on why Jesus taught with parables. The text rang out in complete harmony with my mind:

> You will listen and listen again, but not understand, see and see again, but not perceive. For the heart of this nation has grown coarse, their ears are dull of hearing, and they have shut their eyes for fear they should see with their eyes, hear with their ears, understand with their hearts, and be converted and healed by me.

My forehead tingled. I felt like a prophet. These were *my* words now. Both a challenge and confession. All my past intellectual training, graduate school, my late night self-study of Gramsci and Lacan, seemed but a prelude to this moment. Everything I ever knew or believed seemed contained in these lines, and all my aspirations as an educator poured into those last seven words: "and be converted and healed by me."

But my students were not impressed. This passage didn't seem such a revelation to them. If anything, it was an insult—an accusation, a prelude, no doubt, to more homework or staying after school. I could see it in the way Teddy Latimer doodled with his San Francisco Giants pencil, in the way Marty Shuster looked deeply into his notebook, and in the way Jim Bailey sat upright and petrified.

But I hadn't intended it to be accusatory. I saw the lines as an invitation to change, as encouragement to overthrow the past, as an incitement to see, to hear, to feel anew, to be a part of a new heaven and earth. I was reaching for my messianic moment, but no one was there.

"This passage," I said, "shows us how Jesus taught. He taught with authority, not like the scribes. Jesus didn't threaten people. He liberated them so that they could see with their own eyes, hear with their own ears, and understand with their own hearts."

I was attempting to model this authority myself, trying to enact the role of Christ the Liberator. I had no idea then how vain and presumptuous I must have appeared until a spitwad, very wet and traveling at high speed, suddenly struck the center of my forehead.

I flinched. I heard laughter. Jeers. Shouts of triumph.

And then, almost simultaneously, the bell rang, signaling the end of school. By the time I regained my composure, it was too late. My classroom was empty. All of my students had run out the door.

Now, I could have gotten on the public address system and called them back. I could have waited until later and called all their parents on the telephone. I could have done a lot of things, but nothing seemed to really address the issue.

Sure, I might be able to gain power over these kids. I even might be able to compel them to behave. But I could never force them to learn from me or to care about the things I loved. Besides, who was I to model Christ? Maybe I should adopt the drill instructor strategy that seemed to work so well for Strapp? Maybe that man did know something about education after all? Maybe this whole idea of setting the mind free had to wait until these adolescents had been decanted of some of their sexual energy? Maybe I was just dead wrong about everything? Maybe I was, in fact, just a very silly man?

As I sat at my desk with these thoughts spinning in my mind, someone entered the room. When I looked up, I saw sixty-seven-year-old Brother Blake standing there, his large tummy pushing out his black Christian Brother's robe. He looked like a black dolphin with snow white hair.

"Well," he said, his eyes twinkling, "you look like you've had a good day."

I didn't want to tell him what had happened, but some flicker of intelligence in his face reassured me that there was little he had not seen of classroom fiascoes, so I blurted out everything—my speech, the spitwad, my inaction and resentments—everything. To my relief, Blake was not shocked, nor did he tell me to "get tough."

Most teachers, I found, seldom admit to the psychological horrors in their classrooms or to misgivings about their teaching skills to anyone but a few trusted souls. They do this in self-defense because they are so often blamed for anything that goes wrong. This is why many teachers are upbeat to the point of hyperactivity and stay that way until they can no longer ignore the discrepancy between their positive attitude and the darker realities of their profession. That is when they burn out, quit, start selling real estate, turn cynical or fanatically idealistic, write books, run for the school board, or become administrators. So I was relieved when Brother Blake took my confession not as a sign of personal inadequacy but as an objective description of an entirely logical chain of events.

"Sounds like somebody was listening to your talk on authority," he said.

"What do you mean?" I asked.

"Someone sent you a message about authority."

"And what might that message be?" I asked.

"That you *don't have it!*"

The remark hurt. I knew it was true, but it was still painful to hear.

"But then how do I *get* authority?" I asked.

"For starters, don't resent the kids for pointing out the truth. You tell them to seek truth, don't you? No matter how difficult that truth might be? So don't duck it yourself. You *don't* have authority, but that doesn't mean you will *never* have it. The important thing right now is just to *see* the destruction of your own pretenses and posturing. It's the only way to move from fearing nothing to realizing that there is nothing to fear."

"That's fine advice, Brother," I countered, "but I have to deal with these kids again tomorrow, and I've lost their respect. How am I to teach them about parables? What do I do? Pretend nothing happened?"

"Tell them the parable of the teacher who got hit between the eyes with a spitwad. Ask *them* what it means."

I could tell by the look on his face that he had just given me one of his keys to classroom success: The trick was in providing a link between what the students were feeling and the lesson at hand, and then giving oneself over to the messy process through which that link is explored, expounded, and finally understood. To do this, however, required that you take a risk, leave the lesson open, discover its meaning as you proceeded. Teaching was more like chasing down a metaphor or solving an equation than it was like giving a speech or dispensing information.

I could feel the anxiety melt from my neck and arms and a new anticipatory energy surge within me. His approach just might work. Besides, what had I to lose? The problems of today invent the lessons of tomorrow. There was little else the teacher had to know except the endless varieties of human evasion and perversion as they clashed with the wisdom of one's discipline in the microcosm of the classroom. Errors and miscalculations were part of the lesson, and the subject matter was one with its troubled transmission.

"Youth," Blake said "with all its anarchic energy, impertinence, and physical beauty, is just God's gift to the inane and immature. Don't resent it; it's all they've got."

I began to get my confidence back: being locked up in the ninth grade may not be such a bad destiny after all. I had never thought to connect literature to life in so direct a fashion. I had never thought to see problems as metaphors— emblematic of their own solutions. I wondered how I could have studied for so long and came to know so little.

A teacher was not a scholar or policeman or glorified babysitter. A teacher was more like Virgil or Odysseus: a creature of dialogue. An embodied phantom. Imagination incarnate. Not the Holy Spirit, but its secular double—with one finger pointed resolutely across the cultural abyss at the sacred face of the moon.

The next day, following silent prayer, I announced to the class that I wanted them to interpret a parable. "It's the story of the teacher who got hit between the eyes with a spitwad."

They braced themselves; no one looked me in the eye. Marty started to fidget.

"There was once a teacher who wanted to teach about authority," I began. "Not the authority of power or position, but real authority—the kind one earns through insight and accomplishment. And as he talked about this, a spitwad came out of nowhere and hit him right between the eyes. Before he could do anything the students ran out of the room. And he was left alone and humiliated." I paused for a moment, and then asked, "Now what might this story mean?"

No one spoke for a long time, until Marty Shuster raised his hand. "It means that we should respect our teachers and not abuse them."

"No, it doesn't mean *that!*" I snapped not without a little disgust. "That's not what the story is about! A few days ago, I taught you that one way to unravel a parable is first to isolate the images and then assign them values. Now, who could the teacher be?"

"You."

"Who are the students?"

"We are."

"What is the spitwad?"

There was a brief silence; then everyone had an answer.

"Anger," said Jim Bailey.

"Contempt," said Marlowe Lakes.

"No, fun," shouted Ben Brown.

"Freedom," "power," "truth," "honesty." Concepts came from everywhere, but there were too many to sort out, so I stopped brainstorming and just grabbed one.

"Okay, if the spitwad stands for truth, what is the parable saying?"

Marty Shuster offered his first real idea of the year. "If the spitwad is truth, then the teacher was the one who learned the lesson. He got the truth in his face when he was pretending he already had it in his head."

"But if the teacher is trying to tell the truth," Jim Bailey argued, "then the spitwad must stand for something having to do with students refusing the truth."

"Maybe," offered Marlowe, "truth has nothing to do with it. Maybe the story is about how kids and teachers make contact. Those contacts aren't anything like what teachers want them to be, and that's why teachers pretend to be mean all the time."

I was astounded. We were doing first-class literary criticism now, and my students were actually interested in the debate! Was I finally asking the right questions? Was my two-step strategy for interpreting parables the key? Or was it the risk I took in allowing the discussion to go beyond what I knew? Were my students aware of how profound their answers were? It was hard to tell, but there was no doubt that I had done something right this time.

Such self-congratulatory reflections took my attention from the rear of the classroom just long enough for someone to drop Stevie Chamber's books out the window. The discussion lost its focus, then its energy. But it didn't matter. I had begun to learn my craft.

What that craft *was,* I was uncertain. What I was learning about it, even less certain. Still, I was onto something important here, and I wasn't going to leave this place until I figured out what it was.

4. The Lost Art

Education is not sermonizing to children against their instincts and pleasures, but providing a natural continuity between what they feel and what they can and should be. But this is a lost art.

Allan Bloom, *The Closing of the American Mind*

November

"For some reason," Brother Blake told me, "the kids just love to throw paper. I had the same problem as you did when I first started teaching. At first, I would just compliment the offender, telling him, 'Good, that's right! You are looking for power. But you are looking for it in the wrong place. Its not in spitwads, it's in words! Seek word power, not paper power! Throw words!'

"But they didn't listen. So, one day, I hit upon the idea that I would just let them throw spitwads at one another until they dropped. I picked a Friday before a vacation, when there would be little work to do anyway, and I told them they could throw paper at one another for as long as they wished, provided they stopped ten minutes before the end of class to clean up the mess. They thought it was a great deal, and so the paper began to fly. Somewhere in the back of my mind, I suspected that after twenty or thirty minutes, they would find throwing paper tiresome and inane. But I was wrong. The more paper they threw, the more paper they *wanted* to throw.

"The classroom began to fill up with debris. They emptied their binders of every available scrap of paper, and they began to throw paper *at me.* They were totally out of control. I was frightened and horrified but tried hard not to show it. They would corner one of their friends in the back of the room and, with glee in their eyes, bounce a wad of paper as big as your fist off his head with all the power and violence they could muster, then break out in squeals of delight.

"Ten minutes before the bell rang, I asked them to clean up the room. They did a kind of general sweep of the floor but left thousands of pieces of paper scattered about. The event had effected no catharsis whatsoever; in fact, it made them even harder to control.

"'We'll clean up the rest of the paper, Brother Blake, if you let us throw spitwads after vacation,' they said.

"I was stunned. The more I gave, the more they took. Their capacity for effrontery was endless, and I concluded that my little experiment in excess was one of the stupidest things I had ever done.

"Or so I thought. A year or two later, I was teaching ninth grade English again, and one of the students shot a spitwad across the room. Our eyes met, and a very odd thing happened. As I looked at him, I could see that he knew that I knew more about spitwads than he did, that I'd been through spitwad hell, and that his sorry excuse for a spitwad did not impress me in the least. But more importantly, his behavior did not frighten me as it would have that first year, because I was no longer paralyzed by my own dread as to where his actions might lead. I knew where they could lead. I knew the inner dynamics of classroom chaos better than anyone, because I had already experienced its extremes.

"Before that moment, I never thought that wasted period two years ago had taught me anything, but I was wrong. It had given me an edge, a little extra confidence, a little extra knowledge of what could happen that only an experienced teacher possesses. That brave journey into the heart of spitwad darkness had given me authority, real classroom authority that I could have gained in no other way. And, you know, after looking into my eyes, that little rascal never shot another spitwad.

"That same year, my class simply stopped working two weeks before Christmas vacation. At first, I was outraged by their lack of discipline, until I realized that what was really upsetting me was not their behavior, but my inability to change it. I just could not admit to myself that I did not know how to motivate them, that I wasn't as great a teacher as I thought I was, that there were things I didn't know—that there were things *no teacher knew*.

"Once I owned up to my own imperfection, the class did not bother me as much; it fascinated me. Instead of dreading being in the room with those manipulative kids, I actually almost looked forward to being there to watch them, to see exactly how they resisted work and how they played me off against myself, to watch my own reactions to them, and to fathom the dynamics of classroom insincerity and bogus participation.

"I began to catalog their intellectual evasions. I never took anything they did personally, but I did take it seriously—as a specimen of intellectual rebellion. In fact, this process worked so well that I decided to give up all my cherished notions about education altogether and just watch for my failures. I did this for ten years. It was my cross, my destiny, my power. It became my way."

Blake was silent for a while, looking off in the distance. "When I was younger," he said, "teaching was a kind of game to me. I could afford to take it lightly, because my real life was elsewhere. My real life was in the way I opened doors and tossed myself on the table in front of the room—my real life was my youth!

"Besides, it was fun to be young and have a profession. I played one off the other in a kind of lighthearted dance. No one really expected me to know what I was doing, and, on the other hand, no one really expected me to be so smart. I couldn't lose!

"But now I don't have youth, and my life has become my work. It is as if, in playing at having a vocation, I acquired one. And so now, when I walk into a class, I still toss myself up on the table, but that is no longer what I am there for. I am there to capture and articulate what is *out there*—the creative revelations pulsating in the air. They are what I live for now. What else have I got?"

I asked Brother Blake what to do when the students keep talking after the bell rings.

"Wait for them," he said. "They are not ready to start yet."

"But they will talk all period!"

"No they won't. Just wait. They will be silent within three minutes."

I was skeptical, but I tried it the next day, and it worked. Without my saying anything, the class stopped talking within two minutes, looked up from their desks, and were ready to begin. I was amazed.

"Why does it work?" I asked him.

"When you are patient, you communicate your respect for them. And unless you have totally lost their trust, they will reciprocate. It's only natural."

Not everyone was as impressed with Brother Blake's methods as I was. In fact, Strapp had already formed a committee to look into getting rid of the interdisciplinary humanities program that Blake had designed and go back to three separate courses in English, social science, and religion. The coaches were on his side, along with some of the parents and alumni.

Brother Blake's program, they said, simply lacked any objective measures by which to assess its achievements. It was too subjective. High schools were not built for this kind of education.

But I sensed that Strapp's suspicions of Brother Blake went even deeper than his dislike of the curriculum. You could see it in the way he would bristle whenever Brother Blake would raise philosophical questions at department meetings. Strapp was a practical man. He was interested in meeting the needs of the parents—his clientele—not in some mystagogic interpretation of high school as a living laboratory in philosophical anthropology.

"Teach the basics," Strapp would say. "Teach them effectively. The students will at least know their capitals, read a few short stories, write in complete sentences, spell. That's enough! In fact, that's damn good!"

Brother Blake's approach, I was told, had just confused everything.

Blake and Strapp, I decided, were just two decidedly different kinds of Catholics—indeed, two radically different kinds of men, the mystic and the man of action. Strapp's point was clear: there is a side of life that is not complex or difficult, a side that is straightforward and yields to a strong will. And that obvious side is the side of life we must take on. The rest—literature, ideas, philosophy—distract us from the tough, straight-ahead task of accomplishing the expected. For young boys, abstractions were pure poison, paralyzing the will at the very moment of its inception. What they needed was direction and a *tempering* of the imagination, not incitement to reflection!

But I was not convinced. Brother Blake seemed to be the only person in that school with a realistic assessment of what took place in the classroom, the only one not hiding behind clichés, the only one still intellectually alive. The obvious needs of our students were not so obvious at all. What the parents wanted for their sons was not necessarily what we, in good conscience, should provide.

Brother Blake saw his version of education going back at least as far as the great Mesopotamian and Egyptian mythologies—those first attempts to articulate a spiritual world and lift humanity out of the primordial womb of nature into the life of the mind. For Blake, our adolescent students were still living that primordial existence, most of them still fascinated by the warrior *geist* of the barbarian hordes of prehistory. And our task as teachers was to bring them into the more humane vision of the tribal mythologies as precursor to their tragic initiation into civilization. Teaching ninth grade, according to Brother Blake, was largely the task of spiritualizing the natural man—laying the foundations for some future Age of Greece.

Blake told me, "Mr. Strapp is always asking me how can we better prepare these kids for college. And I tell him that he's asking the wrong question. College professors have a very different job than we do. They take our brightest students and show them how little they really know. They initiate the young into the art of thinking against themselves. Our task is to initiate them into being affirmative. Its a very different thing.

"Have you ever seen those straight-A students who go directly to college and get straight A's there, but yet never experience the *metanoia* or 'turn' that constitutes authentic intellectual awakening? They had high school teachers that 'prepared' them for college—that is to say, inoculated them against radical self-examination. I want my students to go to college more passionate than pre-pared, less defended and more willing to risk failure. There is nothing more obtuse than a self-satisfied college freshman with high SAT scores and narrow careerist ambitions.

"Students need a perspective that allows them to continue to be trans-formed, changed, and renewed by their experiences. Ultimately, we want them to surprise us by their futures, not live out some ambitious high school admin-istrator's dream of a successful life."

I decided that I would follow Blake's lead regardless of the warnings. For as hardheaded as Strapp seemed, his will to discipline bred self-righteousness and sentimentality in those who embraced it. I could see it in the coaches and their following of dependent, once delinquent boys. Besides, Strapp's discipline-through-terror strategy had not brought any real order to my class—nor had it made me a better teacher.

Yet, I also knew that if there was to be a struggle over the curriculum, Strapp and the forces for a return to basics would probably win. And I won-dered if I could teach in a program designed by people like them. Blake's ex-istential pedagogy of the sublime had inspired me.

5. Classroom Praxis from A to B

In all my lectures I have taught one doctrine—namely the infinitude of the private man. . . . I gain my point, gain all points, whenever I can reach the young with any statement which teaches them their own worth.

Ralph Waldo Emerson

November

Try as I might, I was unable to apply Brother Blake's approach to my own classes. The students would come in tired and disinterested after lunch. This in itself would not have been so bad, but I had Jim Bailey in my class, one of the brightest freshmen in the school. And Jim sat there in the front row with such a look of pain on his face and with such disdain at my inability to keep Marty Shuster from disrupting things that I left school every day feeling as if I were an abject failure, a discredit to my profession.

I talked to Marty after school, suggesting that he needed to work harder and stop fooling around so much.

"You don't know me," he said. "What if my parents beat me? What if I was an orphan? What if I was dying of some awful disease? Wouldn't that make school and studying meaningless?"

"Have any of those things happened to you?" I asked.

"No, but they *could* have! How do you know they haven't?"

"You just told me," I said.

"I mean, if I hadn't told you?"

"I'd ask."

"But you don't ask everyone if they've been beaten or abandoned or if they are dying, you just assume they're okay. You just assume that they are essentially like everyone else. But they're not. Everybody's different. So how can I know you aren't assuming other false things?"

"Good question," I said. "You can't. People assume incorrect things all the time."

"So, you see, why should I listen to you at all?" he concluded. "You just might be assuming all the wrong things."

And this impasse left us staring at one another, no closer to any agreement.

"Well, I *do* know some things you don't," I insisted. "I know the assumptions most people make. I know the rules and the conventions."

"In other words, you know how to be a phoney," he replied.

I thought about that one for a while.

"Learning the conventions doesn't have to make you a phoney; you have to know them so you can participate in the culture. You have to know them in order to become *real*."

He looked up at me when I said this, skepticism etched into his brow. "Can I go to the bathroom?" he asked. "I suddenly got this royal pain in the ass."

I told Brother Blake about my problems with my afternoon class.

"Sounds like Marty isn't your problem," he said. "Bailey is. He wants you to protect him from Marty, to be his mother, but now is the time he should start to take on some responsibilities. Instead of blaming *you* for Marty's behavior, he's going to have to fashion his own response to him."

The next day, Brother Blake stopped by my class and sat in the back of the room. We were talking about *Lord of the Flies*, and I asked why, if Piggy was the smartest, wasn't he the leader? And how might civilized Ralph and his friends take over the island leadership from savage Jack and his hunters.

Jim found these questions fascinating, but no sooner had I asked them than Marty started kicking the back of Albert's chair. Brother Blake noted Jim's disgust and anger and so walked over to his desk.

"Do these students *bother you?*" he asked, pointing at Marty and company.

"They sure do," Jim replied. "They act like babies every day, and Mr. Inchausti just lets them get away with it. He tells them to stop, but they don't. He sends them outside, but they just fool around more. I'm getting sick of it."

Brother Blake ignored Marty and concentrated on Jim. "You can't always depend upon teachers and others to protect you. You're reading *Lord of the*

Flies. What does it teach you about leadership? There are going to be goof-offs and troublemakers wherever you go, and the sooner you learn how to accept them, deal with them, and get on with your business, the better off you are going to be."

The class was surprised. This was the first time anyone had lectured Jim Bailey about his behavior, and yet Brother Blake had done it in a way that had put down the class rowdies at the same time. To me, he seemed to be letting Marty off the hook. That is, until I looked over at Marty and found him listening intently to what Brother Blake was saying. It was clear he hadn't ever quite looked at himself in this way.

Jim, for his part, responded with indignation. "Nobody is going to tell me I'm responsible for these loudmouths!"

"No, you're not responsible for them. But you will have to learn how to live with them. And the sooner the better. Think of Ralph on the island in *Lord of the Flies.* Without the adults there to protect him, he wasn't able to take leadership away from Jack. He was the only one there who could communicate with Simon and Piggy and make their gifts useful to the group, but he wasn't able to put Jack in his place, so he wasn't able to lead."

Jim thought this one over. "So you're saying I'm like Ralph."

"You *are* Ralph. And you'll never get off the island if you just sit around waiting for some adult to rescue you. I know it's hard. Barbarians like Jack are everywhere. But that is what it means to go on your quest."

These last remarks, even though they were addressed to Jim, challenged Marty. Marty had always thought that *he* was the one on the quest, that *he* was the adventurer, the brave soul, the one who dared to be different. But seen through the eyes of the text and through the eyes of Brother Blake, he wasn't the hero after all. He was Jack—self-absorbed, self-centered, brutal Jack. And Jim Bailey, Mr. Goody-Goody, *he* was the hero.

Then Brother Blake walked up to the blackboard. He drew two dots and marked one A and the other B. Turning to Jim, he asked, "How do you get from A to B?"

"You draw a line," Jim replied.

Blake tossed him the chalk. "Show me."

Jim walked up to the board and drew a straight line from A to B.

A————————B

"Wrong," said Brother Blake. "The way you get from A to B is like this." And, taking the chalk, he drew a furious array of scribbles across the board.

"Now, why did I do that?" he asked the class. "Marty, you explain it to them."

Marty was surprised to find himself back in the conversation. He didn't know what Brother Blake was getting at. "You're crazy," he muttered.

But Jim Bailey, seeing Marty reject Brother Blake's example, decided that there probably was something to it.

"Are you trying to say that people don't really move in straight lines? That they have to mess up sometimes?"

"What do you think?"

"Well, I guess that's true sometimes. But you can't make a policy of messing up. I mean, you shouldn't plan to mess up; that's crazy."

Brother Blake took full measure of Jim's comment and then said, "Sometimes, the trip from A to B isn't as easy as it seems. Sometimes, it's a circuitous route, a trip up the Congo River. And you're right; you don't *plan* to mess up. It just happens sometimes. But messing up is not a bad thing if you learn from it."

Then Blake drew a whole array of possibilities.

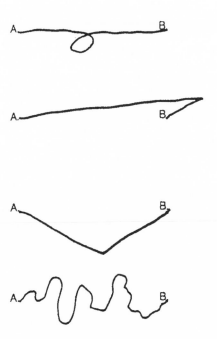

"All of these ways are valid," Blake said. "All of these ways work."

And then he had them open their Bibles to the parable of the prodigal son.

"Here is the story of a classic screw-up," he said. "The story of a guy who took the long way home. Marty, could you read it to us?"

As any master teacher might have done, Brother Blake had turned the class's attention away from the petty problem of "good behavior" to the issues raised by the texts that we were studying. But he did it in such a way that the realities of the classroom became the content of the lesson and we, ourselves, the principal subjects of the literature. My honor student's resentment was distracting us as much as his classmates' lack of discipline. And my tradition-bound views of teacherly authority were making it impossible for me to read the situation as the living embodiment of one of the themes of our reading.

I could not deny that Brother Blake's lesson had touched me—touched me more deeply than any of the lectures I had heard in graduate school. All I could do was stare at those diagrams on the board as if they were the charts of my life.

"Some of these kids," Blake told me, "think that if they aren't successful in the eyes of the world then they aren't worth anything. They believe that only the talented tenth need discipline, that the average person can float along—indeed, *should* float along—that meaningful work and the respect that it brings belong only to the few. So they seek distraction with a vengeance, as if it were their calling—their only compensation for not being superior students.

"We've got to let them know that there is another life, an inner life, a higher life, that has its own heroic dimensions. And that success in this realm is open to anybody."

Brother Blake's impact on the students was profound: here was somebody talking to them about the injustices of the school yard, the presence of bullies, the impotent "superiority" of "smart kids," and the fallibility of their teachers. Somehow, all this became more than just material for class discussions but probes that illuminated the books they were reading. Suddenly, no question seemed out-of-bounds. Everything mattered because there was no place the mind could not go. And the mind mattered because it revealed a way to act.

If anyone spoke out of turn or "messed up," Brother Blake would simply ask, "Does the prodigal son ever talk out of turn? Does his brother?"

Ideas were everywhere and in all things. The key to seeing them was in the quality of attention one paid to one's mistakes, to one's problems, to one's inevitable "messing up."

Brother Blake's lesson brought to mind thoughts of other incorrigible underground souls I had known.

When I was a senior in high school, I was a member of the Key Club, a junior Kiwanis made up largely of kids too inept to be members of any other school organization. We held meetings once a month—the last Thursday night. We didn't do much but drink sodas from McDonald's and plot how to get free lunches from our faculty sponsor. At one of our meetings, none of our officers, the popular kids, showed up. So as a joke we decided to begin impeachment proceedings against them. We thought it would be extremely funny to kick them out of office, since we knew that the only reason they condescended to be in the same club with us was to pad their college application forms.

When we began the procedures, however, Dave Deacon—a bit of an outcast—objected with surprising vehemence, raising his hand and shouting, "Point of order! Point of order!" over and over again. We ignored him and passed motion after motion kicking the officers out of the club, banning them from Kiwanis luncheons and demanding public apologies for their poor leadership.

As we proceeded, Dave got madder and madder. And the madder he got, the more contemptuous of him we got. Couldn't this "dufus" get the joke? Why was he so serious about the stupid Key Club? Didn't he know that the guys he was defending all thought he was worthless? Couldn't he see it was all a hype anyway, that our president only wanted something to add to his résumé, and that for the rest of the members, the Key Club was just a cover for parties and free lunches?

But the more cynically we abused him, the more self-righteous he became, until at last he commanded the floor—standing up on the seat of his desk with his blue parka unzipped and his geeky plaid shirt tail out.

"You know what you guys are?" he shouted., "You guys are a bunch of, a bunch of, a bunch of . . . " And it was obvious he didn't know *what* we were. He had no word for the revulsion in his heart, and he kept stuttering and repeating that last phrase until the word finally came: "You guys are a bunch of, bunch of, a bunch of ASS-BUTTS!"

There was silence in the room. No one could have imagined a more ridiculous end to his dramatic diatribe. It was too good to be true.

Finally a lone inquisitive voice broke the silence and asked "Ass-butts? Ass-butts? Where did you get *that* word?"

The room exploded with jeering laughter. People were falling out of their chairs and holding their sides in mock pain. Whenever the hysterics would begin to die down, someone would utter that word again, "ass-butts," and all fifteen of us would be on the floor, holding our sides again, and laughing until we cried.

At first, Dave didn't laugh. He turned red, tried to make light of his mistake. "Or whatever," he said. But it was too late. For the rest of the year, maybe for the rest of his life, he had acquired a cruel new nickname.

A few years later, I was working at the college bookstore, and as I was walking across campus, I suddenly realized we were experiencing a freak snow flurry. It snows in Sacramento, California, maybe once every twenty years. Being young and high spirited, I decided that the best way to commemorate this event was to make a snowball and throw it at one of my friends. So I padded up snow in my hands and looked around for a suitable victim, when whom should I see walking across campus but Dave Deacon.

I had not seen him in three years, and yet here he was at the very moment I was seeking someone to tease. It was as if God had put him there precisely to be humiliated one more time. I hate to admit it, but the irony was irresistible to me, so I hunted him down, creeping up behind some trees to ambush him at the corner of the walk. When I got close enough to hit him, I called out, "Hey, Dave look out for snowballs!"

He looked up—saw what I was about to do—and the whites of his eyes got large. He knew that if I hit him, the story would somehow get back to all our former classmates, maybe at some future class reunion, and he was determined not to be humiliated again. And so he did something I did not expect: He dropped his books and charged at me with the intensity of several years' worth of resentment and hatred. A raging bull, he leaped upon me, knocking me down and began pummeling me with his cold, wet fists.

"Dave!" I said. "Calm down. It was just a joke!"

But it was no joke to him. And he would take no more from me. He bloodied my lip and punched me until he cried, and then, getting up, he threw a handful of snow on my prone body, saying in utter disgust, "Tell your so-called friends James and Freddy that I beat the crap out of you." And then he walked away with more dignity than I ever imagined he possessed.

Yet, his mentioning of James and Freddy gave him away. He still craved their approval but he was convinced that he would never get it, and so he had built a citadel of scorn to hide his pain. And as I sat there in the snow, all wet, I felt for the first time in my young life abject sorrow for the person I had been and had become. If I could have taken back that snowball, I would have. If I could have erased "ass-butts" from our teenage lexicon, I would have. But I just sat there in that damn snow, bleeding, wishing I would bleed more.

In my night school course (I moonlighted like all the rest of the lay teachers), I had another frustrated "prodigal" who sat in the back of my otherwise very animated and happy English composition class. I could see all the signs of teenage resentment and seething rebellion so common at the high school.

One day, she asked if she could speak with me privately in my office. I didn't like it, but I figured I had to agree. As we walked across the campus, I asked her what she wanted, but she said she preferred to wait until we were alone before she told me. This made me even more uneasy.

We rode the elevator up to the sixth floor without speaking, and when we finally got in my office, she blurted out: "I just wanted to tell you that you are the most condescending person I have ever met in my life. I can't stand your class!"

Although I had many faults as a teacher, no one had ever accused me of condescension before—being too liberal, yes; being too forgiving, yes; suffering fools too gladly, yes; but condescending? Never! So I probed a bit to see if I wasn't the victim here of some grand Jungian shadow projection.

"Do the other students share your feelings?" I asked.

"Those sheep?" she asked. "They don't know anything!" And then she added, as if to clarify things, "I'm an art major."

Her arrogance relaxed me. She felt better just having insulted me, and I felt better knowing that she was self-aggrandizing. It made her criticisms easier to bear. A true underground figure, she felt most moral when she was lashing out. I had to refuse the shame she had thrust upon me, and at the same time, if I could do it, bring her up into the light by giving her a less vicious tool for self-expression.

I was a young enough teacher then to think I could win her back. So I took her insults as if they were observations and tried to practice teacherly satyagraha—Gandhian truth force.

But it didn't work. She continued to refuse to speak up in class or to join in dialogue with the others. She sat in the corner and smirked—continuing to get Cs on her papers and interpreting these grades as indicating her teacher's inability to grasp her secret greatness. She even fainted one day in class—apologizing profusely, saying how sorry she was to put me in such an uncomfortable position, since I obviously could not handle someone so intense, so unconventional as she.

It was hard for me not to hate her when she did these things, but I kept my pledge to acknowledge the underground, to keep the door open that led out of that psychological hell, to include her in our classroom world.

But I was never able to find the path.

It wasn't until Brother Blake had shown me the way from A to B that I began to see how a teacher might provide avenues out of the underground for his prodigal students. For some, the teacher must become the scapegoat—and stand unmoved at the center of their anxiety and contempt. This was not to say that one embraced martyrdom, but one did make it a point to stand outside the students' economy of affection as an independent standard and refuge. In this way, one became both a source of solace for a student like Dave and a contradiction to those who saw themselves as popular and protected.

Blake told me of the time a student had called him a name referring to the female genitalia in front of the rest of his students. Blake responded to this "outrage" by telling the boy not to use words he did not understand.

When the boy announced defiantly, "I know what it *means!*" Blake tossed him a piece of chalk and said, "Okay, then draw one for us on the board."

The class immediately came to attention. The other students were fascinated. Did Joe really know what one looked like? Could he draw one on the board? Would Brother Blake let him do it?

Joe walked up to the blackboard, and after a moment of hesitation, he scribbled for what seemed like a long time. When he returned to his desk, there was a smudge on the board, an oblong dot. The class of pubescent boys was mystified. Was this an accurate drawing?

Blake walked up to the picture, tilted his head to the left and then to the right. "You know," he finally said, "I have been celibate for over forty years, and even I can draw a better one than that!" The class exploded with laughter, and even Joe joined in. His anger was gone and the power of his obscenity defused by the humor.

But if Brother Blake had managed to expose the powerlessness of dirty words before the mind alive, there was one more step to be taken. The dirty words themselves had to be transformed into agents of healing.

Blake walked over to Joe, put his arm around his shoulder, and said, "You've really got to get your shit together, and to do that you need a good asshole. I am going to be your asshole this year. And after me, if you are lucky, you'll meet another asshole and another until your shit is packed so tight it coalesces into a fine powder. And then maybe you will be ready for the greatest asshole of them all."

And with that, Brother Blake stood back and pointed to the crucifix hanging above the blackboard just below the American flag.

The class gasped. It was at once the most sacrilegious and yet mystic moment many of them had ever experienced. If Jesus was the greatest asshole, then maybe they had misunderstood everything about him. What did it mean to be an asshole, anyway?

Brother Blake's image had unleashed a moment of authentic teenage reflection and religious awe. This was not sixth grade catechism, with its platitudes and trite moralisms. This was something that pulled away from schoolrooms and lesson books toward something larger and more profound. Was there nothing so secular that it could not be made sacred? No life so lost that it could not be found?

It was hard to explain to my wife, Linda, what I was going through—the lessons I was learning, and why I was so tense all the time.

The first time my wife met Marty Shuster—we ran into him at the mall—she was amazed. "So that is the kid you've been complaining about, that little four-foot-tall person?"

"Yes!" I insisted. "You don't know him like I do. Size is a relative thing."

But she was unconvinced. She was positive I was overreacting, taking my work far too seriously.

"Relax," she'd say, as if one could will emotional ease. "Don't think about teaching all the time. It's making you a very demented, even boring, person."

She was kind enough not to mention that I was also getting out of shape—gaining weight and acquiring a string of anxiety-related physical afflictions (facial tics, rapid pulse). But I couldn't help it. I had not chosen this fate; it had befallen me. Linda couldn't comprehend my stress. She just knew I was a preoccupied mess who stayed up until three A.M. every night writing and then rewriting chapters of my never-ending dissertation and spending every other waking moment fretting about Strapp, Marlowe Lakes, and Marty Shuster.

When I tried to take an interest in her concerns, she could see it was forced. I just trusted to providence that the lessons I was learning at St. Vincent's would someday pay off at home, that learning to be a teacher in the Brother Blake mold would redeem me as a husband. No, more than that, I trusted it would redeem me as a person.

But I hadn't arrived there yet, and it would strike me from time to time that Linda was wasted on me, that she had unknowingly married some yogic adept who spent far too much time contemplating classroom esoterica. Not that we didn't have our moments that first year; it was just that this teaching job loomed large in my life—perhaps too large.

There are teachers who, in order to survive, become "characters," large dramatic types—Falstaffs and Willard Scotts. For them, being a teacher is playing a role. Their personalities have big handles that the kids can hang on to. And it works!

But these same teachers become hard to live with outside of the classroom. Their family lives suffer. They don't quite fit into "normal" life anymore. It's as if becoming a teacher for them was becoming a performer, and life offstage lacks something. They aren't recognized at home, no one listens, no one has to, and so the gift of a big, easy-to-see self just isn't appreciated. In fact, it's often downright annoying.

This wasn't my problem. I didn't come home from teaching an inflated personality; I came home distracted and preoccupied. Inward. Confused. I felt as though I was fighting for my life, and so I couldn't leave my worries at work.

It seemed to me that each moment I forgot about my classes weakened me. I was at war, and Linda didn't really understand why I felt as though my identity was on the line with this job.

If I could become a teacher, I thought, if I could conquer this classroom of ninth grade boys, then and only then would I be *somebody*. I know it sounds silly and overblown, but that was how I felt, and I sensed that I had a chance to make it if I could follow Brother Blake. I had found something exceptional here, a real teacher, a way out.

It was the first year of our marriage, though, and Linda was working through her own problems of self-redefinition. She couldn't tell if it was our marriage or my job that had made me so distant. Was it her, or was it me? Was she finally seeing me for who I really was—a distracted, dejected, disenfranchised man?

She'd want to go to the movies, out to dinner, dance, have fun, and I preferred saving my life, meditating on my fate, replaying over and over in my mind's eye some trivial conversation I had had with Marlowe Lakes, searching for some edge or angle on the whole thing.

But I would do things with her anyway, halfheartedly, with forced attention—and then I'd stay up late after she had gone to bed, charting my next moves against the enemy, making lists and plans, revising my lessons.

Finally, we had a fight. I came home from work, and the door was locked. I couldn't get in. I knocked, knocked again, the latch turned, the door opened a peek, but the chain held fast. "Go away," she said simply. "I don't want you here."

"Come on," I pleaded. "Open the door, we have to talk."

But when the door finally flung open, I realized that I had nothing to say. I hadn't even been thinking about Linda. My mind was still back in school, on Brother Blake, on discipline problems, on Strapp.

"Well?" she asked.

I stammered. I tried to remember if I had done something or had forgotten to do something, but all I could conjure up were anticipations of tomorrow's lessons.

"You're hopeless," she finally said and walked out the door. I ran after her. "Stop! Come back! Let's talk! This is important!"

She just ignored me. She could tell it was all fake, that I just wanted to think about my class, that I was preoccupied with myself.

A few hours later she came back, although we had said nothing to lessen the tensions. She had just decided to forgive me. No, she had decided to wait for me. There would be a zone in her psyche kept in reserve, a place I could return to if I remembered where it was and if I didn't stay away too long.

I resolved not to forget.

Brother Blake's senior religion class was reading *The Little Flowers of St. Francis,* the medieval compendium of legends and accounts of the great saint's life.

"It's *Don Quixote,*" he told me. "Father Mateo is Sancho Panza, and St. Francis is Quixote. It is one of the first novels, one of the first examinations of the power of a dead mythology to revivify. The kids don't see this because they don't know *Quixote,* but they see the comedy, the farce, the exaggeration, the grotesques. They see the wonderful juxtaposition of the uncomprehending prudent followers of the saint and his outrageous assertion of transcendent ideals. They see the image of a man of passion living a myth larger than life will allow.

"And the sermon to the birds is very moving to them. Francis tells the birds to be happy because they are gifted. They have wings. It's as if he is speaking to our students. Some of us think of them as animals from time to time, but never *birds!*

"I once heard the comedian Jay Leno say that talking to a fourteen-year-old boy was like trying to have a conversation with a chicken. Not only don't they listen, but they even move their necks and arms around! That was as close as I have heard anyone get to the Franciscan concept!

"Well, in the speech, Francis tells the birds to give thanks to God for the freedom of flight, beautiful plumage, and food without labor. He praises their variety and their affection, then makes the sign of the cross over them, and they rise in four separate groups, forming a huge cross in the sky. As they fly off to the four corners of the earth, Francis says, 'Friars, like birds, possess nothing of their own in this world and commit themselves entirely to the Providence of God.' He was providing us with an image as to how to live our lives. The way out is *into the air.*"

6. Ceremonies Sacred and Profane

All I wanted to tell people was, "Honestly look at yourselves. Look at what bad boring lives you lead." That's the most important thing for people to understand. And when they do understand it, they will certainly create a new and better life. . . . Man will become better when we have shown him to himself as he is.

Anton Chekhov

December

Brother Blake's approach to teaching was changing the way I saw things. I wasn't able to teach like him yet, but I was no longer able to teach like anyone else. I was between sanities. I had lost my conventional points of reference, but I had not yet found anything concrete to replace them. To me, Brother Blake's approach was still anchored in the air.

We had a funeral on campus. Brother Bob, the crotchety, white-haired man who ran the ball room and the lost and found, had died in his sleep.

They held the service in the gym, his casket set in the center of the basketball court, a large screen propped up behind him, and a small podium where Brother Blake was to deliver the eulogy. Brother Bob's relatives sat on folding chairs about ten feet away from the casket. A woman in her forties, dressed in black, was crying modestly, but uncontrollably.

My class entered from the rear of the building—happy to have been let out of school for *any* reason.

Strapp had lectured the boys earlier over the intercom system as to the seriousness of this ceremony and the repercussions if any one of them took advantage of the situation to "make a fool of himself." Marty Shuster, however, was willing to take that risk. He saw the whole event as a once-in-a-lifetime chance to be truly outrageous. When he saw the grieving woman, he turned to his friends and mocked, "Boo-hoo! Boo-hoo!"

I couldn't tell if he was just unspeakably cruel or if this was his way of dealing with his own anxieties about death.

For my part, I found it difficult imagining Brother Bob dead. Death still seemed to me a nothing, a cipher, a mere hole in life. But there was the casket before me, the liturgy beginning to be performed, and these awful kids finding it next to impossible to keep their hands off one another.

Strapp came over and stood by my class. He wanted to make sure nothing ruined the mass.

I could not for the life of me understand why *any*one would want to hold a funeral at a high school.

Brother Charlie began to show slides of Bob's earlier years. It turned out Bob had been a fighter pilot in World War II, that he had once had jet black hair and worn a leather jacket, that he had joined the Brothers relatively late in life, that he had a younger sister who was once quite beautiful. (That was probably she, sitting in the front row.)

The slides were projected onto the large screen by one of those machines that can fade one image into the next, and as Brother Blake read the captions, we looked on in amazement at the images of a life and a world now gone.

A high school graduation portrait of Bob that resembled Terry McCloskey.

An air force flight school group photo with Brother Bob's head circled in red.

A portrait of Brother Bob as a child, dressed in a sailor suit, looking frail, hopeful, a little scared. His father, no doubt dust now, stood behind him, full of energy, powerful, strong. And beside him, Bob's mother in a floral print, her eyes sensual.

It seemed so odd. These images had more life in them than Brother Bob ever had working in that stupid ball room, passing out sports equipment. Who would have known he had had a life, that beautiful memories and a glorious history resided in the mind of that frail, if sometimes witty, old man.

My students watched the whole thing as if it were an amateur television show. They were keyed to the emotions of the event—looking to see how Strapp was reacting to things, looking to see if any of the brothers would cry. They were fascinated by adult emotions, as if they held some clue to our weaknesses.

A few of the boys tried to make fart noises without being caught; others tried to be respectful. Both were equally difficult for them—and both reactions equally phoney. I tried to note the most able actors.

Brother Blake led us in a prayer and then communion. Marlowe Lakes went down to taste the wine and returned to his seat laughing self-consciously, letting his friends know that he had participated in the mass for the cheap wine high.

Marty Shuster was still fascinated by the grieving woman. He thought she was funny.

"Where did they get those people? Central casting? Did you see that lady?" he kept asking in astonished tones. "Boo-hoo! Boo-hoo!" And then he'd giggle uncontrollably.

As we left the gym, under the tight security of Strapp's gaze, we were handed holy cards with Brother Bob's name and dates on them. Some of the kids kept theirs, others tossed them unceremoniously onto the ground, while still others waited until lunch to sketch on them. Later, I found one card with a bubble drawn just above the Virgin Mary's head with the caption, "I got Bob, now I'm coming after you!"

Brother Blake came up to me. "Your class handled this very well. Some even took communion." I listened hard to detect any irony in his voice, but I didn't hear any. What was he getting at?

At the faculty Christmas party, our secretary, Mrs. Gray, drank a little too much Christian Brothers' brandy and began to cry. It turned out she was scheduled for a difficult operation in February, and she was afraid that she was going to die.

Brother Blake listened attentively to her confession of fears and remorse, of her desire to see her son grow up, of her anger that she was being cheated by life. I got the sense that they must have been old friends when he cupped his hands as if he were catching water from a faucet and told her, "When you die, you fall into the hands of God."

"Oh, please, Blake," she protested. "Don't give me that! I'm too young. I can't leave my babies yet."

Blake looked at her closely. "But it's true. I'm not trying to comfort you."

Mrs. Gray started to sob, "Oh, Blake, what am I to *do?* What *am* I to do?"

"What *can* you do?" he asked. "I'm not too far from that door myself, but at my age, it is often a consolation to know it is there. For you, there is only faith."

"That's what scares me, Brother," she said. "I don't know if I believe."

"Well, God's there in any case," he said. "It doesn't really matter if you understand it or not, does it? Reality is reality. Death is death. Eternity is eternity. And we are all going there eventually. I'm not trying to make you feel good, Doreen; I just want to remind you that death is not the end of everything. God will still exist, and everything you knew of Him—your love, the people you loved—all *that* will remain. The stars, the sky, earth. All I'm trying to say, Doreen, is that you *can* die, and it won't *kill* you. There are worse things that can happen."

At this, Mrs. Gray laughed, then noticed me standing there for the first time, blushed, and walked away.

Had I been rude?

The Advent assembly was run by the junior class, and their adviser, Dave Rockman, intended to make the event a species of cutting-edge liturgy. The students were picking the readings and the music. Inspired by their etymological dictionaries, they had come up with the theme of *advent*ure. The adventure of Advent—*ad venire*, to come toward, to venture into reality, to journey to God.

"The plan," Dave explained to me, "is to play 'Born to Be Wild' by Steppenwolf as the students enter the gymnasium to symbolize the fact that we are all born as wild animals. The students come to school that way, and most even graduate that way. But the saving grace of Christ remains at the end of their adventure—that's the theme!

"Then right after the liturgy of the word, we play an original piece of music (composed by Jimmy McDermott) for oboe and drums. It represents the chaos of unredeemed experience."

"Sounds great," I said, unconvinced.

"And you should hear the readings the kids picked!" Dave continued. "Unbelievable! A passage from Song of Songs for the sexual adventure. Luke's account of the beheading of John the Baptist for the adventure into violence. And then the account of Jesus' assault upon the money changers for the adventure into history.

"These kids like it straight," he added. "They even suggested we have a human sacrifice, but I had to tell them that's already programmed into the mass."

"You make it sound so *pagan*," I said.

Dave glowed. "Yeah. These kids *are* pagans, primitives. It's not surprising that their liturgies resemble those pastiche assemblage ceremonies some of the

New World missionaries put together with the Iroquois. This is *basic* stuff. Primal energies."

Despite his good intentions, the assembly itself was a disaster.

"What has any of *this* to do with Advent?" asked Strapp, who always stood by my class during assemblies.

"It's the Advent adventure," I replied.

"The *what?*"

We drop everything when the bell rings and march down to the gymnasium for the basketball rally.

Tonight, we are going against our crosstown rivals, the Jesuits. We beat them every year. They are the elite school—more expensive than St. Vincent's, smaller student body, more intellectual curriculum, higher Scholastic Aptitude Tests, more prestigious college admissions, two former graduates on the state supreme court. But they are sissies when it comes to sports.

We are the Christian Brothers school, private but with our roots in egalitarianism. Our graduates enter the police force, take over family businesses, or get jobs as analysts with the state government.

The students are excited today because THE CHEERLEADERS are going to be at the rally. The cheerleaders are from our sister school, St. Theresa's. The boys tell me they are hoping to look up their skirts, watch them do splits and cartwheels, fantasize!

When we get to the gym, THE CHEERLEADERS are huddled together in the far corner of the building. Their adviser stands next to them, to serve and protect. The girls peer out at the crowd from time to time, fearfully and yet expectantly, as if somebody "important" is coming to watch them. A talent scout, maybe?

Brother Charlie nudges my arm. "Are you ready for the $3,000 pyramid?" he asks.

"What do you mean?"

"We sent the girls to cheerleader camp last summer. It cost us almost $500 per girl. When they came back, they were able to form a six-girl pyramid."

The principal takes the microphone in his hand like a lounge singer and shouts: "Christian Brothers High! Are we gonna win tonight?"

There are scattered shouts, a little applause. A disappointing rally opener.

So Brother Nep declaims, "Get it up, men!"

The boys cheer!

I wonder if he knows what he is saying and sadly conclude that he does. He then launches into one of his long-winded orations: one third theological jargon, one third educationalese, and one third misapplied teenage slang. I stand guard over my class, dying inside.

"Well, are we gonna get it up tonight or what?" (More cheers.)

"At St. Vincent's, each boy is an individual, a unique creation of God, but on the basketball court, those unique creations form a community, a team, an instrument of one single will. And we are here today to confirm that commitment, to lend the team our support, to let them know our solidarity with them is absolute."

The students cheer, as if this made sense.

"Basketball is only one part of community life, Gentlemen," he intones. "But it is an important part, because it symbolizes our greater engagement with the struggles of life and our dedication to fair play, discipline, and the love of Christ."

Nep is getting oiled up, but he is going on too long. The students are getting antsy for THE CHEERLEADERS. He senses their impatience, cuts his speech short, and brings out the girls.

Close to a thousand teenage boys crane their necks in hope of catching a glimpse of underwear. The girls, for their part, try to make the best of an awkward situation. They keep their minds on executing the perfect six-girl pyramid and to proving to Strapp and Nep that the money they spent on cheerleader camp had not been wasted. Tracy, Cindy, Patty, Shelly, Debbie, and Brandy are models of concentration.

After dancing around a bit to the pep band's energetic version of "When the Saints Go Marchin' In," three girls hit the mat to form the base of the human pyramid. A second wave jumps upon them, and then the final girl bolts to the top and hangs on. The pyramid is up for maybe a second and then tumbles down in a massive crash.

Cheers ring through the auditorium! The girls bounce out of the hall, none of them seriously hurt (only one bloody lip).

Brother Nep takes the microphone. "Let's hear it for the girls from St. Theresa's!" And the applause rings for three solid minutes.

Outside in the hall, Strapp is organizing the girls for their escape from the school, thanking them and assuring them they had performed wonderfully. In the gym, the senior class performs several skits making fun of the Jesuits. Several students lip-synch to the Village People's recording "Macho Man," wearing little signs that read "Jesuit Student #1" and "Jesuit Student #2."

I tried to see this as good-natured fun, but it just seemed tainted to me. There were dark forces at work here. Every member of the basketball team was wearing a red sweat shirt in occult solidarity. The unexceptional others, the masses, the crowd, chanted their praise and envy. And the principal and the coaches stood there orchestrating it all like some big fascist celebration of the warrior *geist*.

How could Brother Blake accept this? He never made a peep. I saw him standing there with his class, just watching everything, turning his head now and then to take it all in. Holy Mary, Mother, of God, Most Merciful Star of the Sea! Where was the Goddess energy to temper all this bogus, macho, self-regard? Where was our sister of sorrows? Where was our adoration of her mysteries?

I was so upset by the rally that, the next day, I asked my class about their attitudes toward women.

"What do you mean?" they replied. "We like 'em."

"But what do you like about them?" I asked. "What qualities make up an admirable woman?"

To help the discussion, I offered to put their list of traits up on the board.

"Good teeth!" suggested Marty.

But I insisted they get serious, and they did, providing a long litany of "more important" body parts. After they were done, I decided to speak to them straight, man-to-man.

"I'm quite a bit older than you," I told them. "And I've had girlfriends, and now I'm married. So what I'm going to tell you comes from experience. I'm not just making this up. Based upon everything I know and everything I've ever experienced, I can honestly tell you that the qualities that make for an admirable woman are not listed up on the board. They are honesty, vision, humor, and strength of character. The very same things that make for an admirable man."

And you know what? They laughed at me!

I attended the Modern Language Association's annual convention to interview for college teaching positions.

The convention was a disturbing experience for me. Coming back into the academic world after having taught at the high school was almost as unsettling as attending Dave Rockman's Advent liturgy. For one thing, all the men there looked just like me. They all wore beards, Rockport shoes, corduroy jackets, fashionable ties. I was a cliché.

But, at the same time, I felt like I didn't belong. All the other recent graduates seemed to share an idiom, a professional jargon, indeed a collective understanding of things that precluded me and my experiences at the high school.

They all considered themselves "feminists"—even the men, even the *chauvinist* men! And they would talk in shorthand—using slogans like "always already" and terms like "logocentricism," mentioning Lacan, the controversial French psychoanalyst, in almost every other sentence.

It wasn't that I didn't understand them or that they were pompous or self-regarding or even self-deceived; these were *not* extreme people. They were incredibly sane, conventional in most ways, and very smart. And yet, they seemed focused on such a narrow band of cutting-edge thinkers that they felt exempted from thinking seriously about any of the things that mattered to me.

I tried to talk to them about the ninth grade, about Brother Blake, parables, pedagogy, even prayer. They didn't reject my enthusiasms; they just smiled
at them and then gave me titles of books I should read—usually complex,
weighty theoretical tomes, reconsiderations of Heidegger or post-structuralist
analyses of deviant historiography.

I realized I wasn't a part of their world any longer, but I also realized it
wasn't too late for me to jump back into it. I had read many of these books
already. I knew quite a bit of "theory." I could subscribe to the right journals.
I could learn semiotics. I could . . .

No, I couldn't. I couldn't go back.

Brother Blake had ruined me. My ninth grade backwater had chastened
me. I had become too aware of the pretensions of my own profession. Its scholarship seemed faddish to me now—unreal, artificial insights brewed in the
styrofoam coffee cups of conference-crowd prodigies. My only hope was to
connect to a "movement" of some sort—a counter-community, a subculture,
preferably one of the more radical or obscure ones. Basque studies?

But when I was honest with myself, I had to admit that I couldn't really
do that either. I had become a ninth grade humanities teacher, and it was my
job to bring the life of the mind to bear on the lives of fourteen-year-olds. I
didn't feel misunderstood at the Modern Language Association convention so
much as *over*stood—and dismissed.

And yet, had any of these scholars broken up fist fights in the past year?
Had any of their lectures been interrupted by spitwads to the forehead or personal insults tossed from the back of the room?

I listened to their ideas as they read their papers, wondering what they
could possibly teach me about being an educator. Or even about literature?
Who were these pampered aesthetes preoccupied with *epistemological* issues?
How had they come to such status in the unreal city?

There is a kind of arrogance that comes from doing impossible work. You
see it in urban emergency room doctors and nurses, Third World missionaries,
and inner-city cops and social workers. It is a vanity born of self-sacrifice.

As a high school teacher, I was beginning to indulge in this form of self-
righteousness. I knew that I was doing important work that few others wanted
to do or could do. I knew that I was alive in a way others were not, that I was
in the battle, in the action on the socio-historical front. It felt glorious, especially *after* work.

But a part of me was troubled by this feeling. It smacked of a provincial
desire to elevate the value of one's actions to the exact degree they didn't matter. Was this merely a psychological defense against obscurity, or was I really
close to one of the sources of life? I couldn't tell if I was wasting my time on

trifles or doing something important. Would I wake up one morning to find myself transformed into a gigantic insect?

7. Attempting the Impossible

I don't think, amateurs at prayer as most of us are, that we pay half enough attention to pre-prayer. Like all amateurs we see the romance but not the pitfalls, the fears and costly self-giving. We have the audacity to suppose that prayer is something we ought to be able to do.

Monica Furlong, *Christian Uncertainties*

January

At St. Vincent's, every class period began with a simple prayer. The teacher would say, "Let us remember," and the class would reply, "that we are in the Holy Presence of God."

We didn't call it prayer, though; we called it "attempting the impossible." It was a good description of what we did. Just trying to get the students to be quiet for the few minutes it took to recite the prayer was nearly impossible, never mind the exalted ambition of connecting with God.

Some of the students approached the prayers with hands neatly brought together, fingers pointing toward heaven, faces scrunched up in abject concentration. Others took prayer time as a wonderful opportunity to be irreverent: making fart noises, pretending to be asleep, or staring around the room at the "fools" who were taking this hocus-pocus seriously.

I really didn't know how to respond to their varied reactions. Aside from the more boisterous disrupters, I let each student respond to silent prayer in his own way, for I myself had yet to fathom the full significance of this practice beyond its status as an official school ritual. But as the year progressed, I found more and more value in "attempting the impossible."

At first, I wasn't very good at it. I would try to remember the presence of God, but I was more truly just trying to imagine it—trying even just to conceive of it. I knew that this was wrong, so during the prayers, I tried to stop thinking altogether, just stop the chatter of my mind for a few seconds like they do in meditation.

I wasn't able to do this either, so I ended up just watching my thoughts course through my mind, trying not to get caught up in any of them. If I found myself inside some idea or emotion, I would simply return my attention to my breath. After a while of doing this, I noticed the same set of concerns popping up every day: Will I be able to fill up this hour? Will I get some time to relax today? What will I do if Marty acts up? Will I remember everything I am supposed to say? What if Strapp visits my room? Is my lesson plan any good? What do I have to do next?

These same worries arose so often that I soon had them numbered, and so during prayer I could simply let them go. "Oh, there's personal preoccupation #4. No need to bother about that again." As a result, after a while I was able to bring a purity of motive to my prayers that I had never before achieved, and this brought me some profound moments of rest during those three-minute reflections.

But then, beneath those surface concerns, I found another layer of stress. During prayer time, I would suddenly remember some stupid remark I had made to Strapp a week ago, or a look of disdain on a student's face that I had seen last month but had never registered. Or I'd suddenly remember something I was supposed to have done several days ago. During one meditation, I suddenly recalled an argument I had in high school with my English teacher. It was as if my mind simply refused to attend to the reality before me, as if silence and peace were impossible to obtain.

Brother Blake assured me that thoughts and images such as these bubble up in our minds all the time. We just never slow down enough to perceive them. Their logic makes up our moods. When we first try to focus upon God in prayer, we reveal to ourselves the preoccupations of our own preconscious minds. I wasn't to try to move beyond this stage, he suggested. I was to enjoy it, learn from it, catalog my worries as the first step in liberating myself from them.

This was a wonderful time in my prayer life. Every class period began with my opening a package sent special delivery from my deep self. "Oh! I'm still thinking about that? My conversation with Linda affected me more than I thought." "Oh, look at this, a fear I thought I had conquered years ago."

Occasionally, I would grow so bored of all my thoughts, feelings, plans, and obligations that suddenly my mind would become clear and the chatter cease. This would usually happen a day or two after a difficult meditation, when letting go of some particular thought had felt tantamount to dying. The students would sometimes even have to call me back to consciousness. "Mr. Inchausti, the prayer is over. Mr. Inchausti? Are you still here? Earth to teacher, earth to teacher."

When I would emerge from one of these prayers and look at my students, their presence often struck me as miraculous, and I would listen to them with renewed interest and attention in hopes of discovering *who* they were and *how* they got there.

It took me a good three months before my quest for purity of motive got God's attention, but then suddenly—out of nowhere there it was. There was a presence with me—listening. And with God's attention, I suddenly got bigger. I felt less trivial. The classroom became an authentic battleground. Life, the school, my quest for vocation, everything seemed to matter more.

Students often evaluate their days by whether or not their teachers are in "good" moods. At first, I took this as the typical psychological defense of blaming others for their problems, but after a few weeks of silent prayer I could see their point. Events in themselves do not dictate our responses to them. A teacher in a "good" mood simply handles stress better than one in a "bad" mood. Why not simply resolve never to be in a "bad" mood, since moods are merely the result of invidious interpretations anyway?

So I resolved not to get caught up in my own self-drama or thought stream. I tried to stay true to the memory of the presence of God and see each class as if for the first time. I don't think I could have ever remembered to do that if it wasn't for that opening prayer ritual.

As the semester progressed, I began to see more and more of my life as prayer—that is, as attempting the impossible. I experienced my teaching and my praying in almost the same way: as a quest for perfect undistracted attention to the task at hand. With each task an end in itself, a door to bliss— infinitely interesting and complex.

Silent prayer was an activity that was admittedly useless, and so you could not fail at it. It didn't produce anything. It didn't satisfy any requirements. It didn't require elaborate lesson plans, and it couldn't be graded. It simply stopped everything for a minute, punching a hole in my busy, failed day and in any myth of personal or professional progress. It was done for itself and nothing more. It was a great center of calm in my stormy day, and I began to look forward to it.

Once, I promised my class that as long as they stayed silent, there would be no lessons, no assignments, no work. "If you want to," I said, "we will spend the entire period in silent prayer. But if anyone talks, it's over."

Of course, the students tried to remain silent, but they could never do it. Someone always spoke before three minutes were up. It astonished me, but they were simply incapable of being silent for more than three minutes, even when they wanted to be. They found self-control exhausting, and they were quite happy to get back to the routine of classwork after such ventures into the "impossible."

I was beginning to see that prayer was one of the most important but least understood elements in the school's curriculum. It was nothing but silence before the mysteries of life, yet that silence opened one up to infinite intuitions. When the obsessions through which one apprehends the world are allowed to dissolve, everything is revealed in a new light.

Of all the discoveries I made that first year, the power of prayer was one of the most important to me, for it helped me to get out of my mind and attend to the world in its pure, sensuous reality. It provided me with a method that bore in on phenomena instead of carrying me away into abstract speculations. I learned to rest in the presence of things *as they were,* instead of constantly fleeing from them by "figuring them out." I learned, in other words, how to let down my defenses long enough to see through my own grandiose misperceptions. I was beginning to break out of my nineteen years of schooling to a renewed faith in my own native intelligence and its spiritual core. I was at last beginning to *see* my students, rather than merely *think* about them, and prayer was my way back to this kind of independent knowledge.

I looked back into my past to find the reason why it had taken me so long to learn this simple truth. And I had to admit that my ambitions and desires had been the reason. I had sold my soul for success in school, popularity, approval. But through it all, there had remained a part of me unconvinced by the world. And this was the part evoked by prayer, by doing nothing, by attempting the impossible, and I thanked God it was still there.

I saw now that teaching itself was *attempting the impossible,* and so it too was a form of prayer—provided one did not attach oneself to the fruits of one's labors but quietly and continually tilled the soil of teenage awareness, expecting nothing, really desiring nothing, and therefore dreading nothing. Just seeing everything and providing a space for spirit to express itself.

Prayer had taught me that, to be a teacher, one didn't need to act, nor was it enough merely to wait; one could cause things to happen by opening up a space in one's heart to register the subtle movements of the students' souls toward real change. And one could do this only if one remained unimpressed by the old forms of power—progress, ability, ambition, results—and rested in the creative, unique, never-again-to-be-obtained moment of simple awareness of that which is.

My students loved to read the *Guinness Book of World Records.* They could sit for hours, amazing each other by reading excerpts. I tried to figure out why they were so enraptured by the longest basketball game or the tallest human. Then, it dawned on me that what my students were really looking for were concrete examples of human achievements.

What they found, however, was trivia. But this didn't bother them, because at least these were "real" accomplishments. Factual. I knew, of course, that most "real" accomplishments can't be seen, let alone measured, and occur in places of the mind of which my students were only now just beginning to become aware. Most accomplishments are hard to see, because you need imagination and competence to comprehend them. Novels and scientific breakthroughs require imagination to be seen. Most people cannot perceive the accomplishments of Einstein or even Tolstoy. But world records provide concrete, measurable, specific achievements that can be grasped by even the most literal mind. My students' interest in them testified to their longings for excellence and to the paucity of avenues through which they could find it.

I didn't try to change this. I just noticed it.

Maxims, Aphorisms, Insights, and Reflections on
the Art of Classroom Teaching, by Brother Blake

Begin each day by telling yourself: Today I shall be meeting with interference, ingratitude, insolence, disloyalty, ill will and selfishness—all of
them due to the offender's ignorance of what is good or evil. But for
my part I have long perceived the nature of good and its nobility; . . .
therefore none of these things can injure me, for nobody can implicate
me in what is degrading.

Marcus Aurelius, *Meditations*

• It is a terrifying thought to think of our classrooms as laboratories for self-
creation and existential discovery. How could anybody administer that? But
that is exactly what they are! And so the teacher's lessons are never separate
from the teacher's own evolving intellectual identity.

• When you talk to your ninth grade class, talk to yourself as if your ninth
grade self was in the room—only smarter, more perceptive, less emotionally
bound. What did you need to hear? What would have captured your attention?
What would have set you free? This approach works, not because our students
are just like we were, but because kids at this age cannot imagine their own
lives in any historical context, so you must do it for them—only generously,
honestly, perceptively.

• If you stop observing, you're finished. But you don't have to do this consciously, except maybe at the beginning. Everything you see, both inside and
outside of class, goes into the bank of your awareness and will emerge in time,
as needed, if you attend to the business of witnessing to the truths before you.
Teaching, in this sense, is a mysterious process. The mind begins to function
in a different way, making odd new connections, until lessons emerge of their
own accord out of the environment, like leaves from a tree.

• The way I teach difficult material is simply to assume from the outset that
none of them are going to follow me anyway, so who cares?

• The essence of teaching, the soul of the art, is being brave enough, psychologically unencumbered enough, to see exactly what is taking place in the
minds of your students at any given moment and then—like a good psycho-
therapist—speak to and through their defenses to uncover the true promise of
the lesson, its hidden meaning. This significance, of course, will almost always
be different from what you originally took it to be, and it is usually at odds
with the lesson plan. But that is what makes teaching a creative act! One

doesn't just dispense knowledge—one brings it into being. I am surprised by what I "teach" all the time!

• Teachers have to learn to respond to all the intellectual dangers and possibilities emerging around them as their lessons proceed. And if they are good enough, and they get lucky, their responses will sometimes mesh with the truth of the moment, and an authentic insight is powerfully communicated to their students. It might not be the teacher's original insight; it seldom is. It might be Newton's or Tolstoy's—but the teacher somehow connects up with it in her voice or in her gestures or even in her silences, and the idea comes alive; its worth rendered both obvious and profound.

More often than not, however, the teacher's words both hit and miss simultaneously. A few students connect, others do not. A metaphor works—but not exactly. And so choices have to be made on the spot, thoughts recast, the teacher's reading of the moment reassessed. All of this "give" makes teaching an art where one is constantly acquiring new skills and responsibilities.

• Nothing happens until somebody comes along. A teacher is somebody who *comes along*.

• Teachers need not outline great amounts of material. Textbooks do that far more efficiently. Teachers are there to provide perspective. To relate the part to the whole, to link the discipline to the student's life, to connect the passion to the prose.

• I once had a student come to me and ask me what he had to do to get an A in my class.

"I'll do anything!" he said.

So I said, "Okay, run through that wall over there, and when you are done, run through this wall here."

Well, he tried. He bounced off each wall in a mock effort to do whatever had to be done to get an A.

And I said, "Well, now I have to give you an F."

"Why?" he asked incredulously.

"Because the first lesson in the humanities is not to do stupid things just because someone in authority tells you to do them."

• Poets are tempted to destroy language in order to create their own, but novelists are different. They don't have the temptation to destroy language per se, so much as to destroy history, truth, common sense—in order to create a new history, a new truth, and a new common sense. Teachers are closer to novelists than to poets. They are masters of the unreality of the actual and fascinated by the wisdom of exaggeration.

- To be a truly logical thinker, one must be willing to entertain nihilism or at least adopt the role of the nihilist—believing nothing, trusting no one. People with faith are less willing to do this than people without faith, and people with hope less willing to do this than people without hope, and so, by default, the worst among us end up defining what's rational.

- A teacher has not started teaching until she can rise above the narrow concerns of her particular class and curriculum to the broader issues of her discipline and its relationship to her times.

- Just as all art today is "conceptual art," no matter what it may call itself, all instruction today is theater, no matter what anyone says. To teach without theatrical considerations is to become dramatic in spite of yourself. That is to say, to become parody!

- A good lecture-discussion consists in the painting of the mind into corners, followed by a series of miraculous escapes and rescues.

- Teaching—like drama—is an act of pure presence in imaginary time. All delays are overcome in the instant, and it gives us the sense that, at least for the space of one class period, we actually exist.

- I once taught a Virginia Woolf novel at the seminary to the novices. I put a chart of all the characters on the board along with a time line of all the events that took place in the novel.

   One of my brightest students raised an important objection. "Doesn't placing all of these materials in charts on the board violate Virginia Woolf's intentions as a novelist? Doesn't she want us to experience the overlapping, multidimensional nature of experience that defies logical categorization?"

   "That is true," I replied. "But class lectures don't take place in the real time of experience; they take place in the imaginary time of pure presence. When you walk through that classroom door, time stops. And so we can put up on the board structures obscured by the flow of events. When class is over, you will enter real time again. You will read the novel on its own terms, and these charts and time lines will remain in your memory merely as a dream to make sense of the novel as it flies by."

- It is not how much you know, but in what context it is retained and used. This is the essence of talent—the ability to translate, adapt, and refine ideas in the moment as needed. It is grace under pressure, the courage that is authentic thought. We serve our students most when we can demonstrate this value to them.

- A teacher should avoid explaining things. Explanations undermine complexity. Replace them with stories or questions, anything that keeps irony alive. We shouldn't solve problems so much as turn them into significant occasions.

• High-minded teachers keep the dream of a better life alive in the young. And even if you feel unworthy when they project their ideals upon you, remember that there are larger forces at play than your ordinary self. As a teacher, you become a mirror and an icon of their best selves, so let them use you in this way. Just don't ever believe that you *are* your teacherly function.

• One must come to literature from experience, not to experience from literature.

• These kids must be awakened to their terrible beauty.

• You can tell the quality of your lesson by the looks on your students' faces. When you present ideas in the right way, their faces change. They get alert, they listen, they respond more openly, they laugh more easily, they are explorative, likable. But when you appeal to their fears or ambitions, right away they get rigid, defensive, proud, unhappy, and anxious.

• Beginning teachers often underestimate the value of endurance as a lesson in itself. If you fail to inspire your students day after day but continue trying to teach them anyway, eventually, some of them will ask themselves, "What does this guy think he's got that he keeps coming at us day after day?" And then they will ask you and even listen closely to your answer. That's the day you had better be good. They'll give even the most abject loser "one day" to show his stuff, if he persists.

But even if you blow that one day, keep coming at them, and your endurance and conviction will earn you another day, and another, until after a while, your entire year is punctuated by "holidays" of authentic conversations.

• People become teachers for the same reasons people become novelists: out of desperation. But the desperation is a little different in each case. Writing a novel is often a last-ditch effort at making one's life significant. A teaching career often begins as a search for meaningful employment. Novelists are driven by a metaphysical quest, teachers by an untapped energy.

• Some students want you to grade them on their relationship to you as a person. You've got to confront this. Make it clear to them that you grade their work the way a poultry man grades eggs or a butcher grades meat. Too many spots, too little muscle, too much fat, and the work is not grade A prime—no matter how wonderful the steer who gave his life to produce it. Just as there are market standards for meat, so too are there market standards for term papers and tests. Grades just make it clear how to apply the conventional criteria—no more and no less. Students should learn not to take them personally.

• Yeats once said that a man may not know the truth, but he might be able to embody it. Teachers neither know the truth nor do they embody it. For them, truth is like water forever slipping through their fingers. Their only artistry, their only expertise, is that sometimes they remember to cup their hands.

• Teaching, like coaching, is often a matter of speaking the same inner language as your students. That's why administrators place so much hope in finding teachers of the same race, class, and sex as their students. They hope that they can speak the same inner language. But it's not that easy, because coming from the same cultural background does not guarantee that one speaks any "inner language" at all.

• The trick in sports is learning how to forget about the competition and concentrate on running your own race. You've got to focus on the dynamics of the ball in flight, not on the personality or motivations of the pitcher who threw it. When I was young, I was a "thinking" player. But it is far better to be a "thoughtless" one, or should I say "feeling" one, so present to the realities of the moment that you simply act in harmony with the flow of the game.

This is a hard lesson for young athletes to learn, because as spectators, they are encouraged to adopt exactly the opposite interests. They are thrilled by the drama of things, the personalities of the players, the social context within which the game is occurring, even its place in sports history. But inside the game, these interests are vices—distractions. Athletes concentrate on specifics, on craft. Was it Ezra Pound who said, "I judge a man's sincerity by the quality of his technique"? Well, whoever said that was a *player*.

• Many students, like good deconstructionists, spend a lot of time searching for the thread that unties the lesson: the grading criteria, the hidden fetish, what they take to be the real course content. And the teacher, if he is any good, frustrates their bad faith by constantly returning to the mystery of his subject matter.

It is not a matter of techniques or tricks; it is a matter of eluding the students' traps, their nets of definitions, their desire to turn off the dialogue by finding the certainty, the bias, the lie at the heart of the teacherly myth.

• Nothing said in class means the same thing as if it were said in common conversation. The classroom changes the nature of language, making it useless for everyday use but supercharged with a value one might very well call "novelistic" were its ironies not so much more unstable.

• Teaching is a performance in language, so when you speak in class, you cannot just talk like a normal person. Or rather, when you do, you have got to be in on the joke that everything being said is part of a play of invented selves and so bracketed as existing in a universe that is the psychological counter-point to reality—but not reality itself.

• Many students sense that their teachers hold to values that are in cultural retreat and so withhold their allegiance to them out of a false sense of self-preservation. To undo this reticence is, in some sense, the teacher's calling.

• The classroom is a mirror of the self and a window into the future. It mirrors the self in our feelings about it. The students embody all our unconscious traits, and when we can't stand them, we can be sure that an ugly part of ourselves has just been revealed to us and that we are being challenged to own up to some hypocrisy or self-deceit. We are being asked to free up some of the energy we have attached to keeping hold of our own grandiose images of ourselves.

• The key to effective lecturing is to have a purpose, not a message. If your mind is occupied with your purpose, it finds messages to fulfill it, images and examples born of objects and incidents in the room and memories to support your points. This is the key to thinking on your feet and responding to the students' questions and comments. Fulfilling your purpose—to inspire and to reveal, not just passing on information—this is putting cause before effect.

• So often, teachers confuse getting depressed with achieving humility, but real humility comes from seeing how little it is that you actually know and then proceeding to do something about it.

• When we look at students, we see through them into our pasts. But when they look at us, they see through us into their futures. Both acts of the imagination are fraught with the dangers of inflation and distortion. And yet, it's important to know that very little of what takes place in the classroom takes place in the present. The classroom is the zone of imagination—a place of mind, not of fact.

• To take up the possibility of becoming a teacher, one must first take up the responsibility of being a human being. Expertise and professional training can never replace the power of possessing a world view.

• I always have trouble designing tests. The students learn more in my class in fifteen minutes than I would ever have the time to test them on: insights without end, images that reverberate throughout a lifetime, calls to transcend and transcend again, scientific theories whose full implications they may never ultimately grasp. I am not trying to sound arrogant; it's just that our curriculum really is sublime.

• Brother Blake had a quote from Robert Coles (taken from one of Jonathan Kozol's books) pinned tip beside his desk: "In this life we prepare for things, for moments and events and situations. . . . We worry about wrongs, think about injustices, read what Tolstoi or Ruskin . . . has to say. . . . Then all of a sudden, the issue is not whether we agree with what we have heard and read and studied. . . . The issue is *us*, and what we have become."

• Almost always, the most popular teachers are the worst. They are popular because they make thought easy and accessible; they model a kind of intellectual efficiency that is, at bottom, antithetical to real thought. Efficient teachers are, by definition, antiphilosophical.

• Students often feel that they are making great sacrifices to understand us, and we should not belittle what they take to be—however misguided—their own authentic generosity.

• Talking to students outside of class, one can be onself. That is to say, one can wear a mask! But in class, one must use all of one's talents to achieve an authentic speech. The fact that one ends up creating personae anyway need not discourage us, for these selves are dummy selves, props in the search for reality, and the students know that and grant us that conceit.

• The best teachers are not those who amaze us with their eloquence or arrest our imaginations with their brilliance or even get us to work without our noticing it. They are those who reveal some realm of existence previously unknown to us and thereby redeem us from our forgetfulness and lost sublimity.

• Those who believe that it is the purpose of the teacher to impart knowledge fail to see that the domain of the classroom teacher is not the unknown, but the forgotten. Human existence is perpetually being forgotten, insights mislaid, whole civilizations lost, and teaching is the only way through which they can be recovered. We don't create knowledge, we reanimate it. This is why the best teacherly discourse is poetic, metaphoric, but not, strictly speaking, aesthetic.

• You've got to learn to read your students like characters in a Chekhov play—not by their outward appearances, but by their emotional preoccupations. What is fascinating about them is not their ages or their times, not their clothes or their fads, but their feeling life—and that is something secret and often hidden, even from themselves. In conversation, you can sometimes bring it out. In their papers, it will sometimes come through.

• A student is not merely a human resource. A student is a person, and a person is a story.

• A teacher is finally someone who can communicate what it *feels like* to know difficult things. Students who have experienced the power of ideas in this way are infected with intellectual desire—which is something other than curiosity about the way the world works. It is deeper, more profound; it is a longing not just *to know things*, but to fully understand and assimilate the significance of what one *does know*. It is a hunger for meaning and for firsthand, personal experience of the good.

• Culture exists, not only to keep alive the fresh flow of ideas, but also to keep alive a certain level of sensitivity, a degree of intellectual focus, and the will to a precise use of language. After reading Rilke, for instance, I turn back to my world, and everything seems coarse, ungainly, lacking in precise distinctions. My own inner life compared to the jewel-like sensibility of the poet seems splattered and flooded, without significant form, and I am forced to face the message of the Torso of Apollo: "You must change your life."

This is the way students should feel when they leave our classrooms: that they are leaving a golden room where honesty, subtlety, truth, and precision give form to their deepest sense of themselves. And even though many of them will feel those values evaporate into "life" the minute they walk out the door, a residue will remain to be tapped again somewhere else.

• The more you know about a subject, the harder it is to teach it, because you replace the energy of discovery born of risk and error with the deadening surety of statement and expertise. As the teacher gets out ahead of his students, they get left behind—feel depressed, overwhelmed. "He's way out there," they say to themselves, "and I'm still trying to get this basic stuff!"

• Statements are especially tricky, because they exclude as much as they include. As a rule, you should avoid making them, but when you do, it should be done with conviction, and it should be a pronouncement—a summing up.

• We are not the transmitters of a tradition, but workers in a philosophy coming into existence of which "the tradition" is one very important part.

• Teachers must not be afraid of being philosophers, or they will forfeit their functions as prophets and fools.

• The history of "The Sublime Pedagogy" is hidden, because it is disguised as poetics. In other words, all education of the spirit is indirect. It has to be. The soul is shy, like a deer, and can't be approached straight-on. Poetics is the "science" of indirection. Its essence is metaphor, irony, myth—the arts of the tangential. Once you turn teaching into a method with precise definitions and a rigid game plan, you kill it, because you eliminate the "give" inherent in poetic language. You destroy the space within the words where individuals can find themselves. You build edifices of meaning, beautiful, great skyscrapers of relationships, but the deer disappear into the underbrush.

• I am close to seventy years old, and yet even now, when I face my classes, I sometimes have feelings of utter helplessness. I start a discussion, retell a lecture, start a unit, but I know it hasn't been real, and so I have to go home and feel the energy again somehow. Usually I read a passage from Henry James and it inspires me. It reminds me that someone else dedicated his life to trying to express the invisible reality we all live in, and I realize that I am not alone, that if James attempted it, it cannot be futile, and I am ready to begin again.

• When you get older, you do not necessarily get wiser, but you do get stories. I guess the trick of growing old gracefully is learning how not to bore people with them. Staying young psychologically is really about becoming a good storyteller. Taking all those stories and turning them into fresh insights. "Old" people tend to moralize, turn their stories into parables of self-justification—or worse, "proofs" of their own increasingly rigid principles. I've tried to resist that by embracing the ironies and paradoxes of my life. Literature teaches us how to stay young!

• I find it often takes two days to teach a single lesson: one day to mis-teach it, another to correct and transform the original misconception. Beginning teachers don't know this. They always want to do everything right the first time, and it just doesn't work that way. Often, the very best lessons are born of second thoughts, revisions, qualification.

• A person who never experiments in the classroom never finds out that all the old things are true.

• If you are concerned with achieving some specific result, you lose your nerve. You start getting angry, impatient, take shortcuts. You try this, you try that, you never remain faithful to any long-term strategy. But if you can get yourself to give up on success—that is, give up on the success of getting the students to see things *correctly*—you become centered, and this allows you to acquire the peace and poise you need to make discoveries in the moment.

• A teacher is not impressed by her own ideas. She explores them. She feels her way in classroom discussions in an effort to reveal some unknown aspect of the subject matter under investigation. She is not interested in her own voice, but in the form the dialogue with her students seems to be seeking, and only those forms that link the lesson to the life she shares with her students become a part of her work. Such "work" is radically ephemeral, but it's what we do.

• The only context for the evaluation of a teacher's work is the history of the dialogic imagination. The teacher need answer only to Socrates.

• Some teachers play the buffoon or the clown in order to make points and protect themselves from their students. This can work for a while. The problem is that the mask may stick, and pretty soon you find yourself stuck in the role of an eccentric, and you begin to have problems at home and outside of class. You become a crank with a huge mustache!

• We are given freedom so that we can learn we do not need it. Take freedom away, and no one can serve. That's the doctrine of free will in a nutshell.

• One day, I forgot to erase the blackboard before my seventh period class, so I just pulled down the world map to cover all the notes from the sixth period class's discussion. As the seventh period class discussed the book, I noticed they were saying all the same things the sixth period had said. So I let them talk and talk until someone said, "Don't you think we should be writing this stuff down?"

And I said, "I already have!" Then I stepped back and lifted the map to reveal a list of every single point they had made—including some they were just about to make! They thought it was magic! They thought I was a clairvoyant!

"How did you do that?" they asked.

I told them that just because their ideas *feel* new doesn't mean that they are original. We've done a good job of relearning all the old truths and stating the obvious; now let's venture into the unknown.

• A school is not an institution for the training of young minds so much as a living laboratory in philosophic anthropology. That's what Plato's academy was, that's what the Lyceum was, and that's what American high schools still are, in spite of themselves.

• There is a difference between being a teacher and being a friend. Friends pass in and out of one another like air; teachers stick, resist, a part of them always remains unabsorbed and "difficult."

• The idea of the teacher must not be defined but left open, shifting, ever in flux. One can't let one's image of what it is one is doing in the classroom become an attitude or an identity or a profession. Your identity and sense of definition must change constantly as the body changes, as the body politic changes, as the walls of one's classroom implode or expand.

• There can be no political education per se. Education is personal and against any and all repressions of the truth. Political education is a limiting of the subject matter and, therefore, implies some sort of compromise with one's body, with one's dreams and desires. True education is a constant re-creation of fresh visions of the totality of human possibility via acts of bravery and sublime articulation. It is inevitably political, but it is not consciousness-raising.

• For the ancient Greeks, education was preparation for leadership, that meant learning how to respond creatively to chaos and crisis and learning how to take responsibility and stand for values greater than oneself. Odysseus, Oedipus, Socrates—all of these figures model this turn of mind. But it is hard for us to communicate this to our students when there is no one in their experience who models these values. So when we ask them to read these ancient texts, it is almost as if we are asking them to fantasize a kind of being for which there are no recognizable human correlates. That is why I so shamelessly make connections between the action in the novels and the events of everyday life, constantly crossing the border between the imaginary and the real, between historical figures and mythic ones, between actual history and unlikely possibilities. It is the only way to educate the imagination.

• Just seeing the reality before us, registering its paradoxes and contradictions, is a great achievement and pays off in subtle ways we may not consciously realize. It is important to see what is taking place in the classroom, even if one is helpless to change it. *Especially* if one is helpless to change it! For, in the seeing, a kind of emotional distancing and sorting takes place that makes possible new avenues of engagement. Just noticing the chaos is the first step toward discerning a pattern. And when the pattern emerges—that is to say, when the unique character of an event stands revealed—then an imperative emerges, and you know what you must do.

But you have to wait for the pattern to emerge; you can't force it. This kind of thinking is not so much a matter of intelligence or clever problem solving as it is a courageous attention to particulars and the patience to wait for an authentic revelation. It cannot be reduced to a technique, since it can only be acquired through bravery.

• Stand up for the boy and show him that his desires for heroism—up to now imaginary—can become a creative reality.

• Christ does not command; he calls us to him. He does not guide; he attracts.

• Beginning classroom teachers, like new stepparents, find themselves caught inside an odd dynamic. The kind of authority I had over my students, formal and punitive, was not the kind I wanted. And the kind of authority I wanted, informal existential authority, is very difficult to get. And so, as a new teacher I existed in a psychological limbo—perpetually unsure as to my exact role and status. I felt both too powerful and not powerful enough at the same time, like a rebel who woke up to find himself emperor of a realm he had spent his life trying to destroy.

• People with weak egos are tempted to become teachers, because they think having power over others will make their egos strong—having institutional authority gives them the illusion of self-mastery. And so, in time, they become petty tyrants and pass on their victim/victimer ethos to the next generation like the plague.

You should only become a teacher if you have no other choices. If you must be at the scene where learning takes place—if that is the most real place in the world for you. There is no other reason to be a teacher. If ideas are not your passion, do something else. Try acting.

• Fourteen-year-olds are the most interesting people alive—the most honest, the most spiritual, the most idealistic, and the most skeptical.

• Beware of teaching at the university. They have many accomplished minds there, and once a mind is accomplished, it is finished.

• Teaching at a college is nothing like teaching the ninth grade. At a college, the years and the courses fade in and out of each other like so many scattered birds. But ninth graders stay in your mind and memory forever—indelibly.

• The difficulty of teaching does not stem from its complexity, but rather from the fact that it demands total surrender and total vigilance. It is not an intellectual activity so much as a moral and a perceptual one. That is why some of the best teachers are not necessarily the best thinkers. Their genius resides in their capacity to invest so much significant attention to their subjects that the outer world just disappears. They possess a capacity to give their lessons such intellectual urgency that the conventional life loses all its appeal, and students enter into the bliss of pure philosophical absorption. Like a classic work, great teachers fascinate, not by their glamour or flash, but by their intensity, by their focus, and by the perennial worth of their ideas and themes.

• Genius does what it must; talent does what it can. Genius generates imperatives; talent avoids errors. Genius learns from its mistakes to make adjustments to accomplish its own sublime ends; talent learns from its mistakes how to trim its wings to deflect criticism.

• I am bourgeois to the core and parochial beyond belief, and yet I am drawn to great art and scholarship as my anti-type, my shadow, the voice of distinction I never possessed. I don't think of myself as a teacher so much as an impersonator of profundities, inhabiting the wisdom of texts with the naked confidence that the value of the genius I espouse transcends the particular fraud that I am the one espousing it. And it doesn't matter that nobody seems to be listening to me. Those who listen that I don't know about are enough to keep me going, keep me living on the wing of borrowed metaphors.

Eva Brann, *Depth and Desire*

By an old tradition the first lecture of the year is dedicated to the new members of our college, to the freshman students and the freshman tutors. It is a chance to tell you something about the shape and the spirit of the Program that governs St. John's College—and not only to tell you but perhaps even to show you.

I think I am right in this spirit when I begin by examining the class-name I just called you by: freshmen. A freshman, my etymological dictionaries tell me, is a person "not tainted, sullied or worn," a still-fresh human being, where "fresh" means, so the dictionary points out, both "frisky" and "impertinent." Later on in the year you will learn a weighty Greek word applicable to persons of frisky impertinence. They are said to have *thymos,* spiritedness or plain spunk, a characteristic necessary for serious learning. This spirited frame of mind is perfectly compatible with being shy and secretly a little scared. In fact, to my mind, it is a sign of quality in newcomers to be anxious for their own dignity in the way that shows itself in spirited shyness. It is our business, the business of the faculty and of the more responsible upper class students, to help your spiritedness to become serious, to emerge from the shyness—whether it be of the quiet or the boisterous sort, to help you channel your energy into a steady *desire* for learning and to direct your boldness toward the discovery of *depth* and, moreover, to help you without leaving you tainted, sullied, and worn out. I keep saying "help," because although great changes are bound to take place in you in these next years—do but behold the seniors: unsullied, untainted, unworn and transfigured—we none of us know who should get the most credit besides yourself: the Program, our teaching, your friendships or just plain time passing.

At any rate, the spirit of the college is invested in seriousness, a certain kind of seriousness—not dead seriousness but live seriousness, you might say. This seriousness shows itself on many occasions: in deep or heated conversations in the noon sun or at midnight, in marathons of effort and in the oblivion of sleep, in devoted daily preparation and in glorious goofing-off, in the willingness to try on opinions and in the need to come to conclusions. What does your school do to induce this very particular kind of seriousness?

When you chose to come to St. John's you were, perhaps, attracted by the fact that the mode of teaching normal in higher education is quite abnormal here. I mean lectures. Only one lecture a week is an integral part of the Program, on Fridays at 8:15 P.M. Now the chief thing about a lecture is that it is prepared ahead of time. For instance, I began working on this lecture in March.

A lecture ought to be the temporarily final word, the best a speaker has to give you at the moment. It should not matter whether the surface of the speech is brilliant or drab, as long as it is a deliberate and well-prepared opening of the speaker's heart and mind to the listeners. As such it carries authority. These authoritative occasions are obviously important to the life of the school.

Yet our normal way is not the prepared lecture but the focused conversation which is effervescent rather than prepared, provisional rather than authoritative, and participatory rather than reactive. Your tutors will not tell you but ask you; they will not demonstrate acquired knowledge, but the activity of learning. One reason why the teaching of new tutors—and some of your classes will be taught by newcomers—is often most memorable to freshmen is that their learning is genuinely original and keeps sympathetic pace with yours. There is an irresistible but false local etymology of the word tutor as "one who toots," perhaps his own horn. What the word tutor really signifies is a person who guards and watches learning. We are deliberately not called professors because we profess no special expertise.

Since you will not be told things, you will have to speak yourselves. What will you speak about? The Program will ask you to focus your conversation on certain texts—they might be books or scores or paintings. These texts have been selected over the years by us because they have the living seriousness I am trying to speak about. To my mind texts, like people, are serious when they have a surface that arouses the *desire* to know them and the *depth* to fulfill that desire. Here then, is my announced theme for tonight: the depth that calls forth desire.

To delineate that depth I must once again distinguish our kind of conversation, the kind associated with such texts, from the kind of fellowship to be found in other places. All over this country, and wherever the conditions for some human happiness exist, there are people who know all there is to know about some field that they till with a single-minded love. This is the blessed race of buffs, aficionados and those rare professionals who have had the grace to remain amateurs at heart. They study history or race stock cars or do biology or fly hot-air balloons. My own favorite fanatic is the young son of a graduate of St. John's. This boy is persistently in love with fish, with the hooks, flies, sinkers, leaders, reels and rods for catching them, with the books for studying them, with the aquaria, ponds, lakes and oceans for observing them. When I first met him he looked up at me shyly and asked if I knew what an ichthyologist was. Since I knew some Greek I knew the etymology of the word and could tell him that it is a person who can give an account of fish, so he was satisfied with me. This boy may have his troubles but he is also acquainted with bliss.

This kind of concentrated bliss we cannot deliver to you, except perhaps in limited extracurricular ways. Instead we, or rather the Program, will drive you through centuries of time and diversities of opinion, while depriving you of the freedom and the serenity to till and to master a well-defined field of your own choosing. You will study Greek and invest hours in memorizing paradigms, but your tutorial is not a Greek class—it is a language tutorial in which Greek is studied only partly for its own virtues, and partly as a striking and, for you, a novel example of human speech and its possibilities. You will study Euclid and demonstrate many propositions, yet your tutorial is not intended to make you geometers but to allow you to think about the activity of mathematics. In short, you will be asked to read many books carefully and to study many matters in some detail only to find them passing away, becoming mere examples in the conversation. And these fugitive texts will almost all bear their excellence, their worthiness to be studied exhaustively, on their face, for we try to pick the ideal examples. This procedure is practically guaranteed to keep you off-balance, even to drive you a little crazy, since you will not often have the satisfaction of dwelling on anything and of mastering it. How do we dare do this to you?

Here is a strange but unavoidable fact: Those who plow with devotion and pleasure and increasing mastery some bounded plot on the globe of knowledge often undergo a professional deformation. They lose first the will and then the ability to go deep. To be sure, specialists are often said to know their subjects "in depth," but that is not the depth I mean. Let me illustrate with an example I have a special affection for. I began my academic life as an archaeologist, and the first thing archaeologists do is to dig deep past the present surface of the earth, or rather they scrape it away layer by layer. But with every stratum they scrape away they find themselves at a new surface, the surface of a former age. They poke into time—a magical enough activity—but they do not pretend to pierce the nature of things. For example, there would come up from the depths of a well-shaft an ancient pot. I would catalogue it by naming its form, say: *kotyle*, a kind of cup; by giving its dimensions: H. 0.108 m.; diam. 0.135 m; by describing its proportions: deep-bodied, narrow-footed; by interpreting the picture painted on it: a rabbit—this is the pot-painter being funny—jumping a tracking hound from behind; by conjecturing about the provenance and the stylistic influences: made in Attica under Corinthian influence; and by assigning a date: third quarter of the seventh century B.C.

Was I required to consider what I meant by dimensions, proportions, styles, images, funniness, influences, places? Not a bit—that would have meant time out and profitless distraction from my business, which was to know all about the looks and appearances of the pottery of Athens in early times. What this

Program of ours offers you is exactly that time out, and that splendid distraction. People will say of you, when you have graduated, that you have acquired a broad background. But your education will have been broad only in a very incidental and sketchy way—certainly not in the fashion of a close-knit tapestry that is a continuous texture of interwoven warp and woof. Many of the books you are about to read do tie into one another. Sometimes a book written by an ancient Greek will (I am not being funny) talk back to one written by a modern American, or the opposite—the strands that connect these books seem to run back and forth and sideways through time. But some books will stand, at least as we read them, in splendid isolation, and all in all the texts we study do not add up to a texture of knowledge: There is no major called "Great Books." How could there be competence in a tradition whose moving impulse is to undercut every wisdom in favor of a yet deeper one? There is not even agreement whether this tradition of ours advances or degenerates with time, whether its authors are all talking about the same thing, though in a different way, or in apparently similar ways about quite incomparable things.

Here is what the books do seem to me to have in common. They intend to go into the depths of things. All the authors, even those subtly self-contradictory ones who claim that there are no depths but only surfaces, are deep in the way I mean. This desire for depth, then, is what will hold your studies here together. There is a word for this effort, to which it is my privilege to introduce you tonight. The word is philosophy. The term is put together from two Greek words, *philos,* an adjective used of someone who feels friendly, even passionate love, and *sophia,* which means wisdom or deep knowledge.

When I say that your school is devoted to philosophy, the love of deep knowledge, I mean that all our authors want to draw you deep into their matter, whether by words, symbols, notes or visual shapes. Incidentally, in a few weeks a lecturer, a tutor from Santa Fe, will come and contradict me; he has told me that he will say that what we do needn't bear the name of philosophy at all.

Let that be a subject for future discussion, and let me come to the heart of my lecture tonight. It is the question what depth is and how it is possible. I think we are all inclined to suppose that literal, actual depth belongs to bodies and space and that people or texts are deep only by analogy, metaphorically speaking.

I want to propose that here, as so often in philosophy, it is really the other way around: it is the body that is deep merely metaphorically, as a matter of speaking, while the soul and its expression alone are deep in the primary sense.

Certainly the depth of a body or a space is elusive. If a body has a perfectly hard and impenetrable surface, its depth must be forever beyond our experience—a kind of hard, inaccessible nothingness. On the other hand, let the physical body have a hollow in it—such caves are powerful allegories of depth and you will in the next four years come across some famous holes: the grotto of Calypso, the underground chamber in Plato's *Republic,* Don Quixote's cavern of Montesinos. Now ask yourself: Where actually is the depth? The containing boundaries of the hollow are all faces of the body, and no matter how deep you seem to be inside the body, you are still on its surface, just as I argued before about archaeological excavations.

Now consider matterless bodies, geometric solids. Euclid says in Book XI that a solid has length, breadth, and depth, but he gives us no way to tell which is which: it depends on your perspective—in fact all three dimensions are lengths delineating the surfaces that he says are the extremity of the solid. What is inside that solid, what its inwardness or true depth is, he does not feel obliged to say. These are questions you might want to raise in your mathematics tutorials: Can one get inside a geometric solid? How?

Bodies, I am suggesting, are either too hard or too involuted or too featureless or too empty to have true depth. Only divine or human beings and the texts they produce—texts made of words, notes, paint, stones, what have you—can be literally deep or profound. For I attribute depth or profundity to that which is of a truly different order from the surface that covers and hides it. And it must be the inside and foundation of just that surface, so that we can gain entrance to it through that particular outside and through no other. Every depth must be sought through its own proper surface which it both denies or negates and supplies with significance: the surface that hides its own depth is never superficial.

Human beings seem to me the most obvious example of such depth. All human beings have a surface, namely the face and figure they present. I personally think that in real life almost all people also have an inside, their soul, their depth. But there are some famous novels in which characters are described who are nothing but empty shells. Against their impenetrable surface those whom they attract by the insidiously unflawed beauty peculiar to facades that hide nothing break themselves, or if they tear through, they fall into nothingness.

However, these are fictions, and actual human beings have by the very fact of their humanity an inner sanctum. We begin by noting, casually, their face, their demeanor. As our interest awakens we proceed to read more carefully, to watch their appearance ardently for what it signifies. If we are lucky, they may open up to us, as we do to them. If we go about it right, this interpretative process need never come to an end, for the human inside, or to give it, once again, its proper name, the soul, is a true mystery. By a true mystery I mean a profundity whose bottom we can never seem to plumb though we have a persistent faith in its actuality. I think that for us as human beings only depths and mysteries induce viable desire. For love entirely without longing is not possible among human beings. Many a failure of love follows on the—usually false—opinion that we have exhausted the other person's inside, that there is no further promise of depth.

It is not only in respect to living human beings that depth calls forth desire. This college would not be the close human community that it is if you did not get to know some human beings deeply—which is called friendship. But such love is only the essential by-product (to coin a contradictory phrase) of our philosophical Program, a program that encourages the love of certain para-human beings. These para-human beings are the expressions of the human soul, our texts, as well as the things they talk about.

Let me take a moment to ask whether this particular desire for depth I keep referring to is common among human beings or even natural. I say it is absolutely natural and very common. You will see what I mean when I tell you what I think is the nature of desire. Desire seems to me to be a kind of negative form or a shaped emptiness in the soul, a place in the spirit expecting to be filled, a kind of psychic envelope waiting to be stuffed with its proper contents.

Now take a long leap and ask yourself what a question is. A question is a negative form or shaped emptiness in the mind, a place in thought waiting to be filled, a psychic envelope ready to be supplied with its proper message. Questions therefore have the same structure as desires. In fact questions are a subspecies of desire: a question is desire directed upon wisdom or knowledge. Therefore I might go so far as to say that this school teaches the shaping of desire—because here we practice asking deep questions. Now I think that very many, probably all, human beings would like to ask such questions if they only knew how. That is why the desire for depth is both common and natural.

What we most often, or at least most programmatically, ask questions about are those texts I have been mentioning. As I have intimated, such a text, particularly a text of words, is a curious kind of being, neither a living soul nor a mere rigid thing. What a book might be, such that it could have genuine depth, is a question that should arise over and over in the tutorials and the seminars. That books do have depth is shown by the fact that they induce questions, the directed desire to open them up. I want to end by giving a sample of a deep text and a demonstration of the beginning of a reading, a mere knock at its gate, so to speak.

The text is a saying by Heraclitus. Heraclitus flourished about 500 B.C. He was early among those who inquired into the nature of things, and he had a contemporary antagonist, Parmenides. You will see from your sheets that Heraclitus said that it is wise to agree that "All things are one." Parmenides said things that, on the face of it, seem similar, but whether he meant the same thing as Heraclitus, or something opposite or something incomparable—that is a matter of ever-live debate. In any case, Heraclitus and Parmenides together embody the great principle of our tradition that I mentioned before; you might call it "the principle of responsive differentiation." However, I shall not try to talk about Heraclitus's actual wisdom tonight—that along with the previous questions: "What is philosophy?," "What is a solid?," "What is a cave?," "What is a book?," I leave to future discussion. I shall attend only to the preliminaries with which Heraclitus surrounds his wisdom.

Heraclitus's book is largely lost, though as far as we know it was not a treatise but a book of sayings. Even in ancient times it had a reputation for depth; the tragedian Euripides said of it that it required a Delian diver—the divers from the island Delos (which means the "Manifest" or "Clear") were evidently famous for diving deep and bringing things to light.

The saying I have chosen goes:

οὐκ ἐμοῦ ἀλλὰ τοῦ λόγου ἀκούσαντας
ὁμολογεῖν σοφόν ἐστιν ἓν πάντα εἶναι

Transliterated it reads

ouk emou alla tou *logou* akousantas
homologein sophon estin hen panta einai.

On the surface this saying is in Greek and needs to be translated. Since I have argued that surfaces are, like traditional Japanese packaging, an integral part of the contents, they must be carefully and patiently undone. Now to put Heraclitus's Greek into English is, up to a certain point, not hard. Your Greek manual will tell you about the "accusative absolute" and about various infinitives, and your Greek dictionaries will give you the meaning of "listening," of "wise" (which you are already familiar with in philo*sophy*), and of "agree."

But then you look up *logos*. "Logos" is one of the tremendous words of our tradition, to which it is, once again, my privilege to introduce you. Without even looking it up, I can give you the following meanings: Word and speech, saying and story, tally and tale, ratio and relation, account and explanation (that was the meaning which occurred in the word "ichthyologist"), argument and discussion, reason and reasoning, collection and gathering, the word of God and the son of God. As you learn Greek you will see what it is about the root-meaning of *logos* that makes this great scope of significance possible. But how are you to choose? You are caught in a vicious circle: Unless you know what Heraclitus means by *logos* you cannot choose the right English translation, and unless you discover the right English word you cannot know what he

means by his saying. However, sensible people find ways to scramble themselves out of this bind. Try a meaning that makes good immediate sense:
choose "reasoning."

> Listening not to me but to my reasoning,
> it is wise to agree that all things are one.

This yields a saying that is particularly pertinent to us, since although
we look into each other's faces, we must not get stuck on personalities. Each
seminar member has a right to say: "Never mind me, answer my argument."
Heraclitus is introducing a great notion into the Western world here: Not *who*
says it matters but *what* is said.

But there is more signifying surface to the saying. Listen to its sound and
notice that in the second line the word *homologein* sounds like *logos.* "Agree"
is a good first meaning but it does not preserve the similarity of sound. *Homologein* literally means "to say the same." Let me try that, and for "my reasoning"
I will substitute "the Saying."

> If you listen not to me but to the Saying,
> it is wise to say the same: that all things are one.

Now what sense does that make? What Saying? Whose saying other than
Heraclitus's own? Suppose the translation did make sense, then Heraclitus is
saying that there is a saying that can be heard beyond his own, a speech to
which we must listen, a speaking that it would be the part of wisdom to echo
in what we say. What impersonal speech could that be? Heraclitus in fact tells
us not what the logos is, but what it says, for he bids us to say the same: "All
things are one." What if this saying, of which no human being is the author,
were a power whose saying and doing were one and the same? What if its
speech were an act? Let me play with a third, somewhat strange, version:

> Once you have listened not to me but to the Gathering,
> it is wise similarly to gather all things into one.

Here *logos* is translated as gathering or collection. It is the power that gathers
everything in the world into a unified whole, the organizing power we are invited to imitate by giving a comprehensive account of the universe in speech.
The logos speaks primally; *our* logos becomes deep by imitating it.

I think by now the text has begun to draw us through its surface into its
depth. You can see that it demands of you the playful seriousness I mentioned

at the beginning, a seriousness that calls out all your capacity for careful attention to surface detail as well as your willingness to dive into the depths.

Here I shall stop. But although I am ending, I am not finished—and neither, of course, are you. If you have in fact listened not only to me but also to my argument, and if you are possessed by the proper freshman spirit, now is *your* moment, the part of the Friday night lecture that is the true St. John's: the time for questions.

CREDITS

The editor and the publisher are grateful to the owners of copyright for their permission to reprint the following selections:

Agee, James. *A Death in the Family,* pp. 53–62, 80–103. New York: Penguin Putnam Inc., 1957; Bantam Books, 1969. © 1957 by The James Agee Trust, renewed 1985 by Mia Agee. Used by permission of Grosset & Dunlap, Inc., a division of Penguin Putnam Inc.

St. Augustine. *On the Teacher,* translated by Joel Lidov, in *Plato's Meno,* edited by Malcolm Brown, pp. 65–89. Indianapolis: Bobbs-Merrill, 1976. © 1971. Reprinted by permission of Prentice-Hall, Inc., Upper Saddle River, N.J.

Basney, Lionel. "Dream of the School," in *Keeping Faith: Embracing the Tensions in Christian Higher Education,* edited by Ronald Wells. Grand Rapids, Mich.: William B. Eerdmans, 1996. © 1996 William B. Eerdmans Publishing Company, Grand Rapids, Michigan. Reprinted by permission of the publisher; all rights reserved.

Brann, Eva. *Depth and Desire,* pp. 1–11. Annapolis, Md.: St. John's University Press, 1990. Reprinted by permission of Eva Brann.

Buber, Martin. *Tales of the Hasidim: The Early Masters,* translated by Olga Marx, pp. 50–55, 66, 90, 103, 127, 144, 146–47, 300–301. New York: Schocken Books, 1947. © 1947, 1948, and renewed 1975 by Schocken Books, Inc., distributed by Pantheon Books, a division of Random House, Inc.

Fire, John/Lame Deer, and Richard Erodes. *Lame Deer: Seeker of Visions,* pp. 1–6. New York: Washington Square Press, 1978. © 1972 by John Fire/Lame Deer and Richard Erodes. © 1994 by Pocket Books. Reprinted with permission of Simon & Schuster, Inc.

Hoffmann, Yoel, translation and commentary. *The Sound Of The One Hand: 281 Zen Koans with Answers,* pp. 47–51, 219–223. New York: Basic Books, 1975. © 1975 by Yoel Hoffmann. Reprinted with permission of Yoel Hoffmann.

Inchausti, Robert. *Spitwad Sutras: Classroom Teaching as Sublime Vocation,* pp. 23–70, 153–68. Westport, Conn.: Bergin & Garvey, 1993. © 1993 by Bergin & Garvey. Reprinted with permission of Greenwood Publishing Group, Inc., Westport, Conn.

Itard, Jean-Marc-Gaspard. *The Wild Boy of Aveyron,* translated by George and Muriel Humphrey, pp. xxi–xxiv, 3–51. Englewood Cliffs, N.J.: Prentice-

Hall, 1962. © 1962. Reprinted by permission of Prentice-Hall, Inc., Upper Saddle River, N.J.

Jackson, Philip W. "Real Teaching," from *The Practice of Teaching*, pp. 75–97. New York: Teachers College Press, 1986. © 1986 by Teachers College, Columbia University. All rights reserved. Reprinted by permission of Teachers College Press.

Joyce, James. *A Portrait of the Artist as a Young Man*, pp. 127–35. New York: Viking Press, 1982. © 1916 by B. W. Huebsch, © 1944 by Nora Joyce, © 1964 by the Estate of James Joyce. Used by permission of Viking Penguin, a division of Penguin Putnam Inc.

Martin, Judith. *Miss Manners' Guide to Excruciatingly Correct Behavior*, pp. 299–302. New York: Warner Books, 1983. © 1982 by Judith Martin. Reprinted by permission of the author.

Paley, Vivian Gussin. *Wally's Stories: Conversations in the Kindergarten*, pp. 1–31, 194–223. Cambridge, Mass.: Harvard University Press, 1981. © 1981 by the President and Fellows of Harvard College. Reprinted by permission of Harvard University Press.

Plato. *Meno*, translated by G. M. A. Grube. Indianapolis: Hackett Publishing, 1976. Reprinted with permission of Hackett Publishing Company, Inc. All rights reserved.

Rombauer, Irma S., and Marion Rombauer Becker. *The Joy of Cooking*, pp. 9–12, 14, 16–17, 163–65. Indianapolis: Bobbs-Merrill, 1964. © 1931, 1936, 1941, 1942, 1943, 1946, 1951, 1952, 1953, 1962, 1963, 1964, 1975 by the Bobbs-Merrill Company, Inc. Reprinted with permission of Simon & Schuster, Inc.

Ryle, Gilbert. "Teaching and Training," in Gilbert Ryle, *Collected Papers II*, pp. 451–64. New York: Barnes and Noble, Inc., 1967. Reprinted from *The Concept of Education*, edited by R. S. Peters. London and New York: Routledge & Kegan Paul and Humanities Press, 1967. By permission of Routledge.

Thucydides. "Pericles's Funeral Oration," in *The Peloponnesian War*, translated by Rex Warner, pp. 143–51. New York: Penguin Classics, 1954; Penguin Books, 1982. © 1954 by Rex Warner. By permission of Penguin Books Ltd, UK.

Waddell, Helen, editor and translator. *The Desert Fathers*, pp. 76–77, 123–24. Ann Arbor: University of Michigan Press, 1947. By permission of the University of Michigan Press.